The Life of Marie d'Agoult, alias Daniel Stern

THE LIFE OF

Marie d'Agoult

ALIAS DANIEL STERN

PHYLLIS STOCK-MORTON

THE JOHNS HOPKINS
UNIVERSITY PRESS

BALTIMORE AND LONDON

To my children

❧

© 2000 The Johns Hopkins University Press
All rights reserved. Published 2000
Printed in the United States of America on acid-free paper
2   4   6   8   9   7   5   3   1

The Johns Hopkins University Press
2715 North Charles Street
Baltimore, Maryland 21218-4363
www.press.jhu.edu

Library of Congress Cataloging-in-Publication Data
will be found at the end of this book.
A catalog record for this book is available
from the British Library.

ISBN 0-8018-6313-9

~ Contents ~

Contents

Illustrations appear after page 136

~ *Acknowledgments* ~

Over the years in which this book was written, my attitude toward its subject and, in general, toward the historical lives of women has changed. The whole new field of women's history appeared in the 1960s and has been slowly maturing ever since. Therefore, any historian who writes about women is indebted to the yeasting up of ideas that it engendered in the historical profession, through the action of many formal and informal groups.

I would like to thank the New York chapter of the Coordinating Committee on Women in the Historical Profession, which gave birth to both the national CCWHP and the Committee on Women's History. These, in turn, organized the International Federation for Research in Women's History. The importance of these groups is the sharing of research on women, which has made possible the tremendous growth of the field over the past three decades. On the local level, I should like to thank the Columbia University Seminar on Women in Society, which has been meeting monthly during the academic year for more than two decades, sharing research and ideas. The Women's History Seminar of the Institute for Research in History also continues to meet after the demise of its parent organization. And the Berkshire Conference of Women Historians provides regular women's history conferences that feature new research in the field. I count many of the members of these groups among my personal friends.

But it is not only in sharing their research that these groups of women historians aid one another. It is in the working out together of the concepts and theories behind women's history. Not that there is *a* theory, for there are still many. But together we contribute to one another's development of a standpoint from which to view women in the past.

I should particularly like to thank Karen Offen, of the Center for Research on Women and Gender at Stanford University, who has given her time tirelessly to the success of all endeavors that have to do with research and publication in women's history. She was a reader of this book in manuscript, to which she applied her usual thoughtful insight.

I also owe my thanks to my historian husband, who has always put his full support behind both my research and my writing.

Introduction

The lives of women in the nineteenth century are of interest to us because this was the century of the "woman question"—that is, the period when women were beginning to make demands for rights that had been denied them for as long as anyone could remember. Nineteenth-century society was the anvil on which the women's rights movement began to be pounded out, at first in the lives of individual women, then in groups of men and women together, and finally in organizations of militant feminists. This biography is set in the first stage of that process.

The call had first gone out in the midst of the French Revolution, when the English intellectual Mary Wollstonecraft had published her *Vindication of the Rights of Woman*, which laid down much of the program for the century to follow and even prefigured some issues of the twentieth century. But when the revolutionary period was over, reaction set in on all fronts. Views of women traditional in previous centuries were again reinforced, and there were no more declarations of rights from the distaff side. Rousseau had convinced everyone of one thing at least—that women were an entirely different kind of human being from men and should be raised and educated only for the role they were intended to fill, that of wife and mother. Marriage was thus an absolute necessity, but the husband held complete control over the wife's person and property, as well as over her children. For upper-class women, the first issues of emancipation would be maternal and property rights. Meanwhile, women lived their lives under serious constraints.

Most biographies of women in the past need to be rewritten. There are numerous new questions to ask, all sorts of new insights we now have on women's lives. But there are also new women to rediscover, whom we do not yet know. Many years ago I discovered Marie de Flavigny, Comtesse d'Agoult, whose pen name was Daniel Stern. It was the pen name that attracted me, particularly as she was a contemporary of George Sand, another woman who used a pen name and whom she knew well for a time. My discovery had been the mistress of Franz Liszt, to whom she had borne three children. That romantic interlude over, she had experienced the 1848 revolution in Paris and had produced one of its first histories, a source still valuable to historians. She had written art and literary criticism, had introduced the German Idealists to her readers, and had covered the great events of her time in the newspapers and periodicals of Europe. Her second historical work had received a prize from the French Academy. Scores of outstanding persons had made their way to her salon in Paris—not only French, but German, Italian, Swiss, and Russian. She slowly grew in my mind, from a romantic heroine who had run away from her aristocratic family with a penniless artist, to an intellectual who spoke five languages and had correspondents all over Europe.

There are, of course, biographies of her in French: two romantic ones in the 1930s, one highly literary academic work in six volumes, and after the main archives on her were opened in the 1980s, two more modern biographies. Because she broke with both Liszt and George Sand, she has been given a bad press in biographies of both figures. She has sometimes been included in volumes in English on "romantic women." Besides one romantic account of her affair with Liszt, the only complete book on her in English is a Columbia University dissertation on her political ideas, published in 1937.

It took me years to read the extensive public writings of Daniel Stern, but after that, I remained dissatisfied. What was the private life of a woman like this? A woman who left her great love after five years and returned to Paris, not to her husband, who would have taken her back, or to her family, but to an independent life. That is a more complicated question and has taken much longer to answer. Her personal correspondence, in five languages, seems endless; it will never be collected in one place. Her diaries, in tiny, cramped handwriting, are often enigmatic.

One of the first things one must ask about any independent woman in the nineteenth century is: Where did the money come from; how did she support herself? George Sand, contemporary and sometime friend of Marie d'Agoult, went to court and fought her husband for her dowry. She won because he was clearly an unsavory character; she was awarded her children also. But this is an unusual situation. Marie d'Agoult, separated from her husband, ran away with another man. It was only her husband's good will that allowed her to tap her own dowry and live independently. She was not so lucky with her children. They belonged to the men who had fathered them, and limits were placed on her ability to see them or control their lives. Because she did not give in and insisted on living an independent life, she was attacked, by George Sand and others, for lacking maternal feelings.

After asking what a nineteenth-century woman had available to her financially and legally, one must ask what she had to work with psychologically. Given her circumstances, the first desideratum was the right man. A kind and loving husband would make up for a good deal of her lack of freedom. But how was she to know how to pick one, that is, if her parents would let her choose? Both George Sand and Marie d'Agoult failed this first test. One of the requirements for success would be for a woman to have what no woman was brought up to have—a rational view of the world and her place in it. And there were other barriers. The new romantic environment of the century hampered women's ability to see their relationships clearly. George Sand participated in this passionate milieu in her novels and through romantic liaisons. Marie d'Agoult made one romantic love the lodestar of her life and only gradually recognized that the price had been too great.

Neither of these women was a feminist, but both had a good deal to say in their writings about the lives of women. They were individuals who happened to be women, trying as best they could to live successful lives. For in a way then considered uncharacteristic of their sex, each of them wanted to succeed—not in the accepted role of helpmeet and mother for men, but to succeed for herself, making her life count for something on its own. Marie d'Agoult discovered this only after she had failed in one of the great romantic roles assigned to women—that of muse to a great artist.

This female role was another variation on the theme of platonic love, in which the woman served as an ideal that enabled the man to do great deeds (in the Middle Ages) or to attain to the divine (in the Renaissance). Like these women, the muse was always a means to an end, but the end was glorious, allowing her to participate in a greatness she could not herself achieve. For a woman dissatisfied with her life, mired in a failed marriage, the role of muse, combined with a passionate love, seemed irresistible. But could it last? For a Jane Carlyle, perhaps, although she became bitter about it late in her life. At least Carlyle recognized after her death what she had sacrificed for her husband. Cosima Wagner, daughter of Marie d'Agoult and Liszt, was to play the role to the end of her life without ever regretting it. Like her mother, she lacked genius but desired greatly to participate in it.

Posterity has reproached Marie d'Agoult for not having loved Liszt's art sufficiently to sacrifice to it *"une fierté mal placée"* (her misplaced pride). It is true that Franz Liszt needed a woman, not only as soulmate but as a mediator between himself and his musical creation. He also was attracted by titled women who helped him escape the inferior social status assigned to musicians in the nineteenth century. When his relationship with Marie d'Agoult finally ended he developed another, with an even older aristocratic woman, who would also enrich him culturally and provide him with that supportive, almost maternal adoration that he needed as an artist.

That Marie was proud is also true; it was her daughter Cosima, a middle child, brilliant but not self-confident, who made the supreme sacrifice of her whole being to her husband's art. But at least this was done within the context of a real family life; in Germany Cosima had been able to divorce her first husband and marry Wagner. What was required of Marie d'Agoult was more—to love and remain unhappy, in the Romantic mode. As her love for Liszt became—partly by force of circumstance, partly because of Liszt's infidelities—less real and more romantic artifice, Marie finally gave it up, at least outwardly. More lucid and rational than Liszt, she was too proud and gradually became too independent to continue in the subordinate female role required of romantic heroines. Having freed herself from her narrow aristocratic limitations by eloping with Liszt, Marie d'Agoult then freed herself from romanticism by renouncing him.

This did not make her happy. Her diaries regularly display a sometimes severe depression and suicidal tendencies that predated the appearance of Liszt. But she was determined to develop herself, as a thinker and writer. Painfully aware that she did not have genius and could not acquire power, she knew she had talent; she nurtured that talent in her relationships with outstanding personalities and in her historical and political writings. Her chef d'oeuvre was her history of the 1848 revolution, written from original sources available to her; it is still in use by contemporary historians. She also tried her hand at criticism, of music, art, and literature. Her second work of history, on Holland, received the prize from the French Academy that the political situation denied the first.

Besides her writings, it was Marie d'Agoult's ability to bring together in her salon an international assortment of artistic, philosophical, and political figures, and to carry on an international correspondance with them, that made her an unusual figure of her time. She strained against the nineteenth-century limits on women; she opposed in her writings the restraints placed on them. And yet she was not a feminist. Fastidious in her dress, aristocratic in her manners, feminine in her relations with men, she remained an outstanding example of a kind of protofeminism of the period between Mary Wollstonecraft and the feminists of the late nineteenth century. Even her friend George Sand, who dressed in men's clothing and lived a sexually liberated existence that Marie could not approve, never stepped over the line to demand real equality with men, nor did most other outstanding women of the mid-nineteenth century.

If Marie d'Agoult had been a man, her life and works would be deemed worthy of a full-scale biography, set alongside those of the men she knew—Lamartine, Lamennais, Mazzini, Cavour, Renan, Michelet, Littré, etc. This is an attempt to give her her due. In this biography, I have called the heroine (for everyone is heroine of her own biography) by her given name. Although born a de Flavigny and always known under the name Comtesse d'Agoult after her marriage, she left that aristocratic world, retaining only some of its gentle traditions. Although she wrote under a masculine name, she remained completely feminine. Eventually, she belonged to no world except the European one of liberal intellectuals. Therefore, it seems appropriate to call her by her given name, Marie, denuded of any hints of social milieu.

I have also wanted to tell her story using her own words, where possible. These have been taken from her published writings, letters, and manuscripts that she never intended for publication. One must always remember that in her memoir writings, particularly in those she published, Marie was creating her life, tailoring it to her ideal and critical standards—just as she had consciously created her self after the final break with Liszt.

What can we know about the reality of a life, as compared with such a creation? We have the views of other people—often not disinterested, it is true—which help to modify the self-view or the self-creation. We may even have her own modifications. Marie d'Agoult's foray into fiction was marred by her dealing only with situations she had experienced, which she somewhat transparently reorganized. Also there are always some less self-conscious writings; no one can be always on guard. So although letters and diaries are often part of the creation, some are more revealing than others.

Was Marie d'Agoult only trying to represent herself in the most favorable light to the public, as her critics believed? Or was she involved in an ongoing analysis of who she really was, in a world that only occasionally allowed her full expression? Both are surely true to some extent. However, aware as I am of the difficulties of being a talented woman in her time, I have favored the view that she was engaged in a constant self-analysis, in her novelistic writing, in her slightly fictionalized memoirs, and certainly in her unpublished writings. Of course, this analysis was never complete. But her effort at self-knowledge provides a basis for our understanding of the life of an unusual woman trying to fulfill herself despite the handicaps placed on her in the nineteenth century.

One ∽ *"They believe that children born at midnight have a mysterious nature, are closer than others to the spirit world, are more visited with dreams and apparitions."*

In the year that Marie Catherine de Flavigny was born, 1805, one's family origins were an important determinant for future life. In the old world, as Tocqueville would later note, it was not as simple to bridge the gap between classes as it was in the new. Nations were also divided in a Europe torn by the Napoleonic wars. Therefore, it is significant that this child partook of two European societies—the old nobility of France, impoverished and exiled from its homeland by the French Revolution and by loyalty to the ousted Bourbon monarchy; and the new bourgeoisie of Germany, the rising monied class of the Continent. Marie was to manifest aspects of both, valuing the cultures of her two native lands and becoming in many ways a true European in the century of rising nationalism.

The Flavigny family was old and distinguished, noble since the eleventh century and including scholars since the thirteenth. A family member had accompanied Mary Stuart, after the death of her royal husband in France and her royal mother in Scotland, back to Edinburgh to become Mary, Queen of Scots. A seventeenth-century orientalist Flavigny had written Latin dissertations quoted by Pierre Bayle; an eighteenth-century military one had written a protest against the death sentence. Two Flavignys had been executed as aristocrats during the French Revolution, which happily spared Marie's father, Alexandre de Flavigny, once page to the Comtesse de Provence, sister-in-law of the executed Louis XVI. He had joined the royal army under the Prince de la Trémoille as lieutenant-general. Remaining loyal to the royal family and bereft of fortune, Flavigny found himself in 1797 an exile in Frankfurt, Germany, where he was accepted as a foe of Napoleonic France.

He was not accepted, however, as a suitor for her granddaughter by the old Frau von Bethmann, who ruled the family of bourgeois bankers with an iron hand. It was Flavigny's Catholic religion, not his nationality, that determined the attitude of this fanatic Lutheran matriarch, who was also nearly blind and therefore not swayed by his charm and handsome appearance. The Frankfurt Bethmanns were originally from Nassau in the Netherlands; rumor had it that there the family had converted from Judaism.[1] Now they held court in the impressive palace of Baslerhof, where they entertained the best of German society and culture, including the mother of Goethe. By 1808 they would be granted patents of nobility.

Their attractive daughter Marie Bussmann, at age twenty-three already the widow of a man from another banking family, became smitten by Alexandre de Flavigny. To end the relationship, the Bethmanns used their influence to have him temporarily jailed for irregularities in his papers. But the young woman seized upon this as an opportunity. Visiting her suitor in jail, she remained with him the entire day, thereby creating a potential scandal if they were not engaged. It is the most romantic episode we know about this woman, who was depicted by her daughter as dull and unimaginative, a good and careful householder.[2] The marriage took place, and two boys were born before Marie. One of them died. The older, Maurice, was to play an important role in Marie's life. The family continued to live in Frankfurt, while Flavigny continued his military activities on behalf of the French monarchy.[3]

Marie Catherine Adelaide de Flavigny was born in December 1805—at midnight on the thirtieth, she always insisted, although the records indicate it was 4 A.M. on the thirty-first. Whether it was true or not, being a *Mitternachtskind* was part of this child of the century's romantic view of herself as unique, special, and different. The feeling was undoubtedly heightened by her beauty, most notably the blond, curly hair of her Germanic ancestors and the aristocratic features of her French ones. She grew up speaking German with her mother and French with her father. And a key memory of her childhood was meeting at the Bethmann country home the great Goethe, whose countenance fascinated her and who patted her head in what she later considered a benediction.

In 1809 the Flavigny family moved back to France. With the Bethmann dowry, they bought a small chateau at Mortier, near Tours. Its extensive grounds provided for Alexandre's general interests—hunting and entertaining members of the Ultraroyalist nobility. Their winters were spent in Paris. However, the season was cut short in March 1815, when Napoleon escaped from St. Helena and began his triumphal progress north. The family fled back to Mortier, where the young Marie noted that her father did not appear at dinner. He had gone to the Vendée to raise the royalists; that night the family set out on their escape back to Frankfurt.

Then nine years old, Marie found herself terrified of the "alte Frau von Bethmann," who questioned the child harshly about her religion. Marie had been baptized Lutheran as a baby but had as yet been given no religious training in France. Her mother had taught her to read the tales of Grimm, to memorize the monologues of Schiller, and to play the piano rather well. Unhappy at Baslerhof, she was finally sent to an elegant girls' school, the Pensionnat Engeleman, for a year. There also she felt somewhat estranged, for she lacked the experience of her teenaged cousin and even the other girls her age. The tumult of the Hundred Days and her unhappiness with her mother's family had two effects on Marie. It heightened her feeling of being different, and it made her feel detached from her mother and closer to her often-absent father.

In fact, Marie adored her father. When the family returned to Mortier after Napoleon's defeat, her brother Maurice was sent away to the lycée at Metz. Her father, who had hoped for some reward for his loyalty to the crown, was disappointed. He attached himself to the followers of the reactionary Comte d'Artois, younger brother to the king, but spent most of his time at Mortier, hunting and attending to his daughter's French education. Often he took her hunting with him, which led to her great love of the countryside. On rainy days she reproduced on a table a diorama of the fields and woods, with trees and ponds. Her parents sent away to Germany for little animals and figures to put into her landscape. When her brother returned home from school for holidays, he tried to interest her in planting a real garden. But she preferred her idealized countryside, peopled by princesses and enchanted woods. Not that she did not love nature and the natural, but perhaps she preferred a world she could control. If so, she was doomed to disappointment. For the society she lived in was one in which women were subject to control by men.

For the moment, this presented no great difficulty. Marie loved the regular lessons her father provided in her room, with large windows open to the outdoors. There he introduced her to elementary history and geography, mythology, and the classics of ancient and French literature. She became an avid reader, supplementing the classics with novels she found in her father's library. She also read in German and continued lessons in piano, harmony, and solfège (unusual training for a Frenchwoman) with her mother. Later, Johann Hummel was engaged to provide advanced instruction in music.[4]

Marie later wrote: "My father was in complete contrast to my mother. . . . He had all the faults and all the charms of the old French nobility. . . . Sensing a profound opposition of character between my father and my mother, my instinct did not hesitate. . . . The faculties of his mind which recalled, people said, the best society of the eighteenth century, aroused my childish imagination."[5] This period of Marie's life was decisive in making her predominantly a Frenchwoman.

That had already been decided, in a sense, when she had taken the Catholic rite of holy communion. Her paternal grandmother, Madame Lenoir, who had remarried after her husband's death to the former royal Lieutenant-General of the Police, insisted that Marie had no social future in France as a Protestant. Marie remembered her as an indulgent grandmother who served lovely pastries. During the winter of 1816–17 Marie lived with her in Paris while being prepared for entry into the church. She remembered that her grandmother took her to church but complained of the length of the prayers. Although Marie understood nothing of the rite, she was pleased with the spectacle of the mass. Her mentor, Abbé Rougeot, wanted her to be rebaptized a Catholic; her grandmother objected, however. A baptism at age twelve might make people suspect they were Jews! So, having completed her catechism classes, she duly became a Catholic by taking her first communion.

As part of her training Marie also took dancing and deportment lessons from Monsieur Abraham, a elderly gentleman of the old school who had taught Marie-Antoinette and who now wore padding on his elderly calves. She preferred her lessons in fencing, because of the aspect of mock combat. A Professor Vogel continued her studies in German literature, in which she was assigned to compare the *Iliad* and the *Nibelungenlied*. She also attended the Saturday classes of Abbé Gaultier in Paris. He taught Latin, history, geography, French grammar, and mathematics to aristocratic young ladies and young men, accompanied by their mothers. His unique method was intended to make education pleasurable; Marie remembered her history in quatrains and took pleasure in being head of the class.

One day at Mortier when she was fourteen, Marie found her father lying in bed, clearly unhappy. Hoping to amuse him, she detailed her activities of the morning. He replied: "I am glad that you are enjoying yourself. As for me, I am suffering." He died half an hour later, having been mortally wounded in a hunting accident. His death marked the end of Marie's childhood. "My father was my first passion, and therefore the first tragedy [*souffrance*] of my life,"[6] she wrote later. Her adoration of her father may have led to her initial attraction to older suitors. Certainly, it underlay her desire and ability to please men. To some extent, Marie remained her father's daughter, preserving his aristocratic manner and grace, if not his royalist politics, for the rest of her life.

As an adolescent, Marie began to suffer those periods of depression that seemed to run in her mother's family, in which a number of suicides took place during Marie's lifetime. A maid had reported Marie's own attempt to throw herself out a window at the age of eleven. The family tendency, plus the death of her father, inaugurated what she called her "spleen," which was to haunt her throughout her life.

After a year of mourning, her widowed mother returned to Frankfurt in 1819 to organize her financial affairs with the aid of her brother Moritz, taking Marie and her brother. Maurice, who had been a brilliant student at the lycée in Metz and had spent a year learning English in London, took his first diplomatic post in the French delegation to the king of Prussia. In Frankfurt, where the Diet of the German Confederation was meeting, Marie met at the opera her second hero of the century, the romantic novelist Chateaubriand, all of whose works she had read. But the experience was not the same as her meeting with Goethe; Chateaubriand paid no attention to her. She also accompanied her mother to official balls. Too young at fifteen to be allowed to waltz, she spent her time in conversation with the older men of the diplomatic corps, who seemed impressed with her intelligence. Her brother, disapproving, put a stop to what was later to become her great strength as a *salonnière*.

Madame de Flavigny chose to return to France, where her daughter's marital prospects would be superior to those in Germany; she took an apartment on the Place Beauveau in Paris. Marie had earlier met there Auguste, a half-sister from her mother's first marriage. She had not even known of Auguste's existence because of a highly scandalous marriage and divorce between Auguste and the poet Clemens Bretano. Even after her sister's remarriage to August Ehrmann, Marie was not allowed to visit her, not only because of her divorce but also because of the couple's pro-Napoleonic ideas. But as Marie grew older the sisters again began to meet, and Marie enjoyed being an aunt to two boys. When she was not visiting her grandmother, Marie spent Sundays with Auguste, often visiting museums and attending concerts. Auguste later drowned herself in the Main River. When her son Leon Ehrmann came to Paris as a student, Marie took charge of him. He fell violently in love with her and died at a young age, probably of consumption.

As was the custom for noble young ladies, Marie spent a year in a convent before her confirmation. The Sisters of Sacré-Coeur directed a school at the

Hôtel Biron in Paris (now the Rodin Museum). Although Marie had the special privilege of a room to herself, she was shocked at the physical conditions imposed on the young women. Mirrors, which celebrated the body, were forbidden. Only ten minutes a day were allowed for washing out of a small bowl. Baths were reserved for illness, if the doctor ordered them. The food was minimal and bland. (Priests sworn to chastity had long decreed that rich or spicy food heated the blood and was dangerous to adolescent young women.) Marie ceased menstruating for her convent year (probably because of weight loss) and only resumed upon returning home. Worse, there was no real education, as the greater part of the school day was devoted to religion and the *ars d'agrément* (embroidery, dance, drawing, etc.), which were supposed to add to a woman's worth on the marriage market.[7]

Revolting against "the little devotions, the little miracles," Marie refused to join the Children of Mary, an elite, especially pious group of students. She became the protectress of a slightly retarded girl, Adélise, who was mocked by the others. Fortunately, Marie was put in charge of the music and spent hours playing the organ. She developed a "crush" on Sister Antonia, a nun beloved of all the girls, and organized the students to buy a birthday bouquet for her. The Mother Superior chastised Marie as the ringleader of this effort. The blossoms of mixed color, she said, insulted the virginity of the nun, who would have to apologize before the order for inspiring the girls to buy such a gift.[8] Marie, outraged, went on a hunger strike, fell ill, and finally received an apology from the Mother Superior. Both the beloved nun and Adélise appeared later in Marie's novel *Nélida*.

Marie was prepared for her confirmation by Père Varin, a well-known Jesuit who had founded the convent. After answering a few of her questions, Père Varin exhorted her to shun traps laid by the devil, such as the desire to know and the need to understand. He thereafter eluded her questions. "He threw me at the feet of the crucifix, in the arms of Mary, in what he called the being of God, where all reason must perish."[9] She was duly confirmed but was not satisfied. When she returned home, Marie felt she had learned nothing useful at the convent. Also, she had grown further away from her mother, who was living in an apartment in the Place Vendôme. Marie found her mother too bourgeois; she disliked the frilly pink decor of her own room. Worse yet, Madame de Flavigny had been converted to Catholicism by her new daughter-in-law, Mathilde de Montesquiou-Fezensac. Marie was no longer the only daughter, nor could she share her mother's fervent religiosity.

It seems important to recognize that although Marie conducted herself all her life with what seemed like great self-confidence, she probably never completely recovered from the loss first of her father's adoration and then of her mother's approval. Of course, a young woman so striking and intelligent could always attract admiration. She was sponsored by the Princesse de la Trémoille, whose husband had been her father's patron. Marie visited her while at the convent, and the princess read out Marie's letters in her salon as examples of an emerging Madame de Sévigné. The young woman also became known as one of the brilliant pianists of the Faubourg Saint-Honoré. "I played with a relative virtuosity . . . the virtuosity of an amateur and of a noble young woman, which nevertheless, with my curly blond hair, my figure and my air of a Lorelei managed to produce on my audience a certain effect."[10]

There were other young women, although not so noble, who performed in the salons of the time. One was Delphine Gay, who gave recitations of Chateaubriand, Madame de Staël, and even her own poems in various drawing rooms, encouraged by a mother determined to see her daughter shine. Delphine was a great success in the salons of the Faubourg Saint-Honoré; her poetry was published to great acclaim. Marie invited mother and daughter to her mother's salon in 1826, curious to meet this poetic young woman. After a moving recitation by Delphine, Marie went to the piano and played, whereupon Madame Gay, fixing Marie with a soulful gaze, intoned, "Delphine understands you!" Despite the histrionics, the two young women were attracted to each other, and Delphine later proved a good friend to Marie when she needed one. This was a period when even aristocratic women could become artists; Princesse Marie d'Orléans was a sculptress. Marie herself coached aristocratic young women in music and formed chorales for performance. She was very close to the Marquise de Gabriac, renowned singer of the Faubourg Saint-Germain.

Marie's mother encouraged her social success, because it was time for her daughter to think of marriage. Marie herself later described the marriage mart of the time, both in her memoirs and in her first novel, *Nélida*. Her dowry was three hundred thousand francs, with prospects of probably a million more on her mother's death. This wealth created drawbacks, however; Marie could not marry just anybody. (One had to gain in the bargain, either in money or in position.) The poet Alfred de Vigny, for instance, was attracted to her, and the two remained friends throughout life. But his prospects were inadequate. An additional drawback was that such a dowry made any declaration of love suspect. Vigny later told her, "If I had married you, I would never have written a poem."[11] They exchanged letters until 1854.

Maurice and Madame de Flavigny introduced one suitor after another into the picture—admirals, counts, marquis. Marie was uninterested. The only one she became attached to was the Comte Lagarde, age forty-five, whom she met while watching from the windows of the Louvre the procession of the Fête-Dieu with other aristocratic families. For two years he called at the Flavigny home but never declared himself. The family, feeling he was too old (Marie was then seventeen), did not push for a declaration, and he already had a mistress interested in keeping him single. Assigned ambassador to Spain, he came to say goodbye, "unless," he told Marie, "you order me to remain." Unable to say a word, she watched him leave with chagrin. He later married someone else.[12]

Undoubtedly, the count functioned as a replacement for her father, and in him she lost not a lover but a father, for a second time. At this point the young woman turned her back on the whole marriage process, telling her brother to choose whomever he thought best and promising to cooperate. Things then moved quickly. Marie was introduced by the Trémoilles to the Comte d'Agoult, who soon fell in love with her, and they were married a month later. The count admired "her magnificent blond hair, her white complexion, her slim [*élancée*] figure of a dreamy young German girl."[13]

Charles Louis Constance d'Agoult was thirty-eight years old, short and bandy-legged. He limped from an injury in the Napoleonic wars, during which he had served as a colonel in the cavalry. But his family was monarchist, and he had rallied to the Bourbons, serving in the royal army in Spain. Although not a peer, he had connections to the royal court through his aunt, the Vicomtesse d'Agoult. As first equerry to the Duchesse d'Angoulême, he had few duties. In the days of Louis XVIII, when the king wanted his snuffbox, he would peremptorily say "D'Ag, d'Ag . . . ," and the count would hand it to him. This connection was part of the marriage negotiations, which almost broke down over the groom's small fortune, but were resurrected by the Prince de la Trémoille. Marie was guaranteed a place in court, and according to the noble custom of the day, the marriage contract was signed by the king, the dauphin, and the entire royal family (including the Duc d'Orléans, who was to replace the Bourbon king after 1830). The contract thus entitled Marie to be a lady-in-waiting to the royal family; she was "placed in the lap of the dauphine,"[14] the same Duchesse d'Angoulême, by that time wife of the supposed successor to the throne. Madame de Flavigny pledged a dowry of 260,000 francs (worth more than 8 million francs, or about $1.6 million today). The contract provided for a separation of property by which Marie could administer her dowry and also have use of the revenues.

The groom, who was not wealthy, nevertheless pledged a trousseau of jewelry and lace, which he recorded as having cost him sixty-three thousand francs, much of it borrowed from his noble relatives. The trousseau was displayed, according to custom, in an elegant piece of furniture decorated with swords and flowers worked in brilliants. Among the items were two necklaces, one of turquoises, one of emeralds, and a pair of custom-made earrings.

The marriage took place on May 16, 1827, with all of the Parisian nobility in attendance, at the Eglise de l'Assomption in Paris. The couple left for Dieppe, where they rented a house. The new husband wrote to his mother-in-law: "I love her so much. . . . She is now my whole existence." He hoped Marie would not be bored, but her friend Vigny, also newly married, was there with his English bride.[15] The following year the couple made a visit to the count's ancestral area in Provence. The château in Arpaillargues had been sold by his bankrupt father in 1807. They also visited Toulon, where they were received with honors on the ship of an Admiral Regnault, one of Marie's former suitors.

When in Paris, the d'Agoults took a floor of a house rented by the Flavigny family on the Quai Malaquais, at the corner of the Rue de Beaune. There Marie began her own salon. The count continued to admire his young wife. "I appreciate more each day the amiable and easygoing character of the one who will be the companion of my life. She loves the outdoors and activity more than the fireside; but she inherits from her mother a spirit of order at home and in financial matters." Yet he had no illusions about her expectation that he take care of all her needs and give in to all her desires, without her really having to consider his habits and tastes.[16]

Marie threw herself into the duties of her social rank. She made and later described the necessary visits to the grand dames of the Faubourg Saint-Honoré, to be looked over and approved. Prepared by M. Abraham and lavishly dressed, bejewelled, and powdered, she was formally presented to the king, Charles X. The dauphine, daughter of Louis XVI, looked her over first in her own apartment in the palace, making only one comment: "Not enough rouge." Even so, the king was gracious, and Marie became a lady-in-waiting to the dauphine. She later described the stultifying evenings at the palace. The ladies-in-waiting sat in an oval, strictly according to rank, with the dauphine at the head, working her petit point. There was no general conversation. Every so often, continuing her handiwork, the dauphine would launch a brusque question, "seemingly spontaneous, but actually regulated by a strict etiquette," to a particular woman. The answer, resounding in the complete silence, was as brief and banal as possible. Nearby, the dauphin and the old Vicomtesse d'Agoult played checkers in total silence. At the other end of the salon the king played whist with gentlemen of the court, also silently, except when the king exclaimed on losing a rubber and his partner apologized. When the king was through playing, he rose; immediately the dauphine rose also, dismissing her ladies. The game of checkers ended. Charles X spoke a few words to each lady, who was then free to return home to a more normal family life.[17]

It was quite different with the Duchesse de Berry. Marie met her six years after the tragic assassination of her husband, the heir to the throne. Sent from Naples at seventeen to marry a duke more than twice her age, the duchess was never austere enough for the royal family, who criticized her clothes, her hairdo, and her spontaneity. She was later to try, and fail, to put her son, "the miracle child" born after his father's death, on the throne. At this time she was a cheerful and attractive widow. The two women met at Dieppe, where the duchess had made bathing in the sea acceptable for the first time in France. Dutch ladies had also taken up a custom begun at Ostend—that of sitting in little bathing boxes pulled into the sea by horses. At Dieppe, bathing etiquette was different. On the first day of the season, the duchess was accompanied into the water by a doctor, dressed for the occasion in his best suit, who offered the princess his gloved hand. At the moment she entered the water, a cannon went off. After that, professional bathers attached to the establishment carried the young women in their arms and, advancing into the water a certain distance, according to the tide, plunged them in, head first, then set them on their feet. The bathing costume included a taffeta bathing cap and a smock, drawers and thick socks of unadorned black wool. Marie recalled that the prettiest woman in the world, leaving the water with her outfit clinging to her, seemed a monstrosity. The men sat on the hotel terrace with opera glasses to watch them returning to their bathing tents. Once in the water, the duchess splashed happily with her friends, careless of the audience; she even stayed long beyond the four minutes prescribed by the doctors. Marie also was hardy, splashing back and venturing far out in the water. The two women shared bathers and each other's company for the season.

In 1828 Marie's first child, Louise, was born. In a letter written that year the count admitted that his happiness frightened him, that he feared to lose it. "I cannot tell you all that is in my heart; we must never leave each other, right?" He said that he lived only for her and for their daughter.[18] And yet all was not well with the marriage. During a vacation in Switzerland in 1831, as the couple looked down from a precipice, Marie said, "Suppose I should jump!" The count reacted in horror that people would believe he had pushed her. Soon afterward, she had a nervous breakdown and was treated in the Hôpital Saint-Antoine in Geneva by a doctor for the insane, while the count continued the trip with his daughter.[19]

The count recorded in his memoirs that one day his wife entered the room dressed in his redingote and trousers, with his military hat on her head. At first struck dumb, he acknowledged that the costume suited her, that she looked like a musketeer. Marie viewed herself in the mirror, cracked her whip and left, saying, "That's what I need, trousers and a whip!"[20] This incident seems totally out of character for Marie at this or indeed any stage of her life; even if she had heard of George Sand's male attire, she would certainly never have followed her example. But it gives us an inkling of a desire for independence and control of a life that did not satisfy her.

Her husband also began to have second thoughts about his wife, noting that she had great and charming qualities, but that the words duty, sacrifice, and devotion were as strange to her upbringing as to her dictionary. "A cold character, with somewhat elastic moral and religious principles, with a romantic imagination, could well offer some dangers in the future. She does not know exactly what she wants. Her dreamy spirit attached itself to a name and an aristocratic existence, then to triumphs in elegant society, then to the rewards of a musician and writer—to celebrity, for she is a writer and an artist. . . . She writes a great deal, whether to her friends or for posterity."[21] He had already noted that when they traveled, a large receptacle for her correspondance was an absolute necessity.

It is fairly clear that the term *frigide* used by her husband about Marie may be taken in the modern sense of the term. She later wrote, "By what aberration of will did I allow myself, still so young, to marry a man whom I hardly knew, and whose personality formed such a dissonance with mine that the least informed person could have perceived it immediately? By what unbelievable power of custom was a marriage that everything recommended against [*déconseillait*] . . . finally brought about, despite my overwhelming apprehension?"[22] The only answer is that convinced she could never be happy in marriage, she gave herself to it as a kind of social sacrifice, because it was clear that the count was smitten with her. But the intimate aspects of married life were repugnant to her.

Marie read all George Sand's novels. After reading *Indiana,* the story of a woman deceived in marriage who takes control of her own life and asserts her right to love, she urged her mother to read it, noting that people thought she herself must have been the model for the heroine. Another Sand heroine with whom she identified was Lélia, from the novel of the same name, whose frigidity she had probably shared for five years. Marie also plunged into other romantic novels of the period, "which, in exalting my sensibility, innoculated me with a poetic and sickly disgust for life." Books took her out of her unsatisfactory daily existence and allowed her to live in a dream world.[23]

She learned English to read Byron's *Manfred* and went on to Walter Scott and Shakespeare. She even tried to write an epistolatory novel in English. One of her favorite English poems was Thomas Moore's "Loves of the Angels," in which three angels fall prey to seduction. The two seduced by female beauty and intelligence are exiled from heaven; the third, who loves a musician with a melodic soul, is sentenced only to a pilgrimage on earth, because he has loved under the sign of art. Goethe's *Faust* in German was always by her side, and his romantic novel *Werther* was significant for her future; in it she encountered the idea of the woman's role in the life of a genius.

Marie was pregnant again and living in Paris when the 1830 revolution against the monarchy broke out. She watched some of the crowds in the streets from the Quai Malaquais; when she heard shooting, she cried, "The poor people." She felt great emotion—not for the royal family, and certainly not for the revolutionary cause, but for the ordinary people who would die. On July 29 she watched from her window as the Tuileries Palace across the river was taken and the tricolor flag raised over the Pavilion de l'Horloge. Her second daughter, Claire, was born soon afterward.

The revolution changed many things for the d'Agoults, by ending the rule of the Bourbon kings whom both Marie's father and husband had served and replacing them with the Orleanist "Citizen King" of the July Monarchy. Thus ended all the political and social aspirations of Charles d'Agoult, as well as of Maurice de Flavigny. The two families retreated to Mortier. However, Charles suffered by being, clearly, not the man of the house. There were violent quarrels, and finally the d'Agoults returned to Paris. Marie never again lived at Mortier, her childhood home. In 1832 the couple bought from the Trémoilles, with part of Marie's dowry, the small chateau de Croissy in Brie, just outside of Paris, where she began to spend a good deal of time.

The change of regime also affected their salon. The couple had been invited before 1830 to concerts at the Palais-Royal, home of the Duc d'Orléans, who became King Louis-Philippe. This branch of the family had been suspect since the great Revolution, when the king's father had voted for the execution of Louis XVI. Marie had consulted her husband's aunt at the time of the concert. The Vicomtesse d'Agoult, though disapproving, decided that they could not refuse any royal invitation. At the Palais gathered the doctrinaire liberals who were to take over in 1830. Marie was later to judge them harshly, but at this point she wanted to expand her social milieu. The Bourbon family and the old viscountess had gone into exile. There was nothing to stop the young couple from deciding to open their salon to different people—writers, artists, and interesting members of the bourgeoisie.

The salon had been an important institution in French life ever since the sixteenth century and the only one in which women were central. The purpose of a salon was conversation, and women were acknowledged to be masters of the art. A woman had to be clever and fascinating enough to attract to her home interesting and well-known men, including, if possible, one real celebrity, and to keep going a lively conversation among them. Marie's salon was not well known at this time because it lacked the requisite famous man. But it was one of the few that included musicians. Malibran and other singers from the Italian opera would sing; Marie herself sang and played the piano. She excelled at the "Septuor" by her teacher, Hummel. Rossini, hearing her rendering of the overture to his *Semiramis*, was supposed to have exclaimed, "Never has my music been played so well!" He sat down to play, which he rarely did as a guest. Marie was also literary, able to converse in three languages. Her friend Vigny, whose marriage was a failure, had become a literary celebrity with his novel *Cinq Mars*. Marie, wishing to push his reputation, prevailed upon him to read his new poem for a distinguished audience. The reading of "La Frégate la Sérieuse" was, unfortunately, a disaster. Vigny recalled later that his frigate had sunk in her salon.

The count, unlike many husbands, took part in these salons both at the Quai Malaquais and at Croissy; he even wrote poetry himself. He recorded that "no one knew as did Madame d'Agoult how to speak to great artists of their work or their talents. An artist herself, she always found the right word, the precise word about a work. Few people have this talent. . . . Thus these great celebrities, who are often great egoists, were charmed to see themselves so well understood."[24] The celebrated critic Sainte-Beuve dubbed Marie the "Corinne of the Quai Malaquais."[25]

Marie also tried to absorb herself in her children. Like herself, her girls spoke both French and German from the beginning. But it seemed that there was disagreement between the parents on their upbringing. Marie retired to Croissy often, busying herself with landscaping and gardening. She was not happy. In a letter to her sister-in-law's sister, who was considering marriage, she wrote, "It is a word [marriage] which will fix your destiny, for you must not fool yourself, when the happiness of a woman is not *there,* she must not search for it anywhere. And life is so heavy for a woman whose heart is not filled! The unhappiness of most young people is that they get married before they know themselves well, and without knowing what they should seek."[26]

Marie tended more and more to stay at Croissy with the children and nurse her inner distress. Having been taught that suffering was agreeable to God, she first tried to lose herself in contemplation of the suffering of Christ, wept bitter tears, and found some solace. Then she turned to the Bible and the Church Fathers, hoping to understand the mysteries of Christianity, and to gain a kind of strength in resignation to the misery of life. Her confessor, Abbé Daguerry, a frequent visitor, counseled that she take communion often, in order to conquer her tendencies to rationalism and pride. She also wrote a life of Madame Guyon.[27] However, the gift of grace was not given to her; she stopped taking communion, convinced that she had too little faith, and fell into even greater despondency.

There were a number of men eager to try their hand at curing Marie's malady. One was Eugène Sue, the son of a doctor, a dandy, and the future author of *Mystères de Paris.* He flirted with her and wrote her almost daily. He also had his doubts about religion and confided to Marie that he preferred to think of Christ as a prophet, rather than as divine. After reading her essay on Madame Guyon, he urged her to to write, assuring her that it was the only passion she could have of which he would not be jealous. Their correspondence continued until she left Paris in 1835.

One of the important novels in Marie's life at this time was *Oberman* by Senancour. It includes passages about Christianity as a religion fallen into disuse and impossible to recover. The best thing was to sever all ties to religion and the world, to hope for nothing. Only in nature could God be found. Perhaps it could be found in love, but only in a love based on intellectual harmony, on profound sentiments, and on a shared love of nature. In this novel and in Sainte-Beuve's *Volupté* she found a romantic melancholy with which she could identify.

The year 1832 found Marie d'Agoult a wife and mother, admired by aristocratic society for her charm, elegance, musical abilities, and unusual writing ability. Although thoroughly a Frenchwoman, she had absorbed the German language and culture from her mother's side. Her happiest days had been spent under the eyes of her adoring father, who had encouraged the development of her mind and her love of nature. But he was gone. She was unfulfilled in marriage, lost to religion, and beset with nameless romantic longings. It was at this point that she met Franz Liszt.

The turn to Romanticism was a particularly apt solution to an unhappy marriage for an intelligent and emotional woman limited by the social code of her society. Unable to shine anywhere but in her own salon and only as a lesser light even there, the role of patron to a male genius was a logical one, an extension of the role of the *salonnière,* who used her conversational arts to show off the wit and genius of outstanding men. Marie d'Agoult was to move from the role of patron to the role of muse.

Two ～ *"What woman*
would not secretly consent to
live on an altar, mute and
veiled, to breathe the pure
incense of sacrifice?"

Franz Liszt was, with the possible exception of Chopin, the most romantic musician of the period. This Hungarian child prodigy had suffered from his father's brutality but won public adoration for his virtuosity. After his first piano concert at age nine, he had studied with Carl Czerny and Antonio Salieri and been hailed as a new Mozart while on a tour of Germany. After arriving in Paris for further study, he was denied entrance to the conservatory by Cherubini, who refused to relax a rule against foreign students. But he was patronized by the piano-maker Erard, inventer of a new piano with a "double escarpement" that allowed rapid repetition of a single note. Liszt was the first to play it in public. With his Romantic manner he became a sensation overnight and lionized by women. At the age of fourteen he was hailed in both London and Paris. But he was frail and very moody, particularly after his father's death, when he was sixteen.

Shunning public appearances, Liszt began to take pupils from the aristocracy in Paris and fell in love with one of them—the dark-haired Caroline Saint-Cricq, daughter of a count who was in the ministry of Charles X. It was she who introduced him to poetry and literature. Her father ended the romance and married off his daughter. Crushed, Liszt threw himself into religion. He did, however, have an affair with an older woman. In Paris Liszt met fellow musicians, including Berlioz, Chopin, and Paganini. He transposed Berlioz's *Symphonie Fantastique* for the piano. And he imitated on the piano Paganini's "demonic" style on the violin. Liszt was preparing himself to be an artist, not only playing again in public but also educating himself through reading.[1]

When he met Marie in December 1832, Liszt was twenty-one. She was close to twenty-seven. Marie had been invited to a musical evening by the Marquise du Vayer and had refused. At the last minute, she changed her mind. While insisting in letters to her mother that she was sick of polite society, Marie evidently used it to keep up her morale; the Comtesse Dash noted at the time that she was "a ferocious coquette," with at least five or six men madly in love with her.[2] She arrived on the arm of Eugène Sue, who paraded the Faubourg in a white piqué waistcoat from London, while twirling a cane.

According to Liszt's description of her when they met, made long after the relationship had soured, she was "beautiful, indeed very beautiful—a Lorelei. Slender, of distinguished bearing, bewitchingly beautiful and yet stately in her movements, with her proudly carried head covered with a profusion of blond hair that fell over her shoulders like a shower of gold, a profile of classic beauty, a face that contrasted in an interesting and curious way both dreaminess and a hint of melancholy, a manner and dress [toilette] of refined elegance."[3]

Marie's later description of Liszt was of "the most extraordinary person I had ever seen. Tall, excessively thin, with a pale face and large sea-green eyes . . . a physiognomy suffering yet powerful . . . a distracted air, disquieted and like a phantom awaiting the sounding of the hour to return to the shadows." In speaking to him she felt a "force and freedom of spirit which attracted me." He expressed his ideas vehemently, ideas that seemed bizarre to her, almost as if he wanted to challenge her or to provoke her to "an intimate assent."[4] When he was called upon to play for a chorus, she followed him to the piano and joined in the singing with great emotion.[5]

Marie could not sleep that night. The next day the perceptive marquise visited to discuss the genius and suggest that Marie invite him to her salon. After some hesitation, Madame d'Agoult, known for her letter-writing, sat down to write Liszt an invitation. The first two efforts were discarded. Each time, she felt she had hit the wrong note. One reason for this was the position of musicians in the society of the time. When they entered to play in the homes of the wealthy, it was by the servants' entrance. No matter how they transfixed their patrons or their pupils with their music, they left the same way, after receiving payment. Marie was aware that she must not sound too aristocratic or patronizing, nor did she wish to sound too interested. On the third try, she was almost satisfied. And, of course, he came—not once, but many times, often for long afternoon tête-à-têtes.

The conversations that Marie had with Liszt opened up a whole new world to her, as well as to him. Liszt always continued his education with each woman he knew well. A diamond in the rough, he was gradually becoming polished; Marie was for him a giant step in his intellectual development. The two read and discussed the Bible and the works of Shakespeare, Goethe, Chateaubriand, Balzac, Nerval, and George Sand. She shared with him her recent favorites, including Sainte-Beuve's *Volupté* and Senancour's *Oberman.*

One might question whether Liszt was really as cultured as Marie presented him later in her memoirs. In his early letters to her he quoted famous authors with abandon—St. Augustine, Petrarch, Montaigne, Chateaubriand, Hugo, and the Bible. Although he seemed avid to read everything, it is not clear that he had digested much or developed any critical abilities. Even in the springtime of their romance, Marie, always a precise thinker, criticized not only some books he liked but also the language of some of his letters. He begged her not to "treat too badly my poor unworthy endearments; that hurts me."[6]

In certain respects, however, Liszt was more knowledgeable than Marie. He began her education in humanitarian ideas by sharing his enthusiasm for the Saint-Simonians, Utopian socialists who wanted to remake society and inaugurate a "religion of humanity." He actually attended the soirée where their leader, le Père Enfantin, awaited the *"femme révélatrice"* (revealed woman) who would complete the system.[7] Through these conversations about socialism Marie discovered for the first time the world of real physical misery that existed outside her limited aristocratic world. She admitted to being struck by the force, clarity, and justice of most of the Saint-Simonian ideas in Eugène Rodriguez's *Lettres sur la religion et la politique.*[8] Although she never joined them, as did Liszt, the concerns of this group were an avenue to the widening of Marie's horizons concerning society and politics. Liszt also introduced her to the socialist writings of Pierre Leroux.

A republican, Liszt was also a follower of the religious rebel Félicité Robert de Lamennais, whose works he read and quoted to her.[9] Marie was excited by the egalitarian view of society and by the heresy of Lamennais, whom Liszt adopted as his spiritual father. Everything about Liszt fulfilled Marie's romantic ideas—his disdain of convention and of aristocratic society, his concept of the salvation of humanity through art. The theme of the artist's mission was quite frequent in his letters: "What does it matter whether man is happy, provided that he is great! The *bandeau* of inspiration is also a diadem. The artist is the living expression of God, of nature and of humanity."[10] Despite social differences, Marie became a disciple of Liszt, the great artist devoted to realizing the salvation of the people through art. This put their relationship on an equal level. As one scholar has noted, "Liszt and Madame d'Agoult loved each other in books, and it pleased them to extend even into their intimate conversations the echo of the great voices of the century."[11]

Letters supplemented conversations between the two, and they became more than intellectual exchanges. They corresponded in French, and in English and German for more tender thoughts. As their intimacy grew, two friends became messengers for the couple: the Marquise de Gabriac, Marie's musical friend, and Théophile de Ferrière, a young poet who was in love with her. (Throughout her life Marie was able to surround herself with men, usually younger than she, who were willing to express or sublimate their unrequited feelings for her by facilitating and advising on her relationship with Liszt. He, knowing that they were not really competitors, was never disturbed.) Messengers became particularly necessary when the d'Agoult family moved to Croissy in April 1833. From there Marie wrote Liszt, "I would like to tell you that, whatever my present or future sufferings, you need not cry over any of them, because you have done me more good than you can ever do me harm. You have managed to break all the lines that still attach me to the world [of high society], and you have awakened in me that universal charity, that love of all which was smothered in me by the feeling of my own personal unhappiness, which I was offering ceaselessly to God as a sacrifice, believing that resignation was the only virtue possible for me."[12]

Liszt visited Croissy in the spring of 1833, where he saw Marie for the first time her with her two daughters. Suddenly, both of them felt guilty; Marie thought that their relationship changed. After his return to Paris, he wrote her an ironic letter in which he remarked, "A dark reminiscence of Croissy dominates me, persecutes me in a strange way—if you understand it, Madame, tell me in writing . . . if your duties as a governess leave you any time at all."[13] His letters occasionally became cold, angry, bitter, and frustrated. He tended to reproach her for being an aristocrat.[14] He clearly suffered from the separation, begging her again and again to arrange for a few minutes together alone. Some things, he claimed, could not be written. "It is in your power to render me an immense service," he wrote. "My poor and miserable destiny is within your hands."[15]

Marie's letters also reveal an alternation between passionate love and despair. "I am alone, alone with one great thought, and that thought is you!" she wrote from Croissy in 1834. Although his greatness and divine goodness consoled her for being so miserable, sometimes she thought that she should never see him again. "But I love you with all my heart."[16] At some point after Marie returned to Paris that autumn of 1834, the two became lovers. They began to meet at Liszt's apartment, which they called the *Ratzenloch* (rat-hole), in the rue de la Sourdière. Marie suffered greatly from the secrecy of their affair. Liszt chided her. Had she not hidden up to now all that was sacred and pure in her? But Marie was truly disturbed. In one letter she spoke of being haunted by madness, specifically by thoughts of suicide.[17] Certainly, she was hesitant about pursuing this affair, which was nevertheless the first true love of her life and perhaps of his.[18] That Liszt had awakened a volcano was noted by a friend of Marie's, who described her as "six feet of snow over twenty feet of lava."[19] If her husband had seen only the snow, Liszt was to experience the lava.

Liszt's letters throughout 1834 swung from lyrical and joyous to cold and miserable, sometimes within the same letter, as his hopes for the future rose and fell. Many conversations about the future of their love involved the possibility of renouncing it for the religious life; one surmises that Liszt was more attracted by this solution than Marie. Sometimes he talked of their taking holy orders. He wrote in June, "A false need brings us together, a false need will separate us."[20] She, too, was often pessimistic. When she questioned him about his past affairs, he told her about Caroline de Saint-Cricq and also about Adèle de la Prunarède, fifteen years his senior. But he refused to show regret. "Don't you know," he wrote Marie, "that you have the right of life and death over me. . . . I was only a child, almost an imbecile for Caroline, only a cowardly and miserable poltroon for Adèle. For you alone I feel myself young and a man."[21]

It is not clear when the two first began to discuss the possibility of eloping together. A letter from Liszt to Marie at Croissy in July 1834 referring to "the great plan" seems to indicate the possibility that it was this early. He asked her to tell him again that she didn't want to live without him; he had already told her he would never leave her. He promised that the future would be radiant with purity and dignity.[22] Clearly, Marie was wrestling with the problem in terms of the scandal it would cause. Liszt argued that the matter was only between her conscience and God. If she felt that the virtues of her social position were so important, he wrote, perhaps they should separate, but he begged to see her once more. In this same letter he noted that she was still asking about women in his past; did she still distrust him?[23] It is probable that in her moments of objectivity, she did.

By this time the love affair was not entirely unknown to their friends. Eugène Sue advised Marie to go to a fortune-teller, Madame Lenormand, for advice. This famous psychic, whose clients had included Alexander I of Russia, the Duke of Wellington, and Josephine de Beauharnais, first wife of

Napoleon, was then past her prime. Nevertheless, Marie went to her "dark, stuffy room," where she was told that her life would change entirely and that she would love a man who would make a sensation in the world. Marie was not entirely convinced.

In September 1834 Liszt made a pilgrimage with Sainte-Beuve to Lamennais's monastic retreat at La Chesnaie. Liszt had met the great man earlier in the year and considered him his spiritual adviser.[24] Marie was still interested although not completely convinced about the priest, but Liszt insisted that Lamennais's consecration to liberty and equality, "those two great dogmas of humanity," placed him beyond criticism. However, he found the constant discussions of the soul at La Chesnaie wearing and became depressed. "Marie, Marie," he wrote to her, place your hand on my heart, your heart on my breast. I am naked and cold, clothe me entirely with your love. . . . Make me burn again with infinite ardors . . . deliver me for a time from the miseries of the age, resurrect my soul."[25] Had he talked to Lamennais about his love? It was as if he had decided that Marie was his redemption. He returned to Paris early.

As far as one can tell, Marie never hesitated about the elopement on the grounds of her duty to husband and children. But she would have to give up her position of privilege to live with a simple musician like Liszt. Although she claimed that the artist represented the highest realm of society, she knew that this view was not accepted by the aristocratic society of the Faubourg Saint-Honoré, where musicians came and went through the servants' quarter. Marie felt she had transcended this, but she saw the flaws in Liszt, even in her passion for him. Although an enthusiast about ideas, he was semi-educated; his exaggerated mannerisms masked a lack of fine manners. Liszt was enraged by her hesitations. He accused her of viewing him as false and vulgar, and he swore that he could never accept the artificial society in which she lived. At one point when he felt he might lose her he wrote, "However miserable and cowardly the virtues of the woman of the world seem to me, they are the only ones that will suit you henceforth. . . . Madame, you have two daughters and the future looks dark."[26]

During this year Marie lived two lives. One was her life with Liszt, of passion and romanticism. The other was a continuation of her former life. During 1834 she read history, starting with Herder and proceeding through Montesquieu, Sismondi, Niehbuhr, Michelet, and Vico. Since 1832 she had been corresponding with Théophile de Ferrière, who was even younger than Liszt. Madly in love with Marie, he worried about her health and was desperate that she did not return his passion. To please her, he filled his letters to Croissy with news of Liszt. Eventually, he sublimated his feelings for Marie into devotion to the couple. It was he who arranged a quintessential romantic moment for them by gaining entrance to Notre Dame at midnight, where Liszt played the organ and Marie, disguised as a man, came to listen. News of this *coup de théâtre* got out and caused a sensation.

Ferrière challenged Marie on her two lives: either she should accept wholeheartedly the aristocratic world of her upbringing, or she should have the courage to turn her back on it and aspire to higher things. Instead of remaining a cold observer of life, she should live it; she should devote herself seriously to writing.[27] Marie was also in constant contact with Eugène Sue, who was intellectually more her type, worldly and witty. They discussed authors. He flirted with her, but he valued her judgement and taste. He also continued to encourage her to take up writing seriously and reproached her for having no confidence in herself. Like Ferrière and probably for the same reasons, he tried to lead her away from music and toward literature.[28]

In December Marie's daughter Louise fell ill. Brought to the Flavigny house in Paris, she was diagnosed with brain fever. Marie remained at her bedside until she died. The child was buried at Croissy, and Marie went wild with grief and remorse. For some weeks she was intermittently delirious, refusing to eat or to speak, except to cry out in agony. But in contradiction to the account in her published *Souvenirs*, she did resume her correspondence with Liszt. A letter from him in that same month indicates that she had thought of him during those terrible days, undoubtedly with guilt. He had heard from her maid that Marie had lost control of herself, had talked of suicide, and had refused to see her other daughter Claire. He was desperate.

Liszt knew that Marie and her husband had been separated for a year (quietly and without legalities). In her period of mourning, she put Claire into a boarding school, for the child's presence was a constant reminder of the absent one. Liszt therefore knew that the time was ripe for Marie to break all ties to her former life. He sent her George Sand's *Lélia*, telling her to read it when she was alone at night. In it a woman demands the right to fulfillment in marriage. He wooed her in both mystical and sensual terms, insisting that he also had never before really loved. He begged to see her.[29] The letters of this period (they are undated, and we do not have hers) are sprinkled with fervent declarations and determinations—in German and English, as well as French—that their love should survive. Marie began again to visit Liszt's apartment in Paris.

It is difficult to know exactly when she began to live a Romantic novel, but it is certain that this was happening. Undoubtedly, the guilt that she had felt at the death of her daughter led her to push her passion for Liszt, already at a lyrical pitch of romantic fervor, to transcendent heights. Her first writing about Liszt, done probably in the same year, refers to HIM, "that living source of light, of strength and love in which my soul sank under the burden of life. . . . I no longer saw anything except through his love, which extended like an immense veil over the memories, the fears and the hopes of my life, and which mingled them in a harmony sad and austere, but grand and sublime."[30] It was in this period that she began to organize Liszt's thoughts on the higher role of the artist and to ghostwrite his articles, which were published over the next few years under the title "Lettre d'un bachelier ès musique" in various periodicals.[31] But in her passion she was also constructing the great novel of their life together, of the artist and his inspiration.

The dialogue about their elopement resumed. Marie was still hesitant. Such a move would mean breaking not only with her family and her one remaining daughter but also with the world of aristocratic Paris, in which she would become a pariah. And she seemed also to fear putting her whole life in Liszt's hands. He agreed that her whole life was involved, that she should think it over carefully and deliberately. Finally, he wrote that the day that she could tell him with all her heart, mind, and soul, "Franz, let us efface, forget, pardon forever all that is incomplete, sorrowing and miserable in the past; let us be all to one another, because at this moment I understand and pardon you as much as I love you," on that day ("and may it be soon") they would flee far from the world, they would live, love each other, and die together.[32]

By the end of March 1835, Marie was pregnant.[33] It is not clear when she actually discovered this or how she told Liszt. Her enemies among Liszt's biographers see her as ensnaring him through this pregnancy. However, at the time birth control was not used by women of her class; one ended the childbearing years by abstention, as she had done with her husband. The only other means was coitus interruptus, or withdrawal, which would have been up to Liszt. In any case, the discussion about elopement was over; the two began to lay plans to leave Paris separately and meet in Switzerland.

In Marie's *Mémoires* she sets the scene in Madame Liszt's apartment and does not mention the pregnancy. She depicts Liszt as saying: "Our souls were not made for these divisions, for these mute resignations where everything is darkened by tears. We are young, courageous, sincere and proud. We must have great sins or great virtues. We must, in the face of heaven, confess the sanctity or the fatality of our love." In a fragment of an unpublished drama found after her death, the scene shows Liszt as even more heroically roman-tic.[34] Thus she incorporated, without recognizing it, the reality of her situa-tion into the Romantic novel of her life.

The lovers left Paris for Switzerland separately, she probably on May 28. He seems to have left on June 1.[35] Here again, some unfriendly commenta-tors see this as an indication that Liszt was hestitating about the elopement or even running away, although both ended up in Basel, where they met soon afterward. The first biography of Liszt (by Ramann), written while he was still alive, depicts him as leaving Paris to end the affair. There is one incident that has been used to support this view. As Marie described it, a few days before she left for Switzerland, Liszt's confessor, Lamennais, showed up at her door. On his knees he begged her to overcome her passion for Liszt, a passion guilty if she yielded to it but purifying and edifying to others if she did not. He painted the picture of the rebel cast out of society (as he had been out of the church)—of the emptiness, the doubts, the remorse. He spoke of the anguish she would cause her mother and her remaining daughter. The scene went on for an hour. In tears, she begged him to rise. Even if she gave in to him, she declared, she would only change her mind later, and it was unworthy of both of them. The only answer she had to give him was that sin-cerity was the most important virtue for noble souls, which he, of all peo-ple, could not deny.

Lamennais later commented on her refusal, saying he had never encoun-tered in any woman such willful resistance. "At the moment a single chord is vibrating in her. When it snaps, everything wil be shattered." In her unedited memoirs we receive more information: Lamennais first went to Liszt to ask if it was true that the couple was planning to elope. He had been asked by some-one close to the countess to find out and to appeal to Liszt's honor in ending the relationship. Liszt replied that the count and his wife were irrevocably separated and that after trying for some years to convince her to leave with him, he could not change his course. Lamennais asked his permission to try persuading Marie; Liszt agreed, took Lamennais to her house, and left.[36] It was Lamennais who later complicated the question by saying that Liszt had tried everything to prevent Marie from throwing herself into the abyss and had gone through with the elopement out of some false idea of honor.[37] Marie's daughter Claire left a note that Emile Ollivier, Liszt's son-in-law, had asked Lamennais about it much later and had been told that Liszt himself asked him to intervene. However, Lamennais's correspondence of the time indicates that Marie's brother Maurice had sent his friend Denys Benoit d'Azy to ask Lamennais to do what he could to prevent the elopement.[38]

Among the many different rumors about the couple, mostly unfavorable to Marie, was that Liszt had asked Marie to become a Protestant and sue for divorce but that Marie had not wanted to give up a title to become simply Madame Liszt. This story was later refuted by Liszt; no one who knew his religious views, he insisted, would think he could ever suggest such a thing. As an example of the wild rumor circulating in Paris at the time, he recalled the story that he had carried Marie off in a grand piano![39]

One question that has never been answered is who knew of the pregnancy. Did Lamennais, or was it her brother Maurice who called for Lamennais's help? It is true that many people in Paris knew of their affair; Marie had actually left her carriage sitting on the street outside Liszt's apartment. Nevertheless, she would have been forgiven if appearances had been preserved—that is, if she had lived with her husband until the birth of her child, which would then have been legally his. But this would have taken a greater sense of reality than Marie had; it would also have denied her love. Some biographers depict Liszt as taking the chivalrous role by going through with the elopement. For all the attention he later paid to his children, it is possible that he could have allowed his child to be brought up as the count's. But to conclude that Liszt wanted to run away and end the relationship, as some of his biographers imply, would be to view his passionate letters of 1834–35 as completely deceptive. When faced not only with a love affair but with a family, Liszt may have hesitated and wished also to be sure that Marie understood fully what she was doing. But when Marie arrived in Basel, she was able to contact him, which must have been prearranged. Liszt's letters to Marie in 1836 are as passionate as those before. Their correspondence, from this time onward and for many years, amply supports the conclusion that he was truly in love with her.

When Marie left Paris, she left her husband a farewell letter. In it she referred to the failure of their marriage to provide happiness for either partner, and she expressed the hope that her husband would at least find peace. "I do not dissimulate any of my faults," she wrote, and asked him to pardon her "on the tomb of Louise [their dead daughter]." She also swore, "Your name will never leave my lips except pronounced with the respect and esteem that are due to your character; as for me, as concerns the world which will cover me with scorn, I ask of you only silence."[40] This she received. Liszt later insisted that the count never complained but said only, "It's all right; I shall bear it," and, "Liszt is a man of honor."[41]

Traveling in the company of her brother-in-law, August Ehrmann, Marie was supposed to join her mother, traveling from Frankfurt, for a vacation in

Switzerland. Madame de Flavigny knew of her daughter's separation from her husband, but no one knew of her plans. In her fictionalized account of this journey, Marie described herself as trying at first to enjoy the voyage as she got away from Paris, putting herself temporarily in a somnolent state. Then, beginning to converse with Ehrmann, she managed to tell her brother-in-law of her projected elopement by the end of the three-day journey to Basel; horrified, he brought her to the hotel and left immediately, hoping to meet her mother on the road from Frankfurt. In Basel, Marie wrote Liszt, indicating in German where she was, and told him to write her the name of his hotel and the number of his room.[42] Although her brother-in-law had left, her mother had arrived earlier than expected; therefore, he should stay where he was. She had not yet dared to tell her mother but would do so immediately. "It is a last and rude test; but my love is my faith, and I am thirsty for martyrdom."[43]

Liszt's answering letter began, "Here I am, since you have called me." The rest was also in English, indicating the hotel and how to get to his room, and was signed "Yours."[44] German and English had traditionally been used by the couple, partly in case a letter should fall into other hands and partly for emotional emphasis. We do not know the details of the couple's next few days. Some have insisted that Marie descended upon an unsuspecting Liszt, forcing his hand; that she never forgave him for having to do so; and that society (particularly according to some German sources) never forgave her for it.[45]

What we do know is that it took her four days to tell her mother, during which time she did meet Liszt at his hotel. In her account of these days, Marie described her feelings when her mother read the letter she had finally managed to leave in her room. "I felt all of a sudden in the depths of my being a sensation similar to that which a drop of water must feel on freezing . . . a plant which is petrifying, a man suddenly struck with paralysis." Madame de Flavigny collapsed in grief. Marie wrote that she feared her mother would die and that she would be beholden to God for it. Instead, Madame de Flavigny begged her daughter to return to Frankfurt with her before anyone discovered her mistake. Everything could be taken care of, and she need not return to Paris until after the child's birth. At one point, Marie wrote, she actually agreed, but both of them knew she would not do it.

According to Marie's memoirs, Liszt refrained from trying to influence her, so that the decision would be completely hers. But in her other account she wrote, "I was under that occult, magnetic, mysterious force that a strong soul exercises on a soul united to it by a deep love." She also recalled that she saw herself devoting her life to a holy and noble task, a sort of divine mission. She wanted to be able to say to him one day, "What could I have done for you that I have not done?"[46] On the tenth of June she left her mother and joined Liszt in a nearby village. They left Basel four days later.

The lovers spent the next five weeks wandering the mountains of Switzerland, in a romantic haze only heightened by the fact that many people who met them thought they were twins. Indeed, the two incarnated the Romantic ideal; their heads, according to contemporaries, were often depicted in Romantic decoration. Their journey, too, was typical for Romantics, for whom mountains had an almost metaphysical connotation. Marie had written to her sister-in-law on a trip to Switzerland in 1831: "These grandiose sites elevate the soul, and detach it at least momentarily from all earthly thoughts. The snow of the Alps speaks more of God than all the gilt of our chapels, and the roar of the torrent says more to my spirit than all the sermons."[47]

Marie later wrote that she and Liszt wanted to put space between themselves and their past, to multiply their experiences together and to create a "new past" for themselves. Together they experienced a dangerous tempest while traversing a lake, after which they agreed that dying together would have been glorious. But even amid their most idyllic moments, the future weighed upon them. Liszt occasionally spoke of the purification of all love and all glory, of a mutual renunciation and a kind of monastic existence that would preserve their love in some higher celestial realm. This was to be in the faraway future. But even so, it was a solution more acceptable to his romanticism than to hers.

Eventually, even lovers have to come down from the mountains. They arrived in Geneva in late July. For the first time Marie had to admit that although she could sustain her guilty passion in the face of nature, it was much more difficult in society, where at any time she might meet someone who knew her. A malaise descended upon her. This was only heightened by the letters Liszt brought her from the post office. She had girded herself to fight her family, but her mother's letter was not reproachful, only sad. How could a Christian like Liszt influence her daughter to turn her back on a mother's affection? Madame de Flavigny had remained in Switzerland, in Arlesheim, hoping that she could convince her daughter to change her mind before it was too late. Indeed, she did not leave until August. Maurice had counseled her that it was no use trying to change his sister's mind for some months. Nor should she blame Liszt, who had sought the aid of Lamennais at the last moment, "true, after having set the house on fire"; he was, after all, very young.[48] As the older brother, he had sent Marie a letter predicting that for putting herself above the moral law, she would see hell in her lifetime.⁴⁹ In a sense, he was right.

However, both letters tried to assume that Marie would think better of her flight and offered help in reestablishing herself. Her mother recognized that her marriage was over and offered her a home at Mortier. Now at Frankfurt, the mother wanted to return to France with her daughter. Her brother offered to settle with her husband, so that she could live an independent life with her children. He included even a few lines from her remaining child, Claire. These letters indicated that her revolt was known by very few and that if she returned home with her mother, she could get away with her mad flight. For Marie, reading the letters was an agony only further heightened by her recognition that Liszt would not fight any decision she made to return and might possibly be relieved to be free of responsibility for her and their child. But Marie never entirely lost her rational faculties, even when she was overcome by emotion.

She later described the internal struggles of that day as being similar to those of one entering a religious vocation and desperate at the thought of leaving her worldly relations. And indeed, she saw her decision to stay with Liszt as a quasi-religious one. "My passion for Franz . . . verged on fanaticism. I saw in him a being apart, superior to anyone I had ever met. Disposed as I was to superstitions of the heart, I sometimes arrived, in a sort of mystic delirium, at the idea that I was called by God, offered in some way for the grandeur and salvation of this divine genius who had nothing in common with other men and should not bow to ordinary laws. . . . I wished to be a saint of love, I blessed my martyrdom."⁵⁰ Yes, but one assumes she must have also thought, more rationally, that going back to Paris would not solve the problem of her unfulfilled life, and so she allowed her emotions to convince her that continuing the journey with Liszt would. Sorrowfully, she wrote her family that she had made her choice and would keep to it.

Liszt never asked about the letters. She was too proud to reveal her hurt to him. But she blamed him for not recognizing what she had sacrificed for him. It was the first cloud in the romantic aura that the couple had produced around themselves. "I had a friend, but my pain did not have a friend,"⁵¹ she wrote later of this moment. And there were more difficulties to follow.

As Marie saw their future, Liszt, predominantly a composer, would live with her out of public view and produce great musical works. However, Liszt was still a focus of excitement in the musical world. A biographical article on him appeared in the *Gazette musicale* in June; a few weeks later the same journal noted that he was traveling in Switzerland. He had performed in Geneva before, and he was again in great demand. Now visibly pregnant, Marie preferred to stay in their apartment while he took up an active social life, dining out and soliciting pupils to make money. And indeed, after the fund she had brought with her was used up, the couple was in trouble financially.[52] But she could not help resenting his absences at the numerous social gatherings to which he was invited.

One September day Liszt told her he had agreed to participate in a concert, in the salon of Prince Belgiojoso. She was shocked that he expected her to attend. When the day came and he still wanted her to go, she did but remained carefully screened from the general view. As he performed, she saw to her horror that he gloried in the acclamation of the public. She wrote on her program, in pencil: "Aversion for the personality of a virtuoso . . . depravity of a being who performs for money." In her *Souvenirs* she wrote, "It was Franz and it was not Franz. It was like a person who represented him on the stage with much art and likeness, but who nevertheless had nothing in common with him, was only a vain appearance. His playing also troubled me; it was his virtuosity, prodigious, striking, incomparable, but I felt it nevertheless as strange to him. . . . [I felt] an inexpressible anguish."[53] On that evening she saw her future hopes of a quiet life out of the public eye destroyed.

In a later, unpublished work, Marie recounted a dream in which she saw two figures of Liszt holding hands. One was beautiful and radiant; the other was a grimacing and demonic parody. Yet she knew that they were one and that together they would bring her both good and evil. She woke while fending off the clutches of the bad figure. She recounted that Liszt explained dream to her: "Your dream was a presentiment, an only too exact image of a sad reality. The harmonious face, the benevolent power, was I as you would have wished me, perhaps even as God made me; I was also the discordant and tormented figure, as life has made me, as the world and its perversity wished me to be."[54] This passage would indicate that although she was pained by Liszt, she did not so much blame him as she did society for making him a virtuoso.

An additional problem was created by the appearance of an old pupil, Hermann Cohen (Puzzi), who adored Liszt and begged to be near his master to continue his lessons. Although Marie claimed that she resented him only because Liszt did not ask her before saying yes, Puzzi seemed to be always there in their apartment on the rue Tabazan, as Liszt undertook to educate the gauche adolescent in more than music, to prepare him for a musical career. Liszt also offered to teach in the new Geneva Conservatory of Music without pay, in order to attract students; so many applied that he assigned Puzzi to help. Within four months, Liszt became exhausted. He first gave up the male students and, by the end of the term, the post. The conservatory voted him an honorarium.

He was very popular with the refugees in town and particularly with the ladies. Caroline Boissier, who had seen him in Paris, described him: "His appearance is somewhat improved; no one could deny that he looks both refined and distinguished. . . . His clothes no longer have the bad taste which marked him out in Paris; it is easy to see that he has received some good feminine advice. . . . But he is an unfortunate young man, spoilt by the world and by success. His conversation is more wearisome than agreeable. I don't mean that he lacks ideas or wit; he is even capable of attacking profound and serious matters; but he loses his way in them. . . . If it came to it, he would introduce his countess to be, quite unblushingly."[55]

This last was a reference to the fact that Marie was, in Geneva, quite beyond the pale. Although she did not wish to enter Genevan society as Liszt's mistress, it would have been quite impossible for her to do so, which was all the more galling because Liszt wished to appear in society and did. She later wrote that "these rigid Calvinists," disapproving of their relationship but desiring to enjoy Liszt's performances, elaborated a number of stories that exempted him from all blame and attributed all of the initiative to her. "They bitterly reproached me for having snatched Liszt from a brilliant career" to tie him to her own ignoble future.[56]

Left to her own devices, Marie's solution was to create in her "attic" a salon of the men Liszt brought home. Caroline Boissier reported a visit of her husband (she herself would never go) to the fourth floor of the rue Tabazan, where Marie

received like a queen on her throne! Not the slightest embarrassment, not a trace of bashfulness, a dignified, noble, and easy manner. A clever and witty woman, good at repartee; very French, very *bon ton*. No longer young, nor pretty, but with countenance and character. The countess was very amiable, and it was she who introduced the various topics of conversation, holding forth on Paris, literature, the sciences, the passions. She talked about Parisian society as if she were still a member of it.

After a quarter of an hour, her husband reported, one felt as if one was with a married woman.[57]

As so many women had before her, Marie used her salon to expand her horizons. Despite the education she had received, which was far superior to most women's, and her own reading, she felt her ignorance. She began to read German philosophy, translating and commenting on many of her readings in the tradition of Madame de Staël, a Swiss intellectual of the previous generation whom she greatly admired. Then, although she had already read Montesquieu, Niehbuhr, Michelet, and Sismondi, she began a systematic reading of history. She soon attracted Geneva's men of letters, including the same historian Sismonde de Sismondi, the orientalist Alphonse Denis, the botanist Pyramide de Candolle, the philologist Adolphe Pictet, and the politician James Fazy, later mayor of Geneva. Of these, the last two remained her friends and correspondents. She also attracted Louis Ronchaud, a young intellectual of nineteen, who was to remain her cavalier for life.

Guided by her guests, Marie discussed her course of study with them; she also shared it with Liszt. Although he eagerly participated in her intellectual life, joining a reading society to borrow books, he may have resented her salon, for in his later years he gave a very sour description of it.[58] The salon represented Marie's adjustment to her difficult situation in a manner congenial to her. Soon she was using her other talent—writing. Liszt had from the beginning preached to her the concept of art as the saving grace of humanity and the difficulties of the role played by the musician in society. Marie continued to refine his ideas through a series of articles. The first, "On the Situation of Artists and Their Condition in Society," signed "Bachelier ès musique," was published in the *Gazette musicale* under Liszt's name.[59] The series continued for more than six years. Marie saw this effort partly as a service to humanitarian art and partly as a justification of her role in Liszt's life. If he was not to be predominantly a writer of music, with her as inspiration, he could at least be a preacher of salvation through music. She also published, through her new contacts, an article on Victor Hugo's *Les Chants du crépuscule* in *L'Europe centrale.* It was unsigned. *Gazette musicale* published a fifth article signed by Liszt in December.[60]

At this point there were other concerns. On the eighteenth of December 1835, Marie gave birth to her first child by Liszt. She was recorded in the Geneva records as "Blandine Rachel, natural daughter of François Liszt, professor of music, age 24 years and one month, born in Raiding, Hungary, and of Catherine-Adelaide Meran. . . . Liszt freely admitted to being the father of said child, and made the declaration in the presence of Pierre-Etienne Wolff, professor of music, age 25 years, and Jean-James Fazy, proprietor, age 36 years." The reason for the false name of the child's mother was that if Marie's name had appeared, the child would have legally belonged to her lawful husband. As it was, the child belonged in law, as did the other two born to the couple, to Liszt alone.[61] This situation was later to cause considerable heartbreak to Marie, when Liszt used his legal rights against her.

Blandine was for the moment put out to nurse. She would become the favorite of Marie's love-children. Marie has been blamed for her lack of maternal instinct, and her leaving her three children by Liszt with nurses during their infancy supports this accusation. Yet it was customary for aristocratic mothers to do this and to take an interest in their children only when they were ready for a mother's education. Marie fulfilled this latter role with her first two children. But it was also becoming difficult enough to live out the romantic dream with Liszt without adding to it the domestic strain of a baby. We know that Liszt was never really interested in his children, and his indifference may have been apparent immediately. But the year had been fruitful for him as well. During their Swiss idyll he had composed pieces commemorating various places on the way, collected as *Album d'un voyageur.* He added one called "The Bells of Geneva," in honor of Blandine's birth. Published later as part of *Années de pélerinage,* the collection renewed the genre of melody as illustrative and emphasized its correspondences with art.

The year ended with the couple still passionately in love. However, there were certain strains on both sides. Liszt had rediscovered the satisfactions of performance, but his public life was a source of sorrow to Marie, who had hoped that the world of society, which she could not share with him, would not intrude into their life. As an aristocrat, she had never had to think about money, and her natural attitude toward making it was disdain, as her reaction to his first Geneva concert indicates. Nevertheless, she had to concede that Liszt's need to make their living made it only reasonable that he should do so in his own way. A partial solution would be to gain access to the resources of her dowry, but this would involve negotiations with her husband and her family, which were bound to be painful.

A proud and sensitive woman, Marie would have found the situation close to intolerable had she not had faith in the love she shared with Liszt. Yet she could not ignore his lack of sensitivity to her situation. Her frustration made her liable to the old bouts of depression, and her reaction was to find ways to bolster her self-esteem. One way was through writing, by refining Liszt's ideas and contributing her own in the articles published under his name. She would have liked to go further and write completely on her own, but she did not have enough confidence. What she could do was to continue her education, through reading and in her small salon of intellectuals. Thus her basic methods of coping with disappointment throughout her life were established in Geneva, the city that despised her, and that she despised in turn.

Three ∼ *"This need for exclusiveness, this need to be loved totally, has dominated all the feelings of my life."*

In the spring of 1836, Liszt announced to Marie that he had to go on a short performing tour in southern France. He had been absent from public view too long; a new pianist, Sigismond Thalberg, was making a name for himself. It was also time for him to earn some money. Marie could not believe her ears. He intended to leave her alone in Geneva? No, he assured her, not alone. Puzzi, his pupil, would take care of her. And he would write every day. This was the inauguration of the first parting, during which Liszt the virtuoso was drowned in adulation while Marie suffered in a social limbo.

But he did write daily, and the letters were as passionate as ever. "Marie, Marie, teach me the mysterious language of your soul, let us talk to one another in our sleep."[1] When she complained about being left for so long, he exhorted her to apply herself to her writing, to go horseback riding, to give lessons to Puzzi. Although they discussed her going to Lyon to join him, both were hesitant about how it would work out, and she did not go. He began to speak of a possible concert in Paris. His competitor Thalberg had been performing there; he must meet the challenge. Marie was at first opposed to his going and accused him of hungering for fame. He protested that his touring was more for her than for him: "It is my only fortune, my only title, my unique possession. . . . My reputation as an artist is precious beyond all; is it not a jewel that pleases you?"[2]

Liszt had another reason for going to Paris—the need to make some financial arrangements with Marie's family. In what he described as an emotional interview, he met with her brother Maurice and came to an agreement. Marie received an affectionate letter from her brother. Liszt wrote that he and her husband had both behaved like gentlemen. Certainly, the count had; he agreed to what he was not required by law to do in this situation—to give Marie access to her dowry. Some of it had been used to buy Croissy; the count would continue to live there. This agreement eased the financial worries of the couple.

However, the Paris visit was not a short one. Liszt stayed for weeks. He gave two concerts, one in the salon of Princess Belgiojoso, one of the famous hostesses of Parisian society. An Italian nationalist, the princess supported the *carbonari* who were plotting for a free and united Italy, and she sometimes appeared in public with an honor guard of them. Pale and exotic, she could often be found kneeling at prayer in her oratory (featuring Gothic stained glass and dusty folios). Her salon was hung with dark velvet embroidered with silver stars. She adored Liszt. When he wrote to Marie that people in Paris were very sympathetic to her, she could feel only anger at the sympathy of Belgiojoso. There were a number of days when Liszt received no letters from Geneva. A caller at the princess's apartment met him there one morning and was surprised to find them both in casual clothes.[3] Although it is probable that this was little more than a flirtation, it is an indication that Liszt could not forego the attention of women when he was separated from Marie.

Liszt's letters continued to discuss his career and how he had easily won Paris from Thalberg. He swore that he did not go out evenings and spoke of how much he missed her. Why didn't she write? He could not stand being alone in Paris without her. Nevertheless, he had heard that Lamennais was going to be there soon; he was sure that she would approve of his staying a bit longer to meet him. When her longed-for letter finally arrived, Liszt described it as cruel. He wrote that he was looking forward to playing duets with her; she should practice. He emphasized that he wanted to see no one but her for a few days after his return. But he would have to stay in Paris five or six more days. In the next letter he said it would be eight days more.

Marie wrote that if she had known the length of his absence in advance, she would never have been able to face it. If he only knew how desperate she had been. But she knew he loved her. On receiving that letter, Liszt wrote, he cried with joy. However, Marie could not help writing more angry letters, full of "whatever demons possessed her," as she would admit apologetically in other letters written only hours apart. But, she pleaded, he should put himself in her place. Of course, she approved all he had done and rejoiced in his artistic sense. She would wait in Geneva as long as he liked, but she couldn't stand the separation. One day she wrote that she had spent the day in bed because she saw no reason to get up and dress.[4]

As Liszt delayed his departure from Paris, waiting for Lamennais, Marie spent more days in bed, sunk in depression. On June 6 she met the coach she thought would bring him (he had written, "only a few more hours of courage"), but he was not on it. She decided to move out of the hated Geneva, with Ronchaud and Puzzi, to the village of Salève, where she could see her daughter Blandine. Liszt finally returned in the middle of the month. And even then, he had made engagements that required him to leave in a few days for concerts in Lausanne and Dijon. Marie erupted in anger. She later described the two of them: "He, feeling and desiring love as a young man, unconquerable, overflowing with life; I, as a woman defiant toward destiny, broken by sorrow, dreaming and turning my eyes from reality to lose myself in an impossible ideal."[5]

Liszt at least recognized that Marie could no longer stand to live in Geneva; the two began to make plans to live in Italy, after his last arranged concerts. Marie threw herself into writing publicity for him, thus tacitly recognizing that he would continue to perform. Liszt made clear his need for her. "I am not yet really healed from the past. My wounds ache on certain days. Then place your sweet hand on my breast and let me sleep in your bosom," he wrote from Dijon. Thus the two sealed once more their pact as musician and muse; again they seemed radiantly happy. Marie wrote in her diary on August 11 that their life seemed to be "one long vow of love." A few days later, she recorded a comment that seems to have developed out of a conversation with Liszt: "Husbands only die in novels."[6] Hers was still very much alive, and divorce was impossible.

As Marie wrote later, she formed relations at this time that were not solely reflections of Liszt's but were personal: "from that period dated for me some of those strong and faithful friendships which I have always found at difficult moments."[7] The couple made various excursions in summer, including a visit to the home of Adolphe Pictet, one of the stalwarts of Marie's Geneva salon. A major in the artillery and a published author of works on classic and romantic art, Pictet taught esthetics at the Geneva Academy and was writing a book on Indo-European philology. He introduced her to the German Idealists—Kant, Fichte, and Schelling. Marie dubbed him "Universal," and she maintained a correspondence with him that lasted most of her life. Louis de Ronchaud was also a constant correspondent when he was not with her. Marie's letters to him often contained the same information as those to Pictet, but with the younger man she developed a more intimate tone. Ronchaud was selflessly devoted to Marie and did all sorts of errands for her. She described him to Liszt as one of her "transcendent commissioners." Liszt was not the only one who needed the constant attention of the opposite sex.

The couple then began to plan for the visit of a guest whose novels they both admired—George Sand. Liszt had met Sand in late 1834, through Alfred Musset, but he had stopped seeing her in January 1835, at Marie's request, probably because of the false report spread by Heinrich Heine that Liszt and Sand were having an affair. Marie met Sand at the theater, and they dined together at the home of Liszt's mother. Liszt also took Marie to Sand's "attic," where she held her salon when in Paris. The two women were strongly attracted to each other. Sand wrote Marie: "The first time I saw you, I found you lovely, but you were cold; the second time I told you that I detested the aristocracy, not knowing that you were one of them. Instead of giving me a cuff as I deserved, you spoke to me of your soul as if you had known me for ten years."[8]

Sand was excited by Marie's courage in breaking from her past to follow Liszt; she also found her physically attractive.

My beautiful countess with blond hair . . . I can without folly and without displaced familiarity say that I love you, that you seem the only thing beautiful, estimable and truly noble that I have seen in the patrician sphere. . . . At present you are for me the veritable type of fantastic princess, loving and noble artist of manners, of language, and of what is fitting, like the daughter of the king in poetic days . . . sweet as the Valentine [another novel by Sand] that I dreamed of in other times, and more intelligent, for you are much too [intelligent], and it is the only reproach that I have to make to you.[9]

In September 1835, Sand's seventh "Lettre d'un voyageur" appeared in the *Revue des deux mondes*. Addressed to Liszt, it made allusions to his aristocratic liaison, describing a blond vision in a blue dress, "lovable and noble creature, who sat between us like the marvelous princesses who appeared to the poor artists in the joyous Tales of Hoffman." (In a letter, Maurice de Flavigny expressed to his sister his chagrin over this proof of her descent into the bohemian life.) A "Lettre d'un voyageur à M. George Sand" appeared in *L'Europe centrale* on December 19, signed by Liszt. Marie invited Sand to visit them in Geneva, but the meeting had to be postponed. Sand was fighting her husband in court to regain the property she had brought to the marriage.

As a successful author who went where she pleased and wore men's clothes when she liked, Sand was the independent woman of her day. She saw Marie, who had shed her aristocratic ties for love, as a soulmate; Marie admired Sand for her writing and longed to be able to write as well. Liszt urged Sand from Geneva to encourage her. Sand's letter to Marie recommended that she write, "quickly, before thinking too much," and predicted great success for her.[10] Marie's response was prescient. "To become involved in writing today requires either the genius awarded by heaven or the laborious, indefatigable perseverence, the exclusive determination to work, through which one arrives at a special erudition that is out of the ordinary. But genius has not sought me out, and I am too lazy to pursue talent."[11] It was only later that Marie, again acknowledging that she lacked genius, pursued her talent.

Their friendship seemed inevitable. In a three-month correspondence, the two women tested their differences. For Sand, it was Marie's aristocratic background that rankled: "Let me take your countess crown and smash it, and I will give you one of stars that becomes you better." Sand admitted that she herself had a bad character but did not intend to reform; she was "a gross and fantastic porcupine." But if Marie would tame her, Sand was "capable of a complete devotion"; she would serve Marie faithfully, even wash her dishes.[12] Marie replied, dubbing herself a "turtle":

Well, don't let yourself be put off by the shell of the turtle, who is in turn not afraid of the needles of the porcupine. Under this shell there is still life; under this formal and compact exterior, which must be antipathetic to you and which a long constraint of spirit, a long suffocation of the heart made me put on, there is still spontaneity, sympathy. It is something that you must search for a bit, but believe me, it will never betray you. I don't make you any promises; I don't demand any of you. In friendship as in love, the only thing that we should demand and that we can really promise is a constant sincerity, a frankness that prevents the worse or that repairs it; and that sincerity, that openness of the heart, I feel irresistibly drawn to share with you. Why? Perhaps because the North pole attracts the South pole through the magnetic needle. . . . I have felt that the bizarre contrasts between our two natures could and ought to be harmonized one day.

She proposed a treaty of alliance, offensive and defensive.[13]

Sand's new novel, *Simon*, was about to appear in the *Revue des deux mondes*. She dedicated it "To Madame la comtesse ***. Mysterious friend, be the patron of this poor little story. Patrician, excuse the antipathies of the rustic storyteller. Madame, tell no one that you are her sister. Heart three times noble, descend to her and render her proud. Countess, be pardoned. Hidden star, recognize yourself in these litanies."[14]

Her court case settled, Sand was ready to visit the couple. They planned a week together in Chamonix and invited Puzzi, Pictet, and Ronchaud to join them. This journey was recorded by both Pictet and Sand.[15] Marie and

Liszt arrived first with Ronchaud and Puzzi, and awaited Sand with her children, Solange and Maurice, whom Pictet had met at Geneva. They were all to ride through the mountains on mules. From the beginning the party abandoned itself to farce, starting with the registration cards signed at the inn. Sand began it, writing in the hotel register "Name: Piffoël [big nose] family; Domicile: Nature; Coming from: God; Going to: Heaven; Place of Birth: Europe; Profession: Flâneurs; Date of titles: forever; Delivered by: public opinion." Liszt then signed himself "musician philosopher," coming from "Doubt, going to Truth." Sand later wrote that the innkeeper assumed that Pictet, in his major's uniform, had come to arrest them all.

The next day they all set off, dressed in outlandish clothing—all but Marie, who, as usual, looked like royalty at a garden party. Sand called her "Princess Arabella." A tourist pointed her out as "George Sand, the mistress of Liszt," a mistake too often made for Marie's liking. For half the week it rained, but the company continued their buffoonery. Marie, through all the shenanigans, remained her cool self, even trying to discuss philosophy with Pictet, much to the incredulity of Sand. This trip was Marie's real introduction to bohemian life. She wrote later that she had been cold and gauche. "Their childishness put me off; I felt not at all at ease, and consequently I was not pleasant."[16]

Both Sand and Pictet noted Marie's inability to forget herself and enjoy the foolishness. Sand said that the snow on the mountain would never be white enough for her. Pictet wrote later to Marie: "You have an internal standard which, applied to the things of this world, will make them always seem foolish and miserable to you."[17] He was right; Marie could never put aside her critical faculties. Nevertheless, the trip was a success and even seemed to bring the two women closer. George remained with them in Geneva for a few weeks of romantic evenings around the piano and occasional excursions into the countryside. A pact was struck between the Piffoëls and the Fellows, and Sand invited them to visit her at Nohant.

After Sand left, Liszt and Marie put off their plan to go to Italy. They came to an agreement that Liszt would spend half his time performing and half in seclusion with Marie, composing. They also decided to winter in Paris, which would give Liszt another opportunity to challenge his rival, Thalberg. Marie was now anxious to get back to Paris. She told Pictet that she had felt like "a carp on the lawn" in Geneva.[18] She also hoped to see her daughter Claire. Sand was notified of their decision to return to France and replied that Marie should decide when they would visit Nohant. Marie wrote that she had "a great need of solitude to restore to equilibrium a whole part of myself in which three years of passion, of suffering and of superhuman joy have brought trouble and disorder."[19]

In mid-September the couple returned to Paris and took an apartment in the Hôtel de France, on the rue Neuve-Lafitte. Liszt began to prepare for a concert with Hector Berlioz; Marie wrote more articles to keep his name before the public.[20] Perhaps seeking Marie's reassurance, Liszt wrote in their joint diary on November 24: "I am determined to produce my masterpieces, but my incapacity is parallel to my will."[21] In any case, he had no doubts about his ability as a performer. When he and Berlioz appeared in concert on December 18, the audience, at first cold, ended up wildly enthusiastic.

Sand wrote the couple as soon as they arrived that she was housecleaning for their visit, so that Marie would not think she lived in a Cossack camp. However, she soon left for Paris, taking rooms in the same hotel. The two women shared a salon, mainly drawn from Sand's circle and Liszt's: Lamennais, Pierre Leroux, Sainte-Beuve, Sue, Heinrich Heine, Meyerbeer, Rossini, Chopin, Adam Mickiewicz, Victor Hugo, Nicolo Paganini, Adolphe Nourrit, Baron Eckstein, Bernard Potocki, and the writer Charles Didier, who was involved in a liaison with Sand. There is some evidence that the establishment of Lamennais as editor of *Le Monde* was hatched in this salon by Sand, Leroux, and others, with an eye to making it a place of publication for all of them.[22] Here Marie met Carlotta Marliani, a friend of Sand and wife of the Spanish consul at Paris. Determined to become the intimate confidante of both women, Marliani was to be instrumental in the breakup of their friendship. Marie and Liszt were also invited by Chopin, although he disliked Marie and she returned the feeling—a situation that would create difficulties as Sand became more and more attracted to the tubercular musician.

Marie's feelings during the next months are not clear. Malicious commentators insist that it was not she but Liszt and Sand who had planned the common salon, that Marie was unhappy because the two artists had so much in common and because people still thought Liszt was having an affair with Sand.[23] The evidence is ambiguous. An article in *Vert-Vert* described Marie welcoming the author into the common salon: "a divinity blond and well brought up, in Spanish dress, a lace veil on her head, her stockings revealed, and red shoes; she offered me a cigarette and did the honors of her salon."[24] Marie is here pictured as participating in a demimondaine atmosphere that was not natural to her. Was she trying hard to please, or had she for once managed to relax and enjoy being bohemian? There is a letter from Liszt after Marie had left Paris to visit Sand, which is difficult to explain if all had gone smoothly between them: "Oh! Marie, Marie, you could still love me. Despite our past flaws, despite other people, despite all. I would be worthy of you."[25]

It was only after a bout with influenza that Marie was able to accept Sand's invitation to visit her, early in 1837. She was impatient: "I want to see Nohant, I want to live your life, be the friend of your dogs, the benefactor of your chickens; I want to warm myself at your fire, eat your game, and revive my poor machine in the air that you breathe."[26] She did experience a great healing at Nohant in the first months with Sand and felt that their friendship was solidifying. "George is the only woman with whom I could live for a long period without tiring," she wrote.[27] The two would rise early to go riding along the Indre River. Sand, who swam in it until late in life, was fearless. Coming to a precipitous slope that Marie feared would plunge her into the river, Sand took pity on her. "Jumping lightly from his horse, he put one arm in each horse's bridle and ran down the path that Marie would have feared to walk down," Marie wrote in her diary. Thus the two women acted out the roles of male and female.[28] In the evenings Sand liked to brush Marie's long blond hair.[29] The two also engaged in extensive conversations. Sand was working on her "Lettres à Marcie," dealing with what would today be called "women's issues." It is likely that she discussed the letters with Marie, although they certainly did not agree on everything. In particular, Marie felt that it was ridiculous to romanticize maternity, but they certainly agreed on the right to divorce.

Sand had confided to Marie her sorrow upon reading Musset's book on their affair.[30] She had lost her belief that love was the ideal of her life. Marie seems also to have confided her doubts and fears about her relationship with Liszt, including her resentments in Geneva. Still physically weak, she was wracked with depression. And this despite Liszt's constant letters from Paris begging her to return: "Truly I believe that I will fall sick if I do not see you soon." But it was Marie who was too sick to go to Paris. Instead, they spoke of their plans for Italy. Liszt wrote: "Italy, Italy and relaxation and our dear beautiful studies, and our child, and our love."[31] Marie devoted what energy she had to a new "Lettre d'un bachelier," which she sent to Liszt to deliver to the *Gazette musicale.* Usually they were together when these articles were written, which made them to some extent joint products, but not this time. Liszt asked Marie not to betray to Sand that she had written it.

The letter is addressed to Sand, the "*poète voyageur.*" It describes returning from Italy, "which will always be the land of choice for . . . those exiles from heaven who suffer and sing and whom the world calls poets." The author quotes Goethe on "the land where the lemon trees bloom." Paris, in comparison, is criticized as a place of brutal passions, hypocritical vices, and shameless ambition. Liszt is described there, torn from his native Hungary to perform as a child prodigy, prostituting his music for the diversion of society. The letter includes the confession that in order to wring applause from the crowd, Liszt exaggerated and deformed the composers he played, adding rapid runs and cadenzas. One suspects that Liszt would not have made any such confession; the letter certainly reveals Marie's prejudice against performance as compared to composing. There follows a discussion of the musician, who, "as one who is inspired by nature but does not copy it, exhales the most personal mysteries of his destiny in sounds." But the language is obscure, lending itself to different interpretations. The author makes the suggestion that just as a writer adds a preface to his book to make it more understandable by readers, the composer should provide a brief psychological sketch for each work of music, to enlighten those who will play it. The article was popular and brought Liszt many congratulations. Reporting its success to Marie, he joked, "Together we make a great writer."[32]

Despite the friendship of Sand and the love of Liszt, Marie continued to suffer from a bout of "spleen," as she called it. Surely, she must have shared it with Sand. A letter to Ronchaud at this time provides the first good description of it: "I am mortally sorrowful this morning. I have just finished crying bitterly." She went on to speak of her concern that Liszt would be unable to fulfill his genius. "Will my heart be a bottomless vase, in which he vainly throws all the treasures of his genius and his love? . . . And this love, and mine, is it only the sublime lie of two beings who want to give one another a happiness in which neither can believe for himself? . . . Today I feel the venomous tooth of the serpent which always sleeps in my heart; its too violent beating awakes him to bite me." She thought it was perhaps wrong to suffer this way and cowardly to complain of it. But she apologized that she needed to speak to someone who was absent, who could not tell her she was right or wrong. "Is one right or wrong to die?" she asked, indicating that she felt powerless to deal with her symptoms. She asked him not to speak of this letter when they met again; perhaps then she would again be young and full of life.[33]

Although it is impossible to know the basic cause of Marie's tendency to severe depression, which seemed to have some inherited source, we can pinpoint some of the occasions when the crises occurred. They were, it seems, crises of confidence. The trip back to Paris was the first test, in a familiar setting, of Marie's decision to break with her world and run off with Liszt. Living in the same house with him and Sand, she felt how much more both of them belonged to this artistic and intellectual milieu than she did. But worse, she saw, particularly at Nohant, that they inhabited a world of creativity that she did not share. It was also at Nohant that Marie first recognized the possibility that Liszt might not always be faithful to her. These feelings all combined in a fatal mixture of self-doubt, in which she questioned not only her life decision but also her own worth.

When she was thus laid low, it could last for weeks, even months. She could not understand or justify her feelings. On this occasion she thought of joining Liszt in Paris, where he was performing a triumphant series of concerts. Instead, she wrote an article about them. As Liszt said, he couldn't risk doing it himself; the other articles had been such a success. Although he continued to beg Marie to come, she continued to delay, fearing that she would annoy him—rightly, it seems. When Liszt finally joined her at Nohant for a week during mid-March, there were scenes full of anger on both sides. Nevertheless, it is probable that their second child was conceived during this time.

Marie finally did go to Paris, in time for Liszt's final triumph over Thalberg, which took place at the salon of Princess Belgiojoso. It was actually Marie who made the remark attributed to the hostess: "Thalberg is the *first* pianist of the world, but Liszt is the only one."[34] She negotiated with Lamennais to publish Sand's "Lettres à Marcie" in *Le Monde.* Defending the work against Lamennais's disapproval of certain passages, particularly on divorce, she told him that if he was so sensitive he should resign his post. Unfortunately, Lamennais stood firm and did not publish the "Lettres." Sand had other business, with François Buloz, at the *Revue de deux mondes,* and with Maurice Schlesinger, at the *Gazette musicale,* for Marie to handle. She also contacted Musset to try to retrieve Sand's letters. In the correspondence between the two women, Marie provided Sand with all the Paris gossip. Sand pressed her to return to Nohant soon. "Know that your Piffoël loves you and awaits you with impatience. No one has been permitted to breathe the air of your chamber since you have left it."[35] She told Marie to invite "the Poles"—Albert Grzymala, Adam Mickiewicz, and Chopin—to Nohant. Marie was unwilling. Of Chopin she wrote, "There is nothing to him but his cough."[36]

The writer Charles Didier, who at this time was losing Sand as a lover, visited Marie in Paris and felt that she, too was sad. He wrote in his diary, "I like her better than I do Liszt. She is a noble creature and very unhappy. . . . I find their present relationship puzzling, and rather think they are deliberately acting, that their affair is in its last gasp."[37] Things did not entirely improve when the couple returned to Nohant. This was partly because both Liszt and Sand were working; Sand often wrote late into the night, sometimes joined by Liszt. Marie's spleen emerged in the form of jealousy. She began to suspect a relationship between the two, even that Sand was trying to seduce him. Although Sand probably did not really try to take Liszt from Marie, she may have flirted with him a bit. Sand also liked male attention, and her relationship with Didier was over, from her point of view. But the true meaning of Marie's doubts, which came and went over the years, was not so much sexual jealousy as it was a feeling of personal inadequacy. She wrote later, "I recognized how puerile it had been for me to think that only she could have really fulfilled Franz, that I was an unhappy barrier between two destinies made to be joined and complete one another."[38] However, Marie's jealousy was the first worm in the apple of her friendship with Sand.

The three did spend many magical moments at Nohant, with Liszt setting the stage in the evenings by playing the piano for hours. Sand smoked her pipe or cigars, and Marie provided a romantic figure in the moonlight. Sand wrote of Marie in her autobiography: "All her movements had such grace and harmony that one would have said sounds emerged from her as from a living harp."[39] And in her diary she wrote of Liszt: "Powerful artist, sublime in great things, always superior in small ones, sad nevertheless and gnawed by a secret wound. Happy man, loved by a beautiful, generous, intelligent and chaste woman. What more do you want, you miserable ungrateful man? Ah, if only I were loved like that!"[40]

The last comment may have related to the stormy effort Sand was making at the time to capture the radical lawyer Michel de Bourges to replace Didier as a lover. Didier arrived at Nohant to find Michel there; Sand was also being wooed by her children's tutor, the author Félicien Malefille, and by the playwright, Pierre Bocage. Marie found it difficult to accept her friend's easygoing sensuality; disillusion began to modify the boundless admiration she had felt for Sand. She remarked to the unlucky Didier that her friend seemed to be heading for promiscuity.[41] (When Sand, under the influence of her new lover, rewrote the end of her novel *Lélia*, removing her heroine's frigidity, a quip went around Paris: "The style is the man.")

By the time the couple prepared to leave Nohant for Italy, Marie felt refortified by the comparison between herself and her friend. Sand might have the glory, but she, Marie, had a unique and incomparable love. Sand seemed to her a creature of excess—of soul, heart, and senses. Marie wrote later that it was good for her to live with Sand and see her frailties and her inability to control her life. Nevertheless, she admitted that Sand had helped her develop her poetic sensibility and her ability to enjoy. Sand had taught her to analyze her feelings, had urged her to be more confident, and had encouraged her to write. Marie felt that on the banks of the Indre she had found friendship and peace. She cried on leaving Nohant. It was as if she knew that the best time of her relationship with Sand was past. But Marie was beginning another long period of bliss with Liszt. She wrote in her diary:

In traveling the land with him I feel that he is my single support, my unique recourse, my only guide; that my destiny is solely in him, that I have freely and voluntarily given it to him, that I truly have neither temple nor country except in his heart. . . . He says that he needs to see beauty through me, that I am for him like the word through which the beauty of things is revealed to him. Like the statue of Memnon, his soul renders forth divine sounds when the rays of enthusiasm touch it; but, like Memnon, in the shadow of earthly things, he remains impenetrable and mute in his force. . . . It makes me understand what the sybils and pythonesses of ancient times could have been. I do not consider myself his equal, for he has been initiated far beyond me. But at the same time I sense that he attracts and raises me up to him in the immensity of his love.[42]

To some extent, Liszt was now her religion. She had told Sand that she had totally lost the faith of her childhood and was dissatisfied with philosophic systems or the *"vague élan des poètes."* When the couple stopped at Bourges to see the cathedral, Marie recorded that she contemplated a long time, in silence, "but I felt that I did not adore any more. I was astonished at the grandeur of that crucified man to whom they had built more temples than the Caesars had ever had palaces, [but] the terrible words of Pierre Leroux came at the end of all my meditations: And nevertheless, Christ was not resurrected."[43]

Marie was drawn to the social religion of art preached by Liszt and others. It was part of the canon of Romanticism that the artist might, in the waning of traditional faiths, serve not only as genius creator but also as potential savior. On their way through Lyon, Liszt and the singer Adolphe Nourrit, who preached the necessity of saving the working class through music,[44] gave a concert for the benefit of poverty-stricken workers that raised six thousand francs. Describing Liszt at the piano, a reviewer wrote, "The sacred fire flowed out from every pore."[45] Of Nourrit, singing Schubert's *lieder*, Marie wrote, "He was more the priest in that moment than many priests, for if we had obeyed the emotion that he caused in our souls, we would have thrown ourselves on our knees to adore him."[46] She pondered the need she sometimes felt to be part of a community, to connect the little she knew of the good to a unique end, to move from being an isolated individual to being member of a group, "one of the thousand beams that converge toward a center." She was also becoming sensitized to the misery of the poor and rebelled against the idea that suffering was associated with glorifying God. "If I saw Enfantin [the leader of the Saint-Simonian 'religion of humanity'], perhaps I would become a Saint-Simonian, not with a strong faith, but simply because, among the modern social systems, the doctrine of Saint-Simon is the one that embraces all my sympathies."[47]

It has been noted that Liszt's humanitarian projects of emancipation through art and the couple's shared writing about art heightened the romantic relationship of the two, that in a sense the "Lettres d'un Bachelier," which continued until 1841, were actually Marie's love letters to Liszt, her identification with him and his art. In that association of genius and talent, of the mastery of music and the elegance of the written word, she was constantly given the possibility of taking his ideas and molding them according to her own desires and aspirations.[48] As a result, Marie was able to remain for long periods unaware that her Liszt was to some extent her creation and that the more earthbound Liszt might be different and disappointing. It was to her Liszt that she remained forever faithful.

The couple stopped at Etrembière, near Geneva, where Blandine was staying with a nurse. They found her an extraordinary child, intelligent and passionate for music. "What holy joys were embodied in germ for us in that little being still so unformed, so incomplete!"[49] Marie wrote. They arranged that she would join them in Milan. For the moment, however, they were content to leave her with her nurse.

Their Italian journey was planned to include all the notable artistic sites in northern Italy. After seeing Ravenna, they came to Milan, where they found the opera house, La Scala, "sad, monotonous, badly decorated, and horribly lighted." Nor did they like Donizetti's *Marino Faliero,* which they dubbed "anti-humanitarian music." Throughout their trip to Italy the couple criticized Italian music in their "Lettres," causing a scandal in the Italian music world. In the opposition of Italian and German music that raged in France during the nineteenth century, the couple stood firm on the German side. The most impressive thing in Milan was the cathedral, which Marie called a "Te Deum of marble"; it recalled to her the emotions of her infancy at Chartres.

Toward the end of the year, with Marie very pregnant, the couple went to Bellagio, on Lake Como, one of the most romantic spots in Europe, where the mountains seemed to grow out of the lake, which was often wreathed in a mysterious mist. Here they spent an idyllic two months alone, with Liszt composing and Marie writing another "Lettre." It commenced, "When you write a story of two happy lovers, set it on the banks of Lake Como. I do not know a place more clearly blessed by heaven."[50]

Marie spent much of her time reading and sharing with Liszt the works of Bossuet, Corneille, Molière, and above all Dante. With Dante began Marie's love affair with Italy and her lifelong study of the poet, who ranked second only to Goethe among her revered authors. Liszt's longest piece in the *Années de pèlerinage* was dedicated to Dante. The following year, in a "Lettre d'un bachelier" discussing Dante's beloved Beatrice, Marie wrote that she was shocked by Dante's treatment of his muse not as the ideal of love but as the ideal of knowledge: "It is not by reason and demonstration that woman reigns in the heart of man; it is not for her to *prove* God to him, but to make him feel God through love, and to draw him after her toward heavenly things. Her power is in feeling, not in knowledge. The loving woman is sublime; she is truly the guardian angel of man . . . the pedantic woman is a contradiction, a dissonance, she has no place in the hierarchy of beings."[51] This clear expression of the neoplatonic ideal in love would indicate that Marie was still content to assume the role of muse. She had not yet the confidence to feel her strength and independence in knowledge. She was also trying to convince herself that Liszt found the situation sufficient. She wrote in her diary that it was astonishing how happy he was in their solitude with just a bad piano, some books, and the conversation of a serious woman. He had renounced the enjoyments of society without even seeming to know he had done so.[52]

On December 4, 1837, Marie delivered their second daughter, Francesca Gaetana Cosima. This child, musically gifted, was to imitate her mother in leaving her first marriage for a love match with a musician, Richard Wagner. Again, Marie was not recorded as the mother. But the birth was not unnoticed. From the Austrian embassy the news went back to France. The Comte d'Agoult began to be nervous that the fortune of his daughter Claire might suffer from the competing family that his wife was producing. He threatened a lawsuit. It seems that Marie's brother Maurice was able to put it off for some time, but it seemed inevitable. Marie was upset; her mother was angry. The count's lawyer refused to allow him to write to Marie. Finally, six months later, Marie wrote a letter to her husband, begging him not to create a scandal and trying to reassure him while admitting nothing: "If I were to have illegitimate children, could you reasonably suppose, knowing me as you do, that I would by fraud assure them of a part of your inheritance? Would you not be convinced that, on the contrary, I would *expressly* wish in that case to establish an *impenetrable* barrier between them and you?"[53] This seems to have satisfied the count.

After the birth Liszt made frequent trips to perform in Milan, writing regularly, although he complained of sparse lines from her. He referred to her as his angel, repeated often that he was inconsiderate, unworthy of her. Knowing that she was depressed, he insisted on how lucky they were. Their old age would be "like an infinite concert of . . . memories. Now, at midday we suffer and complain, but we are still happy, are we not?" And in another letter he begged, "Let us love each other and then, because we must, know how to bear the rest."[54] Early in 1838, after placing Cosima with a nurse, Marie joined Liszt in an apartment in Milan, where she made what she described as her "third entrance into society." It was a milieu in which having lovers was completely acceptable. She felt that the Italians were sincere and indulgent but not intellectual. The couple composed a "Lettre" on La Scala, emphasizing its decadence, in which the only Italian composer they spared was Rossini.[55]

The two then continued their study of the art of Italy, traveling to Brescia, Verona, Vicenza, Padua, Venice, Genoa, Lugano, Plaisance, Parma, Bologna, Ravenna, Florence, Pisa, and Rome. Pictet predicted that Marie would not be satisfied with Venice, Rome, or Naples. (He added that she would not be content until she entered Jerusalem, not through the gate of Judea but through the gate of the Apocalypse, and even then he wasn't sure.)[56] Although they arrived in Rome during Carnival, the couple headed directly for the ancient monuments. They disliked the Laocoön at the Vatican. Marie accused Bernini of tarting up St. Peter's. They found the church music just as bad as the opera at Milan. But Marie was impressed with the drama of the papal benediction at Easter. The first "Lettre d'un Bachelier à Adolphe Pictet," on the lot of the artist, appeared at this time.[57] Delphine Gay, writing under an assumed name in *La Presse* in Paris, commented that one could find in the article "whiffs of the feminine, of the Muse," thereby hinting at the hand of Marie.[58]

The aesthetics of the articles on specific works of art published by the Bachelier at this time were, it has been noted, those of their time; they analyzed the picture, reconstructed the feelings of those in it, and described the moral impression produced on the viewer.[59] Taking dense notes on the paintings they saw, Marie began to question the absolute influence of religion on Italian art. She saw a paradox in a religion that preached abstinence and unworldliness but inspired sensuous beauty, particularly in Raphael's Madonnas; it was more likely that paganism or even the artist's mistress was the inspiration. It was necessary, she decided, to know the lives of the painters. She felt a tremendous force in Michelangelo. In a comparison typical of the romantics, she compared Raphael to Mozart and Michelangelo to Beethoven. Her favored painters were Titian, Tintoretto, and Veronese— above all, Veronese.[60] Yet, upon meeting the painter Henri Lehmann, she told him that she never permitted herself to have an opinion on a painting, that it was difficult for women to have anything valuable to say about the plastic arts. "We are too subjective, our education distances us too much from reality in the physical as in the moral order; we do not know how to *see.*"[61] An amazing statement for a woman who was writing art criticism under Liszt's name and would later publish it under her own pen name!

Lehmann was a student of the artist Jean Auguste Dominique Ingres, whom the couple met in Rome. Ingres was better known for his violin at this time; he wanted to play chamber music with Liszt. Later, he did portraits of both of them. They also met Luigi Calametta and Ary Scheffer, who did their portraits, and Lorenzo Bartolini, who did their busts. Liszt, with his shoulder-length hair, was the perfect figure of the romantic musician. As for Marie, the Vicomtesse de Poilloue de Saint Mars, who met her later that year, described her: "She was not exactly pretty, but her elegance, her distinction, her blond hair, her eyes and her charm made a beauty out of her. You forgot her thinness, which she angelicized in cascades of muslin and tulle. Involuntarily you looked for her wings."[62]

There were reasons for Marie's wasted frame. She had recently borne her fourth child and was prey to doubts about the future. At this point, she was still caught up in a romantic dream of her own making, which she was not prepared to relinquish. It seemed impossible to acknowledge that she had sacrificed her position and reputation for something less than ideal. But in the year to come she would lose the struggle to maintain the idyll with Liszt, for she realized that it was not only the plaudits of the crowd that Liszt could not give up but also the adoration of other women.

Four ∾ "Alas, alas, where to find again such flights, such madness?"

Marie's first disappointment of the year 1838 was the suspicion that the friendship with Sand might be over. On leaving Nohant, Marie had considered Sand a close friend. Her suspicion of Sand's intentions toward Liszt had temporarily disappeared. Living closely with her idol had led Marie to some disillusionment, particularly over Sand's love affairs. However, she continued to write regularly, as did Liszt, and was surprised when they received no letters in return. Sand was resentful; she knew that her friend was no longer quite so fascinated by her and that Marie's attitude on her multiple lovers had influenced Liszt. Sand had also seen Marie at her worst, in alternating anger and depression, and had noted the strains in her relationship with Liszt. Each woman was to use her knowledge of the other in such a way as to make further friendship impossible. And the result was more damaging for Marie than for Sand.

Marie was quite soon aware of the lack of correspondence from Nohant, since in this period friends wrote each other frequently. They had written almost daily letters when Marie had interrupted her visit to go to Paris. After leaving Nohant, Marie continued to record her impressions on the way to Italy, letting her friend know where she could be reached. Receiving no word, Marie wrote anxiously, "Try not to give away the litle corner that the princess Mirabelle occupies in your heart, because she doesn't want to be dislodged."[1] Some letters may have been lost on the way, as Sand claimed. Finally, Marie received a letter in late September, in which Sand complained about a fancy seal (a present from Pictet but just the type of aristocratic symbol Sand detested) that Marie had used on her correspondence.[2] Sand's next letter was a notice of her mother's death in which she did share with her friends her experience of mourning at Fontainebleau.[3] Marie wrote from Como, inviting Sand to visit, swearing that she found "the waters of the lake blue enough, the fig trees green enough, the sun splendid enough," and teasing her about the writer Mallefille, to whom she had introduced Sand.[4]

By the time Sand received this letter, she had responded to Mallefille's wooing. She did not accept the couple's invitation and enclosed in her very unsatisfactory letter an angry one from Mallefille.[5] When Marie learned of the new affair, she judged Sand harshly, knowing that she had begun by mocking the author. Sand sent Marie few letters thereafter, even though Liszt wrote asking an explanation. In answer, Sand equivocated; she said Marie had needed her letters before but did not need them now.[6] Finally, about a year after she had left Nohant, Marie admitted defeat. Writing to Didier, who was temporarily reunited with Sand, she said, "It is always sad to break with what has been, to deny a part of one's self and one's past. I have never broken a friendship without regretting, not the individual, but the lost affection and the joy of my own heart."[7] She may have been hoping that Didier would convey to Sand the mixed message—that Marie regretted the lost friendship without regretting the friend too much, that she wanted Sand but did not need her.

Then when Marie heard from Marliani that Sand had embarked on an affair with Chopin, she allowed her wit full rein in her reply. She joked that it should have happened a year earlier, when Sand, to cool her sexual ardor for Bourges, was having herself bled. Marie remembered telling Sand then that she herself would rather take Chopin (whom she hated). "How many stabs of the lancet would have been spared her! . . . I assure you it couldn't be funnier."[8] When Marliani rebuked her for speaking of Sand that way, Marie replied that she had never asked for the gossip that Marliani had passed on to her. She was not incapable of loving and understanding her friends. In this case what was so serious was the effect that promiscuity would have on a great writer's talent. Sand seemed to treat love as just a physical matter, like a man.[9]

Perhaps Marie really was concerned about the implications of Sand's promiscuity. She wrote to Pictet that she thought of Sand tenderly but with bitterness. It was terrible to see a person with such intelligence and a heart potentially so noble give herself to a life of sexual intrigue. "Could it then be true that a woman should not have energy and genius, which can only lead her astray?"[10] Here Marie showed her desire to appear a true woman, in contrast to her independent friend. Not that she was totally incapable of recognizing the need for a purely physical love. She was later able to accept the easygoing affairs of her friend Hortense Allart, also a writer, remarking that fidelity in love should be a reciprocal agreement in which the woman should have no greater responsibility than the man.[11] At this time, however, Marie could not conceive of infidelity in her relationship with Liszt. Nor did she expect it of him.

As Sand continued to ignore her, Marie continued her acid remarks and sharp witticisms at her friend's expense. But Sand had already had her revenge, before the fact. First, in her novel, *La Dernière Aldini,* published late in 1837, a friend warns an artist not to marry an aristocratic woman, adding, for those who could read between the lines, "She is neither so strong in spirit nor so free from prejudice as she pretends. . . . She has told me without realizing it . . . hundreds of things that prove to me that she thinks she is making an immense sacrifice for your sake. . . . The day will come . . . when, even without regretting the world, she will accuse you of ingratitude, and it's a sad role for man to be a bankrupt in his wife's debt."[12] But Sand had done worse. In January 1838 Balzac had visited her for a week, during which she had regaled him with material for a new novel—the love affair of Marie and Liszt.

Balzac's resulting novel was first serialized in *Le Siècle,* early in 1839. Entitled *Béatrix,* it was a roman à clef, that form so dear to the nineteenth century. The heroine, Camille Maupin, represents Sand. The villain, Béatrix de Rochefide, represents Marie; she has left her husband for the musician Conti, a man who feigns emotions he does not feel. Béatrix is shown as brilliant in conversation in which she can exercise her critical spirit, but she must have other people in order to shine. She is poised, polished in dress and toilette. Balzac paints her in detail in various situations, as a woman who is prisoner of her own artifices. As their affair cools, the couple resurrects it by traveling to romantic places. Liszt is represented by a combination of Conti and the young, handsome hero Calyste, whom Béatrix seduces away from Camille. When published as a book in 1839, the novel bore the subtitle "The Galley-Slaves of Love," adapted from a phrase that Marie herself had used in a letter to Sand but not in the sense that Balzac used it. His Preface reads: "When a certain woman of high rank sacrifices her position to some violent passion . . . she is attached forever to the author of her ruin like a galley-slave to his companion on the chain."[13]

The question is, how much of *Béatrix* was due to Sand? How had she described the lovers to Balzac? He would not be the only person to whom Sand had denigrated Marie soon after she left Nohant, as her correspondence shows. But Balzac also had an unhappy memory of one of the few times he had seen the Comtesse d'Agoult—before Liszt, at the salon of the Marquise de la Bourdonnaye. The women present had asked Balzac to tell a story; he had been incoherent and was made a figure of fun by the men.[14] His advances had also been spurned by the beautiful Marquise de Castries. Could he have harbored a grudge against all aristocratic women? For Balzac, who had a great need for acceptance by the aristocracy, it was not impossible. In any case, Sand demanded from him a letter swearing that *Béatrix* was not inspired by anything she had told him.[15] He reported to his friend Madame Hanska, however, that Sand was joyful about the novel and that, with some exceptions, the story was true.[16] Later, he told a friend of Marie's whom he met at the Opéra that he had "embroiled the two bitches."[17]

Another question is when and how Marie found out about the work, which first appeared while she was in Italy. Many decades later, a biography of Liszt recorded that Marie had been in tears on hearing of Balzac's novel and its reception in Paris. It also quotes Liszt as saying that Balzac's portrait of Marie was done by the hand of a master; Liszt, who had thought he knew her through and through, knew her better after reading it: "Madame d'Agoult was the cleverest woman in matters of dress that I have ever met, and Balzac knew how to make something of that salient feature. That wounded her to the quick, desirous as she was to be taken seriously, as Muse and as a strong character."[18] However, the source of this information, Janka Wohl, both adored Liszt and despised Marie, so her reportage may not be reliable.

One difficulty about the next phase of Marie's life is that it was mainly recounted by her enemies, like Wohl; by those who had turned against her, like Sand; and by Liszt in his later years. As for her own memoirs, Marie always insisted that they represented not necessarily the facts but the truth. We do know that when the couple arrived in Venice in March 1838, Marie was exhausted. (This was only three months after the birth of Cosima, her fourth child.) She recorded that La Fenice, the opera house there, was less imposing but much lovelier than La Scala. She deplored the Donizetti opera she heard there while admiring the singer, Caroline Ungher, and wrote in her diary that this experience confirmed her idea that none of our pleasures can be complete. The couple could find nothing worth reading in the bookstores. When Marie asked Countess Policastro to lend her some books, she found that her tremendous palace did not contain any!

From the time she reached Venice, Marie felt ill. She deplored the odor of the city, as many have since; it smelled as if "all Venice had the colic."[19] The vapors rising from the water and the thick, heavy air suffocated her. She felt "not exactly sad, but languid, torpid." She wrote in her diary that the sources of life seemed stilled in her; even curiosity, that final goad to activity, seemed dead. However, she and Liszt went to the Pinacothèque to devour the art, they hired a gondola, and they finally found some books. Liszt read *Maria Tudor* aloud to her, and they shared its romantic mood. "How my heart seems poor and sterile when his opens up to me entirely! I immediately compare myself to those artesian wells dug in the hope of finding a rushing spring, where one finds pure beautiful water, but not having its level above the soil, it doesn't gush out."[20] She also felt inferior to Liszt because he was patient, whereas she became annoyed at having to wait for him.[21]

Liszt may have been patient, but he began to chafe at performing only in Venetian drawing rooms. There were conversations about settling down in a chalet in Switzerland but also about another concert tour. Liszt even spoke of their spending some years in Germany, after he made another appearance in Paris. His moment for action came when the Danube overflowed in early April, leaving hundreds of Hungarian victims in its wake. Liszt announced his desire to give a benefit concert in Vienna for his compatriots. Marie was too proud to object, and he left almost immediately, on April 7. He was not to return for almost two months.

This time Liszt left Marie in the company of a new admirer, the young Count Emilio Malazzoni. For more than two weeks he accompanied her daily as she visited the great sites of Venice. On April 25 she wrote in her diary, "I cannot get used to the air in Venice. I am growing thinner and do not feel well, but I am sustained by the poetic sentiment constantly recalled here by art and by nature."[22] Liszt was writing letters to her recounting his triumphs in Vienna. After two weeks he began to suggest that she might join him there. As the month wore on, he made these requests more specific, but he also implied that he was cutting short his stay because he couldn't stand being without her. "You are my country, my heaven, my single love."[23] To these mixed signals Marie did not reply.

Why did Marie not accept Liszt's pressures to join him? Was she really not well enough? Did she feel he was ambivalent about her presence in his public life? Or was the ambivalence hers? In Italy, her presence at Liszt's side was accepted; this was not so on the other side of the Alps. Perhaps she was also aware that the Austrian embassy had passed on the news of Cosima's birth to her family. Preferring to live with Liszt away from the great metropolitan centers of Europe, she was still hoping that he would spend most of his time with her in seclusion, composing and only occasionally venturing forth to perform. But Liszt enjoyed being a virtuoso. And he was to discover on this trip that by giving concerts he could bring in enormous amounts of money, aside from the psychological income of public adulation. Thus he was strengthened in his desire to be a performer who also composed; she was willing for him to perform occasionally, provided he was primarily a composer. So while he begged her to join him, she stayed where she was, hoping to lure him back.

Understandably, there was a certain amount of anger on both sides. Liszt allowed himself to enjoy the company of adoring aristocratic women. As time went on, his letters mentioned their names; one letter Marie received was written on paper with a woman's crest. Many years later, in notes for her memoirs, Marie wrote about this period: "Letters from Vienna to Venice: Strange situation. . . . Proposition to separate 'for a time.' Perhaps his real conception of free marriage. At that time I could not imagine such a thing. It was too reasonable. He always had a profound respect for me. He doubted himself: 'Perhaps I am a vile Monsieur.'"[24] No letter of Liszt's with such a proposition exists. If Liszt did make suggestions for a freer relationship, it would account for the letter in which she wrote him, "I am happy to be your mistress, but not one of your mistresses."[25]

Marie's anger was expressed physically. One day in early May she fell ill with fever. Malazzoni called his family's doctor; after discussing her condition with him, he wrote to Liszt, urging his return. The next letter received in Venice from Liszt asked Malazzoni to bring Marie to Vienna. Liszt may not have received the notification of her illness when he wrote the letter. Or he may have assumed that she had taken to her bed to get him to return. Certainly, his absence contributed to her condition, but her illness was real.[26] According to Marie, he never took her physical problems seriously. In any case, the letter enraged her.

Once he was convinced she was sick, Liszt wrote passionate letters: Why did he leave her? What good are the plaudits of the crowd to him? He has tried to return but found the coach goes to Venice only on Saturdays, and he could not rent one. Also, he has another concert commitment. He is still hoping she can meet him and they can go together to Hungary. If she cannot, he will not go to Pressburg or to Budapest as planned. He would have been back in Venice by now if he had not been convinced that she would be able to meet him. He begs her forgiveness; it is the last time. Pity him, he knows it is unpardonable, etc. In another letter he still hopes she will come. He knows what she is thinking (presumably about his relations with women), but he loves her, belongs only to her. In a subsequent letter he is still explaining how hard it is to get away; he is tied hand and foot. He will leave Saturday. (He didn't.) As he realized the seriousness of the situation, his letters became more passionate. "I love you with all my force. I belong only to you. You alone have rights over my whole being, for you alone have the secret of my life, of my happiness and my sorrows." And, "Finally I will see you again. We will be together once more and for always, right? Oh! tell yourself that we will never part, whatever happens."[27]

Marie, somewhat recovered, was writing letters that crossed his: "After a two day interval I wrote you three days in a row, letters which should have reached you last Thursday, Friday and Saturday. These three letters told you that I could not leave Venice; then I received yours announcing your departure on Saturday evening. I waited for you the day before yesterday, yesterday, this morning. . . . Finally your letter arrived. . . . When are we to see each other then? I am waiting for you. I can not leave my room yet. In the name of Heaven, don't linger."[28]

Liszt arrived only at the end of May, weeks after he had heard of her illness. He described to her his reception in Vienna—the wild applause at his concerts, the money he had made, his entertainment by noble families, who had even found an aristocratic pedigree for him. When he admitted what she had already guessed, that he had been unfaithful, he excused himself by insisting that the women had thrown themselves at him. Marie wrote later that he had abandoned her for such unworthy things—not for a great work, for duty, for patriotism, but for "the successes of the drawing room, the glory of publicity, the invitation of princesses."

It was at this time, when she was desperate, that Marie inflicted on Liszt a wound he would never forget. When she had first left Paris with him, she had been convinced that the social difference between them had become meaningless. Nevertheless, as Sand had inferred, Marie was well aware of the social position she had sacrificed for him. Then he returned from Vienna, elegantly dressed, claiming a kind of aristocracy. And he was so taken with himself that she suspected he was secretly pleased about the titled women who had offered themselves to him. Did he really, as she wrote in a draft of her memoirs, suggest that she take Malazzoni as a lover? In any case, the conviction of being wronged provoked in her a response that was visceral: "Don Juan *parvenu* [an upstart Don Juan]," she called him. The contempt in this retort was like poison on an arrow in its implication that he, the lower-class musician, was social climbing in aristocrat beds.[29] When she later quoted him in their common diary as saying he could not promise not to be unfaithful again, he wrote underneath, "You remember my words, but those you said to me . . . seem to have left no traces in your mind. For my part, I haven't forgotten them, although I have tried. When you can recollect them, they will explain many things you seem to find incomprehensible." Although he admitted that "the three years I have just passed with you have made a man of me,"[30] she had skewered him in his pride, and it would never be the same.

As for Marie, she had been more seriously wounded, in the sense that she could no longer overlook the distance between Liszt the ideal artist she had created and Liszt the fallible young genius, prey to foolish pride and infidelity. And if he was not the ideal artist, what had she done in entrusting her life to him? She accused him of having "snatched from my heart those notions of duty in love that I need, and that form for me an ideal you have treated rudely and harshly."[31] But what was really injured was the ideal of the genius for whom it was only right that his muse should forsake all. Her pride had suffered as well. She felt that she could no longer be happy and therefore could not make Liszt happy if she had to fear future infidelities on his part. She wrote in their diary that Liszt would have to engage himself to be restrained and to conduct himself in such a way as to satisfy "my ideas of propriety, my womanly pride."[32] Much later, Marie recognized that "in the cruel struggle we allowed to develop between us, I have sometimes, often been wrong, wrong not to want to suffer or know how to suffer through you; the expression of my grief has often been sharp and vindictive."[33]

Yet the couple could not yet bring themselves to separate. Liszt felt chagrin, and in August 1838 he lamented in their common diary, "It would have been so easy to place my crown of innocence on Marie's brow. . . . It would have been the most precious of her jewels."[34] From Genoa, Marie wrote to Sand that they were as united as ever, despite false rumors that he had been unfaithful in Vienna and she in Venice. "We have the bad taste to find each other more and more charming, incomparable, and when we try a separation to see how it will suit us, we become splenetic. I begin to think that we are *condemned to love each other in perpetuity.*"[35] In trying to convince herself and Sand that all was well, she supplied the theme for Balzac's subtitle.

Back in Venice, Marie was again stricken by her "spleen," which she described in her diary as "an evil which I have borne since coming into this world. Passion raised me up for an instant, but I sense that I have no longer in me the principle of life. . . . I feel myself to be an hindrance in his life, I am not good for him. I throw sorrow and discouragement on his days."[36] A few weeks later, at Lugano, she recorded the blending of her sorrow and her love in true romantic fashion:

My thought had constructed for itself its own sepulchre. It lay down saying: I don't wish to hope any more, to believe, to search for God, I don't wish to aspire toward Him, I want to annul myself, I want to stop existing. You had to punish such a blasphemy, O my God. And how sweet is your punishment! You make me think that my sorrow is only endless because my love is immortal, and you reveal to me, in the depths of my misery, the sentiment of the eternal infinite which my soul will possess one day.

And then, addressing Liszt: "Mysterious being, angel of anger and benediction, you who attract and repel me; you who bathe me in clarity and who gather the stormclouds over my head, promise and menace, love and hate, joy and sorrow; I want to go where you go, breathe the air that you breathe, speak your word, live your life, die your death."[37] The series of opposites—promise/menace, love/hate, joy/sorrow—although imbedded in a paean of romantic passion, well expresses Marie's ambivalence about the health of their relationship.

One of the problems was that Liszt seemed temporarily blocked in his composing, which was supposed to be the alternative to concert tours. He was profoundly affected by this inability. It became associated in both their minds with his infidelity, an association that Marie retained and expressed many years later. At this point she was trying to be supportive to his genius as a composer, while intensely suffering her own feelings of insufficiency. She was also producing a new "Lettre d'un bachelier," which emphasized Liszt's genius and character.[38]

Did she know at this time that she was again pregnant? She surely did the following month (September) when she spoke of the beauties of nature, which always made her want to mingle her existence with Liszt's. Sometimes, she wrote, she herself wanted to be "a beautiful plant, a flower that *he* would love, that his hand would water and take care of."[39] Liszt would, of course, take care of her until their third child was born. But he indicated in their common diary in November that he would sometimes purposely "forget" to put on the ring she had given him. "I feel a strange pleasure in thus abandoning to chance that sad and terrible sign of our union. Twenty times a day I think about going to get it and I don't do anything."[40] It was a sure sign of his restlessness.

Marie herself had written, back in June: "I love you immensely. . . . There is a part of your heart that remains with me in suffering. My love wrings you out." After referring to his infidelity, she went on:

For five years this [their love affair] has lasted, and perhaps it is enough. Let me go away. When you call, I will come. As for me, I don't know any more how to love, how to love anyone, but why should I deprive you of a love which might be for you a new source of life. At this moment there is a constraint in you, and I fear that if this need is blocked it will . . . produce in you a moral sickness. You should not stop anything that leads to the most complete development of your faculties. If I did not love you so religiously and place you so high, I could not speak to you thus, but I have a profound respect for your freedom."[41]

It was typical of Marie to have put her finger on the difficulty and to have expressed it reasonably. But it was no less typical that she hoped against hope that he would deny her logic. From then on he did so, but sporadically and interspersed with conversations about their separate future that became more desultory as her pregnancy put off the fatal day.

They had begun discussing their separation on Liszt's return to Venice. He urged her to reestablish herself with her mother and brother. Somehow he harbored the unlikely assumption that after such a reunion she would be able to live in Paris with the children and he would be able to go on seeing her whenever he wished. He did not want to end the relationship; he wanted the freedom to take occasional breaks from the close union they had formed, to concertize and make enough to suppport his children, and return as he chose, to warm himself at the fires of their passion. He also urged her to consider her future as a writer. For her part, Marie was prodding Liszt to educate himself with Goethe and Shakespeare, to compose new music. He admitted that he did not always feel his vocation. "I have enough *amour-propre* and enough pride for a great destiny; what I don't have is the calm and sustained conviction." He too was suffering from the crisis in their relationship.

Indeed, although there was no question of reviving their idyll, there were times when they felt the old passion. In Lugano, where the couple spent long hours in the open air, he reveled in the joys of nature. "And I am happy if, at such a moment, she says something to me, anything; her speech is the sweetest light from the brightest of stars."[42] In September, at San Rossore, he wrote that he could not live without her, that all that was good and vital in him would perish without her. "Ah! don't ever tell me that I need something else but you." He protested that he lived only by her and in her, even if he had failed her miserably. He called her little nicknames.[43] In their common diary he agonized that he should have and could have made her happy, but could he still?[44] She, on receiving a letter from him, recorded that his handwriting always caused in her an inconceivable emotion, and his vows of love always surprised and ravished her anew.[45]

We have two descriptions of Marie from people who met her at the end of 1838. One is from the Princess Mathilde, niece of Napoleon I. "There is a beautiful woman with him [Liszt]. . . . She is the Countess d'Agoult. . . . Very tall and thin, she looks like the figure of Hunger, but her face is very interesting and above all noble; of course her conduct is inexcusable and yet when you see her you can't prevent yourself from being drawn to her. . . . At least she has been carried away by genius, not by self-interest; and that makes her guilty but not contemptible."[46] The other is from the French poet Auguste Barbier, in his memoirs: "Madame d'A . . . is a great charmer; she has a fine analytical mind, very erudite, very positive, joined to a lively artistic sensibility and a light grain of German fantasy."[47]

Marie was not, even during this period of crisis, allowing her mind to molder. But her reading, which had started in her youth with Romantic novels, had proceeded to history and philosophy in Geneva, and had encompassed English in order to read Shakespeare, was now returning to the classics of her childhood. She praised not only Goethe but Molière and La Fontaine; she called Bossuet her master, not so much for his content as for his style. Now when she read Chateaubriand's Romantic *Voyage en Italie* she found some of it puerile. As Barbier had noticed, she was becoming more analytical, and what was left of her Romanticism was that bit of German fantasy. It is possible, as her biographer Jacques Vier has concluded, that her disenchantment with Sand may have been the first step in a general movement away from the Romantic writers she had so valued. She came to believe that classical art had produced the truest types of beauty. At the same time, she severed her last ties with Christianity, which she had probably retained longer because of Liszt's religiosity.

Toward the end of the year Marie met the writer Hortense Allart. Cousin of Delphine Gay, friend of Sand, and former mistress of Chateaubriand, Allart preached sexual freedom and "freedom of childbearing" for women. When they met, both women were pregnant; Allart intended to bear and raise the fatherless child herself. At first, Marie found her without grace or style, a bit pedantic, lacking the fascination of Sand. Nevertheless, as she grew to know her, she valued Allart's sincerity and respected her independence, lived out with dignity in near poverty. Summing up her impressions, Marie attributed to Allart a brilliant mind, a diffuse style, and a character reminiscent of the eighteenth century, with a distinct prejudice toward the aristocracy.[48] As Marie approached her time of delivery, Allart invited her to join her and her two children. Marie declined and later invited Allart to join their ménage in Lucca. Allart felt that it would be too much to move with her two babies, her servant, her son's pet lamb, two turtles, and a pile of old books. The very difference between the two women made the friendship last; there was no competition for either. They were to remain friends for the rest of Marie's life.

The year 1839 began with the couple settled in Florence. Liszt wanted to leave Marie there and do another tour. She, having promised to look upon these tours with equanimity, passed a day in bed, sobbing. The next day she admitted in her diary that she had broken her word, lashing out at Liszt because he had spoken of their separation in such a matter-of-fact manner. She was sick for at least three days. But in the middle of January she found that their expenses were mounting, with Liszt buying expensive clothes (something she had certainly not ceased to do herself). The two agreed that he must make money and that he would devote four months a year to doing so, spending the rest of the year with her.[49]

However, a new happiness entered Marie's life when, on January 15, she was reunited with her daughter, her first child by Liszt. Blandine had been left to nurse at Etrembières, near Geneva, under the surveillance of a Protestant minister. But Marie, feeling that the infant had suffered too many illnesses and was not being properly cared for, had decided early in 1838 to take her in. At first, the pastor seemed disinclined to restore the child to her parents; he found numerous reasons to delay sending her. Marie was obliged to write to Pictet, asking him to intervene. Then Blandine contracted whooping cough, which put off the meeting by several weeks, and by then Marie was ill and unable to go to Milan to meet her. It was only in early 1839 that Marie received final word from Pictet that the nurse was on the way with her daughter. She wrote in her diary, "Profound emotion. I sense that I will love this child immensely . . . that my life will change, become better. . . . I feel, in everything that relates to her, a great peace."[50]

Marie was criticized, particularly by George Sand, as unnatural for her lack of maternal instinct. Marie had often made fun of women who celebrated the joys of motherhood. But as a young mother, the countess had devoted herself to her first two girls. It was only in her sorrow after the death of Louise that she had pushed the surviving daughter from her sight. True, she had then left her when she ran away with Liszt and certainly never concerned herself with the physical care of her babies. As was usual with aristocratic women, she did not nurse her children; Liszt's children were also put out to nurse. However, no one has questioned whether Liszt would have wanted or even permitted young children on their journeys. His lifelong treatment of them was uncaring, to say the least. And although Marie would undoubtedly always have sacrificed her children to her love, we do have evidence of her tenderness toward them.

When Blandine arrived in Milan, Cosima was still with a wet nurse. Thus this first child had time alone with her parents at a young age (she was just three) that the other two Liszt children never did. Marie kept a journal of the nine months or so that Blandine was with her. She described the child as robust, intelligent, and beautiful with her golden curls. When the nurse left the carriage to return home, Blandine cried, and she was allowed to cry herself to sleep. When she awoke, Marie played with her. But when she cried again the next morning at not seeing her nurse, Marie did not respond. Gradually, Blandine became accustomed to her mother, who soon pronounced her a very observing and reasonable child. In Rome her parents took her to museums. Marie recorded that Blandine loved paintings and that when given reproductions of those they had seen, she preferred them to her toys. Certainly the report of a proud parent!

There followed a series of occasions when mother and daughter engaged in a test of wills, which the mother naturally won. By late February, Marie was noting the "remarkable spirit of order" in her daughter; she also noted her pride and used it to control the child. In March Marie began to teach Blandine her letters, using the *Journal des débats*; she promised that if she continued to learn, she would be able to read the stories that went with her pictures. Blandine soon learned all her letters. By April Marie felt that Blandine was fully at ease with her, although timid with others. She never spoke, except to her mother. The painter Henri Lehmann was taken with her grace and beauty. He made numerous drawings of the child and agreed to supervise her lessons in drawing and painting. Ingrès, director of the Villa Medici and a friend of the family, also found Blandine lovely—"a Raphaël type." She enjoyed looking at pictures and imitated, in gesture, the figures in them, much to the delight of her parents. However, she never paid attention to music when her father played and could not sing a note. The sculptor Bartolini thought she resembled Liszt. With all this attention, the child became somewhat coquettish; however, her mother noted that she was also happy by herself.

The clash of wills between mother and daughter continued intermittently. On occasions when Blandine's obstinacy succeeded, despite reason and spanking, she was punished with no dessert and accepted the deprivation stoically. By October, Marie recorded that Blandine had almost entirely lost her childish "wildness." But it was clear that she saw her mother, not her father, as the opponent of her willfulness. This was natural, just as it was natural in the nineteenth century for the father to take little part in a child's upbringing and for the mother to believe in the necessity of breaking the child's will.

At this time Marie pondered the ends and means of childhood education, in the sense of training both the character and the intellect.[51] The aim, she believed, was the most complete and harmonious development of the child's faculties, feelings, and energies. For this the parent must have a perfect understanding of the moral and physical constitution of the child. The mother must not be either too severe or too indulgent, using rewards and punishments with an even hand, and avoiding corporal punishment as much as possible. It was important to be sincere with the child—either no explanations for commands, if explanations are inappropriate, or real ones, based on reason. Marie laid out a program of intellectual training as follows: ages six to twelve—development of memory, lessons in arithmetic, geography, languages, history, and some elementary natural science; ages twelve to fifteen—historical studies following the logical order of progressive civilizations, reflective and comparative study of languages, natural sciences, philosophy and literature in their historical order, development of artistic feeling and understanding.[52] One might note that this program roughly followed the first two stages of education preached by the positivists, whom Marie had not yet studied. She was moving away from romanticism into the nineteenth-century alternative.

After 1839, Marie was prevented from personal participation in Blandine's education, or in her other children's, until they reached adolescence. Thus this short experience must have been a more important basis of Blandine's attitude toward her mother than it would have been in a normal family situation. One of the results was that Liszt, who almost never saw the children, although he could have, was adored by Blandine. Marie, whose family accepted her return to Paris only on the condition that Liszt's children be nowhere in view, was to suffer greatly in comparison. Liszt's third child, Daniel Henri, was born May 9, 1839; his birth certificate read "mother unknown." Even more removed from his mother than Cosima, he never knew her until his adolescence.

In September Lehmann did portraits of both Liszt and Marie. Hers shows a thin, almost ill woman, her large sorrowful eyes the only attractive feature of her gaunt face. One is not surprised to find an entry in her diary the same month that read, "First feelings of old age."[53] (She was not yet thirty-four.) The conversations about her return to Paris had resumed. She would establish herself and open up a salon where distinguished people would form an entourage for her; she would go to the theater, to receptions at the Académie, wherever one should go. Perhaps Pierre Leroux might offer a course in philosophy at her salon. Liszt told her to spare no expense in giving dinners, presents, etc. And of course, she would continue writing publicity for him. She planned a book about women's duty to constantly call men to the ideal. (When asked how it should end, Liszt replied, "With divorce.")[54]

Marie tried to prepare herself. She knew that Daniel's birth had made it even more necessary for Liszt to make money. She wrote to Marliani that each joy had to pay its tribute to sorrow; it was their destiny to ensure the children's financial independence. Sometimes she assured herself that she had learned how to live, but when she saw the first wrinkle, the first white hair, she felt that she needed to learn not how not to live but how to look death in the face. At one point she asked the Italian poet, Cesare Boccarella, who was very devoted to her, if he would care for Blandine should she die.

In her dread of the coming separation, Marie again became a coquette, surrounded, as Allart noted, by scores of platonic admirers who hoped to be more.[55] She later wrote that her love and the desire to please Liszt had been her talent.[56] At this point, she seemed to feel that pleasing men was the only talent she had. The lovers still had their romantic moments, of course. They visited the Medici tomb together, and Liszt commemorated the visit by writing "Il Pensieroso." But occasionally, doubt engulfed Marie. "How I regret . . . the blind and egoistic enthusiasm which made me attach myself to him!" she wrote in her diary soon before she left for Paris. It was one of the very few times she ever expressed regret for eloping with him.

Finally, the day came for Liszt's departure. He had learned that the Beethoven monument was undersubscribed. He was to leave on a German tour. Daniel was put to nurse in Palestrina in Lehmann's care. Liszt accompanied Marie and Blandine to Livorno, where they were to sail for Genoa, pick up Cosima and go on to Paris. He brought a bouquet to the boat and waved goodbye with his handkerchief. "That goodbye was, in our minds, only the sign of a temporary separation,"[57] Marie wrote later. But how to manage her life in Paris? Her mother had ceased writing to her, and she didn't even know whether she would be allowed to see her daughter Claire. "What to do? . . . I belonged to no milieu. I had republican ideas but didn't know any republicans. . . . No religious ideas or practices, a character unable to accommodate itself to a petty life of pleasure." In the storm on the way to Genoa, Marie clutched Blandine and half hoped to drown. "Alone in the universe. . . . The novel of my life was over."[58]

A letter from Liszt awaited her. "I only know that you were here, and now are not. Goodbye then, and let me always be yours and only yours. . . . To you, my love, my strength and my virtue. Goodbye, darling Marie. Think sometimes of how much I love you, and let that thought be sweet to you."[59] He wrote that in the concert he played after her departure, he played "Ave Maria" and thought of her. He seemed to begin worrying about what she would encounter in Paris. As far as the two girls are concerned, he wrote, she could get around her family's attitude by having them live with his mother there while supervising their education herself. As for her husband, maybe she belonged to him body and soul by law, but . . . if he should make any demands upon her, Liszt would come to Paris immediately. He missed her. She should keep her diary and send it to him every five days.[60]

Marie's letters seemed, on the surface, more resigned and thoughtful. "How can I leave this dear land of Italy without a last goodbye? How can I see these two years, so beautiful and so full, detach themselves from my life without regret? Oh my dear Franz! Let me tell you, once more in the fullness of my soul, you have awakened there a profound and unalterable feeling that will survive all the others . . . the feeling of a thankfulness without limits. Bless you a thousand times!" She also feigned a self-confidence she did not feel. "How come I feel firm as a rock in thinking of you? I sense in you a firm support, a principle of life that nothing can alter. A disdain, a profound in-difference to all that is not you makes me walk all the thorny places without hesitation, despite all the problems. Try to never make me unhappy if that is possible; I think . . . that I deserve that from you, since I have abandoned myself and my entire life to you." Again she declared her love and begged him to take care of himself.[61]

What, exactly, was the decision that the couple had made concerning their future relations? They seem to have mutually agreed that they must be separated for at least part of the time while Liszt gave concerts and earned a living for the children. They also agreed that Blandine and Cosima, at least, would live under Marie's guidance in Paris. Liszt, recognizing that Marie could not reestablish herself with her family and take her place in society while their daughters lived with her, arranged to board them with his mother. As for the couple themselves, there seem to have been differences in the way they viewed the separation. For Liszt, it was simple. Marie would gather around her, as she always did, a circle of distinguished devotées who would help her to launch her writing career, besides aiding her in placing the articles she wrote about him and in his name. He would, of course, join her for periods between concert tours, probably not in Paris. There is some indication that he expected her to take occasional lovers, which would give him the right to do the same. But their relationship would remain as passionate as ever.

For Marie the separation was a defeat, in the sense that she had to give up her dream of being his absolutely essential inspiration and of fulfilling all his needs. Slowly, she had been forced to certain conclusions. First, since she could not live with him if he was to be continually leaving her for concert tours and if she had to worry about his infidelity, she must learn to live by herself. And second, since she could therefore no longer count all her worth in being muse to a great genius, she must become somebody on her own. She would never turn her back on their love, which she considered unique and unending. But the comfort it provided her was hardly enough to see her through the trials ahead. For a nineteenth-century woman, a lady born, to be in her position was almost impossible. She had no intentions of living a bohemian life. But she was open to the disdain of both those who thought her a fallen woman and those who thought her affair with Liszt was over. She was almost thirty-four years old. How was she to establish herself and retain her dignity in the harsh world of Parisian society?

Five ❧ *"You need wide
horizons, the infinite,
the boundless and the
unforeseen, whereas I
need rules, a full program,
the feeling of doing my duty,
a set pace."*

On arriving back in Paris, Marie faced a myriad of uncertainties. First, she had to be able to support herself. Although her husband would have taken her back, she did not wish to return, so financial arrangements of the greatest delicacy were necessary to ensure her an income from her dowry. Her brother was willing to aid her in these. However, Maurice, married to a highly religious woman who had converted his mother to Catholicism, had certain demands of his own. Their mother refused even to acknowledge the children from Marie's liaison with Liszt. The girls, who had returned with Marie, must be rendered invisible. Hence the necessity to leave them with Liszt's mother, which Marie considered a transitory concession. Even so, her mother and pious sister-in-law were not prepared to see Marie immediately, particularly when they learned that she intended to live independently. "When they saw that I was not entering into a cloister, when they believed me happy, when they discovered my opinions—*fury,*" she later recalled.[1]

Marie's primary concern was still her relationship with Liszt. She warned him that he might find things in her diary that pained him. "Try not to judge it all with your reason, but excuse it with your love, for in the last analysis I have perhaps suffered more than I have sinned."[2] Liszt, meanwhile, wrote with love and advice. He was in tears on receiving her picture from Lehmann; he had been told it looked like him (a reference to the first weeks of their elopement, when they were thought to be siblings). She should not allow Lehmann to exhibit it because she was just taking her place in the world. "In two years all Europe will applaud you and salute you with respect, be sure of it. . . . Remain upright and proud, as you should." She should consult Dr.

Koreff on her health, which was not good.[3] As for her family, he advised her not to get too upset and push them away but to lean on her brother Maurice, who would help if he felt needed. (In this, she was eventually successful enough that her brother became a regular visitor at her salon when he was in Paris.) Liszt also advised her to try to revive her friendship with George Sand. "Above all, and I have repeated this over five years, have confidence in yourself and know your worth, because you are very worthy. And don't worry that my love will be extinguished, it is profoundly rooted in my heart."[4]

Marie's immediate goal was to reestablish her salon, supposedly to create group of supporters for Liszt but for herself as well. She would have to attract as many old friends as she could and add new ones. Of course, the aristocratic circle of her family and husband was closed to her. Fortunately, she had begun to gather a wider circle of musicians, artists, and writers even before leaving Paris. Also, in the short time she held a salon with George Sand, she had broadened her acquaintances. As she and Liszt had agreed, Marie established herself in great luxury, taking an apartment at 10 rue Neuve des Mathurins, hiring a valet, a cook, and a groom and furnishing it with some luxury. Lehmann was charged with purchasing items in Rome for two salons, one in Renaissance style and the other in Moorish. Marie decorated her private study with symbolic citations and bronze medallions of Goethe, Mickiewicz, Byron, Chenier, Lamennais, and Chateaubriand. She said her study was dedicated to serenity—"the rainbow after the storm"—an aim that at the time was wishful thinking. But as in Paris earlier, as in Geneva, Marie attracted interesting men and made her salon a center of intellectual and artistic ideas.

The literary critic Sainte-Beuve contributed a motto in Latin and wrote a sonnet to celebrate this "boudoir." Marie and Liszt had met him in Rome, where they had spent a day together visiting the villa of Hadrian at Tivoli. Sainte-Beuve had written a poem about it, which was published in the *Revue de Paris*. Marie was impressed by the writer; his *Volupté* had been an important book in her life. But she was never attracted by the man. Although famous, Sainte-Beuve was ugly and effected a persona of cynicism and boredom. He had once been a lover of Hortense Allart and kept up a friendship with her. In Rome he sensed the fraying of the relationship between Marie and Liszt, and he positioned himself to take advantage of it, writing flattering letters to Marie and dedicating poems to her. When she arrived in Paris, he rushed to her side. Hoping for a literary career, she retained him in her circle but offered him no hope. Sainte-Beuve courted Marie so assiduously that in three months he was assumed to be her lover. Musset's bon mot made

the rounds of the Paris salons: "It seems that Sainte-Beuve is her consolation! He was born to be the consoler of dead passions."[5] It was to take the critic a long time to accept no for an answer.

Sainte-Beuve was one of a number of men who aided Marie in decorating her new quarters and who danced attendance upon her for the next few years, each hoping to be next in line when the affair with Liszt was over. Another faithful visitor was Count Bernard Potocki, an aristocratic Pole who became so violent in his passion that Marie had to show him the door. After reporting this to Liszt, she wrote, "He is worthy and sincere, I believe. He understands my profound and irreplaceable passion for you." Potocki actually detested Liszt and pointed out how much better off Marie would be with him. He begged to succeed Liszt should anything go wrong. Marie recorded that the count had told her she had made a profound and indelible impression on him: "Each day, I found myself more and more attached. Today all other women seem stupid to me. You have a frankness, an uprightness of character, an elevation of mind which makes you the first woman of the world for me. I do not even mention your charm."[6]

There were also the suitors of her youth, Eugène Sue and the poet Alfred de Vigny. As Vigny's passionate love affair with the actress Marie Dorval had recently ended, he shared with Marie the disillusionment of loving an artist. (Marie told Liszt that Vigny had complained that Sand took Dorval away from him.) Marie and Vigny were also both aristocrats whose disdain of the bourgeois July Monarchy pushed them to republican sympathies. He was from the beginning allowed to see her alone, which in their common milieu did not compromise her. She appreciated his taste, his reserve, and his roundabout, delicate way of communicating. Vigny helped Marie to build her salon; among others, he brought Tocqueville, thus sharing with her his interest in America. A few years later Marie was able put the weight of her salon behind Vigny's successful application (competing with Sainte-Beuve) to the Académie française. Vigny also encouraged her to write, advised her, and later helped her to gain access to the prestigious *Revue de deux mondes*. The two remained good friends.

The painter Henri Lehmann arrived in Paris a few months after Marie. He was an old admirer and confidant who had been present at the conversations leading to her separation from Liszt. When Marie could not keep the girls, Lehmann offered to take them to his sister's; he still had responsibility for Daniel in Italy. Although Lehmann brought her items from Rome to furnish her new apartment, she refused to give him the run of her establishment. ("Since Franz is not here, I want to profit from it by being conven-

tional.") Nor did she want him to hang his picture of her next to that of Liszt in the gallery. She asked him to make her an album of sketches of her friends and a separate one of their caricatures. Lehmann remained, until the late 1840s, a devoted follower. She, in turn, made every effort to advance his renown as an artist.

As in Geneva, Marie filled the empty spaces in her life with men who admired her and also added to her knowledge and understanding. But unable to conceive of a future without Liszt, she made it plain to them that friendship was all she could offer.

Friendship was important at this turning point of her life, when she was viewed by the "best people" with disdain and by the rest as a woman who had probably lost her lover. One friendship that Liszt was urging her to renew was that with George Sand. Although each woman could rightfully claim to have been sinned against by the other, Marie, whom Balzac had subjected to public ridicule using information from Sand, had the major complaint. *Béatrix* had been serialized just before Marie's return to Paris; the book was to appear shortly after. However, Sand, aided by the Countess Marliani, behaved as the aggrieved party. Marliani had complicated the friendship by reporting Marie's acerbic comments to Sand. She had also taken it upon herself to show Marie's letters to Lammennais, for his judgment. Sand then asked the abbé if she should continue to write Marie, adding that she had once loved her fondly but was now disappointed in her. Lamennais replied that Marie was not a good woman—whether because she had denigrated Sand or because she had stolen his disciple Liszt from him, one can only conjecture. In any case, Marliani had made it more difficult for Sand to forgive Marie by extending the circle of those who read her wit at Sand's expense.

As for Marie, she insisted in a letter to Sand that their relationship had been such that she could not end it without knowing the reason. "Certain words were exchanged by us which *still for me* have an unchanging sense," she wrote, creating a link that "ought to last as long as we do." Without mentioning *Béatrix,* she indicated that she too had grounds for complaint. Sand chose to judge the letter only by the angry passage and did not answer. Marie did not yet know that Marliani had showed both Sand and Lamennais the offending letters. On returning to Paris, Marie went to Marliani's salon, where she met Sand. She reported to Liszt that she pleaded with Sand for a meeting, begging her not to "soil and drag in the mud our old and sainted friendship."[7] Sand agreed to a meeting, but only if Marie would apologize. "You will see that I have no resentment toward you," Sand wrote. "But I must tell you that you have put one more pain in my life, and that it was I who received the wound for which you pity yourself."[8] Finally, a meeting was arranged. Because Sand pleaded rheumatism, Marie agreed to go to the mews in the rue Pigalle, where Sand lived with her grown children and Chopin.

Marie stopped at Marliani's the day before to pick up the offending letters. It was only then that she learned how Marliani had given them to Sand, on the advice of Lamennais. Sand had led Marie to believe she had never really seen the letters, so this was news of a double treason. Nevertheless, Marie kept her appointment in the rue Pigalle, where Sand rented an apartment over mews and stables that was reached by a narrow stairway. Sand probably received Marie in her salon, with its Chinese vases full of flowers, Chopin's piano, paintings by Delacroix, and her own portrait by Calametta. Typically, she would be garbed in Turkish trousers, lying on a sofa. (Sand, no less than Marie, liked to provide herself with an exotic background.) Marie described the interview to Liszt: Sand coolly ran down the list of Marie's faults while admitting her character, mind, and grandeur. She had never loved anyone in the same way, Sand insisted. But Marie had never loved her, although for a while Sand thought she did. Marie had cruelly mocked her, judging her coldly, as did the public, whereas Sand had loved Marie blindly, enthusiastically.[9] Marie admitted guilt in mocking Sand but claimed attenuating circumstances. Her letters about Sand were written in anger caused partly by Sand's failure to write to her. She may have said some harsh words. It was a flaw in her she could only deplore in this case, and she begged Sand's pardon. Sand at first refused her. Marie pointed out, still without ever mentioning Balzac, that she had only wronged Sand in letters to a mutual friend and that this should not affect two years of intimacy. After some discussion the two agreed to see each other, but Sand forbade any conversation about her lovers or friends.

Marie said she accepted the condition only because she knew Sand would change it eventually. Perhaps, Sand replied. "I am very accessible to seduction, and you are very seductive, Marie." She spoke of the poetry she had written about their friendship, further remarking that she was an instinctive person and that Marie didn't follow her instincts enough. "She seemed to me exactly the same," Marie wrote to Liszt, "full of *poésie* and charm, lying like anything because in the instant of lying she did not doubt herself at all, flattering with dignity. At bottom, there is something irreparable between us; I think she has put her finger on it in saying that our liaison was artificial, that I yielded to my love for you, to my desire to be agreeable and partake of all your feelings, but that her nature is antipathetic to me."[10] However, on leaving, Marie kissed Sand on the forehead.

When she fell sick shortly after this meeting, Sand rushed to her side. In a letter to Lehmann, Marie wrote that the break had been papered over and might possibly be mended. The problem was that Sand refused to say who told her what about how Marie had insulted her. Liszt warned Marie not to break with Sand until he was around and to wait for the moment when she would have the advantage. When *Béatrix* appeared in book form, Prince Potocki reported to Marie the rumor that she and Sand had enjoyed a lesbian affair at Nohant. Nevertheless, the two women were to appear together at the theater, with Liszt, for the opening of Sand's play *Cosima* in April 1840. They continued to see each other but usually in public, at Sand's salon, or at the lectures by the Polish patriot Mickiewicz at the Collège de France. The glow of mutual admiration and warmth between the two women had dimmed forever. Gradually, people who frequented Marie's salon found a cool reception at Sand's and had to choose between the two. Because Sand was the greater celebrity, Marie was the loser.

The only other woman friend Marie had in Paris was Delphine Gay, the beautiful and poetic prodigy who had enlivened the Flavigny salon in the 1820s. Faithful to her youthful promise, she had become a writer, under the name Vicomte de Launay. Her clever column of Paris gossip appeared in *La Presse,* her husband's newspaper. It was she who had recognized in Liszt's "Lettres d'un bachelier ès musique" the feminine touch that indicated the true writer. But Delphine also wrote plays; her *School of Journalists,* which ridiculed government figures, was accepted by the Comédie-Française in 1839, although it proved too controversial to produce. When she did a reading of the play in her salon, Delphine invited Marie. It was the gallant Eugène Sue who accompanied her, as he had on the evening she met Liszt. Surely, the novelist must have recognized the irony when Emile de Girardin, Delphine's husband, fell madly in love with Marie. This development prevented a resumption of any real friendship between the two women for a number of years.

In falling for Marie, Girardin joined a long line of suitors. But in her first months back in Paris, the most important in both persistence and appeal was the English diplomat Sir Henry Bulwer-Lytton.[11] He had also been a lover of Hortense Allart, who had left the poet Chateaubriand for him. He was then in France to negotiate commercial accords between Britain and France on trade in the eastern Mediterranean. Allart, who had remained in Florence, recommended him to Marie; he soon became a serious contender. He made available to her the diplomatic pouch for items she wished to acquire from London for her apartment. Less willing to engage in delicate flirtation than a Frenchman, Bulwer declared his passion within weeks. Marie had mentioned Bulwer in letters to Liszt and duly informed him that she was working on making him a friend. However, Marie may in this case have been tempted; toward the end of the year she seems to have asked Liszt's permission to be unfaithful. (We do not have the letter.) Or was she simply trying to make Liszt jealous? Gossip had it that he was having an affair with the pianist Camille Pleyel. And since he had not promised Marie fidelity, why should it be necessary for her to ask permission?

Liszt was not happy with the request. He presumed that the "lucky man" was to be Bulwer, who was unknown to him and sounded very attractive. But Liszt followed his own logic in declaring such things unimportant. "You know my way of seeing this sort of thing. You know that for me facts, gestures and actions are nothing. Feelings, ideas, nuances, especially nuances, mean everything. I want and I would like that you always have your freedom; for I am convinced that you will always use it nobly, delicately, up to the day when you tell me: such and such a man has sensed more energetically, understood more intimately than you what I am and could be. Up to that time there will not have been any infidelity, and nothing, absolutely nothing will be changed between us. That day, let me tell you, will never arrive and could never arrive, I am intimately and profoundly convinced." Marie responded that this manner of thinking was incomprehensible to her:

I don't want to reproach you; nevertheless I have to tell you that you have not understood my nature very well, or you have wished to violate it and fashion it after yours. . . . You have torn from my heart notions of duty in love, which I need, and which form for me an ideal that you have treated with rudeness and harshness. You can never know how much you have wronged me, and still wrong me. . . . You must know also that since I have been in Paris I have been continually suffering, suffering very much.

You are right to think that it has to do with Bulwer. I believe that neither you nor I will have anything to complain of from him. He is a man and not a child. . . . Adieu my Franz. Nothing is changed and nothing will be changed.[12]

There were many letters between Marie and Liszt about Bulwer. Liszt stated that if the man were as Marie described him, he would be worthy of her affection; Liszt hoped to meet Bulwer when he came to Paris, as he planned to do shortly.

But of course nothing was changed, Marie promised Liszt. For her, the sin of infidelity to her husband and the scandalous sacrifice of her social position were excusable only for the unique and ideal love she felt for Liszt. She wrote him, "You have power of life and death over me . . . through you and from you I receive unspeakable joys as well as inexpressible sufferings. Ah, I swear to you and I can say to you even today, after this long absence, after all the sadness built up between us, after your faults and mine, a thousand times bigger than yours, never has a man been loved as you are!"[13] To then betray that love would denigrate its great worth. Besides, to live the life of a loose woman, for which she blamed Sand, was against Marie's scrupulous and aristocratic principles. All this pertained, even if Liszt himself did not remain faithful. It was as if the value of their love depended on her. Most of the men who had gathered round to take Liszt's place did not understand this. All they knew was that they were required to think highly, or pretend to think highly, of Liszt. Those who did, like Lehmann and Ronchaud, could remain by her side indefinitely and be treated affectionately as intimates, although not as lovers.

However, Bulwer continued to court Marie. He advised her on her problems, including the children, and even professed himself ready to adopt the girls, presumably with the idea of setting up a household or even marrying her, should her husband die.[14] He went so far as to make a formal request to adopt Blandine. But, unlike her other suitors, there was a limit to how long he would wait for a return of his passion. He abandoned the field when, after a few months, Marie still held him at arm's length. Hortense Allart had by this time become suspicious that her friend was too friendly with her lover and was later to accuse Marie of insincerity on the matter.

One reason that Bulwer may have abruptly left the field was that it was becoming crowded. Although Liszt was always the main competition, Marie was also, by early 1840, undergoing the intense wooing of Emile de Girardin, "the Napoleon of the press." Bastard of the man whose name he finally assumed, Girardin founded *La Presse,* the first mass-circulation newspaper in France.[15] He was hated for his duel with the beloved republican Armand Carrel, whom he had unintentionally killed. When he was elected deputy to the National Assembly in 1839, his enemies managed to keep him from taking his seat by claiming he was not French. (He inherited from his mother a West Indian complexion.) He was elected and refused a place in the Assembly three times; he was finally seated only after being defended by Lamartine, the famous orator who was to lead the republic in 1848. Girardin received constant threats of assassination, but his newspaper made him one of the most powerful men in France. His story exerted a powerful attraction on Marie.

From the beginning of their friendship, the two engaged in a confessional intimacy. Marie sketched for him a psychological portrait of herself as Arabella:[16] "not very susceptible to friendship, because the most imperious need of her heart is enthusiasm and admiration, and she creates for herself *realities* that fall into dust at the first intimate contact. . . . Incapable of tenderness, she only knows extreme sensations; she doesn't live, she aspires to live." Girardin disagreed. To her judgment that her education had falsified her nature, he replied that she should not blame her upbringing. "The horse of breeding does not bolt because it is badly trained, but because it is badly mounted," he wrote, as he became more jealous of Liszt. Girardin also told her that her heart had been devastated. "There are treasures in you, and you are poor!" Now that she had told him her faults, he wanted her to share with him her impressions and hopes.[17]

Marie's interest in her new suitor is revealed in a character sketch she wrote. She often wrote pen portraits of her friends. They remained unpublished, or contributed to characters in her novels. She later used Girardin as the model of a passionate lover in her novel *Hervé* and as a character in an unpublished play. Girardin was, if not her lover, one of the most important men in her life. He not only urged her to write, he opened to her the pages of *La Presse* and educated her in politics. "You and I have been endowed with much imagination; but you, Marie, have put your pride in allowing yourself to be carried away by it; I have employed all my strength in containing it. . . . Do for your reason what you have so well done for your mind, cultivate it."[18] It was advice she was ready to take.

But more important, perhaps, was that Girardin loved her passionately when she knew that Liszt was being unfaithful. After she had invited the publisher and his wife Delphine to dinner, along with Sue, Vigny, Sainte-Beuve, and Potocki, his first note read, "May I return? Whatever hour you like. I kiss your feet." But after finding that he had many competitors, he did not spend much time at her salon. He came when he could see her alone, and his letters were passionate. "What I want is to hear you demand of me something impossible, since I cannot find any more words to tell you that need I feel to make a sacrifice for you that goes beyond my strength." He swore he would joyfully give his life for her, on the spot. "You have aroused in me a singular feeling; it is the ardent desire to disengage my thought from my personality . . . my soul from my body. I feel only my soul is worthy of you, I want to disappear while it remains near you. . . . Marie, Marie, you have aroused in me a feeling that only you could make me understand, explain it to me then."[19] Even he, who had always been tough and a cynic, who had once said that seducing a woman was like corrupting a man, could hardly believe his passion. As for Delphine, she treated the affair with her typical wit: "My husband is having a flirtation with Madame d'Agoult, but that doesn't bother me. With clever women it isn't dangerous; it is only with stupid women that it goes further, because they don't know what to talk about." Marie reported this to Liszt, dutifully noting Girardin's wooing although modifying the tone of the latter somewhat. [20]

Marie seems to have fallen ill at the end of 1839 for about six weeks. Liszt, on tour, was experiencing wild success. His showmanship had developed. He would sit motionless a long time before the piano, as the tension built up; then he would play, fixing his piercing eyes on the ladies, one by one; his body moved back and forth, with an occasional toss of his long hair. The poet Heinrich Heine spoke of "the electrical effects of his daemonic nature on a closely-packed crowd."[21] There are descriptions of a concert in his native Pest: "I was particularly struck by his manner at a ball given him by the ladies of the upper crust, where he was little less than deified," wrote the Englishwoman Julia Pardoe. Liszt was presented with a sword, after which he made a weeping speech and was led back to his quarters by torchlight procession. In Paris the joke went around: "Liszt alone of all warriors is without reproach, for in spite of his big sword we know that it has vanquished only semi-quavers and slain only pianos."[22] Liszt wrote to Marie that his countrymen had even discovered for him a title, and he was planning a coat of arms. While continuing to seek honors—the Cross of the Order of the White Falcon First Class, the Cross of the Belgian Lion—Liszt advised Marie to use her title. "Being nobody, it is necessary for me to be somebody," he added. Marie could only cringe at all this.

But it did not change her commitment to him. "My soul is saturated with you," she wrote him. "I feel more and more that indissoluble links have riveted us one to another. Sometimes I hate you, but I admire you and return to you and love you always." The next day she reported the Paris gossip that he would come back with Pleyel, his mistress. "Once this would have made me shed bitter tears; today it runs off as from oilcloth. Should I be happy or sad about that?" Clearly, she was asking whether Liszt was happy or sad about it. But he probably knew that the bitter tears had already been shed. She spoke of the cruelty of passion and wondered whether he had ever felt it as she did: "My head burns only to think of it."[23] Looking forward to his arrival at Paris in the spring, she wrote, "This long absence will have served me in one thing: that is to give me a very clear picture of my needs, of my tastes, of the fashion of living that suits me, and consequently of the reasons, up to now only vaguely seen by me, for my occasional depression concerning our common life. We will talk about it, and probably about other things, for your arrival will be a moment of crisis . . . for me, and probably for you." She added that she had been to the Bois de Boulogne for the first time, after weeks in bed. Apparently, she was lucky to avoid an operation on her leg. She described a cozy scene with Bulwer and added, coquettishly, "I hope you will find me charming, other men do."[24]

Liszt, challenging her game, replied that Bulwer would be upset by his arrival in Paris and that the matter must be settled. He facetiously offered to act like a brother to Marie when he was there, if she wished. Confident that Marie could not free herself from him, Liszt admitted to her that he had yielded to a two-day affair. So if she slept with Bulwer, it would not affect their relationship. He also commented on a conversation with her brother that Marie had reported to him. Maurice had indicated that if Marie's husband should die, he would give his permission for her to marry her lover. Liszt was supremely confident of Marie's affection for him: "If there comes a time to think about it, I count on the fact that you would do it with or without his permission."[25]

On the same day she was writing Liszt a serious letter. She was dissatisfied with herself because she had done nothing worthwhile. Liszt should push her; she was tired of her freedom. Their two natures were diametrically opposed. He needed grand horizons and unlimited vistas. She needed an ordered life, with the feeling of duty accomplished. Both of them tended to judge people according to their own temperament.

I am truly unhappy about the useless egoism of my life, with so many things begun and left abandoned, because I left everything behind and now lack everything. Choice separated me from my husband and first children; necessity separates me from you and from our children. . . . I need two things: to find a situation that will return our children to me; and for you to give me a positive task, to which I would submit myself, first by obedience and soon by taste and even desire.[26]

Clearly, she was still unable to think of a task in life that was independent of him. She was to find her métier but not through Liszt. Their children would never really be hers. And she had only just received permission to see her legitimate daughter, Claire, at her convent school.

On receiving word from Liszt of his affair Marie commented, "One ceases to be intolerant when one feels in a weak position,"[27] acknowledging her failure to make him jealous enough to be faithful. She was also rightly suspicious that there were other affairs he had not confessed. Liszt continued to talk of Bulwer or Potocki. "If others have the ambition to be a consolation to you, a repose, a sweetness, I want to be your force and your pride," he wrote. This letter seems to have aroused Marie from her pose of tolerant acceptance. In reply to his urging her to infidelity, she raged that what she wanted from him was not force and pride:

Be good to me. Have a little tolerance for my weaknesses. Be a bit tender if you can. . . . You are too preoccupied with being great, you are too much the philosopher. You are so strong that you do not take account of the weakness of others. . . . What afflicts me does not afflict you. What I dream only makes you laugh. What I want you take no account of. You nourish yourself with pride in the consciousness of your grandeur and you do not even appreciate the small pains of feebler hearts.

Scathingly, she warned Liszt that he must be careful on returning to Paris, because people thought he had become conceited from his success; they were joking about the presentation of the sword and nobility to him. He should not try to give a concert right away.[28]

Liszt postponed his arrival in Paris for a month. Then, after promising to meet her at Meaux on April 1, he put it off twice. Finally, he arrived and spent a month in Paris. It was not a great success. Marie, who fought so hard for control of her emotions when he was not there, could not help making scenes when he was. Liszt was not really interested in being en famille with the girls. He spent a good deal of time preparing for a concert, which took place under the patronage of Princess Belgiojoso. In his spare time he attended the Belgiojoso salon and played duets with her. Immediately, rumors started that they were lovers.[29] And the concert itself, which took place on May 1, was reported gleefully in the gossip columns as a duel between the two women. Although Marie had the place of honor, the princess, with her escort of *carbonari*, entered after everyone was seated and remained standing, in great emotion, through the first piece.

When Liszt left for England in May, Marie was not well enough to go with him. For some unknown reason, he asked Princess Belgiojoso to call on her. The princess did, and she later described the visit, giving us a picture of a Marie dressed in black velvet, with black lace on her blond hair, like a queen in her luxurious apartment. Marie wrote of her return visit, with malice, in her *Souvenirs*. To Liszt, Marie conveyed the news that the princess seemed almost ugly and was less witty than she had expected. The guest stayed an hour and said nothing interesting. Of course, she spoke of everyone but him. Marie's letter went on, and she again played her only card: "Emile Girardin dropped in. Like you, I have a weakness for him. He adores you. [There had been a dinner at which the two men talked politics.] People are talking about your affairs. You see that my pride, if I had any, would be a bit dog-eared." Then, taking Liszt to task, she accused him of being surrounded by abject adoration, unable to hear anything but the most absolute flattery.[30] Liszt wrote back that she was a bit hard, both on the princess and on him. He never seemed to recognize, or at least he never acknowledged, that he repeatedly put Marie in an intolerable position from which she could only skewer him verbally in her frustration. She herself recognized this and told him she was determined not to write so often, so as not to irritate him. She wished that she had heard him play more while he was in Paris and admitted that she was jealous of his public.

The plan was that Marie should follow Liszt to England and that the couple would go to Baden after his tour. But again she fell sick, with a high fever and a swollen leg. Nevertheless, she enjoyed a triumph when Sainte-Beuve read fragments of his *Port-Royal* in her salon. Liszt, meanwhile, was playing before Queen Victoria and receiving the plaudits of high society, including one determined Lady Blessington, who had a scarf made for herself in the colors of Hungary, in honor of Liszt. Some of his reviews were less than enthusiastic, however; outside London, in particular, his emotional histrionics at the piano were not appreciated. He had arrived at one concert to find only ten people in the audience, so he invited them to his hotel and gave them a good dinner before playing. Cutting short his tour, he returned to London, where he was welcomed.

To Marie, this change in plans meant only one thing—an involvement with Lady Blessington. Her leg was still swollen; her brother and the faithful Ronchaud were carrying her from room to room in her apartment. Nevertheless, in early June she left for England and installed herself at Richmond, near London. Liszt was surprised and somewhat embarrassed. Marie had not been able to bring enough money to make up for Liszt's lack of receipts, and he was afraid that her presence would cause a boycott of his London concerts. Unable to travel, she wrote in desperation, "I can do nothing else at this moment and probably forever except to remain absolutely alone." When she was able, Marie left her card at the home of certain members of high society. Her overtures were not returned. Only Bulwer-Lytton showed up to take her to Liszt's concert, where she was studiously ignored by everyone else. After the concert there was a party for Liszt, to which she was not invited but Lady Blessington was.

When Liszt returned late that night, he was drunk on Scotch whiskey.

Lady Blessington had, it seems, pronounced some public insult concerning Marie. Liszt had roused himself enough to reply something like, "You want to know what I think of the Comtesse d'Agoult. Well, if at this very moment she asked me to throw myself out that window, I would do it. That is what I think of the Comtesse d'Agoult." We do not know that this story was repeated to Marie. But it was clear that she could not remain in England. Her rage, which had been almost constant since she arrived, must have boiled to a peak. His last letter to her from England returned her anger and admonished her:

Love is not justice. Love is not duty; it is not pleasure either, and nevertheless it contains, mysteriously, all these things. There are a thousand ways of feeling it, a thousand ways to practice it, but for those whose soul is thirsty for the absolute and the infinite, it is one, eternally one, without beginning or end. If it is manifested somewhere on earth, it is certainly in the great confidence of one in the other. . . . Let us not bargain, not measure. If love is still at the base of our hearts, everything is said; if it has vanished, there is nothing more to say.

The letter ended, "Adieu, I am not in despair."[31]

Liszt's next concert stop was Baden, where he awaited Marie's arrival with "an inexplicable thirst." But it was not easy for Marie there, either. Flavigny relatives had snubbed her in England. And on a train from Frankfurt to Mainz, a distant relative of hers pretended not to know her and made nasty remarks about her relations with Liszt. The Russian prince Felix Lichnowsky, another admirer who was accompanying Marie, confronted him and made him sign a letter of apology. There was much talk about it in Frankfurt.[32] Marie followed Liszt until the end of August, when he appeared in Rotterdam. She then left for Paris, he for another English tour. Liszt wrote to her:

We have still many good years before us. This has been another year of trials, of expiation, then . . . calm, deep happiness. . . . If we do not arrive at happiness, it is perhaps that we are worth more than that. There is too much energy, too much passion, too much fire in our depths to settle for the possible in bourgeois fashion. We do not complain, we do not reproach those intense forces of which our misery is the consequence. . . . Let us live, lean your arm on mine, let me go to sleep peaceably on your heart, whose beating is for me the mysterious rhythm of ideal beauty, of eternal love.

Marie replied, "Oh yes, all that has disunited us is just a dream, a frightful nightmare." As long as Liszt was able to woo her with the rhetoric of ideal love, she accepted the misery of her situation. She wrote that what they needed was to live alone together in the midst of nature. It was society that had ruined them.[33] This was partly true. In October the lovers did find peace at Fontainebleau, with their two girls. (Daniel was still under Lehmann's supervision in Palestrina, in the care of a nurse.) They even regained for those few weeks their former idyllic happiness. After leaving each other, Liszt noted, "I am struck with one thing: it is the first time that we have left each other without heartbreak and anguish." It must mean, he added, that they were sure of each other, which made him proud and happy. Marie agreed: "It is you alone who have changed everything by the force of your love. . . . It is you who have crushed the serpent and who for the second time raises me on your wings to the ideal region toward which I aspire."[34]

But a few days later Liszt wrote a letter full of ambiguity. On the one hand he said that it was almost too bad she was such a loyal creature! On the other he warned, "Marie, if ever I surprise you in a lie or even a knowing reticence, I will not say anything, but I will be excessively unhappy."[35] This may all have been a reference to his knowledge that Girardin was still paying court to her. Less than a fortnight later, in an effort at frankness, Liszt sent Marie a love letter he had received from Camille Playel. Marie replied by thanking him for his openness, which she said would render her sweet and even indulgent. She then went on to mention rumors that she had taken a new lover, only to deny them; she also referred to the devotion of Girardin, Lehmann, and Théodore de Ferrière. The sad game had begun again, a game it was impossible for Marie to win.

For Emile Girardin, it was not a game. Sometimes he rebelled against his own desire for Marie, denying himself the pleasure of seeing her. Other times he accused her of immolating herself at the altar of love and insisted that no man existed who was worth a woman's sacrificing herself for. While in England, Marie sent Girardin her pen portrait of him—"master of his destiny, powerful yet surrounded by enemies." He preferred the letters he received from her after she returned to Paris, which, unfortunately, we do not have. "Let us love each other then," he wrote, but as we ought. . . . Be the soul of my life, I will try to be the reason of yours." Unfortunately for him, being with Liszt wiped out any further responses on Marie's part. To prove her loyalty, she asked Girardin to return her letters. He did so, with a note full of pain: "I have solemnly deposited you in that part of myself which is the tomb of feelings for which I have suffered, of illusions for which I have lived. . . . You are for me now only a sorrow and a name, Marie, goodbye. . . . I can only hope that I am at least the man in your life whom you will have esteemed the most and who will have loved you the best. . . . Goodbye, since it will not be the same man next time you see me, but another."[36] Marie wrote to Liszt that she felt she had done the right thing. "I hope that you will judge me thus and that your fears, which preoccupied me greatly, will disappear. . . . Love me and don't doubt of my heart, which is wholly yours."

When Marie was at Fontainebleau with Liszt, Girardin wrote wistfully to ask if she was waiting until winter to come back to Paris. When she did return, he was there each day from 4 to 6 P.M., pressing his suit. Marie, who was very much attracted to Girardin, could at this point only think of using him to spur Liszt's jealousy. In this she succeeded, because Liszt sensed the attraction. When Marie wrote that Girardin had proposed a relationship that would be neither love nor friendship, Liszt became suspicious, admitting that he could not stop thinking about her with sadness and bitterness. He sensed in this relationship a special "persistence and depth" lacking in her relations with other men. But he could hardly forbid her to see Girardin, as he had claimed freedom for himself, so, "Love me and do what you will. That is the only thing I have to say to you." However, Liszt returned to the subject a few days later. "Anything I can say is probably useless; and nevertheless I cannot be silent. One does not with impunity engage in such relations with men like him," meaning, presumably, relations that were not clearly defined. He spoke of his fears, of "doubt spreading in his heart," even of returning to Paris on his way to St. Petersburg. Finally, he wrote, "I want you not to take one step further."[37]

Marie responded that if Liszt wanted it, she would never see the man again. Why was Marie willing to capitulate to Liszt on the matter of Girardin? She certainly could not believe at this point that her giving up a potential lover would cause him to be faithful to her. Was it just because Liszt had ordered her to go no further, and it gave her pleasure to obey him? There are other possibilities. Marie was basically chaste by upbringing. The adventure with Liszt was, to her, an anomaly, something that happened once in a lifetime. Having been unfaithful to her husband, she could not now be unfaithful to Liszt. It is also possible that, although sexually attractive to men, she was not herself a sensual women and needed some overwhelming psychic aid like a great romantic love in order to let go completely. Yet we know through Girardin's letters that during this period she wrote a novella that the editor at *La Presse* refused because it was sexually explicit! However, Liszt seems to have been the key to her desire. Although she may have been tempted, she would not give in to another as long as he remained on the horizon.

But that was not yet the end of it. While asking her to go no further with Giradin, Liszt had also cautioned her not to break off with him. Liszt may have been jealous of the press lord, but he wanted the pages of *La Presse* to be open for his publicity. Curbing his verbal approaches to her, as Marie demanded, Girardin was able to escort her to the grand ceremony in December in which the ashes of Napoleon were returned to Paris by river barge.[38] Girardin also managed to resume the correpondence and to write that he still loved her; he even asked for her letters back so that he could reread them. "See how the union of two *strong wills* comes to an end,"[39] he wrote. The latter remark is interesting because Marie had assured Liszt that she was in control of the relationship with Girardin, whereas in theirs, Liszt was "the master of my thoughts as of my life." But Liszt had also accused her of wishing to dominate: "The need to dominate, to tyrannize even if necessary, is it not the most inherent motive force in your nature? I think so."[40]

Indeed, both Girardin and Liszt saw rightly that Marie was seeking control. But it was her own life she was trying to master. Because she could *not* control Liszt's infidelity, her emotional life would be a shambles as long as she clung to her love for him. Girardin not only saw that but offered her a way out, by guiding her career as a writer. Unfortunately, she was not yet ready to turn her back on Liszt, not ready to accept the passion of Girardin. Nevertheless, Girardin was to outlast Liszt. He and Marie walked together in the Bois de Boulogne as intimate friends in their old age.

Six ⮑ "Daniel. *It was the name I had given to one of my children, the name of the prophet saved from the lions' den. Among all the Bible stories, that one pleased me most.*"

For a year after Marie returned to Paris, no more "Lettres d'un bachelier" appeared in French periodicals. Marie missed this activity—taking Liszt's ideas and putting them in order for publication. By the end of 1840, as we have seen, she was dissatisfied. She knew she could not make a life out of gathering admirers for herself and a following for Liszt. She wrote to him that she had begun a novel. But in the end, it was through the offices of Girardin that she found the opportunity to express her views and to make a name as a writer.

One evening in December 1840 found the renegade priest Lamennais and Girardin in Marie's salon, discussing George Sand's new novel, *Le Compagnon du Tour de France*. Lamennais seems to have turned against Sand after the publication of *Béatrix*. Marie had written to ask him what he thought of it; he had replied that although he had not and would not read it, what he had heard of the book filled him with "indignation and disgust." He was shortly to go to prison for his own book, *Le Pays et le gouvernement*, after having his last dinner at Marie's house, because, he said, in jail he would have no female company. (More likely, since his feelings for her were always ambivalent, it was because she had a superb cook.) When he came out of prison and a friend found him an apartment in her building, he refused it, saying he couldn't live that close to her. In truth, Lamennais did not like any women. Marie scolded him for his misogyny but welcomed him, as a celebrity, to her salon. She even invited Balzac to dinner. He came, more than once, while insulting her in letters to friends.

When Lamennais sharply criticized Sand's novel, Girardin suggested that

Marie might want to review it for *La Presse*. She initially refused, pleading that she needed time for her own novel. But it did not take long to persuade her; she finished the review by the end of the year. The review appeared in January, signed "Anonymous" (*un inconnu*). Marie told Liszt that it was an experiment; she would be able to hear what people said about it. Sand's novel described the love between a high-born woman and a simple artisan. It was not one of Sand's most successful works, and Marie found it unbelievable. Because the review was highly critical and moreover, no one knew who had written it, Marie was able to enjoy the resulting comments. She wrote Liszt at the New Year that she was firmly determined to work and become an author. Of course, she would still write for him. She did, in fact, write two more "Lettres d'un bachelier" that year.[1]

One person who suspected that Marie had written the review was Sainte-Beuve, who had left the scene on Liszt's first visit to Paris in 1840 and returned at the end of the year, when he sensed that Girardin's courtship of Marie was cooling off. As a budding author, Marie wanted to retain the great critic among her admirers; besides, he broadened her circle by bringing into it people like the historian François-Auguste Mignet. Having gratified her by reading his work in progress at her salon, Sainte-Beuve then multiplied his attentions. But he had a new object for his jealousy—the young poet Louis de Ronchaud, now permanently in Paris at Marie's side. Because she tried to avoid seeing Sainte-Beuve alone, Ronchaud faithfully stood guard when he came. Therefore, much of the courtship was conducted by letters, full of the conceits and precious figures of speech of which Sainte-Beuve, an expert on French classical literature, was master. The correspondence lasted, on and off, for more than five years. Not that Sainte-Beuve did not woo other women at the same time. He knew that Liszt was still the "prince-bishop," as he called him, of Marie's life. But his courtship of Marie was more than a literary exercise. It is clear that he wanted what he had described in his novel *Le Clou d'or:* "To possess a woman about the age of 35 to 40 whom one has known for a long time, be it only once, that is what I call planting together the golden spike of friendship."

The task of retaining Sainte-Beuve as a professional consultant while denying him his one moment took all the coquetry Marie could summon up. She wrote to Liszt that she didn't know how to deal with him. "He woos me with madrigals and seventeenth century *bel esprit*. I do not find him at all witty in this circumstance and I fear that this will end in piqued vanity and broken relations." How could a man so sensitive put himself into a situation so stupid? Despite Ronchaud being there from four to six daily to keep Sainte-Beuve from making a declaration, he managed to make one "in silly verse."

Liszt insisted that she put him off while agreeing that she should retain him for his usefulness.

Sainte-Beuve kept Marie's picture on his desk. Once, on returning home from her salon, he wrote to tell her that he had picked up the petals fallen from the camellia she wore and was saving them in an envelope. He then quoted verses from Theocritus about the evanescence of flowers, ending with the words: "And your beauty, however perfect / Cannot last you very long." He went on, "I dare not add what the ancient poet concludes from all this. But why, I ask you, did this camellia take it upon itself, just today, to fall apart all at once? Certainly no one touched it; it was whole and in full bloom when I came in; and *voilà*, all by itself, in the twinkling of an eye, it sprinkled itself over your black velvet dress! It only wished, Madame, to give you a small lesson."[2]

In this back-and-forth relationship, Sainte-Beuve would disappear for a period, and Marie would write to ask why she had not seen him recently. Once he replied with a story about his enchanted island:

It is always the same story. . . . I am in sight of the most beautiful beach. The goddess has, occasionally, smiled at me (yes, Madame, has smiled) and has almost signaled me. . . . I sense that I am going to land and I predict that, once on the island, there await me only troubles, jealousies, ridicule, finally torment. . . . Should one be astonished if, as soon as . . . some occasion permits me to move away a bit, I profit from it with all my strength and try to reach the sea with full oars? Alas, it is undoubtedly all in vain, I can only put off the storm for a few minutes.[3]

There were times when he swore that if he had to, he knew how to wait, "endlessly and in silence." He continued to help his "humble student," as she called herself, with her writing, reading her proofs and paying her court, without success. Marie even backed Vigny for a seat at the Académie française when Sainte-Beuve was also a nominee. His friends pretended astonishment that she continued to support Vigny after his candidacy was known and even teased him about it. One would suspect that this was a worse blow to him than his failure to seduce her. But he never said a word against her, admitting that she had already been committed to Vigny when he entered the competition. (Sainte-Beuve was promised, and received, the next empty seat.) Nevertheless, it was after this that he wrote, "A pleasant friendship, indulgent, ingeniously charming, and which charms so easily, has certain rights over the hearts of friends. For my part I am truly grateful, almost as grateful as if. . . . But actually, did I not one evening have my camellia?"[4]

Finally, Sainte-Beuve gave up and accused her of using him: "O noble and ambitious woman! For I know you now, and that is what you really are."5 Surely, he did not discover this all of a sudden. It was rather that these two had been locked in a battle of wills, and he had believed it possible, up to then, that he might win and might plant his "golden spike." Instead, all he could boast of was an envelope with faded petals of her camellia. Interestingly enough, by this time Sainte-Beuve was beginning to feel isolated from the new literary scene. Marie, who was moving away from Romanticism, was sponsoring a new young poet, François Ponsard. So Sainte-Beuve was still happy to attend her salon for a reading of Ponsard's classical drama *Lucrèce*, performed by the actor Beauvallet, and even to back Ponsard for an Academy seat! However, he gradually retreated altogether.

Marie was to pay for her resistance to Sainte-Beuve. He had aided her greatly in learning to be a professional writer, but he never once mentioned her in his critical works, although she sent him all her books and heard from friends, like Hortense Allart, of favorable comments on them. In his memoirs, *Mes Poisons,* he later wrote: "If I had a young friend to instruct from my experience, I would tell him: You can fall in love with a coquette, with a nun even; you have a chance to conquer her, reduce her to your desire. But if you seek some happiness in love, never love a Muse. There where you think to find her heart you will encounter only her talent."6 So beyond being written off by the friends of Liszt and of George Sand, Marie was obliterated from the literature of her day by its greatest literary critic.

As a woman alone in Paris, who wanted to be independent, Marie needed men—not only for her salon but also to help her make a career and a name for herself. She did not want to embark on new love affairs, but her ability to attract men who could help her was predominantly in her beauty and seductiveness. She developed a method for retaining her suitors without giving in to them, which she described in a letter to Liszt as separating the elements of love from those of friendship, rejecting the first and keeping the second. She was very successful in this method, retaining as friends and correspondents a large proportion of the men originally attracted to her sexually. She did this because she saw it as the only successful strategy for a woman who wanted to move in a man's world while preserving her dignity. Later, she wrote in her *Essai sur la liberté:*

In all civilized societies flirtation has become for women a science as profound as the science of politics. Since society leaves them outside real action, they have easily learned to make use of a man's desires to render him, at least temporarily, her slave; and all their finesse, all their intelligence, all their faculties of observation and calculation are applied to that unique purpose: to inspire love without partaking of it, to excite passion without satisfying it. Out of this . . . [develops] a complicated art, with infinite resources, which partakes of both strategy and politics, where one hundred times more ability, perseverance, audacity, artifice, nuance, deliberation and knowledge is used than is needed to administer a kingdom, discipline a [military] encampment or lead a legislature.[7]

Marie was to use this "woman's weapon" with great success. It became so natural to her that she retained, to her old age, an almost effortless power to charm. Because she remained sexually faithful to Liszt, she was also forgiven by many of her suitors for "inspiring love without partaking of it." But this success became also a trap, preventing her, once the Liszt chapter in her life was past, from ever again allowing the free flow of her emotions. In all her relations with men, she remained in control. And because of the adoration and devotion she continued to receive from men, she tended to value friendships with men over those with women. Thus her emotional life was never totally satisfying.

There was one more blow from Sand before the end of the friendship. Late in 1841 her novel *Horace* began to appear in the *Revue indépendante*. In it the eponymous hero leaves his virtuous and pregnant mistress to join the Vicomtesse de Chailly. Not a main personnage in the story, the viscountess is painted in vicious colors. She is terribly skinny, with bad teeth and long, dry hands. She has an excellent memory but no wit. She prepares beforehand to shine at her salon. Instead of feelings, she has coquetry. She is all pose and lies, and has never really been loved. Liszt agreed that there was no doubt Madame de Chailly was intended as a portrait of Marie. Why was Sand angry enough to do this? There is some indication that she resented Marie's flirting with Didier, even appearing with him at concerts and lectures in Paris after Sand had ended their relations. She might have recognized that Didier, editor of *Le Monde* along with Lamennais, was to Marie a professional, not a personal prize. But Sand believed that Marie took him up just to spite her, his former lover. Unlike Balzac's novel, Sand's portrait was totally negative, pouring scorn on any possibility of a grand passion. In any case, this was the real end of any friendship.

It was around the same time as *Horace* that Marie wrote an article on her own again, rather than for Liszt. She had gone, along with many others, to the opening of a new auditorium at the École de Beaux Arts, which had been decorated by the official painter Paul Delaroche. Marie's taste in art had been formed by the classical style of her friend Ingrès and his student, Lehmann.

When Girardin dropped in that afternoon, she was highly critical of what she had seen. Again he asked her, why not put it down on paper for *La Presse?* This time, there was no hesitation. And this time, Girardin insisted on a name to put to it. Of course, she would not use her own. Aside from the other strictures on women as public figures, she had to consider her family's reaction. Her favorite male name, Daniel, was easy. It is puzzling that for the surname she felt the desire to choose a German one, "Stern" (meaning star). Although she always valued Goethe highly, her literary culture, unlike her musical one, had been predominantly French. Could it be that she felt a German name would make it more difficult to guess the author? She made Girardin swear secrecy, so she may indeed have been frightened as the moment of possible fame approached. But for her friends the pen name lasted only for the first article, and soon her secret was abroad for everyone to know.

The article was a fair success. She described the highly esteemed Delaroche as "the man of his time, but only of his time where a kind of *distinguished mediocrity* reigns. A talent of the *juste milieu*." Marie was referring to the characterization of the July Monarchy as philistine and bourgeois—"no attempt at truth, or the ideal, just agreeable and charming painting."[8] She was not the only negative critic. But there were few, and she was the harshest on Delaroche until Baudelaire's critique of him five years later. Again, she had the pleasure of hearing people comment in her own salon, this time wondering who had dared to take on the eminent painter. Girardin was also pleased. The same month he published Daniel Stern's article introducing Cologne cathedral to the French.[9] In early 1842 she wrote articles on two paintings—Ingrès's portrait of Cherubini, and Overbeck's *Triumph of Religion*.[10] Stern was one of the few critics to insist upon the worth of Ingrès, whose art she judged appropriate to great classical themes and whose disciples she noted with approval. When the annual Salon, in which the great painters of the day showed their work, opened in March, Daniel Stern covered it for *La Presse* in a series of five articles over two months.

The Salons had been covered by the writers Théophile Gautier, from 1837 to 1839, and Eugène Pelletan in 1841. Marie reviewed them for 1842 and 1843.[11] She began her series with the customary exposé of the principles of art. Traditional religious bases for art, she wrote, were no longer appropriate to an epoch like the nineteenth century. Therefore, artists must find inspiration not in heaven but in their own will and knowledge. Marie favored the search for ideal types, which would be facilitated by studying the classical artists for form and for their profound understanding of nature and communion with the universe. The renaissance of painting, she thought, might come about through a pantheistic understanding of nature as spirit. In the second year she began her coverage with a discussion of art criticism. Her standards were purity and harmony of form, vigor, and clarity. She also used in her critique the Germanic notions of the ideal and of immanent truth. The painters she praised most were students of Ingrès—Lehmann and Chassériau, Hippolyte Flandrin and Ary Scheffer. The huge historical paintings so admired in the July Monarchy struck her as "too much."

In each of these years Daniel Stern also covered the Salon of Sculpture. The first year she opined that French sculpture was in a period of such sterility and impoverishment that she wondered if the French really understood sculpture. One exception was a work by Félicie de Fauveau, who had had difficulty with the judges in 1841 over her subject but had made it this year with *Judith*. (This was the biblical figure who cut off the head of her oppressor. She was a popular topic for women painters, who always depicted her at the bloody moment. Here also she was holding the head of Holofernes. Perhaps the absence of color made it possible for Stern to accept this savage and unclassical depiction.) Stern said that the sculptor was "one of the small number of those exceptionally endowed women born with the divine instinct of poetry." One can see that Stern, although willing to deliver herself of daring opinions on art, was at this point far from being able to see women as equal to men, even though she commented favorably on two busts of another woman sculptor. In the following year, Stern found a sculptor much to her liking at the Salon de Sculpture—Pierre-Charles Simart, whose *Philosophy* achieved her standard of grandeur and nobility. The artist was to do a classical head of the critic in 1847.

In 1843 Stern made some suggestions for change in the Salon system, to meet the arguments over works excluded by the jury. One was to include more artists on the panel, another to limit the works of any one artist to three. But she also suggested a solution that would later be used by the Impressionists, in holding their own "Salon of the Rejected." Could not some rooms in the Louvre be opened up to those turned down by the jury, she asked, to ensure that no great work would be lost and that the public would have the opportunity to choose for itself?

Daniel Stern's criticism was that of an amateur, which was normal in those days. Baudelaire, who followed her in commenting on the salons, was the same. Her faithfulness to Ingrès and his school was not connected with the religiosity and political reaction now associated with his school of painting[12] but with her admiration of harmony and the ideal in art. As a result, she missed many of the new trends in painting. (Baudelaire also ignored the great artists of his time. His critical study "The Painter of Modern Life" used as hero a minor figure in the art world.) Remaining interested in art all her life, Stern never again wrote on it, nor on music.

Having done years of publicity for Liszt, however, Marie was often in contact with German newspapers. She produced articles on the salons of Paris, in German and French, for the German and Belgian press. Although Liszt himself was becoming more conservative, he put Marie in touch with the liberal *Gazette d'Augsburg* and with personalities like Felix Lichnowsky, Karl Gutzkow, and Georg Herwegh, who arrived in her salon in 1843. Herwegh was the poet of German radicalism, whose work expressed the ideas of the Young Hegelians, a group including Arnold Ruge, Moses Hess, and Karl Marx. Along with the Russian Bakunin, this group, exiled from Germany, tried to continue their radical journalism in Paris with the *Deutsche-Französische Jahrbucher.* It was a failure. The young Herwegh undertook the radical education of Marie, to whom he was attracted immediately, even though she was twelve years his senior and he had a new young wife. (She was to make friends of both of them.) He urged Marie to rise above convention, to leave dilettantism behind, and to break with the old world. He brought Bakunin to her salon and perhaps Alexander Herzen; there they met the socialist Pierre-Joseph Proudhon and the Russian author Ivan Turgenev.

As France moved into the 1840s, political discontent was growing and was reflected in the more political cast of Marie's salon. The regime in France was not popular, either with the aristocrats who viewed the July Monarch as an upstart or with the republicans and socialists, who found the government still oppressive to liberty and controlled by the moneyed classes. Marie was sympathetic with both groups. No longer an aristocrat, she could not accept the values of the new bourgeoisie. Although she would never be a radical, Marie had become socially conscious through Liszt's connections with Saint-Simonian socialism. Her friendship with Herwegh gave her yet another view of the "social problem" of her time. In 1844, when her friend Eugène Sue was writing his *Mystères de Paris,* about the lower depths of society, Marie investigated an agricultural colony for young prisoners at La Mettray founded by her brother and other humanitarian aristocrats. Daniel Stern praised it in an article in *La Presse.*[13]

France might not yet be a free society, but to the rest of the Continent, Paris was still a center for intellectuals, artists, and political figures. Polish exiles like the poet Adam Mickiewicz, fleeing the unsuccessful Polish revolt against Russia, Russian exiles from tsarist oppression like Herzen and Bakunin, and exiles like Herwegh and Marx from the reactionary German states crowded into Paris and often into the salon of the sympathetic Comtesse d'Agoult. Herwegh introduced Marie to the materialist works of Feuerbach. He also brought her the first two (and only) issues of the *Jahrbucher,* which included articles by Ruge and Bakunin, and two articles by Marx, "Critique of Hegel's Philosophy of Right," and "The Jewish Question," plus some poems of his own. Her reaction indicates why the journal was not a success: "I have read through Ruge and Marx. I am too French to understand what this is *good for.* They are right on certain points, but they betray a great lack of understanding of Christianity, and consequently of the Middle Ages." Daniel Stern, not herself religious, may have been the first critic of many to say that one of Marx's main weaknesses was his misunderstanding of religion. Nevertheless, she decided to present to French readers the thinking of the German Hegelians. Her essay "Georges Herwegh et les hégélians politiques," which included some of her translations into French of Herwegh's poetry, appeared in two installments in *La Presse* late in 1843. Critical of the Young Hegelian movement, these political writings were Daniel Stern's first of a long series. But only with the beginning of the German revolution in 1847 did she turn her attention to the politics of her native land.

Eager to understand the new literary and philosophic as well as political German thinking, she read Hegel's *Aesthetics* and thought of doing a translation but decided that it wouldn't attract a French audience. Her other articles on Germany in this period dealt with the literary and religious world.[14]

Marie's correspondence with Herwegh continued for a number of years. She also shared with him, as a friend, the difficulties of her private life. Herwegh's radical friends blamed her for reducing his revolutionary fervor to mere liberalism and spread the rumor that he was her lover.

Daniel Stern was becoming a real journalist, interested in society as a whole as well as art and music. Already, some of the permanent themes of her work were beginning to emerge—classical idealism, pantheism, and pan-Europeanism. In an article on Meyerbeer's religious songs she wrote that his harmonies reflected both sides of the Rhine:[15] "A propos of which, let us remark how much, over the last twenty years, despite rivalries and antagonisms . . . Germany and France are strengthening each day an intellectual alliance." She referred to Heinrich Heine, then living in Paris, to Schiller's philosophy reflected in the work of Pierre Leroux, to Lamennais's and Hugo's popularity in Germany. There was a place again for a Madame de Staël, she noted, to interpret Germany to France. Clearly, Stern hoped to fill that role.

But she was not yet independent enough in her views on women to be a Madame de Staël. In 1844 François Buloz, editor of the *Revue des deux mondes,* looking to set up an attack on George Sand, commissioned from Stern an article critical of Bettina von Arnim. The reigning grande dame of German letters and friend of Beethoven, Arnim had published her correspondence with Goethe and had recently published an open letter to the king of Prussia. She was the sister of Clemens Bretano, first husband of Marie's half-sister Auguste, and was much admired by Liszt, who begged Marie not to do the article. But Marie, jealous of the great *salonnière,* persisted and sought information from her German sources. Unfortunately, Buloz judged her first article not negative enough. On the second attempt, Stern pleased the editor by excoriating women "who clothe themselves in a system, put on the makeup of erudition and philosophy," and for whom "the spots of ink on their fingers have the same meaning as the pearls at their necks."[16]

Buloz wanted Marie to sign her real name to the article, but she refused. It would have been appropriate, for the type of woman she was ridiculing was what Daniel Stern was striving to become—a successful intellectual woman. "I have been mortally sad for three days," she wrote to Herwegh, who had also recommended against the article, "having been led to reflect on all that mud that I am forced to walk in. . . . I really feel that I was wrong, but . . . extreme pride often leads to extreme cowardice." She told Herwegh that her main aim was to try to gain honestly some credit in those particular quarters that she cared about, "to go around the mountain I do not have the force to scale, to put on shoes because I don't have wings."[17] Although not yet strong enough to stand up to the *Revue des deux mondes,* she was beginning to get some of the recognition she sought.

Her personal life was also gradually expanding. After more than four months in Paris, she had finally been given permission to visit her legitimate daughter, Claire, in the convent; she found a very unhappy and resentful child. Marie's mother did not welcome her until January 1841. When she spent some time at the family chateau the following year, she saw that her sister-in-law occupied her place with her mother, for the two of them shared a religious piety in which Marie could not participate. The situation with her children by Liszt was scarcely better. On her return to Paris, Marie received regular letters from Lehmann about Daniel, who was in his charge. This child, born after the decision of the lovers to part, seemed unlucky from the start. Marie even wrote once that although Lehmann's reports on Daniel gave her joy, he shouldn't bother to keep going to see the child. "That child is of necessity given over to Providence and to chance, and the best I can do is to think of him as little as possible."[18] However, she did ask news of him after that and seemed worried when she learned of a plague in Rome. She planned to bring the child to France when he was weaned.

The girls, by agreement, were living with Madame Liszt in Paris, where they were visited by their mother. Marie involved herself in their education, particularly in languages, introducing them to German, English, and even Latin. She also played with them, engaging in word games, allowing them to dress her hair, "to look like father's," which was, of course, romantically long. She wrote to Liszt that Blandine was her favorite. But within a year there were difficulties between mother and grandmother. Marie wrote to Liszt that something would have to be done; it was mad to think that the two women could cooperate in bringing up the children. At around the same time, Marie told Lehmann she was ready to take Daniel to Paris, but Liszt vetoed the plan. He visited the girls at Madame Liszt's at the end of 1841.

After a week alone with the girls at Versailles in late 1842, Marie wrote in her notebook that Cosima was becoming more and more beautiful, with a regular profile, superb complexion, and lovely hair. But her character seemed "a bit sly and teasing, inclined to solitude." Blandine was perhaps not so conventionally beautiful, but she had grace and distinction. "Her look and her smile express something ineffable." Blandine was also the better student; "her intelligence is open to everything. She asks good questions." In sum, Blandine was loving, extremely reasonable, and desirous of pleasing. "I adore her," Marie wrote. Daniel, only three, she found physically magnificent.[19] The two girls, who visited their mother in Paris, made a great hit with friends. Bulwer was willing to formally adopt Blandine. Ronchaud and Lehmann, as family friends, often had dinner with them. Lehmann drew them and taught them drawing.

Dissatisfied with the education that their grandmother could give the girls, Marie placed Blandine with a schoolmistress in 1843. When the woman became ill, Blandine came to live with her mother, who took over her lessons in German, the Bible, and polite conversation, while arranging for English, geography, and piano lessons from others. Each day, the two visited at Madame Liszt's. Marie gloried in her daughter's clever conversation and word games. Despite the disapproval of Mickiewicz, who refused to give his daughter a "male education," Blandine began Latin. The following year, Marie placed her in the pension of Madame Bernard, where Cosima soon joined her.

In 1841 began the yearly sojourns of Marie and Liszt at Nonnenwerth, an island in the Rhine River, where the legendary Roland was said to have died of love. When Liszt first suggested the place for the summer, Marie was hesitant to go to Germany for fear people would see her as running after him. But the secluded spot, with an old Benedictine convent transformed into an inn, complete with ruins, an old chapel, and a statue of a bishop at the entrance, was too romantic to resist. Marie would dress in a quasi-nun's dress, including a long black cross of something like ebony suspended on a chain of black stones. Perhaps one reason for this outfit was that many of the other guests took her for Sand, a confusion that was frequent and galling to Marie, for it implied a relationship between Sand and Liszt.

One of the guests, Baroness von Czetteritz-Neuhaus, wrote to her daughter about Marie's arrival the first year. "She must once have been a great beauty, although just beginning to fade a little." (Marie was thirty-five.) She immediately took a bath with a quarter pound of starch and lots of perfume in it. Liszt arrived that evening, "the best and kindest man imaginable, generous, liberal, and for all his brilliance, just like a child." A local music class of young ladies came and adorned the doors of his room to welcome him. He played for them. "We admired the tender, affectionate way in which she [Marie] spoke to the children. When she sat down her beautiful features were quite altered, the tears running down her cheeks. No doubt she was thinking of her own children."

The same letter, whose phrasing reveals Marie's influence, provides a romantic view of the lovers:

The passion on both sides is so great, it is as though they were on their honeymoon, although it is not expressed in the usual way and always makes one inclined to consider it a Platonic relationship, because until midday both of them read and write; and then again they spend the evening until late in the night with lively conversation, or reading and writing. . . . Their relationship has now lasted nine years, hallowed by an inexpressible mutual love and respect, indestructible either in this world or the next. She is his FIRST and only love. . . . He can write and compose only when she is here. He sits beside her and sings or plays to her what he has just written.

Describing the books Marie brought—beautiful editions of Byron, Shakespeare, the Bible, books on religion and philosophy—the baroness declared herself frightened by so much intellect and erudition in a woman:

I find it uncanny. . . . What can my company give her? . . . A woman like that sees everything from a different side, has investigated, explored and exhausted everything, and falls from one theory, perhaps from one error, into another. Sometimes I wonder what sort of an end she will come to. . . . I should not like to enjoy her more than I have done already. When the talk is of paintings her judgment is great, just as it is in architecture, landscapes, books, and persons; everything small and petty is banished. Do you know how I should still like to enjoy her? Sitting quietly in a corner when she talks with Liszt about music, with Thorvaldsen about sculpture, with Cornelius about painting; in short, when she talks with great men about great things. When he is away and asks her to work hard, she sits writing until about one o'clock in the morning. She has written a novel here and also a description of Nonnenwerth and the Rhine; of this latter work she read us many pages: glorious and sublime![20]

Despite her original hesitation, which reflects some of the standard fears about intellectual women, the baroness was to become Marie's friend and confidant. She must have noted that the couple always had visitors; Lichnowsky and Girardin arrived quite soon, and Ronchaud became an almost permanent guest. Other friends came and went. By the third summer, Hungarian dancers and Viennese humorists were entertaining them, and a Shakespearean translator from Berlin was reading Shakespeare to them. In the second year, Blandine came with her parents to the island. Marie entertained for a short time the idea of retiring to Nonnenwerth with the children. But Liszt was bored with children and considered family life bourgeois, so it was not a success.

The baroness was also to overhear more stormy moments of the lovers' vacation. Marie had written to Liszt earlier in the year, before a meeting with him, "I yearn for you with all the forces of my being and nevertheless I have the feeling of a destructive element which is blindly making its way and drawing us toward two opposing poles. I think I feel that my chains weigh me down while your wings beat the air with more vigor." Her ambivalence and probably her resentment of his greater freedom was to surface each time they met. Liszt, on the other hand, spoke of the future, when they would live together and be happy. Only he must make money now, which to her meant the competition of other women. Looking forward to the coming vacation, he wrote that he couldn't wait. "You are adorable, and I am madly, foolishly in love with you."[21] But already Marie was guarding herself from taking this too much to heart. She wrote in her diary that he always did have one foot in the exaltation and the other in the comedy of feelings.

The old problem—that Liszt could not resist the plaudits of the crowd and particularly of women—followed them to Nonnenwerth. When he interrupted their vacation to do concerts in nearby German towns, Marie's resentment boiled over. She fled, after sending him a note: "Madness is taking over my brain. I can't hold out any longer. I feel myself incapable of living in these perpetual agitations. You cannot understand that; therefore let us cease these somber, sad discussions and let me retire before those touching devotions which spring up in crowds under your feet. I would be better as a friend than as a lover. I know very well that I have nothing to reproach you for, but I also know—I only know that I suffer and that I will make you suffer eternally in remaining, therefore goodbye then." She indicated that this was not a rupture but an adjournment. "In five or six years we will laugh together at my tortures today."[22] He raced back and went after her. They celebrated Liszt's birthday with with little cannons, oysters, flowers, a treeplanting, and verses from Ronchaud. The autumn finished happily. When it was over, Liszt referred in a letter to how much they fought when they were together but how he knew when they were apart that they were destined for one another.

At the end of the year he wrote that he had finished *Lorelei*, which he dedicated to her. Worried that he had not heard from her for more than eighteen days, Liszt swore that he had not had a woman since he left her. He undoubtedly knew that if Marie had not written for that long, it was probably because she had heard another rumor of his relations with women. Clara Schumann, the German pianist, described Liszt at this time. He had played duo piano with her in public on two occasions and had already visited the musical couple. He arrived at a party in her home "as always, very very late. He seems to love making people wait for him, which displeases me. I find him just like a spoilt child, good-natured, masterful, kind, arrogant, noble and generous, often severe with others—a strange mixture." Another description of Liszt at this period was from the critic Edward Devrient: "He is by no means the charlatan he is reputed to be, although a certain charlatanry has become his truest nature. [He is] strangely volatile, the engagingly attractive hand-in-hand with the demoniacally dreadful. His playing surpasses everything that we have yet known."[23]

For three years Nonnenwerth was the scene of stormy vacations. Liszt became exasperated when Marie wept in frustration. She tried unsuccessfully to avoid hearing those words, "I hate your tears." Liszt suggested she write her memoirs. She produced sixty-seven pages of splenetic anger, started a novel, composed a poetic description of the island that she read to her friends, and wrote delirious incantations to Liszt that sound more like efforts to convince herself of his nobility than anything else. To Lehmann she wrote, "My spleen persists, perpetuates itself and puts down roots; I see no end to it, and don't understand the cause." Liszt, she said, went from strength to strength. "Life boils up in him in large and powerful waves. I have no illusion that he is at a level of the highest grandeur." Declaring that she had all she could possibly want, she added that nevertheless there was that incurable evil, that ennui of life that nothing penetrates."[24]

Marie was by now convinced that "spleen" ran in her family. Her nephew, Leon Ehrmann, whose mother had committed suicide when he was ten, came to Paris in 1842, a tortured and neurotic student. After he had thrown himself into the Seine, Marie, in trying to aid him, became the object of his unstable passion. Instead of keeping him at arm's length, Marie tried to use her influence to push him to finish his thesis. The family became enraged. When Ehrmann, still corresponding with his aunt, died in suddenly in Rome in 1845, Marie was suspected of hastening his death by encouraging his adoration, although he seems to have died of pneumonia. She always insisted that she was only helping him. But she was very much aware of the family instability.

Yet out of the despair of Marie d'Agoult was growing the author Daniel Stern. It was probably inevitable that, not yet freed from Romanticism, she would feel the necessity to try her hand at fiction. Her first novella, *Hervé*, was published in *La Presse* at the end of 1842; it had been written more than a year earlier. The main character was inspired partly by Girardin. In an "Envoi" she dedicated it to him: "To you who have fought alone / Suffered in silence / Triumphed without joy / To you who are my friend." The hero relates to a married woman he loves the story of a former love affair. Hervé, like Girardin, has fought a duel, but for love, not politics. Also married, Hervé does not pursue his love. The character also has elements of Didier, who may have talked to Marie about Sand, and even of Liszt. There are some responses by the married woman being pursued that are interesting in their possible application to Marie's relationship with Girardin: "My heart bleeds sometimes, but my brow is spotless, and the pride of a pure conscience is my force in affliction." Also, "To pass a day quite close to a immense happiness, to see it, to believe that one could seize it by reaching out one's hand, and nevertheless not to take it, that is the unknown heroism of many noble hearts." Many years later, Marie was to write in her diary that for a second time in her life she had felt the possibility of a true love, but the moment had come too late. If she was referring to Girardin, and he is the most likely, then *Hervé* was the memorial to that love.

There was another, clearly personal reference in the novella. When Hervé seeks counsel from a priest, he is told that when the life of the heart has failed, one can find treasures in the mind. Referring to the Tower of Pisa, which seemed to be doomed before its completion, he notes that the architect did not lose courage but instead modified the measurements and changed the lines, completing his tower, which became a marvel to everyone. Life was the same: "First let us shore up our soul, and announce our faults. Let us complete our tilted life so that one might in judging us wonder if were not preferable thus, if a more complete perfection would not have been less admirable." One might see this as Marie's admission that she had to modify her life, give up perfection, and create of herself something different from her ideal.[25]

The second novella, *Julien*, published in early 1843, is mostly a dialogue between an alienated young man and an older woman, who begs him not to kill himself. Surely it reflects Marie's relationship with her nephew Ehrmann; the young man is brought back to a sense of life by the glories of nature. There are also some lines in this work that are interesting for those who want to know the author: "Enthusiasm does not fool us; it is all-powerful; it creates what it affirms." Was she now examining the great enthusiasm of her life? She also wrote, "We do not know what we are . . . we know only what we have been." Another important aspect of "Julien" was the dedication to George Sand:

> To a broken friendship:
> I must write your name at the head of this little work.
> I promised myself I would in a time irrevocably past.
> Today, Madame you will not even divine the name I do not mention,
>   which was so dear to me
> Life passes in vain efforts and in vainer regrets.
> We wanted to love one another.[26]

Daniel Stern was not a good novelist, and neither of these works was a great success. Besides proving to herself that she could produce fiction, they probably served as efforts to give form to the emotional tumult in her life. It was unfortunate that she did not give up writing novels after these two.

*Seven ⌣ "Nonnenwerth,
the tomb of my chimeras, of
my ideal life, the ashes
of my hopes!"*

For more than ten years Marie had remained faithful to her passion for Liszt, and he had returned her love. Their relationship, although physically passionate, was also lived as an ideal love. She was his Beatrice, his muse, his avenue to the higher life, in both a spiritual and an intellectual sense. To this world, defined by Marie, Liszt returned for renewal. But he lived in another world also, in which he gained the plaudits of the crowd and the favors of lovely ladies. He did not want to give up either life. Marie, however, considered her only real life to be the one with Liszt. When in 1839, unable to follow him on concert tours, she returned to Paris, she was still determined to live for him. The salon, the publicity she did for him, the almost daily letters still kept her, as she saw it, totally engaged in his life. And she never intended to lead another. Liszt spoke in his letters about a time when they would live together happily, holding this dream forth to Marie as the reward for all they were suffering in being parted. But for him this time was in some distant future, when all he would desire was his composing and peace with his beloved. For her it was also in the future, but in one that was becoming more and more unreal.

In this situation there were many things Marie was required to overlook. The most obvious was that Liszt did not remain faithful to her. This would not have been so bad if he had been discreet, but Liszt had never learned nor even desired discretion. He was a performer who loved an audience. In Paris there was always someone to transmit the latest rumor to Marie, and she knew that at least some of them were true. Also, the exhilaration of adoring women and enthusiastic crowds often prevented Liszt from rushing back to her at every opportunity; his arrival always trailed days, sometimes weeks behind the promised date. So, although she knew he loved her, she often suffered the humiliation of being, in the eyes of the public, the abandoned mistress. Liszt refused to take seriously the wounds he inflicted on her pride. Instead, he sought a way out by encouraging her, actually against his real desire, to have her own separate sexual life. This would absolve him of the guilt he felt toward her for his affairs. But Marie, by her nature and her breeding, was constitutionally unable to live the life of a loose woman and therefore could not follow his advice. In fact, his suggestions to that effect only caused an additional shock to her sensibilities.

So for years this proud, aristocratic woman suffered from a love on which she could not and would not turn her back, a love for which she had sacrificed her good name, and which she therefore must continue to believe was extraordinary and of great value. But living away from Liszt, Marie began to recognize the reality of her situation. He was not going to change. They were not going to live together, with or without their children. Actually, Liszt was impatient with the children when they were present. The question was, simply, how much could she or ought she accept with bowed head and loving heart? For a time she felt that she had no choice but to accept everything. Tempted but not really interested in taking a new lover, overwhelmingly concerned that her love be ideal and eternal, she tried and failed to restrain her resentment when she was with Liszt. The result was tears, which he hated, and repeated bouts of her "spleen," which marred the vacations, shorter each year, at Nonnenwerth.

A letter from Liszt to Marie in November 1842, just after they had parted separately from Nonnenwerth, says that he has just received an incomprehensible letter from her; she seems to want a rupture. Some weeks later he swore would give up his public life if he truly believed she would still be happy to live with him but said he did not believe he was sufficient for her. Better "this life of vagabondage rather than an unhealthy stagnation which would kill me without making you live." The following year, after leaving Nonnenwerth, he wrote back to Marie with the old exaltation: "I can in no way explain to myself how it can be that you are not here. That urge to see you, that need to live and breathe in you will never subside."[1]

But by now Marie was not as ready to believe him as she had once been. Although Liszt had not had nearly the number of mistresses attributed to him, he continued to be publicly unfaithful to her. The first time that Marie considered not a temporary but a permanent break with Liszt seems to have been in December of that year, when she recorded in her diary a discussion with Ronchaud on her *"affranchissement,"* as she put it. Clearly, she was considering some kind of break.[2] The new element that had entered the equation was that she was learning to stand on her own two feet and be something without Liszt. In January 1843, gratified after seeing through to publication a few articles and a novella, Daniel Stern wrote in her diary, "I am not just a woman, I am a force."[3] She was beginning to feel the strength of her own personality, apart from Liszt.

Then, early in 1844, she heard that Liszt had dedicated a work to Camille Pleyel—which as good as announced their affair and was an insult to Marie. His attempts to explain were useless. Marie had already remarked that constant change and publicity in connection with his "German orgies" seemed necessary to him. Unable to moderate his "performances" in love any more than those on the piano, Liszt was described by Marie in a letter to Herwegh as "half buffoon, half conjurer, who makes ideas and feelings disappear in his sleeves and complacently eyes the public clapping its hands in astonishment."[4] The final straw was Liszt's wild, highly publicized fling in one German city after another with the dancer Lola Montez, who had been the mistress of Duke Maximilian of Bavaria. Now even the friends who had not dared to speak before pushed Marie to break with Liszt. She wrote to Herwegh that she had finally realized that she was a Beatrice without a Dante. To Liszt she wrote a serious warning letter:

Reflect that the difficulties of my life are increasing each day. Claire is going to be 14 yrs old. As for you, it is absolutely impossible that you can be, socially speaking, anything for me. Your plans in that regard have never been made, or, if they were, you have failed to reach any goals. All you can do then is to do nothing, that is, to be wise and prudent and to have taste. But it is difficult at present for me to hope for that . . . and all I have gained by preaching reason to you is to put you into a fury. . . . You have abdicated your last virtue in relation to me, sincerity. As for the rest, I limit myself to a single and final prayer: Try to spare me the grossest publicity.

What is amazing about this mournful letter is that she was able to express her disdain in a bon mot worthy of her salon: "Byronism has had its time, it is a exhausted genre which has also exhausted sympathy. . . . Besides, Byron wouldn't be Byronian now. He would be a member of Parliament and a moderate Whig."

Liszt, at the time being blackmailed by his student Herman Cohen (Puzzi), who possessed some woman's letters from 1840 (so they can't really be important, Liszt wrote Marie) did nothing except plan a visit to Paris; he probably was confident that he could repair things. He loved her and could not conceive of losing her. It would have behooved him to note another part of the same letter: "My courage grows each day. I have no more humor, nor tears, nor joy, nor pain, and it seems that I walk more freely to the extent that I detach myself from those ruined hopes, which follow me like beggars and want a part of my soul."[5] If he had taken these words seriously, he might have made an exception and arrived in Paris on the date he had promised, but he did not. Marie wrote to Herwegh, "Here I am still, Ariadne abandoned on the isle of Naxos. Theseus does not return, and my eyes, red with tears, can see not the least Bacchus on the horizon! I am so sad, so tired of life, and I see nothing changing, nothing to hope for, to desire, to do!"[6]

The chronology of the week Liszt was in Paris, April 8–15, is unclear. Marie invited Herwegh to dinner with Liszt when he finally arrived, probably to have support in what she intended to say. The conversation was continued the following day. And on the next, Marie sent Liszt this letter:

If I did not have the conviction, my dear Franz, that I am and can be nothing but a grief and an importunate disturbance in your life, believe me I would not take the position that I take now in the most profound unhappiness of my soul. You have much force, youth, and genius. Many things will still grow for you on the tomb where our love and our friendship will sleep. If you have the desire to spare me a bit in this last crisis, which I would not have put off so long had I a little foresight and pride, you will not respond with anger and irritation to certain demands that I will have to make of you. . . . [I want] the intermediary of a third party. Chose whomever you wish, Lamennais if you agree, who loves you and has never considered me anything but a misfortune in your life. . . . I want it to be immediately after your concert. It is not good to prolong this state of uncertainty. Besides, I will have to make material arrangements which are better made sooner than later. I ask and beg you until then to tell no one, unless it is Ronchaud . . . and to abstain from treating with a mocking tone what is for both of us perhaps a folly or the consequence of a folly, certainly a serious folly which ought to be respected.[7]

At first, Liszt's response to Marie's letter was abject. "I count, one by one, all the griefs that I have put in your heart; nothing, no one can ever save me from myself."[8] But he resisted a third-party arbiter. If she felt it necessary, he thought Ronchaud would do. What he seemed to want was to get together with her and an intimate common friend, in which circumstance he probably felt he could make her change her mind. There were in the end two intermediaries—Lambert Massart, professor of violin at the conservatory and an intimate of Liszt, and the diplomat Alexandre de Villiers, another friend of Liszt, who immediately fell in love with Marie but nevertheless proposed an armistice. Marie agreed to back down if Liszt would give up his "vagabond life" and devote himself only to composing. Angrily, Liszt declared that all was finished between them. But he later wrote, "The past, Madame, was every day full of a serious and passionate devotion to you. . . . The hand of forgetfulness that you promise to extend to me, I would be happy to seize and hold embraced forever, but I cannot, no I could never say that that hand should have quitted me for a single instant."[9]

Marie dedicated a poem, never published, to Liszt:

> No, with your curled lip you do not hear
> The reproach, the regret in the wrenching goodbye.
> Your light heart feels no pain, no remorse
> In this mute farewell.
> You will believe that she also, with a vain elation
> And forgetful tomorrow of today's tears
> Has with a mocking laugh broken the sworn pact
> And passed on her way.
> And you will never know that, implacable and faithful,
> She leaves on a somber voyage never to return;
> And that in fleeing the lover, in the eternal night
> She takes with her the love![10]

Of course, the "material arrangements" Marie had referred to had to do with the children. She assumed, even though she was not their legal mother, that she would take control of them; Liszt had certainly shown little interest. But he tried to avoid making any settlement about the children. As Marie continued the pressure, he asked why he should put them in her hands if she made herself his adversary? Eventually, he agreed to give over the education of Blandine and Cosima to Marie. He preferred that they be raised in boarding school but tentatively agreed that their mother could have them with her if she wanted. He promised to establish a capital amount that would supply the girls' support almost fully. But he reserved the right to reintervene on this matter later, on the basis that her family would eventually make it impossible for her to keep the girls.

This would have been a fair settlement, had it been real and had it lasted. But it was not and did not. There exists a peculiar letter from Liszt informing Marie that he did not know whether it would be possible to leave the malachite vase at his mother's house: "You can easily see why, and if you want to avoid all scandal, you would do well to leave it in the place it occupied before."[11] Since there was no vase, this seemed to indicate that he had changed his mind about the girls, who were at his mother's house. If so, the letter is the probable cause of the violent altercation that took place at Marie's apartment on the afternoon of May 13. (She wrote to Herwegh that she was fighting like a lion for her children.)

That night Marie opened her door to Liszt's servant, who reported that Liszt was in a delirium and calling for her. On the chance that he had made some effort at suicide, she went to his apartment. He was only suffering from a high fever. In this pitiable state, Liszt importuned Marie for the last time but in vain; she returned home. She had been planning to leave Paris, and Liszt's pleading might have been an attempt to stop her. Had she perhaps been planning to take the girls, which could have occasioned the threat of scandal from him? We only know that the very next day, now ill herself with a fever, Marie left Paris for her family home at Mortier, accompanied only by Ronchaud. Lehmann was to report to her on Liszt's health, but Liszt also seems to have escaped Paris, to the country home of Princess Belgiojoso.[12]

Marie also asked Lehmann to tell Liszt that she would never complain against him. She was not to keep that promise. At the time she made it, she may still have had some hope of a reconciliation on her terms, as Herwegh was soon to be in touch with Liszt. It was not until May 23 that she wrote to Herwegh, "There is nothing to try, nothing to hope, nothing to do but absolutely and courageously to cut off my existence from his." And five days later she finally abandoned any reservations: "What you say to me about Liszt is true and confirms me in the necessity for an eternal and absolute separation. It would be really too naive to preserve the shadow of a hope, and what should I have to do with . . ." and again she said it, "a Don Juan parvenu? . . . Ten years of *illusions*—is that not the sublime peak of extravagance? . . . Adieu, my heart fills with bitterness, the spirit of *revolt* seizes me. Since I have not been able to live for *someone,* will it be given me to die for *something?*"[13]

Here Marie revealed again the nature of her passion for Liszt, a passion rooted in sacrifice that, eventually, she found it impossible to go on making. As she wrote to her friend, Baroness von Czetteritz-Neuhaus, in losing Liszt it was not so much the lost love she bewailed as the ideal embodied in their life together. "I wanted the two of us to make a beautiful and noble protest against prejudice; to show the artist and the aristocrat equal in all ways (except in genius, in which I fully recognized his superiority to me), showing that a free love could be stronger, more faithful, more serious than marriage." She admitted that it had taken her all of the past three years to renounce her dream and to recognize that she was vanquished in the struggle.[14]

Nor did the flight into the bosom of her family offer Marie much consolation. Although opposed to her original liaison with Liszt, they were fearful that breaking it now would cause another scandal. Her pious sister-in-law Mathilde continued to treat her as a fallen woman. A letter to her friend the baroness, who invited her to stay with her, indicates that Marie was still afraid that Liszt might make some extravagant gesture of joining her and so felt safer protected by her family. But Liszt was no threat; in August, asking Massart about Marie, he opined that she would probably return to her husband. He could not have been more wrong. What she was trying to do was to return to herself. She told Herwegh, "Retirement and solitude are very healthy for me. I return to myself; I distinguish there what is really *me* and what is only there by circumstance, and this *non-me* within myself I work seriously and actively to get rid of."[15]

What sustained Marie d'Agoult in these next months was her alter ego, Daniel Stern. Even while she and Liszt were still fighting in Paris, she was researching and writing articles, particularly her articles on German thought. She told the baroness that at this point she preferred books to men. As she reported to Herwegh, her health was improving, and her brain was becoming accustomed to work. Leaving her family in the first week of August, she secretly returned to Paris and rented a little house called the Pavillon d'Armenonville in the middle of the Bois de Boulogne, a great park on the edge of the city. Only Girardin and Vigny knew where she was and visited her. That year, in the less than nine months after Liszt's arrival in Paris, Daniel Stern published two articles and wrote a third.[16] She also wrote a novel. As her strengthening self looked back on the affair with Liszt, she observed bitterly to her friend the baroness, "Liszt wanted to make of me an easy mistress, one more vanity in his life of vanities, a woman good for showing off to others and with whom he could relax agreeably between two orgies. That role did not suit me; I tried it, so hesitant was I to break with the only being that I had loved with passion and grandeur; but the feeling in which lies my strength was outraged, and here I am, as if I were twenty years old, after having lived through all those sorrows."[17]

There were more sorrows to endure, concerning the children. Marie was quite clear about what Liszt's duty was: he was to send some fixed proportion of the receipts from his concerts (whether a quarter, a sixth, or a tenth) to be used for their benefit. She indicated that this was a moral engagement in the eyes of their friends, who would be inflexible on the matter. Liszt did send money. But he absolutely refused the sum Marie demanded for each child and directed Massart to demand an accounting of it. Liszt threatened that if the difficulties become too great he would just take the children to

Germany. At this Marie appealed to their friends, including Lamennais, who said that children should not be taken from their mother. She consulted a lawyer, who judged that Liszt could only legitimize the children as Hungarians and that this was not possible in Hungary. Liszt, in turn, found a lawyer who said it was possible.

Up to early 1845, Liszt seemed truly crushed by the rupture. He wrote to Massart about the bitter feeling of a heart broken forever; the break with Marie seemed at the same time to be the end of his youth and to take ten years off his life. But during the time since she had returned to Paris he had continued to be creative, producing numerous works. Appointed in 1843 as Kappelmeister for the Grand Duke of Weimar, he was responsible for all music programs in that state, which stimulated his creativity. Marie, apprised of all he was doing, rarely commented. It was hard for her to admit that he could be creative without her presence and while living the abandoned style of life she so disapproved of. Even before the split, answering a question from Herwegh about Berlioz, she responded, "I hate music. I loved it too long."[18] Ironically, Liszt's new position, with a guaranteed basic income, was to lead him to a quieter period of greater creativity in the future. But he could not live in Weimar with a mistress, with or without children. And he never lost the taste for an adoring audience or adventures with women.

The fight over the children and the attempts by Marie to turn all their friends against Liszt in the struggle caused an adversary relationship between them typical of a real divorce. Marie had the early advantage. She was able, in her correspondence and her salon, to highlight Liszt's flaws and impose her views. But Liszt still had the strongest weapon—his legal right to the children, who remained with his mother. Just under a year after their separation, in May 1845, he complained to Marie that she was spreading ugly tales about him that were groundless: "I only bring this up to ask if you seriously think that I would want Blandine to be raised by you, considering the war that you have been waging against me." He warned her that she should accept his decision, to put Blandine first, then Cosima when old enough, into a *pensionnat* in Paris. Their lives and their visitors would be controlled by the mistress of the boarding school. "I hope," he added, "that you will finally spare me the unhappiness of recourse to sad necessity,"[19] thus repeating his threat to remove the girls from France altogether. He claimed that he did not want the girls to live with Marie because he would be their sole support and did not want to deal with irritating questions of keeping accounts.

Of course, Marie could not win. When she finally realized this, she wrote to Liszt in a towering rage:

A year ago, Monsieur, you said to me: *take care, you know not what I am capable of.* I know now. You are capable of wiping your feet on an engagement of honor; of proposing to a woman to whom you owe all respect humiliating conditions when she wishes to exercise her sacred rights, which you recognized. You are capable, finally, of the worst of cowardice: that of menacing *from afar* and *in terms of legality* a mother who reclaims the fruit of her womb. You refuse to come to Paris to listen to an impartial arbitrage in the interest of your daughters; you play with their whole destiny without deigning to put yourself out to answer my just demands and and without examining with mutual and serious friends the decisive role you are choosing with a singular brutality. I recognize myself as defeated, Monsieur, in a desperate struggle where I have invoked only your heart, your reason and your conscience. But I protest before God and men, I protest before all mothers against the violation which is done me. The respect that these poor children inspire in me imposes on me the duty not to make a scandal and not to render them witnesses and victims of the *extreme solution* with which you menace me. From now on, Monsieur, your girls have no mother; you have wished it so. Their destiny is in your hands; no devoted heroism will ever be strong enough to struggle against your madness and your ferocious egoism. Please give your orders directly to Madame Bernard [the schoolmistress]; I will go tomorrow to say goodbye to Blandine and pray God that he leaves on her forehead the imprint of her last maternal kiss. One day your daughters will say, perhaps: where is our mother? You will answer: It did not please me for you to have one.[20]

To the baroness she wrote that the conditions Liszt imposed upon her were humiliating. Rather than be controlled by a schoolmistress, she refused to see the girls at all.

For those who have accused Marie d'Agoult of being a bad mother, it is the next years that seem most in question. Was she really going to give her daughter her "last maternal kiss"? Liszt, who took himself to Weimar and from this time on related to his children only by letter, with few exceptions, occasionally asked Blandine about her in a letter. The last report, "Maman is fine," is dated late 1845. After this, there is usually "no news of Maman." The answer seems to be that Marie, instead of using her diplomacy with Liszt, did indeed retreat from the entire situation, physically and emotionally. The restrictions placed on her visits to the school and Liszt's refusal to allow the girls to stay with her even in vacations so disturbed Marie that she did not think of what her withdrawal would do to her children. In letters to friends she made reference to having to wait until Blandine was sixteen, which was the age when the girl could choose for herself. But Blandine was only ten!

One result of the absence of both parents was that the children were thrown on each other emotionally. Cosima fought like a tiger to join Blandine in school a year early. Daniel was bereft when he could not follow them. He was entered into a lycée when he became old enough. Another result of Marie's neglect was that the girls idolized the absent Liszt, who at least wrote to them. But it was a fearful relationship, dominated by the desire to please and propitiate. Blandine, who was the main correspondent for the two girls, announced to her father that she was preparing for her first communion, "to be an angel of bounty and consolation for you." She wrote that she prayed for him, "and for Maman, for I don't forget her." Numerous letters refer to her and Cosima's prayers for him and for their mother. "I have no news at all of Maman, I do not even know where she is, that makes me sad, I think often of you and of her." Blandine wrote in 1847. But she has received permission to write her. (This decision may have been reversed, since there is no indication that Marie ever received a letter from the girls. It is certain that they were not allowed to leave the school to visit her.) When Blandine took her first communion later that year, neither parent was present. In future letters to Liszt, as the years go by, there are constant references to wanting to see him. Almost all were ignored.[21]

In the twentieth century an intellectual woman, after losing her pride, her ideal, the love of her life and her rights over her children, might well go into psychotherapy to try to bring her life back on an even keel. In the nineteenth century she might write a novel. At least that is what Marie did. She had probably always hoped to immortalize her relationship with Liszt. Now she needed to transcend its failure and to cast the blame on him. Accomplishing this in a novel was not uncommon in this period. *Elle et lui*, for instance, celebrated the end of George Sand's affair with Musset. Marie was writing *Nélida* as the final separation with Liszt was occurring. She finished the second version early in 1845, while staying with Hortense Allart at Herblay. Although it is the male characters, each partaking of Liszt, that drew the greatest interest from her readers, it is the female heroine whom anyone interested in Marie must heed.

A young aristocratic woman, Nélida is engaged to the scion of another noble family when she meets again a playfellow of her youth on the estate, Guermann, who has become an artist. Guermann introduces her to Saint-Simonian socialism. Convinced of his genius and deeply in love with him, she decides to run away with him. But when she visits him unannounced, his mistress opens the door. (This is clearly a reference to the mistresses that Liszt had before Marie. He seems to have revisited one of them soon after the final breach.) Nélida tries to commit suicide but is saved by a nearby worker. She marries her aristocratic fiancé, and they do much entertaining. The marriage is not a success; the husband takes mistresses. When Guermann reappears, Nélida is willing to forgive him. The lovers leave for Switzerland.

At this point in the novel the parallel with Liszt and Marie becomes strong. Guermann cares more about showing his works than retiring to produce great art. Nélida, feeling her ambiguous social position, will not follow him into the world of exhibitions. He leaves her in the care of a young suitor to show his art in Paris. She falls sick. When Guermann returns, it is clear that he is impatient with her demands. They settle in Italy, where people are kinder to her than they were in straitlaced Switzerland. While Nélida concentrates on educating herself, Guermann wastes his talent in portrait painting. When he paints a picture of her husband's mistress, it is too much for Nélida, particularly as Guermann, admitting to himself that Nélida is too good for him, takes the woman as his own mistress. Nélida leaves for Paris. But at Lyon she meets a Saint-Simonian and joins a confraternity devoted to social justice. Having received an important artistic commission, Guermann finds he can no longer paint. He falls sick, and Nélida comes to forgive him on his deathbed.

For all the fantasy embodied in the novel (that Liszt could not be creative or could not even live without her), the writing is hardly creative. In her novels Daniel Stern could only combine and depict what she knew. *Nélida* served many purposes in her life, among which may have been a response to recent works of Sand. While Sand was writing novels in which the aristocracy learns from the humble artist, Daniel Stern was depicting an aristocratic woman sacrificing all for the artist and losing when he does not measure up. This mistake is the point of departure for Nélida's new life, as Stern hoped it would be for hers. Although not a great work, it is as good as some of Sand's didactic novels.

Was the book an act of vengeance against Liszt? Marie had begun it at about the same time as she was making the decision to break with him (the first mention is in her diary of November 1843) and continued writing it for the next two years. Her own view of it, sent to Hortense Allart in the hope of stimulating a review of the book from Sainte-Beuve, was: "I wanted to paint a woman possessed with the sentiment of the ideal, believing she would find it in marriage, then in free love; she is mistaken and *should* die, but she lives; she will love again, but not a man (for no man is worth being loved as she has loved); she will love *all those who suffer*; from now on she will act, free and strong."[22] She also described it to Herwegh as the picture of a women who bears in herself the ideal and of her voyage from the heights of society to its suffering depths, the people. In 1844 she read the first draft to friends but gave it up because she feared that people would see Liszt in it. She completely rewrote it in the next two years. It was still too transparent. Buloz refused it for the *Revue des deux mondes* and recommended that she not publish it. So did the famous songwriter Béranger.

The novel appeared as a serial in the *Revue indépendante* in the first quarter of 1846.[23] This socialist paper started by Pierre Leroux was opposed to the regime and in favor of the working class. Stern had already been published in it, as had Sand. As far as her family was concerned, publication in the *Revue indépendante* destroyed whatever reputation she had acquired for publication in the established *Revue des deux mondes*. Liszt, in Germany, read the pieces as they came out, a process that took him five months. He had written Marie at the end of 1845 and asked for her article on Overbeck, as well as "one of those incomparable letters that only you know how to write." When he was in Paris in January 1846, things seemed to have calmed down. She wrote in her diary, "I am persuaded that he loves me."

He continued to keep in touch occasionally, as did she. "What a singular correspondence ours is!—but since we have nothing but words for one another, why not say them? They will not close our wounds, it is true; but they won't reopon them either," he wrote. Even after he had read the first section of *Nélida,* he wrote: "And can it be that we do not speak the same language? That our sorrows and our joys are no longer for each other? For me, I have courageously torn my heart from my body, thrown it to the ground and broken it into a thousand pieces, but it could be that chance will lead you to discover some portions in my life or the products of my thought; you would find there the burning reflection of your radiance and of our young love." This was the last letter in which he did not wound her in some way by mentioning another woman.[24]

As portions of *Nélida* were published, Liszt refused to see himself in the hero. He wrote Marie with great compliments on the work: "You have produced a distinguished book. . . . Continue in this way and try to do better if you can." On finishing the novel, he wrote that he refused to worry about whom the characters represented. He never took that sort of thing seriously. "If you have a good memory, you will recall that I already established this principle when *Béatrix* was published," he added. He always denied that he had been hurt by *Nélida,* although it figured in a scandalous campaign in Germany against him and his life. He called the book a "succès de curiosité, succès de scandale, succès de librairie," and expressed the hope of a most enviable end for Nélida, "for I have never doubted an instant the superiority of your heart and the superiority of your intelligence."[25] But he never forgave her; he referred to her as "Nélida" from then on. In her diary she wrote, "They think that I have ceased to love him, some even think that hate has succeeded love. Profound error. Same ideal always."

Much later, Marie referred to the book as her "first literary sin," which she would gladly forget.[26] She thought that parts of the book represented a dialogue between her passion and her reason. The book was not composed with reflection. "It burst out of me like an eruption, like the measles," she wrote Dr. Guepin. To his self-interested flattering assurances that she would again live and love, she replied, "The epitaph of my youth is complete, I shall never change it; my author's pride shuns it. Here lies Nélida, her son Daniel [Stern] barely regrets her. Cries for her not at all."[27]

The critics were mixed on *Nélida,* but that was mainly because of the efforts of Ronchaud, who persuded Eugène Pelletan to do a favorable review for *La Presse* and who lauded it in his own review, published in the *Revue de Paris.* Learning from Hortense Allart that the long-absent Sainte-Beuve had good things to say about it, Marie wrote to thank him and received a letter that warmed her heart, in which he told her that she had achieved a true success. He went on to say that George Sand had found things to praise in it. But he never wrote about it. Some critics compared her to Sand unfavorably. But the worst review was in the *Journal des débats,* which found nothing good to say about the book, either from the literary or the moral point of view.

Daniel Stern's last novel, *Valentia,* was about a woman who had committed suicide with opium, as told by her doctor. In it appear the innocent maiden, the arranged marriage, the young lover, the romantic trip through the mountains. The novelty is in the vicious nature of the older husband, who tries to prepare his bride for his sexual practices with pornography. Appearing in *La Presse* in 1847, it received mostly negative criticism, particularly scathing in the reactionary Catholic press; *L'Univers* used it to denounce *La Presse* and to comment on the scandalous life of the author. Although Stern produced other unpublished fiction, this was the last effort she made to publish novels. There is evidence that her friend Vigny counseled her to turn in other directions.

Meanwhile, Marie had directed her affections to her legitimate child, Claire, who was sixteen, and therefore free of her aunt Mathilde's control and of an age to be a companion to her mother. Marie wrote her that she loved her more than she could tell her. Early in 1847 Madame de Flavigny died without ever having seen her three grandchildren by Liszt. Under the influence of her daughter-in-law, she left a will that disinherited Marie almost completely, leaving her the same amount as a nephew, about thirty thousand francs in today's money. All the rest was left to Marie's brother Maurice and his wife, including even the linens traditionally left to daughters, except for some clothing (but not the only good cashmere shawl). It was her mother's final rejection. Marie's hatred for her sister-in-law knew no bounds, and she threatened her brother with a lawsuit questioning the will.

Because Claire's heritage was also endangered, Marie consulted the Comte d'Agoult. Amiable meetings resulted in permission for her to see Claire monthly in the convent. As Marie became preoccupied with her, she convinced herself that her daughter really loved her, which had to be unlikely, considering that the child had been literally abandoned. Marie began to take Claire on outings and buy her clothes, which the count adored. He took his daughter, dressed by her mother, to a ball. Because Claire had artistic gifts, Marie took advice from Lehmann and hired an art teacher for her. She also conducted her to exhibits and bought her a monumental tome on the history of painting in Italy. For the rest of Marie's life, mother and daughter were dependent on each other, but the relationship was never a smooth one.

Daniel Stern had been building her intellectual friendships and her philosophical understanding, particularly of the German variety, since the split with Liszt. Besides Herwegh, she was in constant touch with the writer Varnhagen von Ense, a diplomat who attended her salon and became a lifetime correspondent. It was he who dissuaded her from trying a work on Hegel's philosophy. She had also impressed the writer Karl Gutzkow, who returned to Germany from Paris to eulogize her in his memoirs.[28] In 1845 Stern did two articles on German thought for the *Revue indépendante*, beside the one on the poet Platen; they concerned avant-garde rebellion in the Catholic and the Protestant churches in Germany.[29] Her interest in the religion and philosophy of German idealism strengthened her natural tendency toward pantheism. But her articles were not totally successful in grasping the scope of German thought, as her friend Varnhagen gently managed to convince her.

What Stern understood best and personally accepted about German thought was its pantheism and its religious radicalism. She found the missing element, for her, of idealistic philosophy in the New World. Attending the lecures of the historian Quinet she heard about Ralph Waldo Emerson; the feminist Pauline Roland also spoke enthusiastically of his *Essays,* of which only the first volume had been published. Stern read it and wrote to the American philosopher in May 1846. She was pleased with the idea of a pantheism that retained rational analysis. She was also impressed by his description of the inevitable evolution of love into a true platonic love. But the most important concepts for Marie were those of self-reliance and the development of the self toward freedom through experience. She felt that this was the road she was taking. Daniel Stern was the first to present Emerson to the French, in the *Revue indépendante* of July 25, 1847. The following year, on a trip to the Continent, Emerson visited her salon. By this time he had already exerted a great influence on another book by Daniel Stern, her *Essai sur la liberté,* which she was able to give to him. Liberty, and a revolution to accomplish it, were already absorbing her interests and energies.

Eight ∽ *"The people is
an eternal poet, in whom
nature and passion inspire
spontaneously touching
beauties that art only
painstakingly reproduces
through grandiose effects."*

Daniel Stern's *Essai sur la liberté considérée comme principe et fin de l'activité humaine* (Essay on Liberty Considered as the Principle and End of Human Activity) was, as she wrote in the Preface to the second edition in 1863, a means of escape from the calamities of her inner life. She had broken the bonds of religion, class, and marriage, only to fall into the slavery of passion. Her efforts to take control of her life started, rather haltingly, with *Nélida*. But in *Essai sur la liberté* she began to create a personal system of belief, using German idealist philosophy. Eschewing religion, she sought to establish, starting from a purely human point of view, what determined the ensemble of human relations—with self, neighbors, and the world. Her answer was freedom—"that ineffable harmony of which the perishable world is only the form," the principle that ought to regulate relations between human beings. In the early chapters she quoted Kant, Descartes, and Aristotle, as well as Saint Augustine and Goethe. But she disagreed with them on the subject of passion.

Passion, Stern insisted, was not a restraint upon freedom, as philosophy and religion had insisted. Passion was the source of the vital energies necessary for the exercise of freedom. The individual's duty to herself was to search out her own nature and conform to it freely. However, one could only come to self-consciousness in relation to others. Stern conceived duty to oneself as identical to duty to one's neighbor: "to respect and to maximize . . . to the extent one can, what essentially constitutes human life—the exercise of one's faculties, the dignity of one's existence."[1] She emphasized that justice, which established an equilibrium between what one owed to self and what one owed to others, was superior to the renouncement and sacrifice called for by religion.

This statement of a nonreligious morality was published more than a decade before Proudhon's *Justice in the Revolution and in the Church*,[2] which also portrayed true justice as grounded in the rights of each person and then logically extended to all relations of the individual with his or her neighbor. This concept of justice was the source of the movement called *morale indépendante,* which became influential in the 1860s, during the Second Empire. Proudhon was an occasional visitor at the countess's salon in the 1840s, and although he disapproved of much in *Essai sur la liberté* he wrote her a congratulatory letter on her "surprising" ability to assimilate and write about philosophical ideas.[3] However, in *Justice,* Proudhon, basically a misogynist, later condemned women thinkers, citing Daniel Stern, along with George Sand.

One thing Proudhon surely did not approve in *Essai sur la liberté* was Stern's view that the family, which ought to be the basis of the state, as Aristotle said, could not serve this function because it did not adhere to the spirit of liberty and justice necessary to a state. She gave three reasons for this: the unreasonable inequality of women; the indissolubility of marriage; and the failure of the state to educate children. She declared that women, because of the miserable or nonexistent education afforded them, had all the vices of slaves and all the faults of children. Their only recourse was coquetry, the vengeance for their weakness. "Give woman a better means of satisfying her just need for moral equality, and she will take it,"[4] Stern wrote.

For the lack of divorce in a nation that had shed much blood for the principle of freedom, Stern blamed the remaining influence of the church. It could admit separation for physical difficulties, "but not for sterility of the spirit or impotence of the heart." She noted that church control of marriage continued because people believed the priest would control women better than her own reason could. "Strange mistake! The confessor, always stronger than the husband, is always weaker than the lover," she observed.[5] With special bitterness she condemned the irrationality of allowing the husband legal rights to the child born of an infidelity.

Regarding education, Stern noted that what instruction then existed in France was hotly contested between church and state. She called for a system of public education for both sexes. (She was probably unaware that this demand had first been made during the Revolution by Condorcet and that fifty years before, Mary Wollstonecraft had emphasized the necessity for women's education in *Vindication of the Rights of Woman.*) *Essai sur la liberté* blamed the new middle class that dominated the July Monarchy for trying to stop the movement toward liberty at their own class. The people might be patient now, Stern wrote, but would not remain so. She called upon the leaders of her country to educate the people and raise them to their own level.

Women had a role to play in raising everyone to equality, she pointed out, because all women were already equal in childbirth. Here Stern did something unheard of in the nineteenth century. She described, in a romanticized version, but one that still upset many readers, the childbirth that made all women equal. She then went on to counsel unhappy women, actually to counsel herself, not to weep nor bow under the conditions forced upon women. "Above all don't, to escape the intensity of your pain, throw yourself into the drunkenness of vain pleasure. Rectify your virtues, extend your devotion. Learn to love, with passion but without weakness, not one of these chimeric beings that exists only in your dreams, but your country and humanity."[6] It was the route that she had laid out for herself.

The book was attacked on many fronts—for its political liberalism, its support for divorce, and its attack on the bourgeoisie. Her conservative friends, including Hortense Allart, saw it as a book of revolt and unbelief. Lamennais found the description of childbirth vulgar, the call for divorce immoral. She received a bad review in *Le Siècle*, which implied that only someone who had lived her immoral life could produce a book like this. Even the poet Lamartine, a liberal admirer, disapproved. However, some friends, among them Vigny, welcomed her debut as a thinker. Emile Littré, the positivist philosopher and compiler of the first French dictionary, was enthusiastic. Sainte-Beuve admitted to friends that he admired how far her style had progressed in a short time. But he deemed the book "common" and the author "a monster of ambition."[7] The historian Edgar Quinet congratulated her on her courage. But the Mother Superior of her daughter's convent, when asked by Claire why she could not see her mother, replied, "Because your mother has written a book."[8] It was put on the list of "subversive books" by the police in January 1847, as "a passionate satire of society and the institutions on which it rests; exaggerated pictures of the misery of the working classes who have all the more right to goods on earth as the author refuses them all compensation in another life."[9]

Liszt, however, praised the work, acknowledging that the Preface was written on his birthday, and thanking her. He particularly lauded the section on childbearing. "Had you borne three more children to write these pages it would not have been purchased too dearly." (It is interesting that he counted only the children she had borne by him.) He indicated that he thought the book was the beginning of the new epoch that he had predicted for her and offered to have a ring made for her, with a sphere run through by an axis engraved on the ends with the words "truth" and "freedom."[10] Stern had called loyalty "the axis of domestic virtues"; she accepted his praise but refused the ring.

In the same letter Liszt asked her to continue writing to him but not to sign herself as Daniel; he preferred Nélida. As for him, he had not changed and would sign as always. Liszt also told her that he had met an extraordinary and eminent woman, Carolyne Ivanovska, princess of Sayn-Wittgenstein, who was writing a 25-volume history of the Catholic Church. Unhappily married to a Russian, the princess was to remain in Weimar, where Liszt was the appointed court musician, to be near him. By the end of 1847 Liszt wrote to Marie that Carolyne was his new life. Marie inferred that Liszt was turning over a new leaf and would settle down to composing. (His annotation on this: "That's how she reads letters.") Marie admitted her own failure in the task of bringing him back to his best self. "Your pride was on guard against me, and besides, I had nothing more to promise, having given everything." She hazarded that this new woman was of a character that would certainly not be content to be one of his mistresses either.[11] She was right. The princess, aiming to marry Liszt, began efforts to get a divorce from her husband. Marie found this extremely painful. She had accustomed herself to Liszt's affairs, but the thought of a real marriage with a woman of rank provided another level of anguish. She was to suffer for years as the princess worked for the divorce and rumors of an imminent marriage came and went. It is interesting to note that the princess, who was even older than Marie when she met Liszt (at the age of forty-eight, when Liszt was thirty-five), did succeed better than Marie in making Liszt settle down and compose.

The marriage never took place. But its possibility made Marie feel more than ever that she must find her own success as Daniel Stern. She wrote to Liszt, "I sense my ideas growing more precise, stronger; my expression becomes simpler, and what I receive from outside coordinates immediately in what Eckstein calls the interior system."[12] (Baron von Eckstein was one of many mutual friends, an admirer and good friend of Marie.) She was now determined to become a writer and, as she confided to her diary, to get a hold on her life. She was convinced that at this late date she would avoid the faults of her former writing. Romanticism, she insisted, was dead forever. She also swore to be completely independent. But that, as her diary indicates for the rest of her life, was not easy.

The beginning of 1847 found her still at the mercy of terrible anxieties, bemoaning in her diary how badly she had managed her life for twenty years [which would include both her marriage and Liszt], how alone she was. "Life is more denuded than in a cloister . . . it is a prison, a succession of negations. . . . Who would believe my heart's solitude?" She noted that Vigny was courting her again but she was not responding. Still beautiful, she was remarked wherever she went, and she gloried in it. "I like to be seen," she admitted. But she wanted to be a true celebrity while still young. That year, she published *Essai sur la liberté, Valentia* (another short novel), and a series of political articles on revolution in Prussia. Still, she recorded a profound feeling of failure made worse by the specter of old age. "What have I done? *Over whom have I gained authority?* I have only a vain shred of reputation and I am incapable of having anything else," she wrote in her diary.[13] The negative reactions of some friends (including Eckstein) to *Essai sur la liberté* upset her more than she allowed in public.

Her emotions seemed to swing from despair to affirmation; occasionally she would confide to her diary a new sense of authority, a new freedom. But she wanted to vindicate herself, to be more than "the vain remnant of a celebrated name." She also wanted to become a symbol of women's growing influence, along with (and surpassing, she secretly hoped) George Sand. She was desperately jealous not only of Sand but also of Delphine Girardin and her newspaper column—even of her sister-in-law and her religious tracts. Occasionally, Stern would record the conviction that her day of glory would come. By the end of the year she was vaunting her ability to give ten years to the struggle for glory. As Littré had pointed out, she had learned to do what even Sand could not do—to think, philosophize. But her insecurity about her self-worth is the most persistent note in her diaries.

Nor did she have the support of her family. Marie's relations with her brother were considerably strained during this period. Maurice had always supported her to the extent that he felt he could. His letters during the elopement with Liszt expressed sorrow mixed with firmness and tenderness. He had always said that when she changed her mind, his arms were open. When she returned to Paris, Maurice had just been made a peer. He visited her and aided her in drawing on her maternal heritage for funds. Slowly, he brought their mother to accept her daughter's visits. But Maurice, whose wife published pious works, was also very wary of the reputation of his family. When Marie broke with Liszt, friends suggested that when Claire left the convent the two might repair to the family home at Mortier. But even had Marie desired to do this, it was clear that she would not be welcomed by her sister-in-law, who treated her as a fallen woman. When Claire had asked a nun in the convent why her mother and father didn't live together, she had been told that her mother wrote for newspapers, so it wouldn't be proper. There was no way that Daniel Stern would be acceptable to the *bien pensants.*

For her part, Marie held in great disdain the ruling class of the July Monarchy, to which Maurice now belonged. Political differences would have eventually caused a real rift between brother and sister. But already relations between the two were ruptured by the death of Madame de Flavigny, whose will, as we have seen, left her daughter almost completely disinherited. When Maurice was unresponsive to her objections, Marie brought suit for her share. She felt she had lost her brother, that she had once more been betrayed. In a letter to Liszt in 1848 she wrote that she was like a wandering Jew (her friend Eugène Sue had written a book with that title), without family or land. Eventually, she managed to win a capital sum that would suffice if she lived prudently.

At this point Marie was completely cut off. Her father had deserted her by dying in her youth. She and her mother had mutually repudiated each other before death separated them. Marie had made the initial break when she had failed to return with her mother from Switzerland, choosing instead to follow Liszt. When she returned to Paris she could have compensated for this only by playing the role of the dutiful daughter. But she had not yet really given up Liszt and still expected to play a role in the lives of their children, whose existence her mother refused to recognize. Marie tended from that time on to exaggerate her differences with her bourgeois, pious mother, whose own final rejection was in her will.

The shock of being disinherited was compounded in Marie by her brother's willingness to accept the inheritance. This would have been his right under the old regime. Since the time of Napoléon, however, the civil code prescribed equal inheritance, although the law often winked at it in the case of women. Marie, aided by her husband, could and did contest the settlement because it threatened the rights of Claire, the legal grandchild. As a result, she was cut off from her brother also. By 1848 Marie had neither family nor husband nor lover. She was an independent woman. She was, as much as a woman could be in that year, free, and she continued to write about freedom in her effort to learn to live it.

In *Essai sur la liberté* Daniel Stern had written that in her time freedom was turning toward the search for truth, which put everything in question. Her article on the poet Platen had stressed the growing relationsip between France, country of the revolution, and Prussia, which she believed would accomplish its democratic and constitutional reform, with France's help. The moment seemed to have arrived when, early in 1847, the king of Prussia was forced to call an Estates-General in Berlin. Although unable to be on the spot, Marie carried on almost daily correspondence with Herwegh, Eckstein, and another German friend, Varnhagen von Ense, to keep up with events. She began her first article on the Prussian revolutionary events in the *Revue indépendante*,[14] tracing the history of representative institutions in Germany from the early tribes to efforts at reform after the French Revolution. Stern at first judged Prussia ready for constitutional reform because it had a clergy and a bourgeoisie that had kept the misery of the poor to a minimum and had thus not created class hatred. Her hopes that Germany might be united under the constitutional monarchy of Prussia were dashed when Frederick William IV refused to grant national representation and fell back on the Estates-General. She noted that the public had learned that their interests were different from those of the king and had begun to debate, in their estates and municipalities, important subjects—an electoral system, abolition of censorship, emancipation of the Jews. But the king had only called the Estates-General in order to get approval for taxes, and he limited its discussions to that topic.

The article discussed the nature of government based only on property-holding—its lack of mandate from the propertyless and the weakness even of the estates. The king was allowing no public deliberations. He opened the session by invoking God, "the God of armies," as the support of his rule. His address was greeted with a great silence. The constant error of absolute monarchs, Stern wrote, was in counting too much on the incapacity of the masses. She insisted that only the people could dictate the agenda of a law-making body and the only possible agenda for this one was not to grant the king his taxes until he agreed to a representative system. Unfortunately, she could see in the Estates no real leadership that could bring the delegates to feel their own power in the inevitable march toward freedom.

Stern's second article noted that the opening ceremonies of the Estates-General of Prussia clearly marked off the bourgeoisie from the clergy and nobility; this had been unacceptable to the French in 1789 and had advanced the Revolution. She applauded the decision of the Estates to formulate an answer to the king, invoking past practices to demand regular meetings and control of all finances thereafter. "Thus appears to us, from the very beginning, the antagonism of the old society and the new," she wrote, revealing her hopes for progress in her native land. But she was disappointed in the debate, which was weak and ambiguous: the national representatives were yielding already. She longed for strong voices, as in English and French revolutionary situations. Where was the "revolutionary electricity"? Nevertheless, she insisted that the prestige of absolute power, of divine right, had been effaced in the consciousness of the Prussian people.

After outlining for her readers the political tendencies of the different groups in the Diet, Stern described the crowds gathering in Berlin, the riot set off by high prices in the market, and the calling in of troops. She decided that the misery of the working classes was the same almost everywhere, and although perhaps less extreme than in past centuries, it caused more unbearable suffering because people knew that better things were possible. In these articles Stern developed her view that change would come by a kind of "organic necessity" through "these *masses* without form and without name," before whose wretchedness mere charity was impotent. What was needed to prevent these volcanic uprisings was "a heroic effort of public thought which would finally found and organize true justice through an ensemble of institutions." This "social metamorphosis" was the task of all advanced nations. Stern also warned that political questions could be put off, but when the multitude was experiencing "the delirium of exasperated instincts," there was no time to lose. "One cannot negotiate with hunger."

Unfortunately, the disorders frightened the timid in the Estates-General. They were faced with more than four hundred petitions (of which Stern provided a breakdown by subject). They did not know how to proceed with the king. Finally, 137 deputies signed a declaration that the king's order was an abridgement of their rights. But they did not follow it up. In her summary, Stern noted that the king considered that neither of the two houses of the Estates represented the people; only he represented them. Either house could petition the king, but his cabinet ministers were not responsible to them. She described the deputies, patriotic and dutiful, as being helpless under these conditions. Lacking a strong leader, they took only first steps, then fell back into sentimental awe of the monarchy.

Stern tried to be optimistic. The Estates did try to change the law of primogeniture, which strengthened the differences between the classes. Toward the end they voted stubbornly against even things they believed in. However, lacking regularly scheduled sessions and control of the finances, the Estates remained powerless. The one topic Stern found worthy of lengthy coverage was the debate on enlarging the rights of Jews. First providing the historical background, she described some of the speeches and was relieved that at least the opposition, in its support of Jewish rights, saved the honor of the body that voted them down.

After the Prussian king dissolved the Estates-General, Stern pinpointed the mistakes of its representatives. They should have stood up and defended the principle of human rights against that of divine right. They should have based their arguments not on narrow legal bases but on public reason and common sense. There was too much deference toward the king. The only advantage gained was that the political consciousness of the population was raised. The next time they might stand up better. And there would be a next time. According to Stern, industrial development would lead to a more progressive politics, which must in turn lead to the "material amelioration" of the ordinary people. Going further, she declared that while she did not recommend revolution, "a parliament that wishes to establish political freedom cannot operate on the principle that, whatever happens, there will be no recourse to force."[15]

In these articles the aristocratic countess revealed herself not only as a republican but as the more radical brand of republican, recognizing the necessity of social as well as political change. In the late 1840s in France, even political demands on the constitutional monarchy for extension of the right to vote were ignored. (When it was put to the long-standing prime minister, François Guizot, that only the richest could vote in France, he replied, "Well, get rich then.") But many were demanding a republic. Not only Lamartine and Louis Blanc but the great historians Edward Quinet and Jules Michelet produced in the 1840s histories of the first French revolution. The lectures of the two historians were packed with students and the literate public, including Marie d'Agoult, who was to adopt the historians' concept of the centrality of the ordinary people.

In an article published late in 1847, Daniel Stern agreed that the theme of the current epoch of civilization, taken up by poets and thinkers, was "the people."[16] She condemned those who capitalized on the miseries of the lower classes, either frightening the rich by painting the people as dangerous or romanticizing the people as embodying all virtue. Both created arguments for leaving them in their misery. Stern claimed that material well-being favored the development of morality and poverty repressed it. Actually, Stern complained, even the upper classes could not fulfill their potential in the society of the July Monarchy. The education and customs constrained women and children; prejudice blinded men. Again she called for justice, which would give to each person knowledge, work, and wealth that was not equal for all but sufficient for the needs of everyone.

Without social reform, Stern insisted, political reform was useless. Thus Stern called for amelioration of the lot of the poorest class, government provision of work and supervision of the conditions of labor, universal education, and security for the elderly. "If you want to preach to the people the domestic virtues, start by putting wood in their fireplace. . . . If you come to celebrate family values, bring bread for their children. . . . Make sure that air and water circulate freely in the places where they live and soon you will see that their consciences are also cleaner."

It was views like this that placed Marie d'Agoult in the company of those who were working for change; her salon became a meeting place for them as France again verged on revolution. Among them were Adam Mickiewicz, hero of the failed Polish uprising of the 1830s, whose course at the Collège de France was closed down by the government, along with those of Michelet and Quinet. She also entertained the East European radicals Herwegh, Gutzkow, Potocki, and Sandor Telecki. Potocki was Polish; Telecki, Hungarian. Gutzkow was a poet and dramatist, founder of Young Germany, and spokesman for the Left Hegelians in Paris. Believing in the influence of women on art, he wrote about Marie's salon on his return to Germany. Marie herself he described in glowing terms—her beauty, her intelligence, her sorrow, her place as muse of the arts.[17]

On her return to Paris, Marie had met the poet Alphonse de Lamartine at the salon of Delphine Girardin. He began to attend hers also, probably through the offices of Ronchaud, who came from the same region of France. Lamartine was, in 1840, beginning to arouse the French with his oratory. Marie told Liszt that his speech aginst slavery was the first thing that had seized her emotions since her return to Paris. The interest in politics and current afffairs that Girardin aroused in her was heightened by the rhetoric of Lamartine.

Her admiration was matched by his. In 1843 he told someone, probably Ronchaud, who repeated it to Marie: "I am mad about her, [she is] the only woman a poet could love. If I were young! Once seen, two years ago, never forgotten. I will send her my speech. Tell her that I adore her."[18] The speech was the one in which Lamartine placed himself in the ranks of opposition to the regime. He repeated much the same words in answer to Marie's congratulatory letter and asked to visit her. He seemed to see her as an inspiration: "I will carry out your plans, your temple will be mine; women don't think, but sometimes a mysterious voice speaks in them."[19] In 1844 Marie devoted an article to the circle of Lamartine,[20] which she described as "like a vast tent where the soldiers of the new democracy come to rest a bit, get their breath, meet one another, exchange passwords and encourage each other to combat." She noted that Lamartine himself had begun as a monarchist but now recognized the sovereignty of the people.

If Lamartine's visits fell off in the late 1840s, it may have been because he disliked aspects of her new work, which appeared as a series of articles during 1846–47. After finishing *Nélida*, Stern had begun working on a collection of her thoughts, or "Pensées." They appeared first in the periodical *L'Artiste* in the spring of 1847.[21] Additions and reworking of the manuscript appeared in two issues of the *Revue indépendante* in the fall, under the name "Esquisses morales: Pensées sur les femmes." In earlier versions and in her papers there are many sketches, particularly of people, her friends and critics, which she left out of the later book. (Of Sainte-Beuve, she noted: "the master of faded elegance.") Unfortunately, the publisher felt it necessary to add political pieces that Stern had published during the Revolution of 1848 and called the 1849 edition *Esquisses morales et politiques*. Later editions left out the word "politics."

The book was written in the form of aphorisms, often expanded, such as "The life of human beings seems to me like a symphony, composed by a grand artist, it is true, but executed by deaf people." Or, "Christianity has pronounced the saddest of divorces: that of body and soul in the human being." She discussed the proportions of freedom and necessity in human existence, giving a large place to freedom. And again one can see the writer facing her problems. For women, she wrote about platonic love: "Think then . . . that in giving your soul to a lover to whom you refuse your body, you testify to the fact that you value the first much less than the second. If I am not mistaken, that spiritual subtlety has for its principle a gross materialism."[22]

Esquisses morales reflects Stern's movement away from Romanticism, which must have disturbed not only Lamartine but Vigny as well. She credited that school with having cleared away a good deal of poetic undergrowth but pointed out that it had been overtaken by a babble of individual voices that could not express the sorrows and joys of the people as a whole. She declared her return to idealism, a move already seen in her art criticism, and defined it as "choosing, in the reproduction of form, between that which has occurred fortuitously and that which was willed, premeditated, the design of providence. It is distinguishing the eternal creation of God from the accidental work of humanity." She noted that the Romantic writer idealized even the failures of his soul. "What would Cato have thought on reading Werther? How would Alexander have viewed Hamlet or Childe Harold, Obermann or Faust?" The most poetic moments of life, she wrote, were those in which one glimpsed what could have been. She added, "Our remorse is not proportionate to our faults, but to the virtues that remain to us." She also insisted that the ability to face life alone was the essential basis for a worthy and sincere moral character.[23]

Noting that people thought society was falling apart, Stern declared her faith in the nineteenth century: "I think everything is being transformed. . . . Movement is the essential characteristic of modern society." As science clarified the secrets of life, theological views were losing their prestige. "In their place, however, we have the grandeur of human life and its relations with the universal."[24] In her chapter on the bourgeoisie and the aristocracy, Stern bewailed as only a true aristocrat could the growing preponderance of money in public life. She did not ask for social services for the people, except for those things that any enlightened leader would provide them. But she demanded public education, claiming that the upper classes had allowed the lines of community to be broken, particularly in matters of culture, and had rejected the people, forcing them into the shadows of society.

The book was the culmination of a ten-year meditation on life. It was not to be a success until later editions. Stern's social ideas did not seem to fit her social position, which irked many people. She was never completely able to overcome this problem. But she always had confidence in the *Esquisses*. And indeed, it brought her the admiration and friendship of intellectuals throughout Europe. Some of the most important portions of the *Esquisses* were reflections on women.

In mid-1847 Ronchaud told Marie that Lamartine had called her a Madame Roland without the little bourgeois passions and with more talent. (Madame Roland was active in the liberal stage of the 1789 revolution and had been guillotined.) The poet asked about Stern. Had she courage? It would be needed in a revolution. She did. By the end of the year, Marie had the feeling of working with friends toward a dissolution of the government. Lamartine, who would become head of a new provisional government, had already returned to her salon as a regular. Still faithful to the circle of Delphine Girardin, he felt more at home in this year with Marie—another aristocrat converted to republicanism.

By this time the issue of extending the franchise had united against the July Monarchy the dynastic opposition, led by Odilon Barrot, who wanted only the liberalization of the monarchy: the liberals, led by Adolphe Thiers; the moderate republicans, led by Lamartine; the more radical social republicans, led by Ledru-Rollin and Louis Blanc; and the Utopian socialists. Since the law forbade large gatherings, the opposition united to further its cause at "banquets," often free to the working class, where political messages were provided in toasts and after-dinner speeches. At these banquets Lamartine was a star, skewering the government with his oratory.

As she had done with her articles on Prussia, Stern prepared to provide her readers with the background and to establish the situation of the July Monarchy before the buildup of discontent. The election of 1846 had been so successful for the government that Guizot did not feel he had to yield to any demands for enlargement of the vote. "Those who are not content with the actions of the cabinet can go over to the camp of the opposition," he stated arrogantly. Girardin, by no means a radical, was enraged enough at the prime minister to use as a regular motto on the masthead of *La Presse* the answer to a question posed by a conservative in a parliamentary debate, "What has the government done in the last seven years?": Nothing, nothing, nothing. As Stern said, in France, bon mots were an integral part of political history. "The idiom of a people is the people itself."[25] Girardin also accused Guizot of selling peerages. But the prime minister was always able to get a vote of confidence, for he had a majority of the deputies in his pocket. The government was rife with corruption.

The result was the banquet campaign, which Stern would describe, noting that at first the most radical aspect was the omission of the toast to the king and the inclusion of toasts to reform, the press, and the amelioration of the lot of the laboring classes. But she recorded the signs of rising discontent and anger among the people toward the privileged classes. The foreign policy of Guizot had also become less and less successful. And the royal family was distancing itself from the ordinary people. On the intellectual level she noted the influential writings about the first revolution and the journey of Lamartine from aristocratic poet of the Restoration to republican of 1847. Stern recorded his famous speech at the banquet in his own district of Mâcon. If the government went on disappointing the people in every regard, he declared, it would fall, not in its own blood, as in 1789, but in its own trap. "And after experiencing the revolution of freedom and the counter-revolution of glory you will have the revolution of public conscience and the revolution of contempt!"[26] Stern gave the poet full praise at this stage of events, although she would later criticize him.

The banquets continued throughout France, growing more radical as they proceeded, their leadership giving way to leftists like Ledru-Rollin and Louis Blanc and their discourse becoming more antimonarchical, until the day of the forbidden banquet in Paris. In January 1848 the banquet campaign came to a head when a group of the opposition, led by two newspapers, *Le National* and *La Réforme*, planned to hold a banquet in a working-class area of Paris.

The government forbade it, fearing violence. The question was debated heatedly in the Chamber of Deputies, with Daniel Stern in attendance. The government survived the attack of the opposition. It seemed to have no more to fear, except, Stern recorded, the conscience of the country, the justice of the people and the condemnation of history. She wrote to Liszt on January 17: "A revolution seems inevitable and impossible all at once."[27] Girardin tried to organize the opposition to resign and force an election. But he was the only one to give up his seat in the legislature.

Most of the opposition was prepared to back down on the banquet, even if it was to be held in another part of town. But Lamartine declared that he would go to the banquet even if attended only by his shadow. Daniel Stern, already recording the events of 1848, wrote that Lamartine would not be alone; all the vital forces of France would be behind him.[28] At her dinner table five days before the revolution broke out, Pascal Duprat, editor of the *Revue indépendante*, Emile Littré, editor of *Le National*, Anselme Petetin of *Le Siècle*, and Eugène Pelletan of *La Presse* discussed the situation.

When the opposition failed to agree and dropped plans for the banquet, the working class, which had been counting on the occasion as a moment to show their discontent, were frustrated and angry. Many small businesses, fearing disorder, decided to close on the day of the proposed banquet, leaving the streets of Paris filled with angry crowds milling about. The result was a three-day revolt that ended the July Monarchy and a three-volume *Histoire de la révolution de 1848* by Daniel Stern that is still read.

With the greatest of excitement Daniel Stern witnessed the revolutionary days of February and recorded them. The first day, February 22, people gathered in the area where the banquet had been scheduled to take place. Stern gave credit to the students, who marched up singing the *Marseillaise*, for organizing an inchoate mass to converge on the Chamber of Deputies across the river. She was present at the Chamber on that day to hear Barrot attack Prime Minister Guizot. When the army was called out to control the mob, it was cheered and treated the people with gentleness. Stern described the commander returning his sword to its scabbard as "material force yielding to moral force; it was the end of the dynasty."[29] The municipal guard in other areas of the city was not so gentle, wounding many and killing some. The people's reaction was violence, which only ended late in the day when it began raining. But already barricades had been erected.

On the second day more troops were brought into the city, as the National Guard had failed to respond in force the day before. The army again hesitated to march on the people. Stern described the announcement at the

Chamber that the king was planning to form a new cabinet as evidence that he did not yet understand what was happening. Louis-Philippe was still making jokes about barricades. It was only when he heard that some of the National Guard were taking the side of the people that the king began to take seriously the possibility of revolution. Stern, between what she viewed personally and what she heard from others, was able to record what was happening not only at the palace and among the deputies but also on the streets in many areas of the city.

It was in the evening of that same day that the "tragic event" occurred. A ragged column of people, carrying torches and the red flag of revolution, and singing patriotic songs, encountered a command post guarding the Ministry of Foreign Affairs, which tried to turn them back. When this failed, the soldiers were ordered to cross bayonets to hold back the crowd. In the process, a shot rang out; the soldiers, frightened, fired upon the people. When the fusillade was over, twenty-three people were already dead and more were dying. Stern described a spontaneous funeral cortege making its way through the streets at midnight, led by a horse-drawn chariot, on which were laid out five bodies, lighted by the upraised torches of the people. Every so often the chariot stopped, the bloodied body of a young woman was raised, and the cry was heard, "Vengeance! They slit the throats of the people! To arms!" Stern was able to discover the name of the leader and learned that two battalions of dragoons had thought better of stopping this march. The corpses were placed at the foot of the July Column at the Place de la Bastille. Some people went to sound the tocsin in the churches; others went seeking arms and began to make cartridges. "The phantom of the Republic hovered over these sinister shadows," Stern wrote. "The monarchy was tottering. The dead had killed the living. At that moment the cadaver of a woman had more power than the most valorous army in the world."[30]

Stern noted in her diary on the next day that there was already discord among the republicans, some of whom were more afraid of violence than angry with the government. The new cabinet insisted on new elections, but the king still hesitated. There was more fraternization by the troops with the people, who were slowly advancing on the Tuileries Palace. King Louis-Philippe's last review of the National Guard was cut short by their calls for reform. It was Girardin who begged the king to abdicate before it was too late, in favor of his grandson, with the child's mother, the Duchesse d'Orléans, as regent. Stern was able to describe the events taking place in the palace, as the king was slowly convinced by his family and advisers to write his abdication. "Only the queen preferred to die a queen rather than live humbled."[31] The battle for the last redoubt protecting the palace was in progress at the Château d'Eau, one of the fountain houses that dispersed the water brought into Paris. Describing the bravery of both sides, Stern also described the water flowing from the destroyed building, mixed with the blood of the wounded.

Then back to the palace and the flight of the royal family. Stern recorded that although they had to pass through some of the mob to reach their carriages, no one harmed them. When a frightened officer called upon the people to spare the king, a voice rang out, "What do you think we are, assassins? Let them go." The royal grandchildren, in another carriage, peered out the windows in excitement. The last vain resistance at the Château d'Eau was covering the royal departure. The Duchesse d'Orléans, left behind with her two children, made her way to the Chamber leading by the hand the young Count of Paris, heir to the throne. It was just in time. The people occupied the palace. Stern described how, one by one, they sat on the royal throne, and how one of them wrote on it: "The People of Paris to all Europe: Liberty, Equality, Fraternity." And the cry went up, "Long live the Republic!" From that time on, the palace became the scene of "an immense orgy, an indescribable saturnalia," one which Stern went on to describe in unforgettable pages.[32]

In the Chamber the supporters of the monarchy welcomed the arrival of the duchess and the little count, while the republicans made up lists of those who should be in the new government. The arrival of the mob, including members of the National Guard, turned the tide against the regency. Stern gave the stage to Lamartine, quoting much of the speech that led to the establishment of the Provisional Government, with himself at its head. This new government of ten men was chosen by the spontaneous reactions of the crowd to their names when read out at the podium; at the last moment one symbolic working man was added. They then left the Chamber to organize in peace at the Paris City Hall.

But the people followed; in the vast square outside they cried out for the Republic. Stern wrote, "To the demands of the triumphant proletariat, which attached to that word *republic* infinite hopes, the bourgeoisie responded by a silence more of consternation than of consent." She traced the meaning of the word from ancient times to the Americas and the Revolution in 1789. The bourgeoisie, she noted, had lost confidence in its own political theories, which had taken root in the working class of the cities. Stern stressed the distinction between the bourgeois democratic republic, limited to political democracy, and the proletarian democratic and *social* republic, which was an application of the principle that society owes to all its members the security of existence. Since 1795 the bourgeoisie, confusing terrorism with the legitimate efforts of the working people to take their part in society, found this idea menacing. So the Provisional Government, divided, did not at first respond to the demands of the people. Finally, Lamartine, sensing that the moment was overdue, went out on a balcony and declared the Republic. In her diary Stern termed his symbolic act *"très grand."*

But more was being demanded than the Republic. One of the issues of 1848 was unemployment and the government's responsibility to provide work for the people. At one point, an armed worker broke into the room where the government was deliberating and demanded the declaration of the right to work. Lamartine pointed out that the new government could not do everything at once. The man replied that the people would wait, that they would "put three months of misery at the service of the Republic." Louis Blanc, author of *The Organization of Labor,* began writing a decree promising the right to work.[33] Stern felt that ordinary people had made great progress since the first revolution. In 1830 the crowds had howled for the death sentence for the overthrown prime minister, but in 1848 they cheered the decree abolishing the death sentence for political crimes.

Situated politically between the conservatives, who only wanted a minimal political republic, and the radicals, who wanted a political and social republic, Lamartine became the head of the Provisional Government for three months, until the elections. Stern wrote in her diary two days later, "All my friends are going to be in power." Lamartine developed the habit of dropping in at her salon during the evening to relax. His wife was not enthusiastic about the revolution, but Stern gave him constant encouragement. He also used Stern to convey messages to Lamennais, who was serving as the spiritual force of the revolution. As editor of *Le Peuple constituant,* he fought both the reactionaries and the socialists from February to early July. Ronchaud, Marie's most faithful friend, was in the Cabinet, and Lamartine told him to tell her that if Lamennais wanted a ministry, he could have one. The two men discussed a constitution for the new republic at her dinner table in April. Daniel Stern, in her element, prepared herself to be a power behind the new government. She wrote to Claire that she continued to run the Republic by offering dinner to Lamartine and Lamennais. If she could not as a woman have power, she might at least be the power behind the throne.

Marie d'Agoult, painted by Henri Lehmann, 1843.
Richard-Wagner-Archiv, Bayreuth.

The Romantic vision embraced scenes like this one (apocryphal) at George Sand's home in Nohant. *Right,* Liszt, at the piano, admiring the bust of Beethoven, while Paganini and Rossini stand behind. Marie, *lower right,* is limp with adoration. *Left,* Sand swoons in ecstasy, with Alexandre Dumas to her left and Victor Hugo behind. Painting by Joseph Dannhauser, 1840. Nationalgalerie der Staatlichen Museum Preussischer Kulturbesitz, Berlin.

FACING PAGE: On their elopement journey through Switzerland, the lovers were often taken as siblings. Their sensitive Romantic features were seen as emblematic of male and female beauty and were reproduced many times. *Top,* Marie d'Agoult, medallion by Pierre-Jean David d'Angers, 1833. Wagner Museum, Eisenach. *Bottom,* Franz Liszt, drawn by Achille-Jacques-Jean-Marie Devéria, 1832. Bibliothèque Nationale 87C130412.

The painter Dominique Ingrès often depicted Marie and her children. Here is his sketch of Claire d'Agoult, talented daughter and sole remaining legitimate child, with Marie. Bibliothèque Nationale C5119.

Bust carved by Pierre-Charles Simart, 1847. Musée Versailles, R.M.N.

Blandine Lizst, first of three children born to the couple, shone at her mother's salon and later married Emile Ollivier, who became prime minister of France. She died in her first childbirth. Photo by Antony Samuel Adam-Solomon. Musée d'Orsay, R.M.N.

Blandine's younger sister Cosima devoted her life to the genius of Richard Wagner. She lived until 1930, overseeing the Wagner heritage at Bayreuth and entertaining such rising notables as Adolf Hitler. Bibliothèque Nationale 79A43999.

The salon of the Comtesse d'Agoult during the Second Empire. A daughter, probably Blandine, is seated with her, *center*. Note the resemblance of Marie's head here to the one drawn by her daughter, *opposite*. Engraving by Jean Beraud. Bibliothèque Nationale 84C169446.

Engraving after Claire's crayon drawing of her mother's head, incised on Marie's
tomb, 1859. Léopold Flameng. Bibliothèque Nationale 66A155330.

Marie d'Agoult, 1861, age 55. Photo by Antony Samuel Adam-Solomon.
Musée d'Orsay, R.M.N.

Marie d'Agoult, 1865, age 59. Photo by Antony Samuel Adam-Solomon.
Musée d'Orsay, R.M.N.

This strong depiction of Marie d'Agoult, of unknown origin, appeared with her obituaries. H. Roger Viollet, R.V. 349–551.

Nine ⟷ *"All direct action,*
all participation in public
affairs being by custom denied
to women, celebrity is for them
only a vain and irritating
excitation, a resounding
isolation."

Unfortunately, although Lamennais continued to visit every Monday, Lamartine's attendance at Marie's salon decreased. He may have been tired of the constant suggestions of a woman who was becoming disillusioned with the mediocrity of his Provisional Government. From Eckstein she learned that Lamartine was avoiding her because people believed she was irreligious and a socialist, and it was dangerous for him to be overly associated with her. "What a bore to be a woman," she confided to her diary.[1]

Certainly, the new problems encountered by the government were connnected with the rise of socialism, although it was not supported by Marie. The National Guard was enlarged to include all adult Frenchmen, and election of officers was announced. The old Guard, consisting of those who had been able to afford a uniform and a gun, objected to being merged with the new working-class members. On March 16 they marched to city hall to protest. The next day the workers decided to make their own showing. One hundred thousand of them marched up, led by Auguste Blanqui, the most radical socialist leader, whom the revolution had freed from jail. The protesters demanded that the government postpone not only the elections of Guard officers but the elections to the National Assembly as well, so that republicans would have time to educate the people for voting. They also protested the presence of troops in Paris. Although Lamartine assured them that the Republic would never take up arms against the people, this time it took the socialist Louis Blanc to persuade the marchers to disperse.

As a result, ordinary people began to lose hope that their representative in the government was really on their side. The nightly meetings of the numerous political clubs were packed, as they discussed every public issue. Among them were two women's clubs, which publicized the idea of women's suffrage, and Karl Marx's new Communist League, which issued the *Manifesto* that year. However, Marx was a relative unknown in Paris. Blanqui and Proudhon were the leaders of the working class. Proudhon was publishing a newspaper, *The Voice of the People*. Blanqui's Central Republican Society was the most radical of the clubs, although Blanqui was giving the Provisional Government a chance for the time being. Only sworn members could vote in this club, but the nightly meetings were attended by large numbers of the public.

All the clubs were attended by male spectators and by women dressed as men. Stern noted in her *Histoire de la révolution de 1848* that women recognized one another despite their male dress, indicating that she herself may have followed the revolutionary developments while wearing male attire. She described the clubs in great detail, disapproving of those that tried to incite violence. The revolution had deepened the economic depression of the late 1840s, making the situation of the working class worse than before. To raise money the Provisional Government raised the property tax. The ensuing run on the banks was only stopped by a huge financial sacrifice on the part of the Rothschild family.

The "forty-five centime" tax, as it was called, ended any support from provincial farmers for the social republic; they saw themselves as paying for the worthless unemployed in Paris. These unemployed had been meeting at Blanc's Luxembourg Commission, which had been created to respond to his ideas of state socialism and the "right to work" (i.e., the responsibility of the government to set up workshops for the unemployed in hard times). The commission offered the government a plan providing for the support of cooperative agricultural and manufacturing communities. Some cooperatives were actually established, lasting for decades. The government even agreed to cut the normal working day by one hour (from eleven to ten hours, or twelve to eleven). But at the same time the government put the official workshops for the unemployed not under the Luxembourg Commission, as would have been expected, but under another department that organized them into military squadrons to serve as a counterweight to the Luxembourg Commission, and gave them only occasional work.

After fruitlessly demanding a real "organization of labor" (Blanc's terminology), the Luxembourg group organized to march on city hall to press their demands. Another leftist, although to the right of Blanc, called out the National Guard to persuade the protesters to go home. He was Ledru-Rollin, minister of the interior, who had at first been tempted to join the protest with the idea that a more radical republic might be led by him. He was being advised by George Sand, who had rushed to Paris and was putting out the ministry's *Bulletin de la république,* which was filled with inflamed rhetoric. Stern, however, dismissed Sand as a "fuzzy" thinker. Impatient with her own impotence, Stern nevertheless scorned throughout the revolution radical actions by women, including the feminist Jeanne Deroin's attempted candidacy for the National Assembly. It was balm to her spirit when the Utopian socialist Etienne Cabet told her, "You are a political woman. Madame Sand is full of contradictions." But she was disappointed even in her hope to be in on the founding of a new periodical by Lamartine and Lamennais. Stern dared admit her desire for power only to her diary: "I would love to govern."[2]

The Provisional Government did put off the Assembly elections temporarily, until Easter Day, which fell on April 23 of that year. Although all the candidates, even the aristocrats, had run as good republicans, the results of the first national elections by universal male suffrage in history were, to the adherents of the social republic, too conservative by far. Stern noted that the elected deputies were all advanced in years and hoped that this reversed the wisdom about old wine in new bottles. Nevertheless, she missed none of the first sessions of the new Assembly, sitting with Madame de Lamartine at the opening and declaring it "grand" when Lamartine turned over his power to the new Assembly. The deputies made the gesture of keeping him as leader of the Executive Committee, although with the elimination of Blanc and the workingman Albert. (Lamartine insisted he would not serve without Ledru-Rollin.) Stern continued to attend the Assembly daily, although she was soon discouraged and felt that Lamartine was no longer available to her.

Determined to compete in the public arena with her nemesis, George Sand, Stern launched into print on May 27 a series of "Lettres républicaines" that ran in the *Courrier français* for the remainder of the year. Although the "Lettres" show the same firm style used in her coverage of the Prussian Diet, they also reveal Stern's personal feelings about day-to-day events, which she was trying to eliminate from the history of the 1848 revolution she was writing at the same time. In her essays and articles about politics, Stern was indeed able to manifest some superiority over Sand. The "Lettres" show her engaged at one remove in the political drama in which she could take no active part. The first letter was written to a son of the ex-king, the Prince de Joinville, who had announced that he would run in a by-election for the Assembly. Stern lectured him on the true nature of the revolution, which was social, and which the bourgeois friends who had urged him to run did not understand. Not only would he do better to withdraw, but he should, she suggested, seek his fortune in the United States, where he would learn about democracy.[3]

The second letter, on June 5, described to a friend a visit to the Assembly. The tone was ironic, sometimes even acid. Although the result of the elections should certainly calm those who had feared the radical results of popular suffrage, Stern commented, too many such victories would hinder political progress. Any faults the Assembly might have were certainly not from an excess of revolutionary enthusiasm. She then described, one by one, the famous names elected to that the body, beginning with the ineffectual chairman Philippe Buchez, a Christian socialist elected as the result of a compromise. She cast Ledru-Rollin as a melodramatic villain. Lamartine, whose head was in the clouds, she charged, came down to earth only with regret. The popular priest, Père Lacordaire, "his white Dominican vestments a pale souvenir of a dead theocracy," chose to resign. Then there were the royalists who had run under the republican banner ("Paris is worth a *Marseillaise*"),[4] who still displayed on their carriages their coats of arms. "The great breath of February [revolution] has not penetrated this sanctum," Stern decided. She described the Assembly as "defiant of the power that created it, defiant of the People to whom it owes its existence." And this Assembly was to write a democratic constitution! At least the socialists knew what the problems were. But they could contribute to the task only if they abandoned everything in their theories that was false and impossible.

The third letter, published on June 11, was addressed to Lamennais. It concerned the constitutional question of an elected president for the Republic. Stern disagreed that an election would vitiate republican equality. Equality was the recognized right of all to attain the complete development of their physical and moral beings and to raise themselves in the social hierarchy. It was not the apex but the base of a democratic society. As in the United States, the elected president could limit the domination of a single party and prevent domination by the legislature. She demanded of the majority that it *negotiate* with the minority and try to make all the diverse elments of republican opinion live and work together. The following week, in a letter addressed to Proudhon, who was a sitting member of the Assembly, Stern agreed that the people had acted thoughtlessly in voting for Louis-Napoléon in a by-election but pointed out that democracy took a long time to build. All the more reason, she argued, not to allow the relatives of past rulers to enter the Assembly, where they represented an obstacle to democracy.[5] (Louis-

Napoléon, nephew of Napoléon I, sensed that the time was not yet ripe and did not take his seat.) In her letter on the question of the presidential election, addressed to Lamennais,[6] she decided it was not yet time for the people to choose—the Assembly should instead choose the president, at least this time.

On the very day her next letter appeared, June 23, Parisians were building barricades. Their misery was unalleviated, the new Assembly having disbanded the national workshops that had, so far, kept them alive. Addressed to Adam Mickiewicz, who was fighting for Polish independence, Stern's letter depicted Europe in the throes of "a convulsive agony" and asked for reassurance, as the June Days commenced, that their generation not be condemned to bloody violence.[7] The outcome was to be worse than she expected.

As in February, Stern described what occurred on the June Days in every area of the city. From her history we have the account of the astronomer François Arago, minister of the navy, at the barricades begging the people not to attack the Republic. "Monsieur Arago," responded one of the leaders, "we are full of respect for you, but you have no right to reproach us. You have never been hungry; you do not know what true misery is." The great scientist had to turn back. Lamartine, hero of the February revolution, also made an effort. The people crowded around the poet, who reproached them for their revolt. "We are not bad citizens," they answered. "We are unhappy workers. We demand that someone attend to our misery. Care for us, govern us, we will help you. We want to live and die for the Republic." They pressed around him and wanted to shake his hand.[8]

Stern must have heard the story from Lamartine himself. Despite her defense of the rebels, she admitted that the elected government had to defend itself against revolt. But she deplored the total unwillingness of the Assembly to modify their harsh dismissal of the rights of the workers. Indeed, although the entire Executive Committee of the government, led by Lamartine, argued that it was more humane to attack each barricade as it was built, the Assembly chose to put all power into the hands of General Eugène Cavaignac, with orders to crush the rebellion. She described the anguish caused to Cavaignac, who was from an old republican family, by the necessity to fire on the people. But as a military leader, he favored allowing the insurrection to proceed to the point at which it could effectively be crushed with troops. The result was bloody violence. Not only were the troops effective, but farmers and the old nobility also poured into Paris to help put down the leftist Paris workers. Some used the new trains to travel as far as five hundred miles. Fifteen hundred conservatives from Brittany managed to travel for more than two hundred miles without the aid of the railroad, to suppress the despised leftist workers.

In her book Stern was one of the few contemporaries who spoke for those workers. She did not defend their revolt against a republic that was their only hope. But she maintained that they were not a criminal band of rioters; they were engaged in what they considered a just protest against the violation of their rights. Misled by radical leaders and overly violent, yes. But "do not forget that the insurgent of June was the fighter of February, the triumphant proletariat, to whom a government they had proclaimed solemnly assured the modest fruits of their conquest: work to recompense their misery." They had offered three months of that misery to the Republic. One must not forget the dates, Stern pointed out—February 28 to June 22.[9]

At this point the insurrection became more frenzied. The rebels, their backs against the wall, managed to cast a cannon and cool it by hanging it in midair and rocking it while children threw sand at it. Women made bullets and carried sacks of gunpowder under their skirts. A last effort to convince the rebels to give up was made by the Archbishop of Paris. No one will ever know whose bullet mortally wounded him, but Stern describes how the people carried him to safety and swore it was not theirs.

Her letter published the last day of June also insisted that the insurrection that had ended in "rivers of blood" had been grounded in the misery of the people, who had been led astray by Utopians and ambitious leaders. She begged the Assembly to pardon the people. "My hope today . . . is founded on the heroism of battle and the compassion of victory, on the union of all citizens, bound by the common peril."[10] In this letter Stern insisted on the complexity of events, arguing that since the rebels and the bourgeoisie shared the guilt, one should not punish the other. But the Assembly was investigating the leaders of the June Days as well as those responsible for the demonstration of May 15.

Stern took up the question of socialism, which was being blamed for the violence. She began by reproducing the common view: "Have we not seen arise, behind the tottering barricades, over parts of dead and dying bodies, its feet bathed in human blood, the formidable sphinx that cannot be killed?" But she went on to describe the different brands of socialism current in France—Utopian, sectarian, and statesmanlike. In general, she agreed that certain socialist leaders inspired the people to hate and vengeance. But she exempted the Utopians and the two socialists—Blanc, whose theories were peaceful, and Proudhon, whose ideas she knew best. (When her letter appeared, Blanc had been arrested, and Proudhon was soon to be unseated from the Assembly because of his demand for free credit.) Despite her attacks on socialist demagogues, Stern maintained that socialism was being blamed for creating a situation that it had merely recognized. There was, she pointed out, a statesmanlike socialism appropriate to the republic. It had developed out of study and reflection; based on history, it had produced the conviction that political rights were not the definitive aim of the Revolution but the means by which democracy managed to "exorcise the despotism of misery."[11]

By July, Stern saw the forces of conservatism taking over. Her letter of July 17 referred to the tragicomedy France was living through, "where one stage is completely dissociated from the stage before, like a dresser with drawers." She used the figure of Lamartine to epitomize the first phase of the 1848 revolution—republican hope—and Adolphe Thiers (who later became the first president of the Third Republic) to illustrate the "vulgar dénouement" of the revolution—republican deception. Describing the diminutive Thiers at the podium, Stern found him clever but uncultivated, lacking in moral values and devoted to the cult of success. She had always viewed him as a typical product of the bourgeois July Monarchy. It was the figure of Thiers that Stern saw behind the rivers of blood in which the army had bathed Paris. She hoped that the future would not be in the hands of him and his kind.[12]

Stern's next letter was to Emile Littré, who had picked up the work of Auguste Comte and who had introduced her to positivism. "We are in an epoch where the forces of dissolution are more active than the forces of recomposition," she had written in her last letter. She was concerned that the conservative republicans might join forces with the Catholic Church to control the Republic. The original doctrines of Christianity conformed well with the spirit of democracy, she noted; the clergy would be mistaken to separate themselves from the popular cause they had espoused up to this point. Even Thiers was only being used as a republican front by the conservatives, who would cast him aside when they found someone better. Although Thiers would rather be president of a republic than prime minister of a restored monarchy, she stated prophetically, his ascension to power would contain the seed of a regency and lead to civil war. Any party that denied all amelioration of the people's lot would inevitably bring about an explosion of popular despair.[13] This letter attracted much attention and was reproduced in other periodicals, either as a whole or in quotation of its epigrams on political leaders.

In an August letter Stern reflected on the lack of great orators in the Second Republic, as compared with the first. She posited that the rights for which the first revolution had been so passionately fought were now recognized and supported by the dry science of political economy, which did not inspire rhetorical genius. She admitted that Thiers, in his attack on Proudhon in the latest parliamentary battles, had succeeded in appearing as the exterminator of socialism and the savior of property. Socialism had been reduced to silence in the Assembly. Its success, as yet unacknowledged, was in having posed the questions that others would have to answer. In another prophetic statement, Stern picked out Jules Favre (later to be president of the Third Republic) as a coming talent.[14]

Stern was only one of the "three Amazons who dispute over the universe" cited by the popular press, the other two being Sand and Belgiojoso. Stern, however, did not sign a general petition of women on behalf of pardons for the June insurgents. (The government had declared penal servitude in exile for all those caught with weapons or on the barricades. Fifteen thousand men, women, and children had been rounded up. About 150 prisoners were shot or bayoneted immediately, which Stern may not have known at this time.) Instead, she published a letter to Cavaignac. She granted that he had done what he had to do, which was to triumph by force. Now he should treat his opponents with mercy. Surely, he would not exile them to French colonies across the ocean but would allow them instead to colonize in French Algeria.[15]

Stern, the moderate, prevailed among the reading public over the other two women ("over Belgiojoso by talent, and over Sand by good sense," she confided to her diary). Although pleased with the attention she received, she complained, "But I cannot act."[16]

However, she agreed with George Sand's open letter to the nascent women's movement later in the year. The women had called upon Sand to support their demand for participation in the political life of the republic. Sand turned them down, stating that women should not seek political rights until they had gained personal freedom and autonomy. Stern chose this moment to drop her "virile mask" and publish an eighteenth letter, addressed to the women of France. "I know that in a country where women are refused the most elementary rights, where it is judged equitable and necesary to the public safety to humiliate them as perpetual minors, and where, for fear that they might grow up, neither the state nor even the family gives them a rational education," they are not responsible "either for the good they cannot accomplish nor for the evil they cannot prevent." However, there were exceptional women who should speak out. They could not change the laws, but they could make it clear that they ought to be changed.

Stern blamed those "so-called free women" who struggle for as yet ill-defined rights. They had damaged their cause by prematurely exposing it to masculine laughter, which had sent the timid women scuttling back to their state of passive obedience. But one thing women had done before in history: they had been the ambassadors of peace. Therefore, she called them to "their present duties." Let male genius solve scientific and political problems, she urged. Female genius should work on the conciliation of classes, on softening hatreds, on repairing injustice, on preaching real fraternity. Women should demand a reciprocal forgiveness between the victors and the vanquished. "We are all entering upon an unknown path toward an unknown goal. One thing cannot fail us in the face of uncertainty: compassion." Therefore, she argued, although women could not vote or join in political intrigues, they should demand, from whoever is elected president of the republic, "a sage and magnanimous amnesty."[17]

As it turned out, 6,000 of the 15,000 prisoners were released early and more were released in batches over time. Those still held in January 1850, some 468, were actually sent to Algeria rather than to New Caledonia, as originally planned. It was more than a decade before those who survived the exile were allowed back to France.

The Second Republic had arrived at a stage at which fear of the working class had bred rumors about restoring the monarchy—not that of Louis-Philippe but the legitimate Bourbon monarch embodied in the "miracle child" of 1821, who was now the Comte de Chambord.[18] Stern published a letter to the count in September, after he had indicated his availability to aid his country. She first emphasized that she had been raised in loyalty to his house. She also agreed with the royalists that the July Monarchy had been a disaster. But the view of that period that she presented to the count and her picture of the revolution that ended it are a didactic lesson in the pros and cons of inevitable progress—eighteen years of usurpation and bourgeois enrichment, then the revolution of the hungry, leading to the proclamation of the republic, which could not be undone. "The renewing work of the nineteenth century, that great transformation of the whole people's conditions of life, can only operate peacefully in a state that bears the name of no man and that is truly the *public thing*. . . . Only the republican principle is superior to the interest of parties. . . . [A republic is] the only state capable today of embracing the infinite diversity of ideas, of habits, of needs and tendencies that compose and complicate modern civilizations." Tactfully, she added, "Monseigneur, you have a soul too generous to be wounded by that truth."[19]

After the June Days the Assembly, anxious about potential violence, had given over all power to Cavaignac, who, it must be said, did not misuse it. Anxious to lead the people, the Academy of Moral and Political Sciences began to produce simple books teaching values of good citizenship. Stern's next letter noted that the ruling classes were unable to solve their own discords, let alone educate the people, whom they had ignored so long. She maintained that it was the people themselves who incarnated the seeds of the future. "It is in the simplicity of the people's good sense, and not in the systems one works to create for their use, that eternal wisdom resides today."[20] After the June Days, these were inflammatory words. Stern also continued to visit Lamennais almost daily in his slum apartment in Montmartre, where he was putting out a new periodical, *Le Peuple constituant.*

Unfortunately, the eternal wisdom of the people did not extend to the candidates the working class presented for the next by-election. In her letter addressed to the workers of Paris, Stern took the opportunity to chide them for supporting socialist candidates who would frighten the bourgeoisie. Impatient, they did not see that progress could only be made by those who could calculate the resistance against it. Radicalism and the barricades were not the ne plus ultra of politics. "You are being used by ambitious men to prolong France's ills," she warned.[21] Of course, their candidates lost.

Her faith in the people's good sense weakening, Stern addressed her next letter to Lamartine, who was defending election of the president by universal male suffrage. She pointed out the lack of education, particularly political education, among the people. Unsure that they would live up to Lamartine's faith in them, she feared a "ridiculous choice." Stern seemed to feel that the existing Assembly, mediocre as it was, was preferable to any they might have in the near future, that the electorate was not in a condition to make a choice mature enough for the election of a president. Why not, as many urged, leave this first election of president to the Assembly, without compromising the system for the future? Toward the end of the letter she described the excitement of the return of Napoleon's ashes to Paris during the July Monarchy and referred to the possibility of a candidate "whose only value is a name."[22]

Stern attended the Assembly session at which Lamartine spoke for universal suffrage, holding forth the great dream of the republic, and she was impressed by his republican faith and rhetoric. He wrote her a letter, saying that he had seen her there and had thought of her as he answered her arguments. If she realized it, she did not record that universal suffrage was

Lamartine's only hope for the presidency. The Assembly would certainly choose Cavaignac; she herself thought him the better candidate.

But the revolutionary fervor that had sustained her since February was gone. In September Marie fell into another depression. She wrote to Liszt that she was preoccupied with thoughts of death. Liszt, who had become more religious since his relationship with Princess Sayn-Wittgenstein, answered, "Go to Jesus, who is the life." He must have known that this would be of little help to Marie. So he congratulated her on her published letters. Not that he agreed with all her positions, "but to put it plainly, I will tell you that I like what you are doing, because I have loved you—and he who loves understands, as Saint Augustine says."[23]

Despite all that she had thought and written about the snares of marriage for a young woman, one of the tasks Marie set herself at the end of the year was a good marriage for Claire, "to save what can be saved," she wrote in her diary. What did she mean? To preserve the aristocratic family tradition? Or did she believe that she could make a better match than had been made for her? The candidate who soon emerged was Ernest Charles Guy de Girard de Charnacé, who had the advantage of being from an aristocratic family in Anjou and of having been educated in Dresden. He won over Marie, who helped him win Claire. The marriage took place in 1849 in the Church of the Assumption, where Marie had been married, also with great pomp and ceremony. The family was not wealthy, and the couple were to live on the Charnacé estate at Bois-Montboucher. When they left Paris, Marie worried that her daughter would not have enough intellectual stimulation. She gathered books for her to read: Gregory of Tours, Montesquieu, Rousseau, some of Voltaire, Madame de Staël, and some Greek classics. She also drew up a plan of reading, so that Claire would experience ideas in a meaningful order.

Pressed to visit her in-laws, Marie went to visit the Charnacé family, who were still legitimists. (That is, they believed that only the Bourbons could be the legitimate kings of France.) After two weeks Marie reported to friends that her last illusions about aristocratic country life had vanished. She was also worried that the young couple would be unable to fulfill their lives in this backwoods. However, she felt that it was a solid marriage—one instance where her intuition really failed her. She wrote to her daughter, "For the years now that you have become the single object of my life, I have told myself that I had to do two things to prove to you my love and to make up, as much as I could, for the sorrow I have caused you. These two things were to see you married to a man worthy of you, and then to leave behind me a name of which you could be proud. The first, the most difficult and the most important of the two tasks, is accomplished."[24]

By this time Daniel Stern had made progress toward the second task she had set for herself—to make a name of which her daughter could be proud. *Esquisses morales* was published with an *envoi* to Claire, which, after an expression of regret that she could not poetize like the immortals, read in part:

I would sing a young girl, a child; her serious innocence; her brow lighted by thought; her limpid blue eyes; her lips which never tell lies. I would tell the surprising accord of strength and sweetness, of candor and wisdom, of uprightness and clairvoyance manifested in her person. I would tell the maternal thrill when the child, borne in my arms, matured in my absence, suddenly appeared before my eyes in her virginal grace. Thus, after the troubled clouds of a long night, in the sweet light of morning, the lake, surprised and charmed, contemplates the white lotus that has blossomed on its breast during the tempest. First smile of fortune, grace of my unfortunate life, pride of my secret sorrow; pardon, recompense and promise of severe destiny; child of my heart, life of my life, would that I would celebrate you in the immortal mode![25]

France was not the only country in revolution in 1848. The German states had risen up and were seeking unification. So were the states of Stern's beloved Italy. Her friend Bois-le-Comte, who represented France at the court of Piedmont, was keeping her posted on Italian events. Unfortunately, there was disagreement among Italians. Some felt that the country could be unified under the monarchy of Sardinia-Piedmont. But Giuseppe Garibaldi and Joseph Mazzini believed that Italy could only be a republic and were impatient with moderate progress. When the new pope, Pius IX, failed to satisfy the populace in Rome, he was forced to flee. Stern's empathy with Mazzini came from their shared belief in the ordinary people as the bearers of progress. She also agreed with him that Italy had missed essential steps toward progress—the Reformation and the scientific revolution. But she disagreed with his politics. Stern's October 24 letter to Mazzini pointed out that Piedmont, under the House of Savoy, would aid in Italian unification if France would support it, as she hoped they would. Although the Italian revolution failed this time (after the brief Republics of Rome, led by Mazzini and Garibaldi, and of Venice, led by Daniel Manin), and she later chose to support unification under the House of Savoy, Mazzini and Stern maintained a long correspondence based on their mutual love of Italy.[26]

Stern was also interested in the development of the revolution in Germany. One of her letters, addressed to a friend on November 15, expressed her fears of "a struggle of race against race, sect against sect, class against class, monarchy against republic, feudalism against communism." Such complexity could only be solved by a United States of Germany, represented by the Frankfurt Parliament then meeting. But she deplored the weaknesses of this body, which had become involved with menacing neighboring countries and had lost moral authority. In Prussia the king's unwillingness to deal with the people had led to falling back on his one support—the army. In Austria, a spurious unity of disparate nationalities had been broken by revolution. All Stern could see ahead for the German states was anarchy.[27] When she wrote her history of the 1848 revolution, she was to include material on the other European revolutions.

As 1848 drew to a close, the constitution of the French Second Republic was completed, and one more effort was made to eliminate the candidacy of Louis-Napoleon Bonaparte. It was suggested in the Assembly that all members of former ruling families should be barred from running. Cavaignac, who felt that this would show distrust in the voters, opposed it. Louis-Napoléon Bonaparte himself, an Assembly deputy as the result of another by-election, asked to give a speech. He spoke so badly (his French was German-accented) and seemed so bumbling, that barring him was considered unnecessary. The election was set for December 10.

One month before the election, Stern composed a letter entitled to "The people as electors." She wrote that the eyes of Europe were on France, to see what this radical mode of election would produce. She feared that the vote would be a protest by the masses against the successive governments of 1848, whom they blamed for their general malaise. Going over the candidates, she concentrated on Ledru-Rollin, Lamartine, Cavaignac, and Louis-Napoléon Bonaparte. Ledru-Rollin's strength was already vitiated by the candidacy of François Raspail (a medical doctor who practiced in the slums and gave free treatment to the poor), but she considered Ledru-Rollin weak anyway. The present unpopularity of the Provisional Government meant that Lamartine was also a weak candidate. Stern discussed Proudhon's suggested protest against the imperfections of all the candidates—not voting at all—and dismissed it. "Experience has demonstrated a thousand times that the absolute truths of philosophy are the most dangerous errors of politics." One must be realistic; the real contest was between Cavaignac and Louis-Napoléon Bonaparte.

Of the latter, after a witheringly negative description, she wrote: "His followers offer him to France as if the French were a nation of frogs, as a nullity. He will not govern [they imply], therefore we can all govern. Who are we all? Of course, Barrot, Thiers. . . ." The monarchists, she noted, also support him, hoping that once the worst has occurred, the monarchy will have a chance. Stern recognized that the provinces would support him, to have a strong hand at the helm; what people really wanted was another emperor. The Orleanists also believed a hereditary succession was good for property. If they could not have a king, they would take a Bonaparte, even if he would be the laughingstock of Europe. But they hoped that "the nephew of the emperor would make the bed of a king." Therefore, she named Cavaignac as the only possible choice and begged everyone to put aside personal interest and the spirit of party. In her diary she noted that Louis-Napoléon was promising church control over education. "We are returning to Clovis [the first king of France], to the domination of priests and soldiers."[28]

Stern began to keep a journal of the election on November 28. On election day she walked with her daughter Claire in the Bois de Boulogne and the next day in the Place Vendôme. Both days were beautiful. The election results came in the following day, a rainy one: Louis-Napoléon Bonaparte won by 5,434,266 votes to Cavaignac's 1,448,107. Lamartine trailed with less than 18,000. Stern wrote in her journal, "I have to hold back not to burst into tears. Shame on us! Shame on France, shame on the Republic, shame on democracy, shame on the people! The success of Louis-Napoléon cannot be doubted. I long for the reign of Louis-Philippe. At least then we had hope, and illusions about ourselves!"[29]

Although she tried, Stern could not convince herself that the new president would really preserve the Republic. But slowly she came to the conclusion that the election, although it had turned out badly, was the real revolution. She agreed with Proudhon that the people had spoken. It would be wrong to overthrow a democratically elected government, as Cavaignac was urged to do. Yes, it had been a risk to give the suffrage to the people, and they had misused it. But as Raspail said, "Accept the principle, accept the result." Sitting alone by her fire on December 20, Stern cried when she heard the cannons at Les Invalides go off, signaling that the oath had been taken by Louis-Napoléon. It was, she wrote, "the defeat of the republicans and the triumph of the Republic."[30]

Ten ～ *"I have taken more care than necessary in order to be always exact; my research has been minute, even in what concerns inconsiderable persons and facts."*

Despite her disillusionment, Daniel Stern was at the Assembly the next day. She saw Cavaignac, who had been urged by republicans to take over the government rather than yield it to a Napoleon, turn over his powers to the elected president. Stern approved. She hoped his role in the Second Republic was not over, but she agreed with Proudhon that Cavaignac did not understand the revolution of the nineteenth century. The ordinary people, who attached to the word *republic* infinite hopes, understood, but not the bourgeoisie, who found the word menacing. A few days later, Lamartine came to visit her, to discuss the mistakes he had made and his hopes for a future role in the republic. Stern did not encourage him to seek one. She had always admired his republican rhetoric, and she recognized that the word *revolution* on his lips frightened no one, because he presented the idealistic aspect of things. He had played an important role in the early weeks of the revolution, which she highlighted in her history. But she also made clear that his governance as chair of the Executive Committee was weak and ineffective.

In her disappointment over politics, Stern turned more and more to her work-in-progress on the revolution she had just lived through. Her "Lettres Républicaines" had been well received. The poet and songwriter Béranger, who had advised her not to publish *Nélida*, pointed out that she had found her métier. "What you are doing is very good," he had written in November.[1] She continued to gather information on revolutionary events from every source. The poet Auguste Lacaussade, who worked also for Sainte-Beuve, had become her secretary, taking over the most tedious of the editorial tasks formerly done by Ronchaud.

By the end of the year she had become more interested in Louis Blanc, as she learned from the editor of a popular newspaper that some of the workshops set up by the Luxembourg Commission had succeeded and were ongoing. She broadened her historical horizons by reading Blanc's *History of Ten Years* on the July Monarchy, as well as Michelet's and Auguste Mignet's books on the first revolution and Augustin Thierry's *Letters on the History of France*. She may also have read Tocqueville's *Democracy in America,* for he had attended her salon. Stern observed in her notebook that Thierry marked off the most numerous class, the most forgotten, as the one to be resurrected in history. She recorded disapprovingly that Mignet, although revolutionary in principle, justified everything his heroes did. From Lamartine she took the idea of the republic as ideal but did not justify all his actions. In Michelet, whose lectures she had attended, she found echoes of the Hegelian pantheism that had attracted her in her German studies.

Stern's admiration of the Latin historians Livy and Tacitus provided an oratorical style to her writing, with moral analysis and some use of both direct and indirect discourse. She also admired Bossuet. But for Stern, history depended not on God but on a philosophical law of progress governing the lives of peoples. In the introduction to her history she wrote that the republic of 1848 was "the most complete exterior manifestation of that organic movement which, parting from the popular masses, has tried since 1789 to insert them into the social life, to reconstitute the authority of ordinary reason, to procure by the free association of all citizens a new order which would take the place of the old hierarchy, to substitute human rights for divine right; in a word, to organize democracy."[2]

As could be expected, Stern blamed the bourgeoisie, who had failed to educate the people and integrate the nation, for the violence of the June Days. In her Preface to the book she referred to the party spirit which, at that moment, was attacking the popular revolution with such arrogance and bitterness, and which made her feel it a duty to publish, "without waiting any longer, a conscientious study that I think will shed some true light on people and events now strangely disfigured." She swore that she had tried to be impartial and that she would be happy to be shown where she had not succeeded, ending with the words of Machiavelli: "Io mi sono ingegnato, in queste mi deacrizioni non maculando la verita, di soddisfare a ciascuni, et forse no avro soddifatto a persona. Ne quando questo fosse, ne me maraviglierei: perche io giudico che sia impossibile, senz offendere molti, discrivere le cose de' tempi suoi."[3]

It is true that disillusion with the republic was general on both the right and the left at the time she was writing. Because of the violence in June, the revolution as a whole was being attacked by the Party of Order—but not by Daniel Stern. Her history can be considered a permanent protest against the political reaction under Louis-Napoléon. She was one of the minority that continued believe in the republic. She never thought that the red flag seen in popular revolt was a symbol of subversion. In Stern's eyes, the people were not dishonored when they demanded work and bread. She noted how, in the financial crisis of the Provisional Government, the people offered their *sous* to the treasury while the capitalists sent their money out of the country. She deplored the government's failure to enact a graduated income tax—an egalitarian move not accomplished until the twentieth century. She gave serious coverage to the ending of the death penalty by the Provisional Government as a development of civilized society. (Civilized society was not to develop to this point again in France until the victory of the left in 1981, and it has not yet done so in the United States.)

Stern was quite clear that the national workshops, viewed as socialist, had been deliberately sabotaged by the refusal to give them work; it had been a terrible mistake of the government to let so many workers be idle. Emile Thomas, who had directed the workshop for the government, brought a case against Stern for libel on the basis of her description of his actions as a deliberate government policy. The lawyer who fought her case not only proved her right but made a point of "the question of truth and of good faith on the part of the historian."[4] At the end of her second edition, the first document listed the names and vocations of the workers in the national workshops on May 19; the second was the police record of those arrested from May 15 to June 22, 1848, with name, age, party, profession, and reasons for arrest. As Stern insisted and subsequent studies have shown, neither group was a mob of criminals, but solid citizens.

Stern's greatest success was in placing the revolution in the framework of the nineteenth century; she tried to show the influence of all schools of thought. The hero of the story was the people, even though she saw their failures. The Republic was the destiny, the idea toward which France was moving. Freedom was the spirit of the century, and the people were meant to embody it. But the republican leaders were not qualified to lead the Republic.

The first volume of *Histoire de la révolution de 1848* appeared early in 1850. Besides the written sources, which she obtained by engaging in a round of correspondence with people who had been involved in the events, she also used many oral sources. Ronchaud had served as president of the Council of the Provisional Government and had the ear of Lamartine. Her old friend, the historian Louis de Viel-Castel, who had lost his position as a result of the revolution, had from friends eyewitness accounts of the last hours at the Tuileries. Girardin had also to some extent been present at the time. There were other friends: Auguste Barbet, who edited *Le Peuple constituant* with Lamennais; Pascal Duprat, who recounted to her the parliamentary doings of each day; Littré of *Le National;* Cabet of *Le Populaire;* and Guéroult of *La République.* Not being engaged herself, she was able to keep track of events and to generalize and analyze. She also read the other works by Lamartine, Proudhon, and Blanc that appeared during this period. But these books served mainly to justify the authors' own philosophy or role in events.

Stern was proud that she was attacked in the *Journal des débats*[5] for being a socialist and a destroyer of the social order, while at the same time Littré's review was being held up at *Le National* on suspicion that she accepted the idea of a regency. The *Revue de deux mondes*[6] wanted to know how she knew what was going on in the streets and in the corridors of power. The *Revue sociale* thought she was too hard on the left and too soft on the right but called her introduction "a remarkable piece."[7] The *Revue brittanique* had some criticisms but described her prose as worthy of Madame de Staël, George Sand, and even Tacitus![8]

All the critics praised her descriptions of people and the organization and clarity of her work. Some newspapers, like *Le Siècle* and *Le National,* published parts of it. Others, like *L'Opinion publique,* published detailed articles praising her.[9] In August, Adolphe Guéroult printed an accumulation of positive views on the book in *La République.*[10] At the end of the year *La Liberté de penser,* the journal of republicans at the university, lauded Stern's "male and philosophical" mind and her understanding of society.[11]

Stern also received the praise of individuals whose opinion was important to her. The historian Michelet praised the book on many ocasions. Blanc, although concerned about her depiction of him, wrote her from exile, congratulating her. Her German friends were also complimentary. Varnhagen von Ense compared it with other great historical expositions. Hortense Allart transmitted an opinion from Sainte-Beuve: "That seductive writer seems to play all roles and to simulate all beauties, whether in wearing dresses the color of the moment or in putting on the toga."[12] He described the book as full of precious qualities, having a "cold, grand, worthy tone, truly the tone of an historian." But Sainte-Beuve never communicated his approval to Stern herself. Even Thiers expressed admiration of the book to her friend Barchou de Penhoën: "She is not benevolent, but is impartial. That hussy of a woman has a good mind."[13]

In this year of her great triumph Marie was also involved with her children, primarily with Claire. The Charnacé family, far away from Paris, had never connected the Countess d'Agoult with Daniel Stern. After the marriage and Marie's visit, Claire unwittingly revealed the connection to them. The shock of her in-laws was so great that it became impossible for the young couple to remain on the estate in Anjou, and they left for Paris. Marie felt obligated to see them established; they would live in the chateau at Croissy, which was empty. The count had not been able to keep it up, and it was in deplorable condition. Marie and Claire went to look at it and found that two of the towers had fallen down. They decided that Guy could open a stud farm there, one of the few moneymaking activities that an aristocrat could undertake.

The couple was installed at Croissy as it was fixed up. Their first child, born in 1850, did not live. By this time, relations between Marie and her daughter were becoming difficult. Marie, worried about money, felt that Claire was not appreciative enough of what she was providing. Claire, understandably, felt that her mother was too intrusive. Things became better between mother and daughter when a second pregnancy led to the birth of Daniel Guy de Charnacé the following year. Marie was a fond grandmother. Also, as relations between the young couple began to deteriorate, Claire leaned more on her mother. Although Marie's style of life was certainly too lavish for her income, her children also contributed to the financial worries she would have for the rest of her life.

While Claire was still living with her husband in Croissy, Marie had unexpected contact with her other daughters, Blandine and Cosima. Liszt had originally decided that while retaining full control over his son, he would put the education of the girls in their mother's hands. He had written that he was convinced that she, better than anyone, "would know how to direct the education of *my* two daughters"[14] (my italics), and that he would never think of objecting to any plan of education she would choose for them. Daniel would go to the Lycée Bonaparte in Paris. But as relations between the parents suffered, the girls lived at school and did not see their mother for three years. A letter of Liszt to his daughters seems to indicate that this was by his orders.

During their New Year's school vacation in 1850, Blandine and Cosima, who had managed to learn their mother's address, persuaded the maid at their grandmother Liszt's house to bring them to see Marie. The children seem to have known this would not please their father. It was an unexpected and therefore emotional meeting as Marie opened the door and saw her two girls standing before her. She confided to Hortense Allart, "Since I wrote you a great happiness has been given me, I have seen my children again. I found them all mine, and I don't dare say even to you how much they appear fine and lovely to me; but I can confess to you that love has reentered my life through them. . . . It seems to me that I am being reborn to love all and understand all."[15] Blandine registered her mother's happiness in a letter to her father: "She was truly moved and astonished to see us again, above all she felt a great joy in seeing that our feelings for her were just as strong and tender as always." Blandine added that the happiness of the meeting made up for all the time they had missed seeing their mother.[16]

Marie went twice to see the children at Madame Liszt's house, reviewed their studies with them, and was pleased with them, Blandine reported. "We always try to prolong her visits and we are very sorry to leave her."[17] Daniel also visited the girls at their school, and all of them were together with their mother on one visit. Blandine added that she would be just as happy to see her father; her joy would then be complete if she could share her kisses between the two.

Liszt, however, did not feel his daughter's joy at all. Although he had not bothered to see the children himself for over five years, he wrote, "I must not only scold you, but blame you severely, for you have done wrong." He ordered the girls to cease, for as long as he would order, all visits, all correspondence, and all relations with their mother. He pointed out that he had supported them financially from their birth, while their mother "judged it appropriate to accord you only the benefit of her beautiful words." Therefore, he was not flattered by sharing their affection with her and would not accept "the expression of your *divided* feelings."[18]

Tearfully, Blandine wrote that she would obey. "I admit that I was wrong, but at the time I went to see Mama I heard only the cry of my heart, the natural feeling that led me to love her." She had written to him immediately after. If he had written back right away, she would have obeyed, but she had seen her mother since then. "However, since it gives you pain and makes me feel guilty toward you, I submit to your will and will not see Mama any more. Nevertheless, I admit to you that I have shed many tears on learning the orders you have given."[19] Liszt also removed the girls from the school, depriving them of the pleasure of beloved teachers as well as their mother. They were to stay at home with Madame Liszt. Despite begging letters from the girls, which only made him angrier, Liszt refused even to allow them back to school.

Thus Marie lost her girls again. In August she lost the first grandchild at

Croissy. When it was all over, Marie set out on a trip to Brittany, where she probably visited Barchou de Penhoën. He was the author of *Histoire des doctrines hindoues*, which she had read in Switzerland. She had met him in Milan in 1837. An old legitimist, he had written to compliment her on her *Lettres républicaines*. She sent him a picture and a model of her hand. Their correspondence was extensive. In the process of trying to convert her to Catholicism and democratic monarchism, his letters became very passionate. Barchou was to die prematurely.

Stern also visited Normandy, from which she crossed over to talk to Louis Blanc, in exile on the island of Jersey, about the revolution. This visit punctuated a correspondence between the two that began with his sending her documents for her history. It extended over thirteen years, despite his rage at "the grace with which you have assassinated me."[20]

On her return, the ever-waiting depression overtook her. It seems to have manifested itself first in difficulties with her eyes, which made her incapable of working and frightened her. She retired to Croissy for a week. After that situation cleared, she remained depressed, fearful of death, and recorded in her diary the entry "extreme sadness, uncertainty, uprooted life without action, what to do?" A month later, in September, she wrote, "The evil in me is recognized and unhealable."[21] This refers to Marie having sought help; for the next three months she was treated by a Dr. Emile Blanche at his clinic in Passy.

Her disappearance led to a curious and negative result for Blandine and Cosima, who were suffering further for having enjoyed the time with their mother. Now that Liszt was completely involved with Princess Sayn-Wittgenstein, he had followed her advice and sent her own governess, Madame Patersi de Fossombrini, to look after the girls' education. The new governess, seventy-two years old, moved into an apartment with them in Paris; the children were told to obey her. In a letter to Liszt in January 1851, Blandine confessed that while still at her grandmother's, she had written her mother and made a rendez-vous. But when she arrived, her mother was not there. "My mother must have understood my duty better than I," she concluded. Repenting her former ideas, she promised to ask counsel only of Madame Patersi thereafter.[22]

One wonders if Blandine ever knew that Marie was in the sanitorium of Dr. Blanche at the time. From her diary we know that Marie was dreaming of the death of Liszt and of friendship between Blandine and Claire. Blandine, meanwhile, had made the mistake of weepingly complaining to her grandmother about Madame Patersi. Madame Liszt, who was probably on the girls' side, reported this to her son, who demanded that Blandine apologize to the governess. Liszt wrote his daughters that he hated women who cry and that "both of you must learn to make life sweet and easy for those around you, for that is the destiny of women."[23]

In 1851 Marie bought a house from the painter Claude Jacquand; it was isolated in an unbuilt area near the present Arc de Triomphe. She dubbed it the Maison Rose, after the pale color of its bricks. There was a garden in back, entered from the artist's large atelier, with mimosas, rhododendrons, gardenias, and a small fountain. A good deal of work was needed to make it suitable for a *salonnière*; for weeks, Marie lived with alterations going on around her. On the ground floor she decorated the large room for a main salon. A smaller, octagonal room, reached from the front door by four steps under a marquee, formed her Renaisssance salon. Her own room was on the first floor, reached by a small stair. She and Claire would sit on the little stair and make plans. Marie was to live and entertain there for nine years, until Baron Haussmann's urban projects in Paris doomed the Maison Rose.

In August Marie was at Croissy for the birth of Claire's second child, named Guy Daniel. Then she left for Great Britain, taking the train from Paris. She was no more impressed with train travel than Flaubert, deploring "that prodigious speed which in accelerating and multiplying communications between people only isolates them in an inferior kind of activity. . . . The exchange of ideas and feelings that animates the intellectual life of societies seems to slow down and lose its charm to the extent that the exchange of material products takes place with greater speed and freedom." She felt that this gave modern civilization, admirable as it was, "a sad quality felt deeply by the noblest and most delicate souls."[24]

Marie visited the London Exposition but did not stay long. The city, which she had seen first on her honeymooon and later on the unhappy visit with Liszt, aroused in her a repulsion, "more lively than accords with philosophy." But Edinburgh, with its grand site between mountains and sea, attracted her by its combined history and poetry. Extending her stay in Scotland, she pushed into the Highlands, whose scenery she pronounced different from any in Europe. Not only did the people, the bagpipes, and the kilts charm her but also the castles, the legends, and the stories, immortalized in the works of Sir Walter Scott.

In her extensive coverage of this trip, never published, Stern combined descriptions of landscape with historical references and comments on the use of steam power in Glasgow, which she found dehumanizing. She agreed with those who linked industrialization with the Reformed religion and blamed "the rigid figure of Knox, who from the heights of the city of Glasgow dominates the city of the living," for holding at his feet the "humiliated cathedral" and forbidding forever all fantasy, beauty, and grace. She also criticized the use of Greek and Roman architecture by a "culture without a priesthood," in those temples of commerce, the banks. Edinburgh, however, she described as truly the modern Athens. She claimed to be haunted throughout her visit by two figures: the beautiful, touching, voluptuous Queen Mary Stuart; and her austere persecutor, the zealous promoter of Presbyterian independence, John Knox. The queen, of course, caught Marie's imagination.[25] She visited all the places connected with Mary Stuart's history and conceived the project of writing a drama on her life.

Receiving news that Claire was not well, Marie rushed back to France. Fortunately, both mother and child had improved. However, at Croissy the stables of Guy de Charnacé, financially backed by Marie, were failing. Not only that, but the marriage was no more successful than the business. It was clear that Marie would have to take care of her daughter and grandson. She returned to Paris, and after supervising the completion of renovations on the Maison Rose, she was able to give a dinner party there early in December. Then the second volume of *L'Histoire de la révolution de 1848* was published. This time, there was less discussion of it in the press as Louis-Napoléon took over complete power in the government a month later.

Although she had predicted the coup, Stern was angry. In a letter to Herwegh, who had written to ask her if there was any hope for the Republic, Stern replied in the negative. The parliamentarians would make some noise, she wrote, but only for show. The shopkeepers and businessmen were content because order was now ensured; they saw the end of the Republic as "a slight evil on behalf of a greater good [the end of socialism]." The army officers were completely devoted to the president; the peasants, except for some sporadic rioting, would give a Napoleon their vote in the plebiscite, she predicted. The workers were confused between a royalist parliament and a despot who offered universal suffrage. The population of Paris had not yet recovered from the June Days: "Some brave republicans [fighting against the coup] got themselves killed on the barricades for honor. The police left these barricades alone, in order to give the troops the opportunity to *save French society from pillage and anarchy.*"

Pointing to the willingness of Russia to help crush revolution, Stern stated that any uprising at this point, either in Italy or in Hungary, would be a disaster. She found the political atmosphere intolerable. "The democratic group in France has been led by simpletons, by braggarts, by traitors," she wrote angrily. She feared her letter might be censored and spoke of the numerous arrests being made. Still writing the third volume of her history, Stern felt that she had "augured too well for the people, and believed too much in the power of principles alone. All worn out with our own enthusiasm, we misunderstood the customs of our times. There is no hope that we are going to see them change. What we took for *heroism* was only *bluster,* and for *free spirit,* only disorderly minds. Let us live as long as we can, to see if our children at least, will want better than we."[26]

Nevertheless, she asked for news of Mazzini. She had visited her old friend Cabet in prison during that year and partook of his bitterness about the fate of the Second Republic. And she hid Leroux, socialist editor of the *Revue indépendante,* for twelve days after the coup and then gave him money to get himself and his family to England.[27]

In 1852, Claire and little Daniel finally left Croissy for Paris. Marie had a small apartment built for Claire in the back of the garden, called the *"maison grise."* But Guy de Charnacé was using up their fortune; it became necessary to sell Croissy to pay the bills for his stable. Marie was concerned about the future of young Daniel. After much expense, the young couple were finally separated in 1855. Marie wrote to Ronchaud that the business part was over, although not the suffering, and that it had required the sacrifice of a great deal of money. "She will live independent," Marie said, "and will find under my roof the benefits that I have acquired, also at a very high price, but which I prize more every day: a peaceful physical existence and a free moral life."[28]

Stern continued to use her mind as she pondered the revolution and politics in general. She wrote to a friend that politics consisted in "leading people to your house while persuading them that you are going to theirs."[29] As Louis-Napoléon proceeded to convert the Second Republic into a Second Empire, the coterie at the Maison Rose became more frustrated and angry. In 1852 Stern made a trip to Holland. She visited Bruges, Gander, Rotterdam, Leiden, and the beach at Scheveningen. She found the terrain fascinating and was excited by the idea of a people in constant combat against the sea. The Dutch revolution of the seventeenth century had resulted in a republic. Stern was interested in how this small nation had managed not only to create a republic but also to preserve it. To research the topic, she began to add Dutch to the German, French, Italian, and English of her linguistic repertoire.

The third and final volume of Stern's history appeared in May 1853. Among the descriptions in the later volumes were those of the constant displays in early 1848 of popular homage to the Republic by a people who believed that they had become free. Almost every evening spontaneous processions would form, directed toward some popular revolutionary site, with singing and banners. One song declared the willingness of the people to die for the Republic. Although not a socialist, Stern described the socialism of her time and was impressed by certain leftist leaders. Both Leroux and Proudhon had attended her salon. She thought Proudhon's newspapers were the year's best. (They kept being closed down and then reopened under new names.) She recognized but could not wholly condemn the fact that the main aim of this anarchist was to disorganize government and destroy anything that impeded the instincts of society. Stern also espoused the radical opinion that the conservatives in the Assembly had feared writing a republican constitution and wanted to see class war break out so that they could modify the constitution in such a way as to limit democracy. Hence the closing down of the workshops, which led to the June Days.

Stern's history also reported on events in the provinces during 1848. She had initiated correspondance with a Dr. Guepin in Brittany asking for information; he sent her newspapers of the year. She read the papers of other areas of the country as well, and tried, as she wrote Guepin, to check every fact from a second source, since she had not been there at the time. He helped her with information on the families of revolutionary personalities and with events in Algeria. He also read the chapter once she had written it. Eventually, the correspondence broke down, as Guepin became a suitor and made tactless advances. Another of her correspondents was the young Emile Ollivier, who had made himself a name in Marseilles in 1848 and was known as "the Lamartine of the Midi." He was to become a frequenter of her salon and, later, prime minister of France. Through other correspondence, she researched and covered European affairs; her letters went everywhere. Blanc, in exile, was concerned to change her opinion of his actions, already published in her first volume. As a result of her visit to him, she changed in her second edition some but not all of the judgments that had upset him.

Stern was the only contemporary author of the 1848 revolution who appended a clear and detailed list of her written sources of information. She also reproduced documents, proclamations, letters, and decrees. Her history is still probably the best study of the 1848 revolution done at the time; certainly, it has been pillaged ever since by historians for its vivid descriptions, usually without attribution.

As Marie recognized that Claire and little Daniel were now her financial responsibility, she also worried about what would she would be required to contribute to her three children by Liszt. He showed little interest in even seeing them, describing them as being so little a part of his life that it was better to love them at a distance.[30] Finally, in 1853 he decided to make a journey to Paris, but in informing the children about it he was very cool. He was coming on business and they might be able to see him, he wrote Blandine, but they shouldn't count on it; they had to learn to get along without him. He eventually did arrive with Sayn-Wittgenstein and her daughter, some of his students, and the young Richard Wagner. Despite some initial stiffness, Liszt's charm made the visit a success. The girls became attached to "Magnolet," as they called the princess's daughter. Cosima, then fifteen, met Wagner for the first time.

Stern was not in Paris at the time but on an autumn visit to the south of France. She had published, besides her third volume, a review of the German historian Georg Gottfried Gervinus's *History of the Nineteenth Century* in *Le Siècle*.[31] She had also completed *Trois journées de Marie Stuart*, which was to be part of a trilogy of historical dramas, along with *Jeanne d'Arc* and *Jacques Coeur*. As she wrote to Michelet, the idea was to raise the popular interest in French history.[32] In June, *Marie Stuart* was read in her salon on two days, one by the celebrated actor Bocage, before an elite audience of littérateurs. Michelet told her that she "carried with a light foot the burden of history."[33] But when the administrator of the Comédie-Française offered to put the work before the committee that chose plays for performance, she first accepted then withdrew the play from consideration.

Stern seemed suffer from both a lack of confidence in her play and a pride that refused to put herself in a position to be turned down. She knew rejection was a real possibility, since her enemy Buloz, editor of the *Revue de deux mondes,* was on the committee. Later, she wrote to Bocage that she had wanted it to be known that she had written a fine work but that she had resisted the temptations of theatrical success. "What gives me, not happiness, but strength, calm, a certain pride necessary to my nature, has been work . . . without illusions, often without success."[34] Three years later, however, she published *Marie Stuart* in the *Revue de Paris,* with a preface saying that her desire had been to represent only the truth and that the complexity of her thought did not fit the necessities of drama.

It is understandable that for those who did not know her, Stern had the reputation of being haughty. It is more likely that this complex woman used a pride that was real to compensate for feelings of insufficiency that were just as real. Her diaries show an overwhelming desire for greatness and recognition, a constant measuring of herself against others, particularly Sand. She had replaced dedication of herself to love with dedication to making a name for herself. As in love, the outcome was not sure. She may have been right to refuse the nomination of *Marie Stuart*. The play on Jacques Coeur was refused by the Comédie Française in 1858, despite the support of the house administrator and of the actor Edmond Jeffroy, who wanted to play the leading role. The text of that play has been lost. *Jeanne d'Arc* was to be staged only in Italy.

In 1854 Lamennais became ill, and Marie rushed to his side. She considered him the "only guru" of her life, despite his misogyny, and she seems to have aided him financially. His illness was mortal, lasting a couple of months. Later, she described him to Mazzini as "occasionally rude, violent and tender, unjust and passionate for justice." She said she had tried to interest Lamennais in writing the story of his conversion from Catholicism to "the modern faith," because she thought it would be a testament to the time they lived in.[35]

In this year there was a cholera scare in Paris, and Claire fled with her son to Spain, followed by her mother. They spent two months at Biarritz in a fisherman's house isolated on a promontory by the sea. Biarritz was in full season, and the imperial couple was in residence. Louis-Napoléon seems to have visited them. To get away, Marie took trips to parts of Spain. But she hated the country, with its exaggerated Catholicism and its bullfighting. When the empress's mother visited, a bullfight was held in her honor. Marie attended out of curiosity and abhorred it. "Six bulls were killed and as many horses, or almost as many, disemboweled. I found this spectacle disgusting and monotonous. I thought I would feel here something of that attractiveness, of that depraved curiousity that Saint Augustine has painted for us so well, but I remained stupified and indignant."[36] She was grateful that the French had never taken up the sport.

This same year Marie decided to try her hand again in the education of Blandine and Cosima. Through the original mediator, Théophile Ferrière, she sent Madame Patersi a memo on her requirements for the girls, then eighteen and sixteen years old. She also claimed the right to see them. Liszt could hardly ignore the cultural advantages that Marie could offer his daughters, but he set unpleasant conditions. Madame Patersi, the governess, was to be invited and received by Marie alone first. Liszt warned Marie that she had better get along with the governess, who would have sole responsibility for the children. Nothing would prevent Marie from visiting the girls at any time of day she judged proper. But Liszt presumed that such visits, at either home, would include Madame Patersi. If, on exceptional occasions, she wished to see the children without the governess, she must go to the apartment and pick up them up herself, not send anyone for them. Liszt also told Marie that he intended a dowry of one hundred thousand francs for each daughter. Marie indicated that she had kept aside enough money from her heritage to promise eighty thousand francs for each.

A letter from Blandine to her father in November 1854 seems to be the answer to his letter informing them of the conditions and of the dowry arrangements. After expressing the joy of the sisters at the expectation of seeing their mother, she asked her father to think well enough of them to know that no idea of material interest could be connected with such happiness. As for her marriage, she was not concerned with it and did not think that several francs more or less would contribute to her happiness.[37] It would seem that Liszt had put it to the girls that he was allowing the relationship with their mother so that they could get a dowry from her.

Liszt, whom Marie referred to in her diary as "the great shadow," had insisted that Marie must render the governess the respect that a woman of her age and position warranted. It is not at all clear that Marie followed this direction or that she included the governess in all the activities she undertook with her daughters. A letter from Blandine to her father early in 1855 reported that they had been to see *Il Trovatore* after dinner at their mother's; they seem to have been prepared for the opera by one of her musician friends. Marie had delivered herself of negative views on Verdi that amused them: "detestable, and good only to make the bears in the zoo dance." Another day their mother had taken them to lunch and discussed with them the poem "Tannhauser," which she found superb. She asked them what they read and promised to get them a particular history of architecture. Marie also took them on visits to the Louvre. When she brought them to Sainte Chapelle, she lent them a brochure about its history.

Daniel seems to have been included on that day, probably on vacation from the lycée. Marie asked him a lot about his studies and was delighted that he did so well in science, as that indicated a good brain. "We then discussed the universality of genius, which is not confined to any one area," Blandine wrote. Marie also seems to have included Madame Patersi in an outing to see the *Barber of Seville* ("Badly done, but amusing," Blandine judged. Was it her own opinion?) On another occasion, Marie gave theater tickets to the girls and presumably the governess, for she herself could not attend. In March Blandine wrote that they had dined at their mother's, with only her and Claire. "She read us the Prometheus of Aeschylus, in which we were keenly interested." At another dinner Marie discussed architecture, showed them pictures of Chartres and Rheims cathedrals, which they then compared to the architecture of the Arles cathedral. She also visited the girls and heard Cosima play in a Schubert trio, which delighted her.

Blandine also played the piano in her mother's salon, to the plaudits of those present. Her letters to her father reveal a heady social life in which the girls, along with Claire, were now involved through their mother:

Tuesday evening at mother's—many people, including General Czetteritz, whom we had met before. I played chess with him. Also Monsieur Ratisbonne, who writes in the *Journal des Débats* and is translating Dante into verse; also Renan; and the Baron de Penhoën, who was quite anxious to meet us. Long discussion of a prose translation of Lamennais. Next Sunday we go to the Assyrian museum. Mother gave us some books to look over to prepare us. We are now launched on the divine Plato, have read the Crito, the Apology of Socrates, and the Euthyphron, with the comments of Cousin which are very well done. We have also read Sophocles; besides Oedipus the King and Oedipus at Colonna, we are now doing Antigone.

Another letter read: "Visited mother recently. Renan there, spoke of things he knows so perfectly, a very interesting conversation. Also J. Simon. Discussion of new play on which much said pro et contra, as always. We are launched on reading Maistre and Bossuet. Mother leaving Tuesday, we'll have plenty of time."[38] In this letter, however, Blandine expressed alarm that they had not heard from their father for such a long time. The girls were happy, however, to be immersed in a culture that was not only French but cosmopolitan. Daniel Manin, in 1849 head of the short-lived Venetian Republic, instructed them in Dante. For a while, their life was like a dream.

In her memoirs Marie described the Maison Rose "animated by a flowering of youth" seated at the piano and the easel, singing and laughing in charming groups, "a lovely young woman with her child, arms and legs uncovered, rolling on the floor or sleeping on velvet cushions, two gold and white girls with blue eyes, their adolescent brother, with pensive brow." She described it as a marvelous accord of intelligence and love, "a springtime, a dream of maternity."[39] This experience of having all her children—Claire, Blandine, Cosima, Daniel—and her grandchild all together was hers for less than a year, from late 1854 through mid-1855.

For "the great shadow" was clearly not enjoying the excited news from Paris. Whether Liszt had complaints about Marie's meeting the conditions he laid down or just wanted to put an end to the pleasure the girls were having in their mother's company is not clear. In any case, he decided that the girls would make an extended visit to Germany. Blandine's next letter was intended to soothe, expressing her need for him only and how happy she would be under the same roof as her father. She even seemed to be critical of her mother, referring to her as Daniel Stern and using the male "he." But Liszt did not intend to bring the girls to Weimar, where he was Kappelmeister and was living with Sayn-Wittgenstein. They were to go to Berlin, where the mother of his favorite pupil, Hans von Bülow, would take care of them. Liszt seems to have felt that he could marry the girls in Germany without a dowry.

Marie was on another visit to Holland when she heard the news by a letter from Blandine. "Each time I begin to breathe a little, a new blow of the hammer knocks me down," she wrote to Claire.[40] The girls first visited Weimar with Daniel and then were shipped off to Berlin. Meanwhile, Madame Patersi forwarded to Sayn-Wittgenstein, who gave them to Liszt, three letters that their mother had sent the girls after learning of their departure. Marie had assumed, with horror, that Liszt was bringing the girls to live with him and the princess, and she delivered herself of strong opinions on such a situation:

I received your letter. I remain so upset that I can say nothing. He waited until I was absent, my children, to have you do something against honor. . . . I make no appeal to your affection. I have never doubted it. But your youth, your inexperience, your blindness frightens me. You will be brought, unawares, to do things unworthy of you. Both of you know how to comport yourselves so that the person who betrays and oppressses and dishonors you will herself want to see you far removed from her. The rest is up to me. I am yours in heaven and earth and you are mine. Oh! my noble children, remain forever proud![41]

Actually, Sayn-Wittgenstein had not been present when the girls arrived to visit Liszt. But once they were there, their father found them time consuming; they took up too much of his day. Besides, as he told a friend, the children took after both sides at once—but too much after their mother for his taste. By the time Liszt received Marie's letters to the children, they were already shipped off to Berlin. Liszt wrote them angry letters:

From your birth to this day your mother has not concerned herself in the least about the *bread* you eat, about the *place* you live in, etc. Although she has always tranquilly enjoyed a fairly considerable income, she has seen fit to spend it on her personal pleasure, and to leave me, for nineteen years, the *entire* and *exclusive* burden of providing for your needs as well as for all the expenses of your education. . . . Since she wishes me harm . . . she takes pleasure in attacking me in your affection, and in the respect and profound love I retain, as the purest passion of my life, for a woman who should be *holy* to you too in view of the devotion she has so nobly shown me for nine years, through incessantly renewed trials, sacrifices and sorrows."[42]

He also sent selected portions of Marie's letter on to the girls with his comments. He admitted that Daniel, still with him, had at first declared Madame Patersi's "espionage" as disgusting police methods. But he argued with the contents of the letters. He had planned their visit to Weimar and move to Berlin for a long time and had not waited until their mother left town. He would never fight for the affection of his children. "If in the last analysis you think that your affections should be equally divided between the parent who fulfilled his duties with conscience and devotion and the one who forgot hers, I will have no objection to your making whatever choice you wish when you are grown up."[43] Even now, if they insisted, he would let them live in their dream world, because it was too discouraging for him to discuss such a ridiculous letter. The girls, although accepting their father's decision, agreed with Daniel about Madame Patersi's betrayal of the letters.

As for Daniel, who returned alone to school in Paris, he had been the child of a disintegrating love affair and abandoned by both parents. Nevertheless, sensitive and precociously mature, he felt the ambivalence between being faithful to his father and yielding to the charm of his mother. Although he chose Liszt, he felt strongly about the bad blood between his parents and even called openly for their reconciliation. Only sixteen, he wrote to Liszt that it was difficult to resolve his respect for Sayn-Wittgenstein and his love for his mother. He pointed out that the princess really disliked Marie. Could he be an intimate of someone who would harm his mother?[44] There is no evidence that Marie was ever aware of her son's inner conflict.

Although she agreed that the girls could complete their education in Berlin and find good husbands who might marry them without a dowry, Marie wrote to Claire that she had an extreme need to repeat this to herself constantly, "since my soul is bitterly sad, and I see no great justice in the arrangements of Providence."[45] So Marie fell back on Daniel Stern and the solace of work, particularly her history of the Dutch Republic.

Eleven ⟿ *"I love politics.*
It is for me the greatest
of the arts: architecture
with the building blocks
of knowledge."

Originally, the salons of the Comtesse d'Agoult had somewhat resembled those of the seventeenth century. Attracting knowledgeable men and encouraging conversation among them was one of the ways that women, shut out of the education provided to men, acquired knowledge in their own homes. Certainly, from the time she was living in Geneva, Marie had learned from educated men and proceeded to read the books they recommended to her. Adolphe Pictet, in his memoirs of that time, wrote: "Cleverer and more feminine than Madame de Staël, the Comtesse d'Agoult gathered her acquaintances for her own instruction rather than trying to teach them. Thus she never lacked professors."[1] Back in Paris, she had continued this practice; she had also used the writers, educators, and critics she attracted to help her sharpen her writing skills. The faithful Ronchaud read every word she wrote. Sainte-Beuve served for some years as her editor; the poet Lacaussade was as much an editor as a secretary. And Girardin gave her important lessons in both journalism and politics.

During the Second Empire Daniel Stern came into her own as a *salonnière*. The description of a salon by one contemporary observer was of "an intimate meeting place, lasting over the years, where people know and seek each other and have reason to be glad to meet one another." The *salonnière* was the link among those invited. Relationships were established quickly, and the exchange of ideas determined the value of each participant. But "the veritable king of these kinds of republics is wit." In the most successful salons, wit, often provoked and quickly multiplied, was the lingua franca of the gathering.[2]

In the early 1840s the countess's salon emphasized the literary, which was traditional for salons. A reading of a play by Ronchaud in the Romantic mode was given there before a sizeable audience in 1842. Victor Hugo then commented. Ferdinand Denis noted, "The real drama came after the play. Victor Hugo spouted theory. I only remember these words from the oracle: *"émouvir les chiffoniers."* The following year the actor Beauvallet read from François Ponsard's *Lucrèce*, written in the classical mode toward which Stern was returning, to an audience including Lamartine, Eckstein, and Sainte-Beuve. There was always intellectual discussion as well. Denis, who frequented her soirées regularly at the time, declared that "the spirit of the eighteenth century flourished in the Countess' salon in the form of lively and pleasant witticisms."[3]

Eighteenth-century salons had changed focus, from the literary to the political, as the Revolution drew near. That of the Comtesse d'Agoult had done so as a new revolution threatened in the late 1840s and as she developed a taste for politics. It has been said that the eighteenth-century *salonnière* could serve an important and constructive role because she lacked the competitive spirit resulting from the education in dialectic and rhetoric that males received. The function of the *salonnière* was to restrain such tendencies, "suppressing her own ego in order to manage that of others." She thus created a setting for the peaceful exchange of ideas necessary to the evolution of new political forms.[4] Stern had served a similar role in 1847–48, creating in her salon a center where political dialogue thrived, where Lamartine and Lamennais could be brought together to discuss—and disagree on—a new constitution.

News of Louis-Napoléon's coup in December 1851 frightened Stern, for she knew the change in regime would affect her republican friends. As the president transformed himself into Napoléon III, many republicans, unwilling to take the required loyalty oath to the emperor, were forced to give up their positions in government and the university and even to go into exile. Stern wrote to Claire that she herself thought of "passing over mountains and seas to be able to write freely."[5] But she did not do so. Instead, she completed her history of 1848, putting out the third volume as the government reached its most repressive stage. Automatically in opposition to the Second Empire, she extended her salon to embrace republicans of all stripes and to become a center of political dialogue. She referred to it as the "Abbaye-aux-Bois of democracy."[6]

Stern's preference was for elliptical formulations that hid a profound subtext, perhaps because the entire salon might be considered subversive. Reclining on her divan or leaning back in an armchair of red velour, she listened more often than she talked. Probing for people's opinions, she questioned them rather than discussing. When the conversation took a turn that did not interest her, she never interrupted but let her thoughts wander. Never encouraging a unity of views, Stern occasionally came out with something maladroit, exasperating those who did not know her well. Those who disliked her thought she struck poses; among some she never completely lost that reputation.[7]

Her guests were not homogeneous; although most were from political circles, there were still a great number from the arts. Emile Ollivier recorded in his diary in 1853 that he had stopped in at the Maison Rose and found a circle of republicans expressing "sadness and dissatisfaction about present conditions, fear rather than hope of the future."[8] He was to play an important role in the future, both of the nation and of his hostess's family.

It was a family again split. After rejoicing in their presence for a time, Marie once more lost Blandine and Cosima to their father's control in 1855. Liszt accorded his daughters a short (only three-week) visit in Weimar and then shipped them off to the home of his young pupil, Hans von Bülow. It took the girls a while to recover from their exile to Berlin, which they rightly connected with Princess Sayn-Wittgenstein. The line taken by Liszt under her influence was that while he was expected to provide for the girls, Marie, purely for the adornment of her salon, wanted to take over their lives without really caring for them. It was to him that they owed their allegiance and their affection. Although Cosima continued to write to the princess's daughter, Blandine grew cooler to Liszt's other family. Nevertheless, both girls obeyed their father and never stopped adoring him from afar. Marie wrote angry letters to Berlin that Cosima answered in the same vein. Nevertheless, Marie showered the girls with gifts, including hats, umbrellas, books, and articles on Semitic languages.

What was happening in Berlin was that Cosima, only seventeen, was falling in love with Hans von Bülow. Within two months of her arrival in the household, the two were engaged. Hans was nervous and depressive, which seemed to arouse Cosima's protective instincts. She herself, according to her mother's description, was prone to ecstasy and depression. Because Hans was his favored pupil, Liszt was not averse to the marriage and asked only that the couple wait for a year. In this period Cosima was victim of both her fiancé's emotional problems and the overbearing nature of her future mother-in-law. She declared her impatience in a letter to "Magnolet," adding that, after all, she had "not yet become engaged to Hans' mother!"[9]

Marie probably learned of the engagement from Daniel, who had returned to school in Paris. It may have been on this return that the only surviving informal note from son to mother was written. The most surprising thing about it is that, alone among the children, he used the intimate *tu* instead of the more formal *vous*. The use of the nickname is not unusual; it was a family custom to use nicknames: "My dear Mimi, I remember very well the face you made last year because I went to Madame Patersi's before calling on you. This time I will be at the Avenue Sainte-Marie [her house] Saturday at six thirty A.M. . . . [There follows a gloss on a nursery rhyme about opening the door because his candle is not out but still lit.] Adieu dear Mimi (I have prepared answers to all the questions you will address to me and I hope to be *Clear* [his nickname]). Your son." Marie was proud of her Daniel, who distinguished himself at school, but she confessed to Ronchaud that in mind and character he was as much a stranger to her as "the presumptive heir of the celestial empire."[10]

Maintaining that Cosima was not in good mental or physical health, which was probably true, Marie immediately opposed her engagement with Hans, declaring that such a union, born simply of propinquity, would bring happiness to neither party. That the marriage would put Cosima permanently in Liszt's circle was also a factor in Marie's disapproval, which she voiced in letters to Berlin. Although not as fond of Cosima as of Blandine, Marie had always believed the younger to be more intelligent and more musically endowed; she held out the idea of a musical career for her rather than marriage. Cosima continued to respond to these letters by merely inviting her mother to come to Berlin and meet Hans. Furious, Marie insisted that she not write again. Cosima continued writing. She was coming into her own as a determined young woman.

Marie still had one daughter in Paris and a grandson. Claire continued to develop her talent for art and writing. Her pencil portrait of her mother was engraved by Leopold Flameng and distributed to friends. Marie helped her to publish under the name C. de Sault (a territory near Carpentras that had belonged to the Agoult family). Extremely proud of her, she called her daughter, baptized Claire-Christine, "Christin," thus providing her, also a superior woman, with a male name. C. de Sault would make her debut in *La Presse* in October 1856 (on Saxony and its monuments). As she was setting off to Dresden in the spring of that year, Marie asked her to drop in and see her sisters in Berlin. She was hoping that Claire, whose own marriage was unhappy, could convince Cosima not to marry precipitously.

The visit had a negative effect. Blandine wrote to her father that Madame de Charnacé had arrived like an aide-de-camp to the general back in Paris. The two girls had told Claire that they would accept no intermediaries between them and their mother who, if she wanted to convey something to them, should come to Berlin.[11] (Blandine seems to have learned that reporting mainly negative things about Marie to her father was pleasing to him. Most letters from this point on tend to be negative.) While refusing to go to Berlin, Marie declared herself ready to take complete charge of Cosima in Paris and help her regain her equilibrium. As she told Claire, she was trying to avoid being seen either as a mother who didn't care or as a mother who didn't count.

At Easter Daniel received Liszt's permission to spend the vacation with the girls in Berlin as long as he didn't come to Weimar(!), but the son was able to get around his father and spend a few days with him.[12] As for his sisters, they longed in vain to visit their father. While he was in Hungary and Hans was taking a cure in Baden, Blandine and Cosima made plans to visit their mother and grandmother in Paris. Liszt was enraged. But he relented enough to give them a sojourn in Weimar, after which he was glad to see them go, even to Paris. The girls never admitted in writing that they resented his attitude toward them. Blandine's letters always expressed not only the obedience he demanded but the adoration he also accepted as his due. Upon her arrival in Paris Blandine wrote about "the emptiness we feel around us since we can no longer see you, no longer hear your sacred voice speaking holy and venerated words, no longer say: this is the air he breathes, the atmosphere he fills, the space he brings to life."[13] For some reason, Marie had not and never did receive the girls' letter from Weimar, so she had not expected them. Was the letter deliberately not mailed by someone, in the hope that their mother would be absent when they arrived?

Marie was happy to see her daughters and told them she had suffered from the separation; she hoped they would come often from their grandmother's, where they stayed. The next day at lunch, however, she took Blandine aside to complain that they had ignored her and that Hans had not even written her. She asked Blandine if Cosima really loved him. Blandine said yes, and she was determined to marry him. Marie replied that she could understand it all but that she could not pardon Cosima for acting without her consent. The next day she said as much to Cosima, adding that it was ridiculous for her to think of marriage. Cosima was immovable, insisting that she loved Hans and that she had not come to Paris to talk about it. The three went out together; Blandine reported that their mother had showed them great affection, declaring that she hoped they would end by understanding one another. Marie proposed that the three of them pass several days at Fontainebleau the following year, which pleased the girls.

Blandine and Cosima arrived in Paris in time to witness the scholarly triumphs of their brother, who had always won the prizes in Latin and was being feted as the top baccalaureat student in rhetoric of all Paris. This meant dinner with the archbishop, reviewing the Garde Nationale, and other great moments, which Blandine reported with enthusiasm to their father. At the Maison Rose, the girls celebrated their brother by playing Beethoven, which was also a success. Marie then whisked Cosima off for a four-day visit to Compiègne to try to convince her not to marry yet. It was all in vain. Marie had to give in to Cosima, who planned to leave at the end of the month to meet Hans in Berlin. But she begged Blandine to stay longer at her grandmother's, so that she could spend time with her. Blandine reported to her father that she and Cosima found it so difficult to think of separating; what did he think?

Liszt wrote from Baden, where he was now taking a cure, that he did not object to whatever plans the girls made. But he did not want Blandine to stay with her grandmother. (For reasons he indicated he had told her verbally.) Her mother should keep her instead. We do not know what his reasons were, but a month later Blandine was still at her grandmother's, waiting for her mother to make arrangements for her. In November Liszt expressed his anger and set January 1 as the final date on which she must move. Blandine began to resent the pressure from Liszt as well as the failure of her mother to provide for her. She reported that her mother could not keep her, that all convents or pensions seemed less proper than her grandmother's apartment. Although there were families who would invite her, it would look odd if she lodged with strangers, aside from the pain it would cause her. "On the other hand," she wrote, "I have now received offers [of marriage] from two honorable persons," so she didn't want to leave Paris now. "If when you come to Paris, you find my staying at Grandmother's not proper, I will do whatever you counsel me to do."[14] Although Liszt replied with another angry letter, Blandine stayed at her grandmother's well into April, when she seems to have settled down for a short period with her mother.

One may perhaps explain this tug-of-war between the two parents in terms of money. Liszt was not known for paying his bills. Later, when her sick grandmother was living with a married Blandine, the daugher had to remind her father what that cost the young couple. Part of Liszt's insistence on Blandine's living with her mother may have been an attempt to make Marie underwrite the costs of launching a young lady in Paris. Marie, on the other hand, while willing to spend for clothes and culture, was not going to take over Blandine's support. Even though she did not yield to Liszt, her financial situation was deteriorating. Guy de Charnacé had made a big hole in her fortune, as had reestablishing Claire and her grandson. Her capital had been badly invested and had lost value. The Comte d'Agoult, living on a military pension, needed and received her financial help. And worse, she was losing the Maison Rose, on which she had spent a great deal. In 1856 Baron Haussmann, remaking the center of Paris, began tearing down the entire neighborhood of the Arc de Triomphe. Unfortunately, Blandine's resentment of her situation between two parents resulted in Marie's receiving more of the blame.

However, when Daniel Stern published both her plays—*Trois journées de Marie Stuart* and *Jeanne d'Arc*—in the *Revue de Paris* in July and September, Blandine was impressed enough to inform her father about it. Stern was also working on a new edition of *Esquisses morales,* which appeared in 1857 with the subtitle *Pensées, réflections et maxims. Jeanne d'Arc* received two readings in the Maison Rose, the second by the famous actor Bocage. Many of Stern's political friends were there, including the historian Michelet, Jules Simon, Henri Martin, and Ollivier. When it was published in book form, it did not sell. But it gained her the recognition of someone whom she had only ocasionally been able to lure to her salon, who belonged to that of Sand. Victor Hugo, who never thought of her as a real author,[15] wrote, "I have just received and read your Joan of Arc. I write you my feelings. You have created a great work. The poetry of woman traverses the history of man. . . . It is beautiful, it is right that this great drama be written by a woman."[16] *Jacques Coeur*, Stern's third play, of which no copies survive, was read by the Comédie-Française in 1858 and accepted, if certain corrections were made. Stern did not make them.

Blandine's social life in her mother's salon must have been intoxicating. She was a beauty, a tall, willowy blonde like her mother, with her mother's complexion but a nose like her father's. Alfred Darimon, a leading republican who frequented the salon, wrote, "I have never seen so much grace together with so much simplicity. She is at the same time an excellent musician like her father and a woman of high intelligence like her mother." Vigny also found her "tall and lovely, blond like her father and mother, with a Germanic quality, intelligent, energetic and candid at the same time."[17] It was clearly the time to arrange a marriage for Blandine, who was twenty-two and beautiful but born out of wedlock. Marie planned a setting in which a suitable if not brilliant solution could be found.

One of the great discussions taking place in the countess's salon in the 1856–57 season was whether republicans, in order to take part in politics, should run for the legislature and, if they won, take the loyalty oath to the emperor. A list of potential candidates was drawn up by the editors of republican periodicals who frequented the salon. Of these, five were elected to the Chamber in 1857, including Emile Ollivier. Stern had already marked the young man as a potential success, for his role in the 1848 revolution in Marseilles and his brilliance as a lawyer in Paris, where he had come to make his way. She had dubbed him "Tree of Judah," a nickname of intimacy and favor. His father, exiled for his role in the revolution, was living in Nice, then part of Italy; the son planned to visit him there during the summer. Marie, about to leave Paris with Blandine, arranged to meet Ollivier along the way.

For the final months, Claire rented out the Maison Rose to a Russian noble, who took most of the furnishings when he departed. With the money she received for the property Marie later bought a plot of land nearby to build on, but she never managed to do so. Later, in *Dante et Goethe,* Marie wrote of her many conversations about Dante and Italy in the Maison Rose, "that house which was so dear to me and in which were concentrated joys today dispersed to all the winds of fortune and death. I search in vain for a trace of it." It was razed by the zeal of "the embellishers of Paris" and yielded to "the straight and implacable line of a noisy and dusty boulevard,"[18] which is today the most famous street in Paris—the Champs Elysées.

She and Blandine set out for Switzerland in June. At this point Marie had not decided where to settle on her return; her home would be gone by then. Mother and daughter went first to Divonne, accompanied by Ronchaud, Ponsard, Eckstein, and Girardin (newly married to a young woman after Delphine's death). There Blandine entered into an amateur theater group. Marie was visited by the Swiss Henri-Frédéric Amiel, who had written a rave review of her *Esquisses morales* in the *Bibliothèque universelle de Genève.* They discussed Goethe, Renan, and Michelet. Amiel noted in his celebrated *Journal* that Stern was as he had expected—aristocratic, svelte, and dignified, her white hair in long bandeaux, "blue eyes with long lashes, a pensive brow, an aquiline profile, a meditative and tranquil expression, but an unhappy mouth." She was, he thought, a representation of her life: "elegance, audacity, regret, and profound thought."[19]

After five weeks, mother and daughter moved on to the Hotel Byron on Lake Leman, a most romantic spot, where they were joined by Ollivier. Having been elected to the Chamber of Deputies, he held a long discussion with Stern on whether he should take the oath or resign his seat. She agreed that although it was a compromise, it was sensible to take the oath and be a republican presence in the government. But all was not politics in this meeting. Ollivier had undoubtedly met Blandine many times. In this romantic setting he found her even more desirable than in Paris, particularly in those magic moments of the evening when she played Beethoven. The three moved on to Como, where Marie could remember her own romance and Cosima's birth, and then on to Florence via Milan and Genoa.

In Switzerland Blandine lost contact with her sister; Cosima and Hans had been married on the nineteenth of August. Liszt never did give his final permission for the marriage, saying he was worried about Hans's depressions. Clearly, he was not prepared to sign a marriage contract obliging him to pay a dowry. However, after receiving a letter from her future son-in-law, Marie accepted the match. Who knows, she wrote to Claire, this marriage may succeed against all predictions. She had Blandine choose a modest but tasteful trousseau and send it to her sister. When the two finally married, it was in the Catholic rite to suit Liszt, although Hans was a Protestant. The couple left for Switzerland to join Marie and Blandine but missed them because Hans's papers were not in order. Instead, they visited with Wagner in Zurich.[20] Hans became ill, and the two returned to Berlin without joining the family.

Meanwhile, Blandine, Marie, and Ollivier were met in Florence by Ollivier's father Demosthène, nicknamed "the River" for his flowing beard. Ollivier proposed marriage on September 12; Blandine consented in Italian verse. She had written to her father at Aix-la-Chapelle, where he was taking a cure, asking the whereabouts of her sister and brother. Two weeks later she had not heard from him but wrote that she had Cosima's address. She also told him that they had traveled with Ollivier and that although she never thought she would find anyone to match her father, she was in love. She asked him to bless their union.[21] Liszt wrote back with questions. What was her mother's attitude to the marriage? What about his family and financial arrangements? Perhaps Ollivier should come to Weimar to see him.

Blandine replied that Emile was a native of Marseilles, thirty-two years old, with three brothers and a married sister. Her mother was satisfied, as was Emile's father, and they hoped to marry in Italy to avoid the expense of a Paris wedding. But Emile, a lawyer, had a case pending in Paris, which gave them only a month. It could be be arranged if Liszt consented. Ollivier went off to Weimar. Marie had promised the couple forty thousand francs and a trousseau. Ollivier returned properly impressed with his future father-in-law but somewhat disturbed about Liszt's refusal to make a marriage contract. In effect, this meant no dowry; Liszt sent them about five thousand francs for expenses. Blandine, who intended to celebrate her marriage on her father's birthday, was disappointed that he would not attend.[22]

Marie, who had made all this possible, began to behave irrationally. As soon as her daughter and Ollivier became a couple, without her participation, she seemed to try to set them at odds with each other. As they drew away from her, she tried to separate them, for example, by discussions of religion. (Blandine was Catholic; Ollivier, deist). Ollivier wrote in his diary, "The conduct of Madame d'Agoult is becoming incomprehensible. She viewed my marriage with pleasure as long as she believed that it was for her an instrument of domination. Since she sees that it cannot be, she is becoming cold, restrained, almost an enemy."[23] Two days before the wedding, Marie wrote to Claire that the marriage was off, even though it was not.

What can explain Marie's behavior? It is possible that Ollivier was right—that Marie wanted to live the couple's life or at least control it. But, more likely, her spleen had risen because Liszt had refused to promise the couple any money, whereas Marie, faithful to their agreement, had contracted for forty thousand francs that she could ill afford. This was even more wounding when Blandine insisted on marrying on Liszt's birthday, despite her mother's protests.

Nevertheless, Marie participated in the evening candlelight wedding in the Florence cathedral, on the arm of Ollivier. Demosthène took Blandine down the aisle. Marie described it to a mystified Claire as "truly lovely." She wrote also to Emma Herwegh that same day: "I greatly love and esteem Emile Ollivier."[24] The Olliviers left to meet Cosima and Hans in Berlin; Blandine stayed with her sister when Emile had to return to Paris for his case (which helped make even more of a name for him). But even before Blandine returned to Paris, there was unpleasantness about the dowry, which Marie could not pay.

Now Marie seemed to be cut off from her children. She had wanted to gain entrance for the brilliant Daniel to the Ecole Polytechnique, where his future in France would be assured. (Even though the elite school did not take foreigners, she tried to pull strings to gain him entrance, sure that the school would take the year's top student.) Liszt had other ideas that would lead his son away from France. Daniel, pondering his future, thought for a time of going into the church. But in the end, he gave in to his father and entered law school in Vienna. Marie complained to her friends that Liszt wanted to make an Austrian of him (presumably because Liszt, a Hungarian, belonged to the Austrian Empire). Early in 1859 Daniel asked Blandine in a letter: "What has become of Mimi? Do you see her often?" He avowed that he had not written his mother for two years. "You will ask me what she has done to deserve that? I am embroiled with her in my mind . . . a complete mental block." Was Blandine also detached from her mother? Daniel would not be surprised: "She is too worthy (deserving) to be worthy of us. We are all three of us too good for her. We get that from Papa."[25]

At the end of the year Daniel arrived in Berlin to spend Christmas vacation with Cosima. He was seriously ill and coughing. Cosima tended him and demanded that Liszt come. For once Liszt did, despite his hatred of sickness, but returned immediately to Weimar. Marie, in Nice for the winter and ill, did not go to Berlin. Finally, when the doctor said only a miracle could save Daniel, Cosima notified Princess Sayn-Wittgenstein, who insisted Liszt go to Berlin. Two days later, Daniel died of tuberculosis. Marie notified her friends that her son, whom she had described as "a force, calm, magnificently organized," was dead. "The sweetness of his big eyes, the serenity of his face, the tenderness of his smile cannot be described,"[26] she wrote. But he had been from the beginning the child of bitter unhappiness, never of joy.

In Nice, relations with the Olliviers were growing worse as Demosthène demanded the dowry promised; so far, Marie had been able to pay only interest on the forty thousand francs. The Ollivier family was in financial straits, and he had counted on the money. Clearly, he thought Marie was a great lady and had more resources than she did. Marie never intended to go back on her word, but she had to have her husband's permission to release the funds. She consulted her friend Jules Grévy (later president of the Third Republic), who felt she had a right to demand how the money would be used. In Paris, Blandine and Claire exchanged heated words. Marie finally got her husband to agree to her taking the eighty thousand francs she had reserved for the girls from the settlement and notified Ollivier that he would have the money the following February. This did not prevent a new fight between Claire and Blandine.

When she returned to Paris at the end of the year, Marie moved into Claire's apartment in the rue de Courcelles, where she set out to publicize Claire's talents and place her articles on art criticism. Blandine, from her new home in Paris, wrote to her father, "Now that she sees that neither one of us [Cosima nor herself] wants to serve as the pedestal to her maternal statue, she poses with Claire, and in recompense for her good will, flatters her and goes on ceaselessly about her genius and true goodness. . . . Vanity of vanities."[27] Blandine knew that she had been her mother's favorite; she was afflicted with anger at Marie and jealousy of Claire. After much pressure, Marie managed to pay Ollivier the dowry; he bought property at Saint-Tropez and the Chateau des Salins nearby. This property, rounded out later, became the Domaine de la Moutte, which his descendants have tried to conserve by creating a foundation there.[28]

Cosima's husband, Hans, on the other hand, was attracted to Marie. He was impressed by her works and fascinated by her relationship with and physical resemblance to Liszt, whom he worshipped. Marie recorded in her diary that this marriage might at least make a transition for Cosima to something else. (What she meant is unclear, but Cosima did not receive her dowry at this time or in her mother's lifetime, although she did later have access to the interest. The principal was left her in her mother's will as a debt of honor.) Concentrating on this member of the family, Marie was on the platform when Cosima arrived in Paris the following spring; so was Blandine. Each was determined to take her home. Cosima finally gave in to her mother, to Blandine's fury. But Marie could never really separate the two girls and only lost by such means. Thus, even after the financial settlement was paid, the bitterness of the favored daughter remained. As it turned out, Blandine never saw her mother again.

At the end of 1858 Marie took an apartment next to the land she had bought, at 15 avenue de l'Impératrice (now avenue Foch). She called it "my slum" but reopened her salon nevertheless. Alfred Darimon, one of "the five" elected republicans and a frequenter of both the Stern and Ollivier salons, noted that Blandine arranged the furniture the same way her mother did—no chairs, only velvet couches along the walls, with a piano before the window. But he complained that Blandine no longer played the piano. "Too bad, for that charming young woman was a born virtuoso." He also felt that she no longer showed her former gaiety, that she effaced herself in her husband's presence, never speaking but seeming to drink in his words. He found himself wishing she had spoken more and put some idealism into the young men of the time, who thought only of success.[29]

During this period, while Marie was having difficulties with home and family, Daniel Stern remained busy. The second (1856) edition of her *Esquisses morales,* unlike the first, which took eight years to sell, sold out almost immediately. A third edition appeared in 1859. Stern was also involved in politics through the visitors to her salon. She welcomed the new young writers and republicans, some of whom created a kind of Stern cult, based on her history of the 1848 revolution and her *Essai sur la liberté.* The second edition of the latter, published in 1863, was dedicated to them. Stern always supported the young, hoping for a better generation of republicans than those who had lost the Second Republic. She wrote to Herwegh in 1857, "May this generation not be as ours, prey to chimeric ambitions, and to love of the impossible."[30]

Stern wanted to think of herself as a second Madame de Staël, the intellectual woman who opposed the first Napoléon and who revealed the culture and literature of Germany to the French. While she was still working on her history she had been preparing to write an article about Staël. The last *salonnière* of that circle was still alive. Marie acquired from Ballanche an introduction to the famous Madame de Récamier, but she came away disappointed with her visit. The former great beauty, mistress of Benjamin Constant, had become a conventional conformist of sixty-one who was primarily concerned about her respectability. Three weeks after the interview, Récamier died of cholera. Marie gave up the project of writing about Staël, whom she described in her notes as having to struggle against the mockery of eminent men and who triumphed "not as they said because she stopped being a woman, but because she was a woman of greater power and grandeur than the others."[31]

Marie felt that she was following in the same tradition by nurturing intellectual, literary, and political genius in the young and also by interpreting German culture to France. Thus she was happy to be present at the birth of a periodical, *Revue germanique,* that promised to accomplish both these ends. Two men were primarily responsible for the founding—Charles Dolfuss and Auguste Nefftzer. Both from an area of France that was partly German, these young Alsatians shared with Stern the desire for a rapprochement of the two countries. In 1856 she read Dolfuss's *Lettres philosophiques* and *Essais de philosophie sociale* and wrote to the author expressing her desire to know him better. She considered him a young genius whom she could help to develop and be recognized. He soon became strongly attached to her: "I bless the destiny that gave me such a travelling companion," he wrote, "but I bless it even more for the tenderness which you pour out on me. I need it; my mind lacked a mother, you will be the mother of my thought, and for me thought is very close to the heart."[32] She wrote to him as an intimate, as she had for many years to the poet Herwegh—particularly because Dolfuss shared with her that tendency to depression that became worse as she got older.

Through Dolfuss she came to know Nefftzer, an Alsatian journalist who had been jailed for his ideas. At the time editor-in-chief at *La Presse,* he had been influential in the election of "the five" republicans. Nefftzer was particularly interested in the history of religion. Stern admired his taste and judgment, and she discussed with him the whole range of religious issues of the century. Both were opposed to the power of church and papacy; Nefftzer was an ex-Protestant and a follower of the Young Hegelians, whom Stern had read and written about through the urging of Herwegh. In Germany the radical scholarly treatment of religion was the source of critical scholarship in history and radicalism in politics. It was this approach that the new periodical aimed to introduce to the French. As Stern wrote to Herwegh, the time was ripe for the work of Madame de Staël. He should look for books to translate and articles to write for the new review.

Two other friends of Stern collaborated in the founding of the *Revue germanique.* One was Emile Littré, disciple of the positivist philosopher Auguste Comte but actually an expander of the positivist doctrine to fit the new republicanism. Stern had attended Comte's lectures in 1847 and met Littré that year. He told her that Comte would like to know her, but there is no indication that the two ever met. In 1848 Littré was editor of *Le National,* and Stern applied to him for information while writing her history. The two shared a hostility to Louis-Napoléon, an appetite for knowledge, and the ability to make up for lack of genius with hard work. Stern asked him to help her educate herself in the sciences. He set her to work on the program of Comte, taking the sciences in their proper order, from mathematics through astronomy, physics, biology, psychology, and ending with sociology.

Littré had also translated the works of the Young Hegelian David Friedrich Strauss, who wrote the first modern biography of Jesus, picturing him as a man. Stern did not entirely agree with Littré on his view of Jesus or on positivism. She took from positivism the formula of seeking laws, not causes. And she contributed to a fund to erect a statue of its founder, Comte, as well as to another fund for the support of his widow. As for Littré, he reviewed her history of 1848 with enthusiasm and responded to her plea for help on a work she intended to write on public education.[33] The only salon he was interested in attending was hers. This was probably just as well, since he cared nothing for his appearance and probably would have been unacceptable in most drawing rooms. He often visited at odd hours, carrying piles of books. Once when he appeared at Stern's apartment house thus encumbered, the concierge directed him to the service entrance. So much for the man who was the Daniel Webster of France, producing the first French dictionary!

Whereas Littré was Stern's senior, Renan was the youngest of the collaborators on the *Revue germanique.* Best known to us as the author of *La Vie de Jesus,* he was a young scholar of Semitic languages when Stern discovered him. She offered to have his first tome in philology reviewed, but he expressed distaste that it should be presented in a popular periodical. The poor young man then discovered that she had been planning to do the comment herself. He recovered by praising her new edition of the *Esquisses morales*, "so strong, so true, so profound," with reference to particular *pensées*. He spoke of the "grand manner" that characterized all her works, something that was becoming rare in their time.[34] Stern was fascinated with the brilliant young man, who became a regular at her salon. Both were interested in the history of religion and discussed an article Renan was writing on the American Unitarian William Ellery Channing.

In the first issue of the *Revue germanique*, on January 31, 1858, Renan published "Lettre aux directeurs," stating that they should present a complete tableau of the intellectual movement in Germany, beginning with the criticism of religion. This caused a scandal—not among Catholics and orthodox Protestants but among Protestant liberals and professors of the university (who had, of course, signed the oath). They accused the *Revue* of pantheism and of being too much influenced by English ideas and German materialism. Proudhon, a friend of Nefftzer, demanded that the editors defend themselves. One result of the scandal was that solid backing of the Institute, from the historian Hippolyte Taine, for instance, dissolved. This left the editors without a historian. Marie was to fill in by publishing pieces of her history of the Dutch republic in the periodical.

Although taken with Germanic culture, Stern was not interested in Germanizing French culture. As a result, she questioned the name of the periodical in a letter to Nefftzer, even before publication commenced. When Herwegh and his circle in Zurich, who were counted on to write for the periodical, warned against any German chauvinism in the *Revue*, Stern admitted that she agreed somewhat. "I combat to the end Germanic tendencies in my own family where I see them arise from time to time at the expense of taste and French good sense; however, in insisting above all on scientific works and on criticism, and in representing what Madame de Staël neglected, we can profit, we [French] who are much too disposed to consider ourselves as possessing the exclusive privilege of thinking and acting on the destinies of the world."[35] After the first dozen volumes, the name was changed to *Revue germanique et française*.

Cosima, encouraged by her mother, offered for publication her French adaptation of Friedrich Hebbel's *Maria Magdalena*. Unfortunately, her mother criticized her translation, and she had trouble with Dollfus and Nefftzer over corrections they made. That was the end of her writing for the periodical. But on his visit to Berlin she did introduce Nefftzer to the poet Gutzkow, the writer Varnhagen von Ense, and the critic Adolphe Stahr, all of them friends of her mother. Stern wanted the journal to underline the new role of German liberalism in Europe, through the vitality of Prussia.

Claire also contributed to the *Revue*. But she went on to publish much more in the new paper founded by Nefftzer, destined to become one of the great newspapers of France—*Le Temps*. By 1860 Nefftzer was predicting war between France and the new Germany coming into being—something that was unthinkable to Stern. He gave over the running of the *Revue* to Dolfuss, who doubled the issues with the idea of expanding it into a great liberal journal. But it was *Le Temps*, with an editor who favored constitutional monarchy over the republic, that actually became the great opposition newspaper of the Second Empire.

Stern began by supporting the program of the first issue in April 25, 1861. It preached the education of the masses as the answer to the dichotomy of liberty and equality. It supported the politics of the possible. It also preached cosmopolitanism and intellectual exchange. Nefftzer actually attributed the program of *Le Temps* to Stern. Nevertheless, the two disagreed on politics. He thought that constitutional monarchy was best for France at this time, although he was insulted when Stern accused him of supporting the Orléanists of the July Monarchy. He considered both Stern and her son-in-law Ollivier too radical. The argument continued over many articles Stern submitted on political subjects. However, she provided her daughter Claire to write on art, her former son-in-law Guy de Charnacé to write on horse-racing, and Louis Blanc to provide regular letters from London. Stern herself published a few long articles on literary figures and summaries of current musical, literary, or historical subjects.

Occasionally, disagreements between Nefftzer and Stern would lead her to threaten to separate from the periodical. But Nefftzer would insist that she could not do so just because of a difference in views. She continued to advise and aid *Le Temps*, although the distance in political outlook remained a problem. Stern also criticized the periodical's heavy Germanic style, which she said lacked *"électricité."* Thus, most of the publication of Stern's later years was in the *Revue germanique*. Dolfuss continued to seek her advice about the publication and to confide in her his hopes and fears. She was always supportive, although as she told Mazzini, she refused to be responsible for everything published in it. The name was changed to *Revue moderne* in 1865; it did not survive the Franco-Prussian War, which began in 1870.

Renan was also more politically conservative than Stern but remained a good friend. He encouraged her to pursue her Italian and Dutch works. She discussed with him his multivolume *Origines du Christianisme,* particularly the third volume, devoted to the apostle Paul, which she reviewed. She followed closely Renan's course at the Collège de France and the problems it brought him. Publication was suspended in 1862 because of Renan's insistence on providing the traditional scholarly apparatus for his analysis of the New Testament. After his *Vie de Jésus* was published in 1864, he was suspended from his post. The clergy was against him for his views on religion; the republicans opposed him for having held a post that required him to take the oath in the first place. Stern saw the importance of his work in opposition to an empire that rested on clericalism. But she had to disagree with Renan's article in the *Revue* in which he attacked the republicans and denied complete equality.

Stern, although in opposition to both the July Monarchy and the Empire, was not totally against constitutional monarchy. In the case of her beloved Italy, where her friends Mazzini and Manin had established republics in Rome and Venice during the 1848 revolution, she favored a united Italy under the constitutional rule of the king of Sardinia-Piedmont. Victor Emmanuel II had been a leader of the rebellion against Austria in those years. It had failed, but he had given the people under his rule a constitution. He had also appointed a prime minister whom Marie, informed by her friends in Italy, believed might be the hope of a new nation—Camillo Cavour.

While in Florence after Blandine's wedding, Stern had resumed her study of Italian art. She had also pondered the lack of a republic in Florence since the Renaissance and attributed it to the Medici rule. What would be necessary to arouse Florentine republicanism from its slumber? Not revolution, Stern insisted, but perhaps the example of the renewal that was taking place in Piedmont. Her "Fragments d'un voyage en Italie," sent back to Paris, were not published in 1857—because, she believed, they discussed republics and were written by the republican historian of 1848.

However, her friend Pascal Duprat published them in 1858 in *La Libre Recherche*. In this year it was revealed that Stern's vision of a united Italy was shared by her emperor: Louis-Napoléon had, when young, fought with his brother in the uprising against Austria of 1830, in which his brother had died. He agreed with Cavour that France would join Piedmont in fighting Austria but only if Austria attacked first. In 1859 Cavour was able to provoke Austria to do so and France was able to join Piedmont, soon backed by many northern Italian states, without the censure of the rest of Europe. At the same time, Mazzini and Garibaldi returned to Italy, landing with their followers in the south. They were determined to press through the Papal States and join all Italy. Louis-Napoléon, who had come to power with the aid of the Catholic Church, knew that he could not remain in this battle; besides, their victories had been won through luck, for the French army was weak and inefficient. He therefore withdrew, demanding Nice and Savoy from Piedmont to round out French borders.

Articles on Italy were now welcomed by French periodicals. Stern began a series, somewhat like those she had done in 1847 about Germany, to inform the French about Italian politics. Occasional "Lettres écrites d'Italie" ran in *Le Siècle* from late 1859 through 1860. In the first, she agreed that the forced retreat of the republicans from the south was politic. She recalled that her friend Manin had said to Victor Emmanuel: "Make Italy, and I am with you, *if not, not.*" Stern adopted this position, adding that if the legitimate desires of the constitutionalists went unfulfilled, revolution would break out again. "And the revolution in Italy is the revolution in Europe; who does not know that?" Only those countries with the mass of unorganized democrats on their side would win out.[36]

Stern was to return to pan-Europeanism in other "Lettres." "Europe wants peace, all civilized people want peace. . . . Under the triple inspiration of science, philosophy and faith, Europe considers itself more and more as a vast family and tends . . . to form . . . the United States of the European Republic." But first each state must belong to itself, establish its own peace and order. Thus it was in Europe's interest to "restore Italy to herself." She pointed to the establishment of constitutional government in northern Italy, whch avoided both reaction and revolution, as the ideal. Austria, Stern insisted, should give up a useless province that hated her. The papacy should sacrifice a part of its temporal power in order to retain its spiritual power; otherwise, it would subject the church to a "persecution without grandeur and a martyrdom without sanctity." It should spare Catholics "the spectacle of blood shed for the defense of that kingdom [of this world] that Christ declared was not his."[37]

In the unification of Italy, Stern's hero was Cavour, whom she hailed as a great statesman with an open mind. He had proclaimed to the Senate in Turin the necessity to ameliorate the lot of the masses through more productive labor and universal education. Stern had finally found herself a truly modern statesman.[38] In April 1860 she traveled to Turin to see for herself the new Italian government. On May 16 Cavour received her. New "Lettres" on Italy followed. She reported that the Italian people were in accord with their government. They had put up with many things since the victory over Austria: abandonment by an ally, cession of territory to France, attacks on the royal house by the Pope, and a rupture between Cavour and Garibaldi. But

Cavour took on himself the discontent of the people, who remained faithful to the monarchy.[39]

Stern recorded that her life had had five passions: God, Liszt, the Republic, maternity, and Italy. "Only the passion for Italy has not deceived me. It has offered grandeur for my enthusiasm."[40]

King Victor Emmanuel II received the Comtesse d'Agoult on June 10. Yet even this was not the point of her visit to Turin. For a long time she had been in correspondence with an Italian who was translating her *Jeanne d'Arc*. Now the play was actually ready for a performance in Turin! The first performance took place on June 3. Both translator and lead actor had taken care to present the story as a saga of Italian liberation; the English were called "the enemy" (read Austria) and the heroine's country was merely "the homeland (read united Italy)." To Stern's great distress, her name was linked with that of Rossi, the famous actor, on posters throughout the city. She was told she would have to go onstage and hold hands with the actors at the end. This she could not do. Hiding in the corridor at the end of the performance, with the exuberant Italian audience shouting "Author!," she was able to be seen bowing only through the door of a friend's box. For an aristocratic Frenchwoman, it was an Italian nightmare. And yet it was the greatest public recognition she ever received.

Twelve ~ *"Differently, but as*
completely as man, woman is created with
a view to rational activity, whose principle is
freedom, whose aim is progress, and whose
exercise, within a society perpetually being
transformed, cannot be arbitrarily
circumscribed or determined."

Although the Second Empire was a very productive period for Daniel Stern, family affairs often overshadowed her life. In the middle of 1860 she spent several months with Claire in Nice, which had just become French as a result of Napoleon's aid to Italian unification. Separated from her husband, Guy de Charnacé, for five years, Claire was having an affair with a physician, Eugène Dally. She planned to live with him openly on returning to Paris, particularly as she suspected, toward the end of the year, that she might be pregnant. Marie, still in touch with Guy de Charnacé, opposed the open liaison. Claire, of course, pointed out that, with her history, Marie was not in a position to criticize. But Marie did not want to see her daughter suffer what she had suffered; she warned her that the bourgeoisie now dominating French society was more prudish than the old aristocracy. Claire would be unable to create for herself a milieu. And what about Daniel? Marie feared that Claire would lose control of her son to his father if she was not careful. When Claire told her that she was putting Daniel into a boarding school, Marie erupted, "You know very well that the danger of boarding school is, to call things by their name, homosexuality and pederasty, both more to be feared when living together in the dormitory and recreation than in the classes."[1]

Mother and daughter were in unalterable opposition. Marie moved to Pegli, near Genoa, where she tried to recover her weakened health. Meanwhile, Cosima had borne her first child in October 1861 and named her Daniela, after her beloved brother. Toward the end of that year Marie learned that Liszt was planning to visit Paris to attend the opening of Wagner's *Tannhauser*. As she wrote to Tribert, "The great Franz is coming to Paris to assist at the triumph of the great Richard."[2] (Unfortunately, the performance of 1861 was to be hissed by a cabal of the Jockey Club, for which Wagner would never forgive the French.) Marie began to dream of Liszt again, dreams in which "the great shadow," as she referred to him in her diary, rejected her and from which she awoke sobbing. She wrote to Cosima to tell her father that she would be happy to see him when he came to Paris.

Liszt insisted on a written invitation, which Marie provided. He had to put his visit off for a month, but on May 27, 1861, he came to the Hôtel Montaigne, where she had an apartment. It was more than fifteen years since they had seen one another. Marie wrote in her diary:

I went into the salon and, turning the door, found myself in the presence of Liszt! I offered him my hand. He remained silent, visibly moved. 'It's a long time since you last came to Paris . . .' and our conversation went on in this fashion for an hour. He has aged greatly, but has not lost his looks. His face is bronzed and his eyes no longer have their fire; but he is still young in demeanor. His beautiful hair tumbles down in long flat locks on both sides of his noble, saddened face. He spoke animatedly but quite without naturalness, in a manner that sought to be trenchant and sententious. Not a word about either Blandine or Cosima, although I mentioned Herr von Bülow. He was astonished at my [strong] feelings for Italy.

Marie asked if he still saw Sand. He said that Sand had been somewhat cool toward him, because he had taken Marie's side in the quarrel, even though he thought her in the wrong. Marie said she had believed the contrary. He said she was wrong, as before. "When he left I offered him my hand again with emphasis. He will be coming to lunch on Friday." And the next day:

After seeing him I have not stopped thinking about him. The first night I had difficulty in sleeping. Identifying him with what he was is still not easy. Although he has aged as we all must, with nothing violent or contrary to nature, the picture of his young, lively self was so deeply impressed on me that I am unable to bring it into accord with this new image, grave and quiet. I still feel a force there; but I too have become a force, equal if not superior. What was—still is—the mysterious bond of sympathy between us, despite the contradictions that burst out so obviously in our opinions and our pride?

The planned luncheon with friends was agreeable. Marie recorded that Liszt was still slightly on the defensive, uneasy about what one thought of him, ever engaged in repelling any innuendo. He congratulated her for the delicious meal, and they exchanged a few friendly words, some gracious or courtly memories.

I went to table alone; returning from it, I passed my arm through his. He squeezed my hand effusively! He is certainly very pleased, or rather, very proud, about our reconciliation. As for me, I find him still very handsome, very remarkable, very engaging. I feel more pleasure in his presence than in that of anyone else; but the great ideal he personified has vanished. Who would have ever said that we would meet again like this! It is at once sad and sweet. Above all, it cuts human things down to size: the great passions, the great sorrows, the great ambitions that rend and tear—they all come down to a chicken à la portugaise eaten together in the company of people who are complete strangers to the whole of a long life past.

At the third meeting, Liszt arrived unannounced. Tribert was there and left immediately. The conversation was more intimate, about the girls, but not Daniel. Each thought that Cosima resembled the other. "In saying goodbye to him, very much moved, I rose spontaneously and kissed him; he was also moved, and left me with a kind of vow or *benediction,* whose words I cannot remember. Imperishable charm! . . . It is still he and he alone who makes me feel the divine mystery of life. When he was gone I felt the void around me, and I shed tears."[3] As Liszt described it to the Princess Sayn-Wittgenstein in his report back, Marie had begun to cry as he talked to her of how his true self had not changed direction. He had kissed her on the forehead and said: "Come, Marie, let me speak to you in the language of the peasants. May God bless you! Wish me no evil! She could not respond at that moment—but her tears flowed more abundantly."[4]

Ollivier wrote of Liszt after this visit to Paris: "His is a weak character, spoiled by admiration—but upright, loyal and charming. I have come to feel a most warm and genuine affection for him; and how transported, moved and filled with wonder I have been by his truly supernatural playing, it is impossible to describe. . . . Unfortunately, nowadays he finds playing tedious, and has wholly given himself up to the pursuit of glory as a composer."[5] This is what Marie had wanted of him, what greater maturity and the Princess Sayn-Wittgenstein had brought about. Ollivier was later to observe that Liszt had never provided either of his daughters with the dowry of one hundred thousand francs that had been promised in the contract made with Marie.[6]

The following January (1862) Blandine announced to her father that she was pregnant. This was when Ollivier demanded the whole of the dowry from Marie. (Juliette Lamber recorded that Marie feared he knew of something wrong with the pregnancy and wanted to collect before a possible death of his wife;[7] however, her memories were not always reliable.) Marie gave in so as not to upset Blandine further. But when she found that Blandine was planning to have the child in the south, attended by Ollivier's physician brother-in-law, she strongly declared her view—that Blandine should give birth in Paris with the best doctors. Her insistence was futile and, in effect, ended the relationship. Blandine chose her father and Cosima as projected godparents for the child, who was born in July in the small town of Gemenos, near Marseilles, and named Daniel, again for the dead brother. All seemed to go well at first. But Blandine was unable to continue nursing the child and did not recover her strength. She lingered on, sick, until September 11, when she died. Ollivier wrote to Marie the next day.[8]

Again Marie notified her friends in a few words that she had lost a child. But this time she poured her grief into her diary, noting how beautiful, talented, and lovable her daughter had been. Of all her children by Liszt, this was the one she had really spent time with and nurtured. "O my sweet Blandine. . . . Somewhere in the infinite, do you feel how dear and sacred you were to me! . . . I remain all day in bed, lacking the *will* to get up." She tended to think of Blandine along with Louise, the first daughter whom she had lost. In each case the remaining daughter had not been the favorite and was undoubtedly aware of it. Claire and Cosima, who kept in touch with each other, were the only ones of Marie's five children who outlived her.

Ollivier and his mother-in-law, who no longer had anything between them but sorrow, were reconciled by the end of the year. Early in the following year, Cosima bore another girl, who was named for her dead sister. Blandine was her last child by von Bülow. Her next, Isolde, was the daughter of Richard Wagner. Cosima duplicated her mother's maternal career by having two more children, Eva and Siegfried, with her famous lover. Marie was not disturbed; she had never thought that von Bülow was the man for Cosima, and in a Protestant country, divorce was possible. This finally took place in 1870, and Cosima became Frau Wagner. She then went on to succeed where her mother had failed, becoming the permanent muse of a great composer.

Liszt was in Paris again in 1864. Marie found him aged in the years since she had seen him. He had given up his plans to marry the Princess Sayn-Wittgenstein.[9] They met at Ollivier's home, in the bedroom of Blandine. She reported to her diary that Liszt told her he had loved her profoundly and felt that he had recently become more worthy of her. She noted that he spoke in "Roman Catholic" language and was still very much preoccupied with the aristocracy. "Life is a dream," she concluded.[10] The two saw each other for the last time in 1866, when he came to present his *Messe de Gran* in Paris. He came dressed as Abbé Liszt, although this was not necessary or even appropriate for the minor orders he had taken. Ollivier, who had heard of his action from a tearful Madame Liszt, had notified Marie, calling it "a spiritual suicide."[11] When Marie visited his mother, with whom she always kept up relations, Madame Liszt had shared with her letters from both Cosima and Sayn-Wittgenstein, and she told Marie her son had always wanted to be a priest. She died two months before his visit. It was Ollivier who arranged and spoke at her funeral.

The presentation of Liszt's Mass was an event attended by all Paris, including Marie. But the reviews the next day were unfavorable and included one written by Guy de Charnacé, Marie's ex-son-in-law, who had become a critic. Liszt always thought that Marie had dictated it to him and had orchestrated the hostile press he received. Many of his followers agreed. However, her son-in-law, like many critics and even Berlioz, associated Liszt with Wagner, whose music they despised but Marie did not. There is no evidence in her writings even of any joy at the poor reviews and certainly none that she could have been so powerful as to organize a cabal against Liszt. On the contrary, in the memoirs she was writing at the time, she was idealizing her memories. And finally, in her old age, there is not one hint of criticism of Liszt in anything she wrote, despite the unpleasant stories about herself circulated by him, usually to his woman friends.

We have two records of the visit Liszt made to Marie in 1866, neither by herself. Liszt, reporting to his princess, represented himself as telling Marie off. When she told him she was writing her memoirs, he replied that it was impossible for her to do so, because what she would record would be reduced to poses and lies. There is no record that this was a faithful account and nothing about it in Marie's diaries or letters. There is another description of the meeting, by the somewhat unreliable Juliette, which she claims to have received from Ronchaud. He had lived a good portion of his life in the aura of the lovers and said he was "stupified that they could love each other and detest each other and still meet calmly and talk about their children, living or dead, with such serenity." When Marie asked why Liszt had taken orders, he had indicated it was to avoid marriage. Ronchaud described the two looking at each other, "smiling, with a little self-mockery," and he felt that each was pleased that the other had remained attractive and distinguished, which justified their affair.[12] Both stories may be untrue; this one is surely the more romantic. Some months later, reading the diary of their travels together, Marie wrote in the margin, "What has he done with these twenty-eight years? And what have I done? He is Abbé Liszt and I am Daniel Stern! And what despair, what deaths, what tears, what mourning separate us![13]

As for Claire, her predicted struggle over control of young Daniel de Charnacé was not long in developing. Marie and her brother tried to mediate between the parents, proposing compromises that Claire refused to accept. Again Marie was in a familiar situation. She herself had not been as diplomatic as she might have been in her struggle with Liszt over the children. Claire felt that no one could be a real help and that her mother, who had maintained a correspondence with her son-in-law, was against her. Marie, angry at her impotence with her daughter, wrote to Cosima that Claire had taken up with with inferior types. Claire fought her mother by constantly blaming her for having left her as a child. By 1867 she seems to have broken with Marie almost completely, as well as with her uncle Maurice.

Although Marie had good relations with her daughters for only very short periods, she sustained and valued friendships with other women throughout her life. Some were literary women. In 1843 Sainte-Beuve introduced her to the poet Marcelline Desbordes-Valmore. Marie invited her to dinner with Lamennais and Vigny. The poet memorialized her hostess in a poem,[14] and the two women entered on a correspondence. Another gifted friend was the poet Louise Choquet, Madame Ackermann. Her husband, librarian and editor of the French library of the king of Prussia, had been a friend of Proudhon. Widowed, she moved to Nice, where Stern visited her in the winter of 1859–60. The two corresponded until Stern's death. Known as a poet to a small circle in Paris, Ackermann was launched into a wider group by Stern, who reviewed her *Contes* in *Le Temps*. Although Ackermann believed women really were inferior, meant only to reproduce the species, and was a great supporter of marriage, the two became close friends and intellectual companions. They shared an interest in Germany. Stern was more radical politically; Ackermann, religiously, as an avowed atheist.

Ackermann was proud of their friendship and of the articles that Stern wrote about her. She called Stern an "Amazon of thought" and dedicated her poem "Promethée" to her. She did have reservations about her friend's pushing herself to the front in some of her works—as *Nélida*, or as Diotima in *Dante et Goethe*. But it was Ackermann who arranged Stern's stays at Nice during her attacks of neurasthenia, and Stern had no pretenses with her friend. Writing two years before she died, she exclaimed, "Mon Dieu, que nous avons été sottes, vous et moi, et qu'elles ont dû se gausser de nos imbécillités! . . . Et sommes nous bien sûres de l'avenir?"[15] In the condolence letter she wrote to Claire after Marie's death, Ackermann said that the pleasure of visiting Daniel Stern was for her one of the greatest attractions in Paris.[16]

Some of Marie's relations with women were, in their own way, as complex as those with men. She began, typically, by viewing them as potential competitors, as can be seen in her mean-spirited article on the *salonnière* Bettina von Arnim in the *Revue de deux mondes*. In a letter to Sainte-Beuve in 1842, she described a visit of the feminist Flora Tristan, "a green feather in the hat on her head, eloquence on her lips," pleading for money to propagate the cause. Marie treated her to a sermon on the woman as wife and mother, whereupon Tristan "hung her head with its green feather."[17] It is a familiar example of a woman's willingness to make fun of another woman to please a man. There is a letter of 1844, evidently replying to one from Sainte-Beuve on the von Arnim article, in which Marie agreed that women should not atttack one another. "There are in me two penchants that fight each other: enthusiasm and irony, faith and doubt. The irony ought to be restrained and will be."[18] It is true that Marie easily took the cynical view, which often harmed her relationships and her happiness.

In writing her account of the 1848 revolution, Stern played up the role of women. She emphasized the bravery of the Duchesse d'Orléans in going to the Chamber on behalf of her child, the royal heir. She featured the prostitute who stood as Liberty during the invasion of the Tuileries palace—a pike in her hand, a red cap on her head, lips shut, immobile for several hours, with the people making signs of respect. "The prostitute is the living symbol of the degradation of the poor and the corruption of the rich,"[19] Stern wrote. Insulted in normal times, she had her triumph in this great moment of popular frenzy. In her book Stern provided a fairly accurate review of French feminism in the 1789 Revolution, focussing on Condorcet, Madame de Staël, Madame Roland, Olympe de Gouges, and Wollstonecraft's *Vindication of the Rights of Woman*.

However, she did not support the women who formed clubs in 1848 and tried to take a political role. "But I will say nothing harsh, at least I will try not to," she wrote to Hortense Allart, who agreed with her.[20] She believed that the only result of the demands women had made in 1848 was that they were ridiculed. Women should have spoken to the issues of female education, possible careers, wages of women already working, or the place of the wife and mother in the family, "that is, proceeding in logical steps as public opinion gradually changed." She believed that popular sovereignty would lead to greater freedom for women, because working-class women worked alongside their men.[21] Stern's negative views on women in politics were only heightened by the failure of men, supposedly practiced in politics, to succeed in maintaining the Second Republic.

Known for her writings on women in the *Esquisses morales* and in *Essai sur la liberté*, Stern had been invited to feminist meetings during 1848. Jeanne

Deroin, founder of the Union for the Freedom of Workers of Both Sexes and associate of the newspaper *La Voix des femmes* had received, in answer to her call, an invitation to dinner. When Deroin arrived, Stern was taken aback by the actual appearance of the woman who attempted to run for a seat in the National Assembly. Petite and pale, extremely straightforward and honest, she won her hostess over to her character, if not to her ideas, in a long evening. By the end of 1850, Deroin was in prison. Stern went to see her, admiring how heroically she bore her confinement; she sent her the history of the revolution they had just lived through. Deroin was enthusiastic. "We have poets, artists, moralists, philosophers, scholars; we can now be proud of having an historian that the other sex will envy us!" she wrote Marie, insisting that this was a step in the freeing of women.[22]

Pauline Roland, with whom Stern was associated on the *Revue indépendante,* was one of the founders of the Association of Male and Female Socialist Teachers. She was also imprisoned during the revolution and was free for only six months when she was arrested again after the coup d'état of Louis-Napoléon. Marie had originally visited her in prison and asked what she could do to help her. When the new regime sentenced to exile a whole group of women, twenty-one of them besides her, Roland sent a moving message to Stern on their behalf. Could Stern do anything for them before they were sent to African colonies, where many of them would probably die?[23] We have no evidence of an answer; Roland herself did die after returning from exile.

There was certainly nothing Stern could do for anyone once Louis-Napoléon took complete power. She felt that even continuing to publish the volumes of her history might be dangerous. She wrote to Allart, "Actually I believe it is an act of courage, and as I have been well informed about the possible consequences, I have not done it heedlessly. I confess then to you, but only to you, my dear Amazon, that I feel some joy in showing that a woman can, on occasion, equal, and perhaps slightly surpass men in the battle. And that battle is great and beautiful, for it is no longer over this or that form of government; it has to do with freedom of conscience and the dignity of the human spirit."[24]

The two friends did not agree on everything; Allart did not see the republic as the best form of government for France and was willing to accept Bonaparte. She was also critical of her friend, particularly when Marie did not apply her principles in family matters. She wrote to Marie about her daughters: "Will one of them become a fine and independent woman? And are you afraid of that? Do you believe that marrying them off is your first duty?

Women would be the queens of the world if they began without bonds."[25] Allart remained a friend until the end. Her own numerous works on history, sociology, and metaphysics were almost never published. Yet she always praised Marie's work and kept her going in times of discouragement. After the separation from Liszt, Marie spent two summers with her friend, recuperating and writing. And despite what must have been jealousy originally, Allart continued in vain to urge her ex-lover Sainte-Beuve to write about her friend's books.

Stern shared many of her views on women with her first real friend, whose loss she regretted greatly—George Sand. Although Sand had taken a more radical role in the revolution, she agreed with Stern that women were not ready for political participation until they had educated themselves. In her history Stern spoke highly of Sand, only regretting that she had leaned toward communism and disorder. Allart wrote to Stern, at a time when she was trying to bring the two women back together, that she hoped Sand would not object to the treatment given her in the book. Stern replied that she should not, as she had chosen her words carefully. "No doubt the past binds us together and perhaps the future will join us together again. The middle periods are most difficult in women's friendships. . . . Madame Sand sincerely cared for me, and I feel for her a profound friendship. What evil genie embroiled our spirits and our hearts, created to understand one another better? I don't know or I want to forget."[26]

Actually, Marie had forgotten nothing. While consumed with jealousy of Sand, Marie missed the frank friendship the two had shared. She seems to have written to Sand in October 1850, using as an excuse something mentioned by the actor Bocage, who frequented both salons. The wrongs that had been committed on both sides, she wrote, should be attributed to their immaturity. It was clearly an attempt to reach out to her old friend.[27] An incomplete letter of Sand to Marie exists, which may have been the answer, whether or not she sent it. Bocage had, it seems, conveyed to her Marie's desire to renew the friendship. Sand's letter first recalled the past and Marie's tears when she left Nohant. It went on to recall her feelings on reading the fateful letters Marie had written about her to Marliani.

I was giddy, humiliated. I went fifteen days without wanting to read those letters. Finally I read them. . . I pardoned everything, I wished to forget everything. You became sick, I went to you. And during those few weeks of unsettled, blighted friendship . . . the words [of the letters] came and went, causing me new sorrow and chagrin. . . . I felt then an invincible need to forget you, and I disappeared. . . . [Hearing from Bocage that Marie was] "happy, calm, surrounded with friends and family, respected," my reaction was real joy. He said you still cared for me.

I said, "No, she never seriously cared for me; she lives in her imagination, she has infatuations followed by hate and disgust." Bocage asked, "You see her as bad, false?"

"No, I neither say nor think badly of her, you know that, but there is something between her and me which is not good, not right; admitting that this could be the only bad action of her life, and I hope it is, it is I who suffered from it, and when someone recalls her to me, I feel bad; let's not speak of it any more."

Bocage insisted, told me many wonderful things about you that did not touch me. But then, some words broke through: "When she speaks your name, she cries. She cries real tears that she does not try to hide, that she does not wipe away. . . . She is profoundly grieved by your not liking her."

I wrote Bocage that if by his telling you only the truth, that I had nothing against you, he could make you feel better, he should do so. I think that is all, Marie; I would not be sincere if I were more loving . . . than the truth. You should understand that this heart . . . does not return with enthusiasm to the passion of friendship. . . . Perhaps in your presence it would awake as on the first day, perhaps not.[28]

There is another piece of a letter that we know Marie received, in which Sand assured Marie that she should have no illusions—that she really hated Sand and had probably always hated her. Why? Sand went on to presume that it was because of Liszt. But, "You could not have been jealous of me, who never felt the attraction (outside of the friendship that united the three of us) for the man that you loved."[29]

Marie replied by recalling that some "very serious, very precise accusations [about Sand and Liszt]—to which the opinion of the public, of all my friends, and even of some of yours gave weight—raised in Italy those first bouts of anger whose expression [in the famous letters] was tinged with an irony *that was not mine*, which contrasted with the nature of my feelings, and whose injustice I did not hesitate to recognize on my return to Paris." She went on to say she did not now believe Sand had been trying to seduce Liszt, but she was persuaded that any other woman in her place would not have had even her hesitations. "As for me, I believed one day and doubted the next." She also referred to a letter Sand had written Liszt. "In the very time that we [Marie and Liszt] were trying to get together again, a letter from you to Liszt was shown to me by him. I have kept it. . . . This letter treated me with a severity that was cruel and, pardon the word, *perfidious*, for it was addressed to a man passionately in love with me and tried to take from me his love and his esteem!"[30] She went on to say that she did not want to continue trading accusations [which, considering the betrayals of Balzac's *Béa-*

trix and Sand's own *Horace*, she certainly could have done], recognizing that it would only separate them further rather than bring them together.

Seeing that Sand could recognize fault only on Marie's side and had no real desire to transcend their differences, Marie regretfully gave up the idea of a rapprochement. "Between us there are great and good similarities; I believe that our ideals differ very little. But in the down-to-earth aspects of our lives, in our tastes, our habits, our secondary opinions, our entourages, there arise contrasts to which you attach, I believe, greater importance than I."[31]

This was the last attempt to renew the friendship. When Sand began publishing her *Histoire de ma vie* in 1854, Marie feared, needlessly, that she would be attacked again. This may have been why she made some highly critical comments to Allart on the first installments. However, she later praised it in a letter to Ronchaud. But she was always measuring her own progress against the reputation of Sand. She confided petulantly to her diary in May 1862: "It is unbelievable that with this growing talent, this persistent beauty, noble and elegant manners, I do not achieve greater results. I sense that the least fault will do me in, that I can be excused nothing. Madame Sand [remains] today incontestable, despite [failures in her publications] . . . despite a growing obesity and materialism. What is the secret of that difference? In her great fecundity (one of the signs of genius)."[32] Marie always maintained that she herself had to make up in talent and hard work for what came so easily to the genius of Sand. The difference in the recognition given the two women was a constant source of frustration and lack of confidence for Stern. This may have been why she was so proud that she had retained her beauty. She read everything Sand wrote and praised most of it. Yet she looked forward, in private, to the day when Sand would lose out on the ground of character. Sand was not quite so restrained. While praising Stern for her beauty, her mind, and her charm, she warned Prince Jérôme Bonaparte, "She is very demanding. If you offend her, she will cut you down. Be warned."[33]

In June 1862 Sand sent a notice of the marriage of her son Maurice. Marie took the opportunity to send a congratulatory note ending with the assurance that "time has not changed my feelings for you" and that she remained "more than ever your sincerely affectionate . . . ." Sand responded, in part, "When one is freely loved, I believe that one is always loved, even during the time that one believes oneself forgotten. I do not know what has happened; life is always for me the present hour. This hour is such that today you could read in my heart without finding anything there that would afflict or disturb you. Then, as always. . . ."[34] Marie answered in a light, affectionate vein and with the hope that when Sand came to Paris, they would see each other. In

October Marie received from Sand a letter of condolence for the death of Blandine. "It is in these sad shocks of life that one feels the continuation of lines of affection and a kind of reawakening of all the joys and sorrows that are mingled together in the heart." She hoped that Marie had come to believe in a life hereafter. "I bear you a great respect for your tears and a great tenderness for your heartbreak."[35] These were the last words between the two former friends.

In 1859 Marie met a young woman for whom she was to conceive more than a friendship, almost a passion. Juliette de la Messine, lovely, intelligent, and seeking separation from her husband, had come to Paris, as Marie had twenty years before, to make a name for herself. With the help of Marie, among others, this young woman from the provinces would do just that and become the premier *salonnière* of the Third Republic to come. As a start, she had taken on Proudhon, whose *Justice dans la Révolution et dans l'Eglise* had attacked women writers—notably Stern and Sand. In her memoirs Juliette described her attempts to publish her response, including the patronizing attitudes she met from editors, even though she was prepared to pay for publication. *Idées anti-Proudhoniennes* defended the women Proudhon had scorned, noting they were intelligent enough for him when their arguments supported his own ideas.[36] When the book was finally produced under her maiden name, Juliette Lamber, Stern, whom she had defended, wrote to her, assuming she was addressing a man posing as a woman. They soon met, and Marie saw in Juliette a resemblance to Blandine, from whom she was then estranged. When Marie retired to Nice for her health in 1859, she continued a correspondence that was addressed successively to "Juliette," "little Juliette," "my little cat," "my little white cat. . . ." Juliette became her protégée; Marie educated her in the arts, as she had her own daughters. She encouraged, developed, and advised her and showered her with affection.

Juliette responded, submitting to Marie's editing of a novel she had undertaken, weeping over *Nélida*, and seeking advice on extricating herself from her marriage. We do not have her letters, but we have those of Marie. One written on November 24, 1860, while she was again recuperating in Nice, illustrates not only the relationship but also the complexity of Marie's affections:

Ma chère enfant . . . to *write* certain things is delicate. One can never be sure of being really understood when one can add neither the accent nor the facial expressions to the words. . . . So first of all to your question, Do you love me truly? I should, if I believed my visualization of you—charming, lovable, among the most lovable—answer *yes*, three times yes, without hesitation or reticence. But reason and especially experience are there to warn me and tell me that perhaps I love in you the person that I create, with elements too little known as yet. . . . I do not mean that you are *worse* than I see you, I mean that you are *other*. Therefore, for one who has a need for complete sincerity towards herself and toward others, the unpleasant and peevish necessity to respond to your sweet question: I *think* that I love you, I want to be able to love you. May the gods smile on me![37]

Was this somewhat unsatisfying answer the reason that Juliette wrote to Sand, seeking entrance to her salon? She received the answer that no meeting between them was possible as long as Juliette had a relationship with Daniel Stern. However, Sand did send the young woman her works as they appeared. Juliette never told Marie, but she reported in her memoirs that Marie warned her against Sand, who, she said, betrayed a good background both in the way she dressed and the way she behaved. And Juliette was for a while content, for she could read in a later letter from Marie: "Count on me: I hope to aid you in the complete development of your rich nature. I hope to lighten your sorrows, give you courage. For me it is a hope full of sweetness, for I love you. . . . Darling Juliette is sweet as a lamb and truly lovable for this old nomad called Daniel Stern. I love her then, and will love her as much as it will please her to allow herself to be loved."[38]

Marie saw in Juliette herself twenty years before—trying to remake her life and establish herself in the literary world, surrounded by adventurers waiting for her to fall again. Juliette confided in her, was happy to be led by her. When Marie returned to Paris, there was a place for her protégée, not only in her salon but also in her household. "Never despair of yourself; don't forget that you have to fight for yourself and for others; to expand in yourself the honor of women, put yourself in the service of great causes. You will be happy, or you will not be. *That is not the question.* You must make those who love you proud of you and be content with yourself."[39]

Marie taught the young woman everything she had learned. Advising her to write less but only things of high quality, Marie had her stories published in *Le Temps* and *Revue germanique*; she had Henneguy touting them in Italy. She launched her young friend at dinners with critics; she introduced her to the young republicans, among whom Juliette found her next husband, Edmond Adam. Juliette appears to have really admired Stern, whom she presented in her novel *Le Mandarin* as a superior being. She later wrote a description of Daniel Stern at that time:

Her mind was most elevated, very mature, quite individual, and possessed a rare cultivation. Curious about others, she revealed little of herself. Firm, resolute, sometimes wholly devoted to her opinions, she practiced a singular tolerance. At first view Madame d'Agoult revealed something virile, strong, mingled with a distinction so perfect that she seemed to have lost none of her femininity; she said willingly, "I have reached the age of man." Tall and supremely elegant, with the incomparable manners of a great lady, when she called herself a democrat, which was true, one could not prevent a smile, as this word in her mouth seemed, if not an anomaly, at least a contrast. Dignity dominated in her, even in those rare moments of expansion, and sometimes attained to majesty. It was astonishing never to see her betray the passionate character which had brought that violent storm [of Liszt] into her life.[40]

But Marie was to reveal her passionate character. Juliette, having been coached by her mentor, began to set up a salon of her own. Members of Marie's salon attended. Marie learned (again, as with Sand, the story came from a mutual friend, this time Mlle de Pierreclos) that Juliette had in her salon publicly criticized an article by Stern on the Dutch Republic. When Juliette denied it, Marie accused her of using her as a steppingstone and trying to set up a salon in opposition to her own. Counseled by Ronchaud, the young woman withdrew for a period. We have only her description of the supposedly final scene of the friendship—a scene in which Marie, told of Juliette's plan to marry Adam, attacked her with frenzy for so soon giving away the independence she had finally won. After using unpardonable language, she ended with the words, "I never wish to see you again!"[41]

This story would be possible, as Marie could lose control, particularly in the case of someone she cared deeply about—except that Juliette's husband did not die until years after her split with Marie and Marie approved of Adam as a suitor. There are letters from Marie to Juliette that go on to 1864, becoming cooler and sadder, to be sure, and indicating other possible betrayals. In one of the last letters Marie wrote:

Believe me, it would be impossible for me to blame you. I have only regretted not making myself better understood. My friendship for you was both maternal and paternal in its indulgence without limits, and because of its solidity I was astonished to see that you hesitated, after all that had passed between us, to be sincere and that, at the first test you preferred, instead of speaking to me of what only concerned the two of us, to speak *against me* to other people. Shall I say it? I am saddened to see you lose, in the same year, by death [Juliette's religious advisor Jean Reynaud died this same year] and by a misunderstanding, two affections whose very nature was to excite in you noble ambitions of mind, those ambitions that fortify us against the blows of chance and the problems of life in common.[42]

It is more likely that the final scene presented by Juliette was created to justify her turn to the bosom of George Sand, which she made about the time it was described.

Another young woman whom Marie greatly admired was Clémence Royer. An intellectual, Royer had followed Pascal Duprat into exile in Switzerland, where she had introduced a course at Lausanne on the philosophy of women.[43] Back in Paris she presented it in the form of public lectures. Stern attended them and wrote to her. She admired Royer's knowledge and her articles in the *Journal des économistes.* (Not that Royer had a formal education; it was only in March 1864 that courses were organized for women at the Sorbonne. Before that, they could only attend lectures at the Collège de France.) Royer told Stern that reading her *Essai sur la liberté* had been of tremendous importance in her life. She also valued *Esquisses morales,* "the book that does women the highest honor."[44] Stern was able to introduce her as a writer at the *Revue germanique* and the *Revue moderne,* its successor.

Royer's greatest accomplishment was translating Darwin's *Origin of Species* into French. When she brought Stern her published translation in 1862, its introduction shocked even that avowed agnostic. "She talks as if Catholicism were a party and Christianity a fatal error of humanity that should be torn out and destroyed," Stern wrote in her diary.[45] She corresponded with Royer, who went on a study trip to Germany. The serious young woman was shocked by the students, who ignored the library. She also confided to Stern that she felt like an outsider, "walking on a sea of ice." She was sure that her friend had also experienced "that sense of limitation" because she was a woman.[46] Back in Paris, Royer wrote a novel, which she sent to Stern with the reservation that she might find it too masculine. It was badly received, although Ronchaud wrote a review that praised the ideas in it, if not the form.

Stern was so admiring of Royer that she tried, in vain, to find her a husband. She also aided Julie-Victoire Daubié, the first woman in France to receive the baccalaureat (from an unwilling academic jury in Lyon in 1862), by working to get reviews for Daubié's book *La Femme pauvre.* The young woman from the provinces, smitten with Stern's intellect and cosmopolitanism, urged her patron to apply for entrance to the Académie française and, later, the Académie des inscriptions.

In 1868 Stern began to collect material for a history of the feminist movements in France, England, and the United States. She solicited the aid of the feminist Pauline Beauchet, whom she called upon to aid her in research, while encouraging her to write on her own. "There is much to say and to do for women and by women," she wrote her. And later, "The soul of women must spread itself out when the spirit of men becomes sterile."[47]

It was probably in this way that she developed an interest in the writings of the leading feminist of the time, Maria Deraismes, founder of the Société pour l'amélioration du sort de la femme et la revendication de ses droits, and active in the Ligue française pour le droit des femmes. Born of a wealthy bourgeois family, Deraismes was beautiful and well educated. She shared with Stern the ability to put pen to paper, at first as a writer of plays. She also shared Stern's limited feminism, demanding for women social rights, marriage rights and education but not political rights. The younger woman was more radical, however, in being willing to lecture in public—at first on literary or philosophical subjects, and then on the condition of women. She also wrote for the periodical *Le Droit des femmes.* Stern seemed to appreciate her work, and the two became friends and correspondents. Deraismes was concerned about Stern's health, which she had to preserve "for the cause of women, since no one could better demonstrate the intellectual equivalence of the two sexes." She prescribed a verveine tea and a diet to bring back Stern's appetite.[48]

Stern's views on women's position in society can be abstracted from her book originally subtitled *Pensées sur la femme. Esquisses morales,* almost ignored at first publication, was popular in its second and third editions under the Second Empire. Stern rewrote the book many times, and some aphorisms in her notes never made it into print. In it she asked the basic question: Is woman equal to man? In most of history, she agreed, inferiority had been ascribed to women, and it was true that no women had reached the heights of invention or discovery. But past inferiority said nothing about the future. What had happened was that man, physically superior, was able to prevent woman from participating in intellectal conquests by denying her all means of development. And despite this handicap, women had arrived at a position of understanding their duties and demanding their rights. As a result, some men recognized them as partners—subordinate to be sure—mainly because of their importance to the family, in their roles as devoted wife and sacrificing mother.[49]

But Stern took issue with the principles of renunciation and sacrifice. She placed justice above a devotion practiced in an absolute manner without discernment or measure. Unfortunately, "love is the whole ambition of woman. For the man, on the other hand, it is most often only the momentary sleep of ambition." And love often perished because of too little pride in the woman and too little delicacy in the man. Men might place women upon a pedestal, but as they bowed before them, they deposited at their feet, "like the tide saluting the river, the sludge [*limon*] of their corrupt habits, the spume of their memories." Women needed to develop a proper sense of their own worth.[50]

As for motherhood, Stern declared it false, as some had said (including Sand), that maternity was the unique vocation of woman. "However profound or exalted one supposes it to be, the love of children cannot, to the exclusion of all other loves, absorb all her powers of being, nor fulfill her destiny." She pointed out that maternity took only a small portion of a woman's life. "Before, during, and after, woman exists by herself and for herself, as a human being. No less than man, she is endowed with quite varied faculties, which create duties and rights for her in the home, the nation, and in humanity, duties and rights that clearly call her to multiple functions."[51]

The fundamental equality for women would be the equal possibility of intellectual development because it implies all the others. "The Scythians struck out eyes of slaves so they would not be distracted from their work. Some do the same with nightingales to make them sing better. One is tempted to think that an analogous reason accounts for the kind of education given to girls." Such education produced, Stern declared, women who still manifested all the vices of slaves and all the defects of children. Neither church nor state had any serious plan of education for women, that is, for half of the human species. As a result, thinking was for a great number of women "a happy accident rather than a permanent state." What was necessary was a vast system of universal education provided by the state for both sexes.[52]

Stern deplored the fact that many women were still childlike. "Don't demand of them logic; if they arrive, by means of study, to put it into their writings, they never put into their lives, because they never seek their point of reference in themselves; it is always in some one else that they place their center of gravity." Women who were unhappy in marriage often wished divorce, but the ability to change husbands under current conditions was only the ability to change masters. "More important is the divorce from ignorance, frivolity, puerile passions. Without this divorce the other is useless." In the future, Stern predicted, when woman would be, "not only in a manner of speaking, but truly and in her mind half of man, the sentiment of love, up to that point only sensuality more or less refined, or passion more or less visionary," would become, "in its constancy and its plenitude, the supreme harmony of human life."[53] (Like Condorcet, Stern had great confidence that through knowledge all life would be changed for the better; a great traveler, she even predicted air flight.)

In 1857 Stern repeated her thoughts about the woman problem to Herwegh: "If I include in my program and sustain with some liveliness the equality of women (even their present superiority—more lively inspiration, greater moral delicacy, *good* desire, *good* will, the faculty of devotion, etc., etc.) it is not, believe me, that I want to see reborn from their cinders those sad phoenixes of the revolution of 1848, women's clubs, women candidates, women's periodicals, etc., etc. No, I hate *le tapage revolutionnaire* more than ever, I simply return to the thought of Condorcet: equality of education. After which, let us see what women are capable of."[54] Although she thought it stupid that women were not admitted to the Académie française, she ridiculed tokenism. On hearing that women were to be allowed into the Austrian Society of Antiquarians, she wrote to Nefftzer that her heart beat only to think of the perfect felicity an Austrian woman would have in the circle of the Academy of Antiquarians!

In one dialogue of *Dante et Goethe,* the leading character, Diotima, apologizes for lecturing, saying that she would be ridiculed for it in Paris. Asked why it is ridiculous to the French that women teach what they know, even lecture in universities on what is found perfectly natural and agreeable that they say in salons, Diotima answers that even Madame de Staël, who argued with statesmen and diplomats, would have been considered out of place mounting the tribune at the Assembly to present her political views. "And yet she would have been truly in her place, beautiful, with the beauty of Mirabeau,[55] bearing as he did conviction in the clarity of her glance, in her gesture, in her manly voice." In this conversation Diotima also recalls that when women opened a club in 1848 and were laughed at, Emerson asked what was so funny. Foreigners do not view direct intervention of women in education and politics as bizarre, Diotima explains. In the United States god-given talent was not to be wasted. She quoted Henry Ward Beecher and Wendell Phillips on women's rights and duties. Women, she said, could even be professors at universities, and she mentioned the names of Olympia Morata and Helene Piscopia of the Renaissance.[56]

Stern seemed to grow more radical, at least on the role of women in society, as she grew older. At the age of seventy, when she was willing to accept a very conservative republic, she seems to have expressed the belief to her friend Viel-Castel that women should be allowed to become members not only of the Académie française but of the Assembly as well. When he objected that women would lose their charm if they became legislators, she replied that already (in 1875) they were becoming professionals, doctors, for example.

Stern also believed that ideas of the virtue necessary to women were exaggerated. "Thus modesty, one of the graces of chastity, has become exaggerated and almost degraded into the feeling of guilt in love." Women should be able to enjoy their sexuality in marriage. She named as the most satisfying sentiment of the soul "the friendship that follows love between a man and a woman, who don't have to blush either at having loved each other passionately, nor at having ceased to love each other with the first ardor of youth."[57] However, she saw marriage as a trap for women; her last writings in her diary, on the subject of divorce, dealt with the necessity to change the conditions of marriage.

Although education was the centerpiece of her demands for woman, she went further than other merely "liberal" feminists in her demand for what would be called today *autonomy*. She rejected any custom or law that implied the husband's control over the wife's body. In a letter to Mazzini, who had said that women fell all over Napoleon, she wrote that she didn't like the concept of women fainting in ecstasy. "I have never fainted. I like to remain standing up, in full possession of my thought and my will," she declared.[58] In December 1861 the pioneer photographer Adam-Salomon asked to do her portrait. Félix Nadar also took her picture in 1863. In 1865 Salomon decided that his first portrait was too dreamy, too sweet, and asked to do another with her standing, displaying more force, more will. She posed gladly; she was just short of sixty years of age.

Thirteen ～ *"When a woman has created her life herself, and that life has not been governed by the common rules, she becomes in everyone's eyes responsible for it, more responsible than a man."*

I n Paris Marie's salon was more brilliant than ever. George Sand described it as "a gathering of the elite that she presides over with exquisite grace, where she treats all important topics through the breadth of her mind and the variety of her abilities, at once poetic and serious."[1] What Liszt called *"la glu de la comtesse"* joined together in one room many different types of persons—diplomats, foreigners, academicians, political refugees, and artists. Stern felt that they represented different aspects of herself that became unified in their presence. She sometimes referred to her salon as her "laic vespers." Juliette Adam later recorded her mentor's written advice on how to go about creating a salon:

To gather around you a number of men and a few women [Stern suggested twenty men and five women] you must maintain a serene and happy appearance.

In the eyes of others your life must seem unified, not complicated, no matter how troubled it is. Create a peaceful and impersonal atmosphere to retain your friendships.

Consult the early members of the salon on whom to admit as you enlarge it, so that there are some who feel like founders [of your salon].

Avoid confidences which, if exchanged, create exaggerated intimacies and oblige you to give advice for which you will someday be blamed.

Be modest without self-effacement, simple but elegant. Provide confidence by the solidity of your opinions, so that people may feel you are both resolute and tolerant.

The first duty of a person who tries to preserve her salon is to support the intellectual curiosity of those she has gathered.

Make those whom you invite feel, and prove it to them, that you are more concerned with them than with yourself.[2]

One activity common to salons was reading letters from those not present. (The young Marie's own letters from the convent had been read in the salon of her patron, the Princesse de la Trémoille.) This was a way of spreading news interesting to those present, particularly news from abroad. Stern read selected letters from her correspondence with the Italians Mazzini and Manin, the Hungarian Lajos Kossuth, and the exiled Frenchmen Louis Blanc and Edouard Quinet. Her German correspondent, Varnhagen von Ense, was the husband of the late Rahel, the famous Berlin *salonnière*. Polymath, diplomat, and Goethe scholar, Varnhagen published his correspondence with Humboldt and two books of memoirs in the *Revue germanique*. A suitor of Marie's before and after Liszt, he corresponded with her until his death.

Another of Stern's faithfuls, the historian Louis de Viel-Castel, brought his brother Horace, as well as Bois-le-Comte and Vicomte Freycinet of the diplomatic corps. The Marquis de Lagrenée, envoy extraordinary to China, was probably introduced by Théophile de Ferrière, who went there as first secretary. These diplomats all corresponded with Stern. Horace Viel-Castel, diplomat, caricaturist, and writer, had recorded the court life of the Restoration. Stern called him "Vieux-Château." He was one of the best actors in plays put on in her salon. In 1866 the actress Mlle Favart played a leading role in an act from Corneille's *Psyche* and from Ponsard's *Agnès de Méranie*. The latter was performed not only for literary reasons but also as a riposte to the Comédie-Française, which had refused Ponsard's work on political grounds. Favart participated with the actor Coquelin the elder in the salon's homage to Ponsard after his death in 1870.

Although her dramas were never played by the French theater establishment, Stern did present her own *proverbes*, or salon plays, along with those of others, including Alfred Musset and Girardin. One of hers, "Ninon," dealt with the youth of the famous seventeenth-century beauty Ninon de Lenclos and how her friends persuaded her not to enter the convent. Its moral was that one should always be available to one's friends. Other outlines of plays can be found among Stern's papers, none completed. But she did publish in 1859 another novella, *Boîte aux lettres* (Post-box). Composed as a series of letters, it recounts a story that ends in the death of wife, husband, and lover and represents a return to romanticism, a recall of that true passion which is always fatal. The lover writes in phrases reminiscent of the early letters of Liszt; the date on the letters is May 1839. It is as if Daniel Stern was recalling the days when Marie d'Agoult nearly died of love. Or perhaps it was inspired by the last (unnamed) man who proposed to her.[3] In 1863 Stern made her debut as a poet in the *Revue germanique*, with three poems—"In Alta Solitudine," "Sérénité," and "Oceano Nox" (or "Adieu").[4]

The Second Empire was Stern's period of plenitude, in which she fully developed her talent and acquired a measure of inner peace. She returned to the European authors who meant the most to her and finally found her literary style—as critic, not novelist. *Dante et Goethe* was dedicated to Cosima:

Your birth and your name are Italian; your desire or your destiny has made you German. I was born on German soil; my star is in the Italian sky. [Performances of her *Joan of Arc* were taking place in Italy at the time.] That is why I wanted to address these memories, which mingle Dante and Goethe, to you—a double cult, in which our souls meet, an ideal homeland, where, whatever happens, and when everything here below would separate us, we will always remain united in an unchanging love.[5]

Claire and Cosima, her only remaining children, were the only ones to whom Stern dedicated books.

The work was presented in dialogues, a form in which she could set a readable background for what was a piece of literary scholarship. Over five days three friends picnicking on a mist-covered beach in Brittany discuss the two greatest authors of Europe with Diotima, who has spent her life reading and rereading them, along with their commentaries. Named after the wise woman in Plato's *Symposium*, Diotima is clearly the professor of this seminar and represents Stern. But the other women also participate and move the topic along, while the man provides challenges that Diotima easily answers.

The first comparison Stern made between Dante and Goethe was that both dealt with human destiny on earth and beyond—not, as in the ancient poets, with war and the founding of cities or states but with the problem of good and evil in the human conscience. Although both poets expressed permanent and universal preoccupations of the human spirit, each represented a particular epoch and nation, basing his metaphysical poem on a popular legend. Both were the principal actors in their works. And both expressed the same ideal: the infinite, absolute love of an eternal god who draws to himself the love of mortal creatures. Diotima provides her listeners with a short history of Florence and the life of Dante before discussing his work. She does the same with Goethe and Frankfurt, telling the story about meeting him as a child. She says she still attaches a kind of superstition to that moment when he patted her curly head, as if he were her good genie bestowing on her a benediction.

It is woman who serves as mediator between human love and the divine love that informs both *The Divine Comedy* and *Faust.* This leads to a discussion of platonic love, described as a mixture of asceticism and sensuality.

Diotima notes that Héloise, in her love for Abélard, refused to think of sharing with him the petty round of domestic life. In those days marriage had nothing to do with real love; even today, Diotima adds, it is only a shameful contract of sale. The group also discusses religion. Diotima calls Dante's work the bible of the Florentines, which, like any bible, needs exegesis. It uses the symbols of his time; although they may not be our symbols, they arouse in us the basic emotions. Dante used the language of freedom of thought—Italian—and therefore was considered suspect by the church, which also condemned polyphonic singing as too free. Diotima quotes Cardinal Pacca, sent from Rome to convey papal condemnation of Lamennais's *L'Avenir,* on the theology of civil and political freedom: "If in certain circumstances prudence demands that they be tolerated as a lesser evil, they can never be presented by a Catholic as a good thing, or as a desirable state of affairs."[6] She says that Mazzini thinks Dante is Christian but not Roman Catholic, noting that a current edition of *The Divine Comedy,* edited by Protestants, is on the Index of Forbidden Works. Diotima thinks Dante's work is Catholic but mingled with unorthodox elements in Italian society—the influence of Arabs and of pagan antiquity.

She describes Goethe as having a Unitarian type of religion, in which Christ was a central figure but other saints, martyrs, and prophets had their place as well—rather like the ancients who took everyone's gods into their pantheon. The book is full of aphorisms, for which Stern was already known, for example, "Prudence is negative by nature, from which it follows that generally the feeble do well to follow the advice of counsellors, but the strong do better to pass beyond them." When asked if universal suffrage is any more meaningful to people than their local myths, Diotima answers: "Believe me, before long that [electoral] urn . . . will constitute an irresistible magic; that square of white paper where the peasant, with his rude hand, will one day write the name that pleases him, according to the dictates of his conscience, passion or interest, will give the republic to govern it a Cromwell, a Lincoln, a Medici or a Bonaparte!"[7]

On Faust as the modern man who wants to make a terrestrial paradise out of chaos, who has in him the disinterested love of generations to come, Diotima quotes Emerson on not dragging after oneself the corpse of memory,[8] and she declares that the sentiment of anyone animated with the genius of life and matured by conscience should be to repair evil rather than cry over it. To Goethe, the true morality was that of compassion. Diotima insists that both poets saw life as a cult, an offering, and a perpetual sacrifice to God in which the human being is priest and victim at the same time.

An idiosyncratic work, *Dante et Goethe* is a testament to Stern's broad European culture. For most of her life the two authors' works had been her bibles. She had read all of the commentators on them up to her time and worked to recreate the context of their works. She did obscure passages that disagreed with her thesis and also emphasize certain aspects of the two lives to make them comparable. But to her they provided a humanistic ethic that she shared.

The greatest critic of her day, Sainte-Beuve, recognized the quality of Marie's work. He wrote to Marie that he had always admired her as Diotima [the wise woman], although it was true that he was attracted by her blond hair. "But today I am happy to listen to Diotima in her purest, severest, most lovable form yet: this latest work in which she has summed up all the education of her mind, all the honey of her doctrine and her wise poetics, enchants me; it instructs me, and I cannot do better from now on than to take the author for guide whenever I desire to travel in these lovely regions. . . . Diotima has created there a work that only she among us could create."[9] And to Allart he wrote, "Diotima has recalled all of Dante to me, and has conducted me further than has any other commentator into the sense of the great work. How she walks with firm pace and serene brow! For Goethe she recalled, or completely taught him to me."[10] And yet, still punishing her for rejecting him, he never published a word about the book.

By the late Second Empire, Marie had completed her religious evolution. Early in her life she had set off in good faith on the quest for God, with meager success. In *Esquisses morales,* she wrote that faith was often only an illusion of the heart and, more often, a revolt of imagination against reason. She blamed the Catholic Church for no longer addressing either the heart or the mind of the faithful; it only demanded resignation and obedience, making women and the proletariat the victims of modern society. Devotion to the Virgin Mary she dismissed as the remnant of an old nature cult that had been Christianized. Opposed to the miracle of Lourdes and all miracles, she blamed priests for using supernatural stories to gain ascendancy over their parishioners. "Liszt returns to the folly of the cross! His letters have no interest," she wrote in her diary in 1847.[11]

However, Marie still sought signs that the Catholic Church might reform itself. She could not envision Italy becoming Protestant, as she wrote to Allart, "our lovely pagan Italy in the clutches of St. Paul." She became interested in the Italian Ausonio Franchi, a brilliant young priest who became an apostate. He reminded her of Lamennais, and she encouraged him. In an article for *Le Temps* she asked why the Catholic Church was unable to keep such men; she treated their apostasy as one of the defining traits of nineteenth-century thought.[12]

Protestantism attracted Stern because she felt it preserved the dignity of human thought and did not bend itself to a universal and unchanging dogma. In the Preface to the second edition of the *Esquisses morales,* she praised the reform religion for rejecting the despotism of the Bible, for freeing the spirit of Jesus from his flesh, and for allying itself with science. Applying the Darwinism of the time, she added that science taught that the ability to vary is in nature a characteristic sign of superiority. Many of those who attended her salon were Protestants—Henri Martin, Lazare Carnot, and Eugène Pelletan. Jules Simon saw it as a road to natural religion; Favre was a convert.

Of course, Stern referred only to liberal Protestantism.[13] She was attracted to the most liberal Unitarianism of Emerson and William Ellery Channing in the United States. She was also interested in *morale indépendante,* a French ethic current at the time that was based on the rights of the individual and on reason, which recognized that these rights must be reciprocally accorded. Completely secular in orientation, *morale indépendante* was drawn from Proudhon's *Justice dans la Révolution et dans l'Eglise.* Stern met Alexandre Massol, executor of Proudhon's will and the leading proponent of the doctrine, as a neighbor in the Boulevard Poissonière and was impressed by him. Two of the regulars at her salon were also propagandists for the new movement—a Doctor Clavel and the young republican Henri Brisson. Stern was therefore approving of the first Advent sermon of Père Hyacinthe Loyson at the cathedral of Notre Dame in December 1865, which found some virtues in *morale indépendante.* However, the church hierarchy did not approve, and the chastened cleric had to back-pedal for the remainder of the sermons.

Attracted to Protestantism, Stern was opposed to any Protestant fanaticism. She disapproved highly of Quinet's writing on Holland, because he pictured the wars of liberation from Spain as fanatical Protestantism triumphing over fanatical Catholicism.[14] The first result of her research on the formation of the Dutch Republic appeared in 1855, the year after his articles. She published seven articles and a small book on the subject over the course of nine years.[15]

Unlike Quinet, Stern preferred to see statesmanship triumph over fanaticism. Henry IV and Elizabeth I were her models; they demonstrated a religious indifference that she saw as the very foundation of statesmanship. She portrayed the failure of Phillip II of Spain to bring the Dutch to heel as also the failure of the medieval church in the modern world, a process still at work in her time. "We are living through a slow decomposition of Catholicism, without seeing anything ahead that will take its place. We don't know how to attack it passionately, as in the eighteenth century; we feel it is too wounded," she wrote in her diary. Nevertheless, she hoped for a schism in the church at the death of the Pope.[16] Published between others on Italy, on Dante and Goethe and other subjects, the series of articles on Holland was completed by three in 1863, which were very much admired. (Littré was so admiring that he memorized whole portions of them by heart and would recite them on the slightest provocation.) But although Stern continued to work on her Dutch history, she was not to publish the first and only volume until 1872.

Stern's religious ideals, as stated in *Dante et Goethe,* were based on Spinoza. From Spinoza she drew certain conclusions: the infinite development of intelligence, an underlying harmony that resolved the opposites of freedom and necessity, and a commandment of love unaffected by fears of eternal damnation. God was the soul of the world, the living law of the universe, the eternal Becoming, the supreme reason and virtue of all things. This pantheism she shared with Dolfuss. The Germanic side of her also tended to the belief that God, singular or plural, seen indistinctly in the mirror of nature, was revealed only progressively, in history. This "mute god" was the subject of a poem Stern wrote and published in the *Revue germanique.*[17] She dedicated it to Madame Ackermann.

Stern had written in *Dante et Goethe* that belief in immortality through one's works dominated the whole of Dante's poem. She was, as she had mentioned to Liszt, preparing her memoirs—collecting material and asking people for her correspondence. She used her brother Maurice as a source of information about their old acquaintances and their childhood. Claire researched the family background. Marie felt that in writing her memoirs she would make Blandine and Louise live again. She wrote in her diary, "If I retrace in my memory the face of Blandine, I will have given her life for the second time." She also recalled Louise's last cry in her mortal illness: "*'Mama!'* That profound cry of human distress in the mouth of a child, I will hear it over again forever."[18]

The first volume she had completed in publishable form by 1866—"publishable in the sense that it does not take up any *delicate* matter,"[19] she wrote to Claire. It covered her infancy and the world of the salon in the early years of her marriage. The only part she saw published was a description of the Faubourg Saint-Germain in the 1867 *Paris-Guide.* Ronchaud, who was the executor of her writings, published this first volume after her death as *Mes souvenirs;*[20] it went into a second edition within the year. It is, besides the history of the 1848 revolution, the book for which she is best known, because of her witty and revealing descriptions of the monarchy and aristocratic society in France during the Restoration.

In her Preface, she discussed the pros and cons of autobiography. A woman, who could hold no public office, had no need to be forthcoming, to render account to society. But by breaking out of the normal life of women she had perhaps contracted masculine duties. She noted that influence in public life was not only exerted in war or public office. A woman might also make people see things in a new way. She suggested that in her time women sensed the problems of society better than men did, for they suffered more than men from a world that had lost its faith and its respected customs.

There were other reasons for writing memoirs: "When you look closely at a life, it is unbelievable—complicated, irrational, having no plan or law. But at a distance, viewed from above, its main lines stand out, an ensemble appears."[21] Autobiography cannot, then, consist of photographic images of real life. Like the poet or artist, the biographer eliminates all prolixities and redundancies, distributes light and shadow to achieve the simple expression, the simple unity that strikes the senses. She referred to Goethe, whose memoirs, *Dichtung und Wahrheit,* were a combination of truth and poetry. In *Dante et Goethe,* she had described him as a person for whom the ideal and the real intertwined inseparably, "forming in the depths of his being a tight weave and composing a harmonious design." When asked if this was not lying, Diotima replied: "To put all one's art into one's life and all one's life into one's art . . . is a divine lie . . . through which one gains immortality."[22] In this, and in the assertion that women might also influence public life, Stern came close to admitting her own desire for greatness and immortality.

As she proceeded, friends were consulted on the project. Girardin encouraged her, on the condition that she treat her passion for Liszt with frankness. He said she would not be courageous enough. "You will come up to the edge of the ditch and you will not jump."[23] Marie herself wished to explain and immortalize her relationship with Liszt. She admitted that the first product of that desire had been the somewhat vengeful roman à clef, *Nélida.* Now she emphasized that their love affair had to be understood in the context of the time. In the Preface to the second volume she described the era of Romanticism, when, with all traditions overturned by the Revolution of 1789, people sought the ideal, the sense of divinity in everything. In this time of overwrought passions, she and Liszt had met each other, and their love had "all the characteristics of the milieu in which it was born."[24] Pondering the proportion of freedom and of necessity in human actions, she asked how, since it was impossible to know, could one make moral judgments, particularly on matters of the heart and the passions? Stern looked forward to a better time—when religious morality would have given way to an ethic based on reason, and when men and women, more similar in their culture and more equal in their rights, would no longer misunderstand one another. In that ideal society, passion would not be so destructive.[25]

This second volume was never published until her grandson, Daniel Ollivier, edited it in 1927. The main reason was the opposition of Ronchaud who, unlike Girardin, was against the kind of revelation that he felt would be held against her. As a result, she left at her death some finished sections and some fragments of the whole work, which she kept rewriting until the end. When finally published, *Mémoires, 1833–1854* did not include everything she had written. One notable omission was about Liszt: "It is to *him* that I owe everything; he inspired in me a great love. He weaned me away from the vanities [of my life], then he weaned me from himself, cruel but salutary. If he had been what he should have been, I would have stayed. My name would never have emerged from obscurity."[26]

It was Ronchaud who held her back from publishing about Liszt. Faithful preserver of her memory, he had met Marie and Liszt in Geneva when he was nineteen. A lyric and dramatic poet, he managed to tranform his passion for Marie into a platonic devotion. His value to her was greater in that he knew and appreciated Liszt also, had been witness to all stages of the stormy relationship, and understood it completely. During her time with Liszt, Ronchaud had tended Marie through outbreaks of fever that had brought on delirium. Two of the "Lettres d'un bachelier" were addressed to him. Called "Quotidien" by the couple, Ronchaud was always there to run errands, first for both of them, then for Marie. Although he had encouraged Marie to leave Liszt, he continued to value the musician's genius, which pleased her. She referred to him in her diary as "the vibrant and conciliating connection" between her past and her present. A literary critic, he became secretary general of the Beaux Arts in 1879, then director of the National Museums after her death.

In all but conjugal rights, Ronchaud was Marie's husband, devoted and adoring for forty years. Despite her aging—by the 1860s she had lost some teeth, had weak eyes, had gone white, and had deep lines in her face—Ronchaud danced attendance on her daily, the same courtier he had been decades before. He only left her to take care of his estates at Saint-Lupicin, near Sainte-Claude in the Jura. She passed many summers on this estate; from 1865 on, when she was often unwell, she would retire there. She found it romantic, though spartan, like Ronchaud himself. Actually, he entertained her in a grand style that he could ill afford. In his library she reread Spinoza and Marcus Aurelius while convalescing.

Thus Ronchaud's whole life, in art, letters, and politics, was devoted to serving Marie. She never published a single line that he did not read first; he tended, unfortunately, to praise rather than criticize. In the 1840s he was the indispensable proofreader and negotiator with editors; later, she hired secretaries. The papers she left him as her literary executor passed to his brother, a *conservateur* at the Louvre, after Ronchaud's death in 1887. A fire in the Louvre destroyed many documents, including some of Marie's. After that, the rest were given to the family.

Younger than Marie, Ronchaud was seconded by a man fourteen years younger than she—Louis Tribert, a distant relative through Marie's grandmother, Madame Lenoir. A traveler, Tribert had been to Asia and North America, and he shared Marie's attachment to Italy. He sent her passionate letters and spent with her as much time as possible. He was another of those whose passion Marie transformed into ardent friendship. Although upset that he was assumed to be her lover, she often traveled with him, to Brittany in 1847 and later to England. She found him necessary to her in a different way from Ronchaud. They went to lectures and plays together, read the same books, and exchanged impressions. He also entertained her on his estate in summers or when she was recovering from illness. Like Ronchaud, he was always available to her. Tribert remained a bachelor until after Marie's death and then at age fifty-seven married her chambermaid! Marie refused, after Liszt, to accede to men's desire and offered them instead friendship and an intellectual relationship. As one of her biographers noted, "That is the secret of the crowd in her salon and the solitude in her heart."[27]

One of the reasons for the hospitality Marie accepted more and more often from Ronchaud and Tribert was her financial situation, which had seriously deteriorated by the late 1850s. From this time on, she rented an apartment during the Paris season and traveled a lot out of season, living *en pension*[28] in the provinces with only one servant and with a smaller wardrobe, so that her diminished lifestyle would not be obvious to Paris society. She explained to Claire that because she was too poor to keep up an acceptable establishment at Paris, she found periods of absence strongly advisable. She chose Italy for its climate and its cosmopolitan society, impossible to partake of in Paris without a good deal of money but easily available in Italy with little. By the mid-1860s, Marie was bankrupt, and all Paris was aware of it. Without complaint, she began to sell her jewelry, with the permission of her husband who was also poor and needed some support. She lived on a small pension, aided by Ronchaud and Tribert in case of need.

This situation produced the last word we know of on Marie from her old friend, Sand. In a letter to a third party she wrote:

I feel sorry for Madame d'Agoult. They say she is ruined. For her that must be a true unhappiness. I saw her, still young, brave and in love, surrounded with everything and beautiful in her insouciance. But love and youth have fled. She needed golden luxury and to lose it today is not easy. I think however that she will triumph because she has a great aspiration to be more than herself. I know her bad side, but I also know the good ones, and without wishing to ally myself with her again, I hope that she will be happy. She searched too much for a role in the world; she didn't need to, being herself above what she dreamed of. By collecting her thoughts at her advanced age, and by not tormenting herself about others in their relations to her, she could have found herself naturally quite high in relation to them. It is not too late, she will survive if she wishes. Poverty is so healthy for those who embrace it strongly.[29]

Unfortunately, Marie was not healthy. Throughout her entire life she had experienced the darkness of depression and the temptation of suicide. Even while living with Liszt she had suffered severe spells of depression; after returning to Paris without Liszt, these spells descended upon her regularly. She began a process of self-analysis, through her diary and through letters and conversations with intimate friends, to clarify her life to herself and others. Ronchaud was her main confidant, but there were others. As attacks of what she called her "spleen" occurred in 1842 and 1843, she recorded their effects:[30] "Torpor. Decline. Total loss of memory." Around this time she began a regular correspondence with Louis de Viel-Castel, an old suitor and her link with the aristocratic world of her childhood. With him, she shared her feelings for the rest of her life.

Even while she was writing her history of the 1848 revolution, she occasionally had to forego her salon, complaining of "uncertainty, an uprooted life without action," of "mental collapse, the evil in me recognized and unhealable." During a three-month siege in 1850 she entered a clinic and began to understand something about her symptoms. But again in 1851 she spoke of "infinite melancholy, unspeakable regrets . . . cerebral prostration," of being "more and more inert, cold, without action, incapable of anything."[31] It is true that she was at this time in her mid-forties, Liszt's marriage seemed inevitable, and Claire's seemed to be ending. She was deprived of her children by Liszt and had temporarily lost her relationship with her brother. Her mother had died and disinherited her. She wrote to Allart,

"When one lives a long time, one is always in a state of mourning that keeps on getting longer. . . . I am looking for you to tell me great and profound things about death."[32]

As her history of the 1848 revolution was being published, volume after volume, to great acclaim, Marie found herself more and more "the prey of bewilderment and imbecility." She felt her brain was in atrophy, causing her to lose reason and memory. She wrote that an identical sterility reigned in her mind and in her heart; the universe had lost its interest and charm for her. She referred to her attacks as the bankruptcy of the nerves and tried to understand her situation. "What is this spleen?" she wrote. "How does it happen? Should one see in it a movement of blood which leaves the brain or which pours into it in too great a quantity? But what causes this movement?" No doctor could answer these questions.[33]

Marie knew that the germ of mental illness was in her family. In her diary she listed the suicides in her German family, including her half-sister Auguste, who had jumped into the Main River. However, after a three-month crisis in 1852, perhaps the first of such a serious nature, she tried to discover external causes. She blamed overexcitement while in Holland, or perhaps too much wine, coffee, or cigars, or finally, "a closed-in life" weighing down her brain. She often confided her feelings to Herwegh and his wife, then back in Germany. She wrote that she was "peaceful as a cemetery, resigned as a bird that has broken its wings against the bars of his cage. . . . Life is really nothing but a foolish lie." To Madame Herwegh, who had said women had to put up with half-rations, she replied: "Talk about half-rations, next to what we wanted out of life in our youth it is more like a third, quarter, twentieth. Let us be honest, Emma, sooner or later life deals us slim pickings, which in the beginning we would have rejected fiercely."[34]

Marie seems to have been ill through much of 1856 and 1857. Yet in these two years she wrote a review article on Pictet, her two plays on Mary Stuart and Joan of Arc, and an article on the Dutch revolt. She wrote to Dolfuss, who suffered similar attacks of spleen, from Claire's house at Versailles: "And in truth I do not know, in this beautiful countryside, under these cool shade trees, in the bosom of that radiant nature where all is joy, perfume, heat and light, how I could be so feeble as not to know any more, from moment to moment, why or how I should go on living."[35] In 1858 she remained in a state of lethargy until May, then recovered, only to sicken again with the return of cool weather. She lay prostrate for days on end, yearning to die. Gradually, she was able to get up and walk, but she felt that her intellectual life was over. She dreamed of those she loved, of the places she had visited and wanted to visit. She wanted to die, yet at the same time she strongly wanted to live. "A means of action!" she wrote in her diary. If the gods would send me a means of action I would live and I would spread life all around me."[36]

And that is what usually happened. When she had her crises, she locked the door; when she appeared again to her friends, she had totally recovered. Not only that, but she was optimistic and full of new projects. In 1848, in one of her last letters to Liszt she wrote, "I will tell you that today I have the certainty that in these next ten years, if God lends life to the little fish, it can become big,"[37] and shared with him her confidence in her work on the revolution. In 1852 after a conversation with Ronchaud, who told her she had arrived at a true self-consciousness, she wrote, "I sense that I have always lacked [true self-understanding] and that only this can give me the kind of satisfaction which is possible and necessary for me."[38] She seemed to use these periods of recovery to reassemble her psychic energies.

Marie not only valued her own writing, but she was also a patron of budding writers. It has been suggested that having fallen in love with a man six years younger than she helped her to be sensitive to the qualities of young men of talent. A group of them followed her up to the time of her death. A letter from her distant cousin Charles Söhnée to his friend Henri Charomet speaks of a friend of Lamartine, Madame d'Agoult, whom he and Henri Boucher had wanted to meet. Boucher finally tracked her down to her home and introduced himself. She knew his book and was enthusiastic about it. Each time the shy young man rose to leave, she sat him down again and involved him in conversation about his ideas. He was there for two hours and promised to return, bringing Söhnée. The young writer described her ability to converse about "everything philosophical" in a witty and very impressive manner. Clearly bowled over, he returned with his friend again and again.[39]

The writer François Ponsard was a provincial, uncomfortable everywhere in Paris except at Marie's house. He wrote, "I remember that from the very first day, I set about telling you quite openly all my impressions. I had never met anyone who gave me the same feeling of confidence and ease. . . . On my third visit you brought words to my lips, and my heart in the words." She was his "first tribunal" for anything he wrote. Many of the problems of the artist unable to produce in *Nélida* were actually those she had helped Ponsard to overcome. The young writer spent most of his time back in Vienne but corresponded with her regularly. She gave him her constant and faithful support in his work and eventually helped him get a seat in the Academy.

She wrote an article on him for *Le Temps* in 1867, the year his *Galilée* was produced by the Comédie-Française.[40]

By the 1860s Marie felt she had made a place for herself in the world, without either returning to the aristocrat milieu or descending into the bohemian life that many had assumed for her after Liszt. As she wrote to Mazzini, "If for the pain of my intimate life I have sought the consolation of writing, it is much less in the hope of the good that I can do to others than in the *pride* of not descending to lesser consolations or alleviations."[41] She was proud that she had retained her freedom and her dignity and had attained some success as a writer. She felt she was creating herself. Although she acknowledged to herself that none of her books was a masterpiece, she saw her life as one. Conscious of herself as different, both in running away with Liszt and in parting from him, she also felt that in making her own life, she was acting in conformity with the new morality of her time. She recorded that the positivist Célestin de Blignières called her one of the three figures possessing the true social instincts of the coming age, along with Littré and John Stuart Mill.

When she had returned to Paris without Liszt, Marie had taken as her motto "In alta solitudine," to protect herself and because she felt herself unique in her implacable demand for truth. She felt her character had matured. "I was sweet and submissive, I have become good and remain true; I was passionate, I have become generous." She wanted "to radiate more and more, to act on the spirit of my time,"[42] and felt she had established the ability to stir people with her writing. In a conversation with Ronchaud she concluded that her nature was masculine in that her reason, imagination, and heart were separated. In her mid-fifties, Marie did seem to have achieved a serenity, an almost virile strength from her victory over herself. She admitted that she lacked tenderness, what Eckstein called *sensibilité,* and that was why certain men were not charmed by her friendship, which, she wrote, was masculine. "Only my senses are dominated by imagination. . . . Intelligence governs all. What is lacking in my style is a bit of what Lamartine and Sand have too much of. I never write something when carried away by nature; I always know why I write things."[43] Or, as she put it another time, "I was born with reason and imagination. I have put the imagination into my life and the reason into my books."[44]

Nevertheless, she was still beautiful; no longer slender to the point of evanescence, she retained the aristocratic carriage and demeanor of her youth and her impeccable taste. White had taken over her blond hair early, so she moved to darker colors in clothing (purple velvet was a favorite) and to black or white lace over her head. In 1862 she recorded some compliments in her diary. Girardin brought one from the Marquise Du Bellay, who said that with her Germanic air, she was even more lovely than her portraits. Félix Henneguy, seeing her on the street, told someone that she affected him like "a spurt of light, a swift bedazzlement." Tribert found her beauty at age fifty-six surprising.[45] That was the year the photographer Adam-Salomon asked to capture her on film.

But she had not conquered her inner demons. In 1862 she confided to her diary that she had no longer the desire to write, let alone publish. In 1863 she spent three months in the clinic of Dr. Blanche in Passy, where she had been before.[46] Her period of depression plunged her into sorrow; she felt she was crazy and losing her memory. The following year she wrote in her diary, "How to end with dignity is the question I ask myself. I yearn for solitude but I don't dare." Was she contemplating suicide? The next year, in a letter to Henneguy in Italy she wrote, "The sight of an inkwell arouses horror in me, and the scratching of a pen on paper gives me a fever."[47] Yet in these three years she put out new editions of her history and of *Essai sur la liberté,* both with new prefaces, published seven articles on various subjects, three poems, three parts of her work on Dante and Goethe, and three of her work on the Dutch revolution!

In 1865 she wrote in her diary, "For the first time I feel that I have a great talent, a superior *demon* in me. [I feel] my authority, my influence. I am full of joy, and I thank God for it."[48] She stopped worrying about her finances, which were getting worse and worse. In fact, it seemed that Tribert was subsidizing her "in a kind of common ménage," as a somewhat shocked Claire wrote to Cosima. He kept his own apartment while actually living in and sharing the expenses of hers. She had a chambermaid; he had a cook and a domestic. In 1865 he seems to have lent her thirty thousand francs, which she repaid in small amounts.[49]

One day in June 1867, with Tribert away, Marie dismissed her coach at the Suresnes bridge, to walk along banks of Seine River. When she arrived home hours later she was out of breath, haggard, and without her cloak. She said she had returned running, fearing that a policeman would stop her on the way. Her intimates suspected a suicide attempt, but no one could be sure. Ronchaud stayed with her until she was more calm. The following April an attack rendered her prostrate for some days, unable even to read, let alone write. She later wrote to Tribert, "Between two horrible crises from the bottom of my heart [I send] thanks and ardent good wishes to you, incomparable friend who would have saved me if that had been possible, you to whom

I owe so many happy hours in a life that is today so somber."[50] It was after this crisis that she went off to Ronchaud's estate in the Jura and engaged in a campaign for the election of Jules Grévy to the Chamber. She then proceeded to Nice, where she visited Ollivier and her grandchild; she stayed there with Madame Ackermann until the new year. Somehow she had published three articles that year. But the following year, 1869, was to be the worst of Marie's life, again beginning in April.

Claire described it in a letter to Cosima. While at home in the rue de Presbourg, "Mother must have made some public manifestation of madness. The neighbors complained. They notified my uncle [Maurice] Flavigny." He called on Guy de Charnacé, Claire's ex-husband, to share the responsibility of committing her. Her obsession was that they were going to dissect her alive! "Mama was put in a straitjacket, and rose out of her stupor only to cry out or to push her head out to butt something or someone with her forehed." Her agitation increased when her hated sister-in-law showed up to give her the comforts of religion, seeking some form of profession of faith. Claire, called from Versailles, intervened and sent her aunt away. Unfortunately, a surgeon had to be called to the clinic to operate on a carbuncle. Considering Marie's hallucination of being dissected alive, the operation must have been an excruciating experience.

When Marie returned home, Claire spent all the time she could at her mother's side, until she got the impression that "my presence upset her more, excited her, did her harm. Therefore I limited myself to being in the apartment without entering her room. Mr. Tribert found also that that was better."[51] Marie later wrote to her daughter from Saint-Lupicin, where Ronchaud had taken her when she was well enough:

My dear child, if I have not written you before, it is not that I have not thought of you and of the signs you have recently given of your affection. But it seemed to me that after so many terrible moments for which I have been responsible, a little silence would be better for you than the revived memory of those sad hours. I only just learned here that you had, for the sake of my peace, strongly protested against a certain too-Catholic zeal, and I sincerely thank you for it. I intend to write some lines for you on that subject which in a similar situation, soon or later, will give you still more force and authority, for hypocrisy in death appears to me more detestable than in life.[52]

The promised authority gave Claire "the absolute right to prevent anyone from introducing to my bedside a Catholic priest." Marie indicated that she denied neither the moral law nor the hope of a future life but that "my law, my hope, my ideal of justice, finally my God has nothing in common with the laws of a church with which I parted voluntarily and seriously many years ago." She declared that she wished to leave at least "the example of sincerity of conscience, persuaded that, if this became the law of the majority, our society, worn out with superstition and hypocrisy, would recover the moral vigor it has lost." She also asked Claire to destroy all correspondence in which she had said anything bad about anybody.[53]

In September Marie had to return to Paris because of an abscess on her breast; it turned out not to be malignant but led to another crisis. This time it was Tribert who took her to his tiny Henry IV house with four towers in Puyraveau, in the Deux-Sèvres region. Each day they went out in the carriage, but the least incident plunged Marie into terror. She finally seemed to recover, and Tribert reported to her friends that she had sat quietly in the courtyard during the afternoon, where for the first time in two weeks she showed an interest in the newspapers he read her.

After this series of bouts with her malady, Marie seemed to be relieved of her demons. Even her handwriting became rounder and more legible. Whereas her signature had been a tiny squiggle before, she now began to sign with her whole name. Her correspondence with her daughters lost its heightened tone and became calmer. Claire, who was never to lose her persistent hostility toward a mother who had abandoned her at a young age, had her own view of Marie's psyche, as revealed in her comments on her mother's illness. Claire insisted that there were "two Madame d'Agoults," totally separate, of which the tenderhearted one was the sickest. In any case, one personality always destroyed the projects of the other: "*She was always unhappy.*" Perhaps Claire was impelled to this description of a split personality by a letter to her from Ronchaud, written from Nice after a bad period of Marie's. He wrote that her mother was worse in the morning, during the period she was accustomed to working. She was better in the afternoon and evening, when fatigue set in.[54]

Was her problem really, as one biographer has said, that she had staked her all on her romance with Liszt and that she was sickened by a "pathological love" because she could not emotionally admit what her mind recognized—that what she had made her reason for living was over?[55] It is true that Liszt—less as a reality than as an ideal—continued to occupy an important place in her life. Marie never gave up her dream of ideal love, which she was better able to retain in Liszt's absence. Even though in later life she was prey to new humiliations from Liszt, who ridiculed their life together for the pleasure of the princess and other women, Marie still tried to preserve her belief in the purity and the ideal nature of her one love. Nor would she sully it in her own mind or anyone else's by taking a new lover.

However, Marie was gradually able to disconnect Liszt himself from the ideal that she retained. Portions of an unpublished novel in her papers describe a dream in which Liszt (called Wolfram) appears in two persons—one "all radiant with a calm seraphic beauty," the other "possessed by some demoniac power." The heroine, Palma, awakes with a start, bathed in perspiration and trembling all over, in the embrace of the demonic figure. When she told Wolfram he smiled bitterly and said that the two figures were himself, the one as she would like him to be and the other as life had made him.[56]

It is also true that the terrible decade of the sixties was one in which she saw Liszt again on his three visits to Paris. She also decided to put out a new edition of *Nélida,* which greeted the abbé on his third visit. The dates of his visits—1861, 1864, and 1867—do not in any way fit with those of her psychological crises. And yet it must have been difficult not only to be faced again with her failure as a woman but also to have the Abbé Liszt imposed on her ideal. Perhaps one can see the attacks of the 1860s to some extent as a final purging of the past, since they were never again as bad in 1869.

There are possible sources for mental illness in a woman other than heredity and disappointed love. Louis de Viel Castel, whose courtship was frustrated, put his finger on one aspect of the relationship when he accused her of never having known true love with Liszt. "At the moment you are making those immense sacrifices to your love, inspired by a delerious exaltation, is it not true that your soul, always proud, does not bend under the yoke of his? Your heart, your mind, your feelings, are they confounded with his? . . . His opinions, tastes, preferences, do they become yours without effort, and do you find in that abnegation of your moral being the significant sensual pleasure that would be the most certain sign of love?"[57] Surely, Marie must have recognized that he was right—that she was unable to sacrifice to Liszt her judgment or her persona—even if she did not concede that such a sacrifice was necessary to true love.

Even before meeting Liszt, Marie wanted her life to be meaningful. She did not find meaning in marriage, motherhood, or aristocratic life. She also wanted to be *somebody,* beyond the importance of her birth, beauty, and charm. Liszt provided the possibility of meaning and importance—as muse to a great artist. Perhaps the most important aspect of her desire to be muse to Liszt had been that through him she had expected to be great, to give direction to her world, and to have what women did not have—power.

She first accepted indirect power, the inspiration that she as a beautiful woman could provide to a great artist, but inspiration came to include an element of control. After all, she was more than a muse to Liszt. She completed his education; she wrote his articles. Of course, their love had to be ideal in order to justify devoting her life to it, and ideal love could not be indefinitely sustained. Therefore, Marie had to seek other meaning, becoming a writer and intellectual. But she learned that she could not ever *control* the actions of others—not of the artist Liszt and, during the 1848 revolution, not of the politician Lamartine. Unhappy with the leadership of the Second Republic, she dreamt of running it herself. "I would love to govern," she had written in her diary in June 1848.

It is becoming recognized that women in the nineteenth century did sicken because they could neither have power nor recognize publicly that they wanted it. Marie was at least able to admit it to her diary and, occasionally, to friends. Why then did she not follow the more radical feminists and seek power directly? Because she had a good sense of how ridiculous she would seem and how she would lose the little influence she had slowly built up. Better to keep the power one has than lose it all. Better to reach as high as possible in what one can do, by educating oneself, by writing articles and books, and by presiding over a salon.

There were some in Parisian society who sensed the countess's desire for influence and, because she was a woman, made her suffer for it. The critic Barbey d'Aurevilly, in his series on bluestockings, described her books as pretentious and then attacked her as a woman "once beautiful, but with a metaphysical beauty . . . with a face correct as a medallion, unwarmed even by her blond hair quickly turned white between old age and [too much] thinking." He called her an Amazon whose left breast had been withered by philosophy and indicated that sensual men were not attracted by her. "They say that in her faraway youth she committed follies of passion. Follies [would be] astonishing with that face. But she must have committed them coldly, like her books."[58]

There were others who, entertained at Marie's table, were put off by her encyclopedic knowledge, her ability to discuss abstruse topics, and her willingness to make judgments. They associated these qualities with men and instead found them manifested by a highly gracious woman, beautifully dressed, still reflecting the aristocratic world of her birth. Although some men, particularly the young, were captivated, some of the older generation could not forgive her what they saw as her pretension to be more than she was—which was, after all, only a woman. The real hubris, which they may have only intuited, was that she, like them, longed for power and glory.

Some glory Stern achieved, from her books. And yet it was not enough, particularly when compared, in her typical ruthless honesty, with the fame of a George Sand. Some of Marie's worst attacks of spleen came with the publication of her works, because the fame they brought her was not enough. Although Marie might seem to have been physically fragile because of her mental instability, she was actually robust most of her life. She had borne five children, done a great deal of traveling, and written reams of books, articles, and letters. If she had been a man, she would have put some of that energy into a life of politics, which was of overwhelming interest to her. As a woman, she did what she could and manifested her frustration in spleen.

Fourteen ∼ *"I have never
felt entirely French or entirely
German but apart, isolated,
somewhat foreign as well in the
country where I was born as in that
where destiny had me live."*

D aniel Stern's articles about Italy continued to appear in *Le Siècle* in 1860 and in *Le Temps* in 1861.[1] She stopped sending them to Mazzini, confessing that although still a republican, she disagreed with his intransigence; she preferred the flexibility of Manin, who had been willing to put his republic of Venice under a federation led by Victor Emmanuel. Stern published her Italian articles in a book entitled *Florence et Turin*. In it she pictured the large number of revolutionaries proscribed by their different countries, who joined together in the free places of Europe, forming a kind of community, "a laic church, fortified, like all churches, by persecution." From this group was proceeding "one of the most profound transformations that the world will perhaps ever have seen. . . . The establishment of a vast republican confederation of all western nations is being elaborated almost before our eyes."[2] Thus she treated the changes going on in Italy in the context of a larger European movement, whose representatives she knew personally.

Stern was still seeking to play an active role in society, particularly in politics. As a center of the liberal opposition to the Second Empire, her salon drew like-minded editors, such as Jules Simon, Pierre Lanfrey, Louis Ratisbonne, Paul Janet, Léon Pascal-Duprat, Laurent Pichat, Dolfuss, Nefftzer, and occasionally Girardin, who was not a republican. There were authors, such as Ponsard, Edouard Grénier, and Leconte de Lisle (who taught her Latin), and political writers, such as Henri Martin, Pelletan, Laboulaye, and Prévost-Paradol (who was for some time her secretary). Littré, Renan, Vacherot, Laboulaye, and others were preparing the great *Encyclopédie de xixᵉ siècle*.

Stern was asked to write the articles on modern religion and modern revolution.

There were also budding political figures like Ollivier, Simon, Hippolyte Carnot, Floquet, Jules Ferry, and Grévy (who, she correctly predicted, would be president of the next republic). Stern began to have two salon days, one for artistic types and the other for political figures. In the final years of the Empire her different salon days served to separate the various republicans of the political spectrum. This spectrum extended more as Ollivier and his followers grew closer to working within the empire. As more republicans became willing to take the oath to the emperor, those who refused turned their backs on them. Stern herself was torn between her opposition to the Empire and her desire for political change. As the most intransigent republicans moved away, her salon was more popular with the moderates, led by Ollivier. Even Prince Jérôme Bonaparte, partisan of a liberal empire and the bane of his cousin's existence, wanted to be received by Stern.[3]

Ronchaud was absolutely against any contact with a Bonaparte; her republican credentials would suffer if she received him. Girardin, himself a partisan of a liberal empire, pushed it, but on the first occasion, Stern backed out. Finally, a dinner was arranged at the Café Durand during which the three talked politics until midnight. Stern was impressed by the prince's appearance and his desire to please her. He asked again to visit her at home. Finally, she invited him in the company of her friend Alix de Pierreclos, a niece of Lamartine. There are indications that the emperor himself approached Stern, through a go-between, to talk to her about Italian policy.

Although a republican, Stern was not holding out for complete democracy. She wrote to Mazzini, "Our democrats are limited and gross, they oblige us nevertheless to love the republic."[4] Although she was against the ultraleft republicans, who she felt had buried the Second Republic, her politics were somewhat to the left of her son-in-law Ollivier.[5] He shared with her the dislike of a society founded on money and of the Orleanist clique. Both preferred to see movement in the right direction rather than the status quo. Ollivier believed that political action should aim at enlarging freedom within the empire rather than at overthrowing it.

Unfortunately, the young republicans who had now joined Ollivier in the Chamber—Floquet, Ferry, and Gambetta—tended toward militancy; the old ones tended toward a liberal Orleanism. Ollivier stood between the groups. Stern noted that although by her white hairs she was with the old, she was with the young by her militant nature. But she always saw the virtues of compromise. She kept an affectionate eye on Ollivier and was never hostile when he disappointed her; she encouraged him but didn't expect too much. By 1863, with so many of her republican friends in the Chamber, she was looking forward to political activity.

She was practicing on elections to the prestigious Académie française and working for her friend Ponsard, whose inaugural speech praised Voltaire. She was later to support him when he ran for political office. She still discussed politics with Girardin, who initially supported Olliver but grew more radical. The press lord continued to buy and sell newspapers as his opinions changed. Even when not in agreement, Stern always valued the opinions of the friend who had introduced her to journalism and politics. Another editor friend, Pascal Duprat, was in exile with Clémence Royer. He started a periodical, *La Libre Recherche,* with Arnold Ruge, Quinet, Michelet, and others, in Switzerland. Stern published in it, along with democrats from Hungary, Poland, and Italy. She was also a collaborator on *Le Siècle* (with a circulation of thirty-seven thousand), the only republican paper allowed to publish in France.

Stern did became involved in politics again, to a great extent through Ollivier. When Thiers joined the republicans in the Chamber in 1863, he tried to put together a third party. Stern had never liked Thiers, but she saw him as one of the few republicans likely to be a successful leader. Again she was perspicacious; Thiers would be the first president of the Third Republic. The problem for Ollivier was to carve himself a niche in the political spectrum. Like Thiers, he was an excellent orator, but his appearance was more statesmanlike than that of the diminutive Thiers. Stern began giving Ollivier regular advice in her supportive letters.

He gave a speech introducing a coalitions law that would liberalize the empire. The intransigent republicans, led by Jules Simon, attacked him; they did not want liberties from the hand of the emperor. Stern, who was in the Chamber at the time, wrote Ollivier her congratulations for his eloquence and measure; she felt that he would emerge from the situation with honor and predicted for him a great career. Although she preferred a republic, she did not think much of the possibilities of radical republicans for real action. During the fall recess of that year, Ollivier retired to Saint-Tropez to lick his wounds and prepare his counterattack. Stern wrote him encouraging letters in which she counseled him not to attack his enemies but to rise above them.

In 1865 Ollivier gave an address asking the emperor to add real political rights to the civil rights he had already granted. Stern, who had been given a copy of the speech, contacted him the morning he was to give it, advising him not to beg favors from the emperor. "The country should not beg from the Bonapartes, as its interests are not mingled with those of the dynasty. . . . The Bonapartes can be temporarily useful, but never indispensable, to France. It was here before them, and will be here afterwards, still quite healthy when they are all buried."[6] That evening, she said she was content with his speech. But his name as republican was dead. He was invited to call on the empress, who hoped to convert him to a defender of empire. Later, while visiting at the palace, Ollivier met the emperor; the two seemed impressed with each other.

Again Ollivier wrote Stern during the autumn recess, presenting her with his program. She was much impressed by his eloquence and knowledge. But she thought him perhaps not quite prepared for power; there should be more clarity to his program. Quinet, whose history of the Revolution was opposed to the radical Jacobin republicans, was urging him on. Ollivier wrote Stern that the preliminary to any durable freedom was the condemnation of jacobinism by democracy. Stern was not enthusiastic about opposition to the republicans. However, the following year, in debates on the demand for a free press and responsibility of Cabinet ministers to the Chamber, Ollivier took the lead. Although the amendment lost, sixty-two members voted for it. As the emperor weakened, physically and otherwise, he drew Ollivier closer to him, which earned him enemies—Prime Minister Rouher on one side, Thiers and the republicans on the other.

By 1867 Stern was able to write to her friend Henneguy in Italy that the emperor had decided to change the form of government. She approved, preferring to go the way of the liberal empire than to return to a defeated royalty. She feared above all the followers of the last king, the Orleanists under Thiers. Unable, as a woman, to run for office herself, Stern worked, through others, for the candidature of those she supported.

In 1868 there was an election for a vacancy in the Jura, where she was staying with Ronchaud to recover her health. She had been writing "Lettres villageois" for *Le Temps* and had become a partisan of local government and decentralization.[7] Her articles had made her a person of note in the town of Saint-Lupicin; the town council and mayor visited to thank her. She wrote to Ollivier that she was beginning "*la vie politique des femmes*" and added that "if it weren't for the Salic Law and the Constitution of 1852, I really think I would be elected leader of Saint-Lupicin unanimously."[8] When the local deputy to the Chamber died, she urged Ronchaud to solicit the candidacy of Grévy, who had refused to take the oath; of all the republicans, his politics were most like those of Stern. Now Ronchaud and Grévy started a newspaper to support his campaign. (Ronchaud, pushed by Stern, was hoping to run himself in the following year.) She was passionate about Grévy's campaign, which was successful. Up to then extremely ill, she immediately recovered her health. Unfortunately, Ronchaud was to lose in 1869.

At the end of the year, reviewing Dupont-White's book *Official Candidacies* in *Le Temps,* Stern wrote that freedom should not be an expedient but "the permanent necessity of societies founded on the sovereignty of the people." Electors should know what is going on, so their votes would signify approval or disapproval. For instance, they should be informed on such subjects as the budget, relations with Germany, and the aims of foreign policy. "That is what they will not tell you, indiscreet children that you are, and that upsets you."[9]

Ollivier continued to use his considerable oratorical skills to attack Prime Minister Rouher for his hesitant administration of the new reforms. Ollivier was so eloquent that even the republicans were beginning to hate him less. Still, opposed by the extremely republican Freemasons in the 1869 elections, he lost in Paris and had to take a seat from his home *département* in the Var. At the first meeting of the new Chamber, the opposition, including Ollivier, demanded of the government a ministry responsible to the legislature. The emperor responded by another Senatus-consultus with new reforms, which Ollivier convinced them to accept. Stern, while not thinking this document ideal, felt it would at least arouse political interest and participation in the country.

That year, when Ollivier remarried, Marie sent her congratulations. As he became master of the political situation and clearly a candidate for prime minister, Stern grew nervous. Wondering aloud to Prince Jérôme, she asked whether Ollivier, without a revolution, could provide the French with the rights they had always acquired by revolution. Would the emperor allow it? Or the empress? Would he not be considered a hostage of the right? Would the left-wing republicans allow him to operate? The problem was that Ollivier had no party behind him, and as Stern probably recognized at least vaguely, he could not fill government posts with followers to back him.

Nevertheless, on January 2, 1870, Olliver was named prime minister by the emperor and wrote a new Senatus-consultus, actually a constitution for a liberal empire that became the basis for a new regime. It was ratified by a plebiscite of the citizens, who broadly approved. Stern herself remained ambivalent; it satisfied the majority but consolidated the regime. She wrote to Dolfuss, "Whatever happens, in one way or another we are advancing; we are now out of the mire we have been wallowing in for twenty years."[10]

Her ambivalence about the new government did not stop Stern from asking the new prime minister for a position in the appointed Senate for her brother Maurice, who had been allied to the Orleanists since the July Monarchy. Liszt went further, asking Ollivier for the archbishopric for a friend! Because the new regime extended political freedom, the republicans decided to give Olliver a chance. It was not they but the international situation that eventually led to the precipitous downfall of the government.

By the late 1860s Daniel Stern's hopes for a "vast republican confederation" of European nations were collapsing. The *Revue germanique* had changed its name to *Revue moderne*. But Stern rejected as long as possible the idea that her two native lands, France and Germany, might go to war. It would be "against philosophy, against history," she said.[11] In 1868 her friend Prévost-Paradol predicted the war and France's defeat in his work *France nouvelle*. The events of the decade were leading her to a definitive choice between her two native lands.

A long-range trend toward the unification of the Germanies under Prussian auspices had been taking place. The Napoleonic wars had already reduced the number of small Germanic states. A commercial treaty joined the northern states, mostly Protestant. During the revolutionary year 1848 a German parliament had met and failed to unify the country. Prussia had been organized into a constitutional monarchy in which real power remained with the king and his prime minister, Bismarck. The latter took the unification of Germany in hand—and it was not to be under liberal auspices.

In a war with Denmark, Prussia allied with Austria to regain the former German states of Schleswig and Holstein. Then Bismarck saw to it that the two allies fell out over the administration of those states. This resulted in the Austro-Prussian War of 1866 in which Prussia, allied with the northern German states, defeated Austria. France had been neutralized by secret promises of land along the Rhine river. But when Prussia took only seven weeks to crush the Austrian forces at the battle of Sadowa, Bismarck decided that France would get no rewards. This was one of a series of foreign policy defeats for France, including the collapse of an imperial foray into Mexico.[12]

When Thiers made a speech warning of the dangers to France of German unification, Ollivier agreed but pleaded for Franco-German friendship. Stern herself supported German unification, as she had the Italian; she even preferred Prussia to Austria as its leader. In a series of articles in *Liberté* she wrote that Prussia, though militaristic and even feudal to some extent,[13] had produced geniuses and independent minds. It had some parliamentary experience and a liberal (Protestant) religion. However, she was disgusted with the wars Bismarck had provoked throughout the 1860s. Gradually, she came to see that war between France and Prussia was inevitable. In a letter to Claire she quoted her friend Edmond Schérer to the effect that old Europe was entering a period in which it was to be shaken to the marrow of its bones. The same was to apply to Marie herself, then in her sixties.

Bismarck kept the correspondence in which Napoléon III demanded the Rhineland, to make it unlikely that any other nation would help France in a war with Prussia. For there was to be a war with France. Bismarck figured that in defending themselves against the French, even the reluctant states of the Catholic south would be drawn into a German union. Therefore, he waited for an opportunity to provoke France into declaring war on Prussia. It came in 1870, with the question of the throne of Spain. All monarchs in Europe were related, so the crown could be worn by someone from any royal family. Bismarck put forth the candidacy of a Hohenzollern of the Prussian royal house, knowing that France would not accept a Prussian king replacing one of the house of Bourbon on the Spanish throne. Nor did the king of Prussia expect them to; he withdrew the candidacy.

That should have been the end of it. But the French, seeking greater advantage from the situation, insisted that Prussia promise never to support a Hohenzollern candidacy for the throne of Spain. The king refused and sent Bismarck a telegram describing his interview with Gramont, the French ambassador. Bismarck, by editing the telegram, managed to make it sound as if the ambassador had hounded the king (which he had somewhat) and the king had insulted the ambassador (which he had not). He then sent it off to both German and French newspapers. In the nineteenth century, insult was cause for war. The Germans were enraged; the French felt their honor was involved. Napoléon III, who knew from experience in the Italian war that France's army was weak and who had been unable to get the money for modernization that he knew the German army had achieved,[14] opposed war. But the legislature and a jingoist French public were determined to make Prussia pay. In the new liberal empire, the emperor was overruled. France declared war on Prussia, led by Prime Minister Ollivier (who foolishly declared that France went to war with a "light heart"). Bismarck then released the correspondence of the Austrian war, thereby ending any possibility of allies for France.

The emperor, painfully ill from gallstones, nevertheless felt he had to go to the front two days after war was declared on July 26, 1870.[15] The French troops did no better than he had expected, although they fought valiantly.[16] At the end of August they lost the battle of Sedan, and the emperor himself was taken prisoner. This was the signal to Paris for the overthrow of the Second Empire. Ollivier, who had sent the nation to war with optimism, re-treated to Italy, scorned by his countrymen.

Marie was summering at Saint-Lupicin with Ronchaud when war was declared. For her there could be no favorable outcome. Cosima had just ob-tained her divorce from von Bülow and was living with Wagner. Claire's son, Daniel de Charnacé, had just been graduated from the French Naval Acad-emy. Maurice de Flavigny headed up a committee to care for the wounded. After the Battle of Sedan and the declaration of the Third Republic, Paris was besieged by German troops, as was Metz. Marie began to look for a safer place to stay.

This led to an interesting exchange with Cosima in November. At first Marie thought of taking refuge with the couple. Cosima wondered if her mother would be happy "in our milieu," that is, in an exultantly German atmosphere. Marie decided against the visit. Cosima, who had confided to her diary that the French were "the rotten remains of the Renaissance," com-mented, "We are too German for her." Not only was her mother on the French side, but her father was also sympathetic to the French. Cosima con-cluded, "So the gap between us is now beyond repair!"[17] Marie decided to pass most of the winter in Switzerland. Although she invited her daughter to visit her there, Cosima would not think of leaving Wagner and her children.

Cosima was able to judge her mother's position by the article her mother sent her from *Le Temps* in September. Despite her condolences to Ollivier on his political demise, Stern was excited by the declaration of a new republic (the third) in France on September 4. She demanded that peace be declared, since any possible gains had been accomplished on both sides—unification of Germany and a republic in France. "I was born in the land of Goethe," she wrote. "Throughout my life I have fought constantly, as far as I was able, against the old prejudices of the French mind." She declared that Germany had the right to desire its political unification and its proper role in the mod-ern world. But the unity of Germany was no longer in question; whatever the outcome of the war, it was accomplished. Also, the France of monarchies was ended; "only republican France is standing . . . cruelly punished for faults it has not committed, with a large bleeding wound in its flank," it could itself not end the war with honor. "Republican France, peaceful in heart and mind, fights only for the independence and the integrity of the nation," she declared. Any monarch would be foolhardy who thought he could "crush under his feet with impunity a nation still all pulsing with life and honor."[18]

Stern kept up on events in France through her various correspondents.

By the end of October Paris had been besieged and bombarded by the Germans; the last remnant of the French army had capitulated to the Germans at Metz. The new French government was ready to sue for peace, although the people of Paris, who had formed a citizen army, did not agree. In an article published in the *Journal de Genève,* Stern was favorable to peace negotiations. But she wanted a kind of international court of arbitration to be set up, particularly because there were rumors that Prussia would demand the formerly German territories of Alsace and Lorraine. To counter such a demand, Stern pointed out that France had favored Prussia in the Austrian War and had received no territory for it, whereas she had received land (Savoy and Nice) in remuneration for her cooperation in Italian unification. France should not have to suffer for the sins of a Bonaparte, she wrote, piling the responsibility on the emperor by noting that the prime minister had sought both peace and freedom for France.[19]

Stern feared that if the new republic did not negotiate with Bismarck, the Prussian prime minister would make a deal with the emperor. Writing to her friend Charles Söhnée, who was head of France's War Ministry Office, she pointed out that suing for peace would avoid more bloodshed and also save the new republic. In November she left Saint-Lupicin for Switzerland and settled near Geneva. She admitted that she could hate the Prussians and did hate the arrogance of the German nationalists. But she still believed that the interpenetration of French and German culture would render a service to civilization. Corresponding with a committee set up to prevent the reunion of Alsace with Germany, she wrote to its representative, Eugène Poujade, that it was too bad Franco-German relations were drowned in rivers of blood. She regretted that the efforts of *Revue germanique* and *Le Temps* had not succeeded in helping the French to know Germany. If they had, the French would not have been so surprised by their technological efficiency.[20]

Another Alsatian friend, Edouard Schuré, wrote a brochure protesting Bismarck's demand for Alsace. Stern sent it to be published in the *Progrès de Lyon* in December 1870 and later produced a summary of it in the *Journal de Genève.* "One finds no more at this hour, except in some rare spirits, that Germany so just and loyal, so religious and peaceful, which in its arts and its philosophy offered to the world the highest ideal of humanity, that Germany of Herder, of Lessing, of Goethe and Beethoven," she added.[21] In the end she did not join the committee because France seemed about to accept Bismarck's conditions and the committee consisted mainly of Catholics. Stern was much disturbed by the attempt of religious Catholics to see France's defeat as punishment for a society that had turned its back on true religion.

Nevertheless, she denounced Bismarck. After failing to capture Paris, armed to the teeth by its citizens, the Prussians began to bombard it. In the nineteenth century, it was unheard of to bomb civilians. The ladies of the court waited upon the Prussian king to protest. In her "Lettre à Sir Henry Bulwer Lytton" in the *Progrès de Lyon,* Stern wrote that since Sedan, Bismarck's war, "defensive and in a certain sense legitimate and political in its origins," had become a war of conquest.[22] Instead of a generous peace, he had

unleashed upon a confused and disarmed France—without a leader, without a voice, and almost without a law—innumerable troops inspired by a vengeful spirit. They were commanded to perpetrate devastation and ruin everywhere on the soil of France. They were told that they were one race, the French another; that they had one religion, [the French] had another religion; and that these opposed races and religions ought to hate one another until death. These simple [soldiers] have been persuaded that the German nation cannot live as long as it has at its side a French nation.

While recognizing that Alsace and Lorraine had belonged to Germany more than two hundred years before, she insisted that "the populations that they want to annex to Germany by force are passionately French in heart and spirit" and urged England to end its neutrality.[23]

Her friend Jules Favre negotiated with Bismarck to end the war. The Parisians refused to accept the government's peace and formed the Commune, literally seceding from France. They were seconded by Marseilles and a few other large cities. Marie was anguished. She wrote to Söhnée that if there were still fools mad enough to attempt civil war, they were irredeemably lost. But that was exactly what had happened. The Parisians took over their city; the new government of the republic, sitting at Versailles, had to take it back by force, with German troops sitting in wait in case they should fail.

Daniel Stern missed it all. There were to be no descriptions of the Commune from her pen. But unlike those (almost everyone) who voiced strong opinions for or against the Commune, she said nothing. Did she perhaps hesitate, despite her disapproval of radical republicanism, to damn "the people" whom she had glorified in 1848? Her greatest concern now was that the new republic not fall prisoner to the royalists, who dominated in the newly elected Assembly, or to the Bonapartists. In her article "République ou monarchie"[24] she declared that after all the chaos, what most French people wanted was security and a moderate government. After the disorder into which the empire had led the country, universal suffrage would never again choose a dynastic government, royal or imperial. Therefore, a democratic republic was the solution. She thereby agreed with the famous pronouncement of Thiers that the republic was "the form of government that divides us least." Stern only regretted, privately, that she could see no one on the horizon better than Thiers to lead the nation.

While she was in Switzerland, the Wagner family settled near Lucerne and invited her to visit. Marie had already met Wagner while visiting the von Bülows in 1858. When Liszt implied that she had tried to turn Wagner against him, Wagner, insulted, replied, "She [the Comtesse d'Agoult] came many times to make music with her daughter. . . . In the course of the moments I was able to pass in her company I could appreciate her reserve, full of distinction, and the judicious character of her words. She never spoke of you."[25] In 1869 Cosima, preparing to marry Wagner, had asked Marie for the capital of her original dowry. Marie had given orders to her lawyer to make the transfer. Unfortunately, the outbreak of war prevented the payment, and Marie was unable to spare the money; probably she needed the interest.

She found the Wagner family peaceful and happy, "corresponding to the ideal of life that I conceived in my youth: a poetic retreat and intellectual influence over a whole society," she wrote Claire. "Wagner is more than amiable with me; and the intimacy among the three of us, despite [political] circumstances so unfavorable, is true and charming."[26] Cosima had achieved with Wagner what Marie could never have managed with Liszt, for two reasons. First, divorce from a Catholic husband was not available to her. But more important, Marie had not been willing to dedicate herself unconditionally to Liszt, as Cosima did to Wagner.

Marie and Cosima spent the days talking and playing with the children— Daniel and Blandine von Bülow, Isolde, Eva, and Siegfried Wagner. Evenings were consecrated to the "music of the future." When Marie heard Richter play from Wagner's work, she seemed overwhelmed by it. Wagner read Marie the first act of *Tristan and Isolde* one evening. On another, he played her the prayer from *Lohengrin*, which caused her to weep. She wrote to her friends that she considered him one of the finest minds she had ever met. Cosima recorded in her diary, "She likes it here. I feel very strange toward her, but she is pleasant company because of her broad education." Cosima recorded that Wagner avoided being alone with her mother. But Marie did not discuss politics. "She is well in spite of what she has been through and now faces," Cosima concluded.[27]

What Marie faced was probably a reference to the fact that Paris was in the hands of the Commune and civil war was pending. Nevertheless, Marie knew now that she was French, and the whole environment of the Wagner household was anti-French and anti-Semitic. Although her grandchildren wanted her to stay longer, Marie felt she had to leave. Mother and daughter separated with emotion and never saw each other again. Cosima wrote of her mother's leavetaking, "I am very moved as I embrace her for the last time; all the sadness of life overcomes me." Cosima remained with the belief that only Wagner had ever really loved her.[28]

By June 1871, the Commune had been defeated and Marie, at Saint-Lupicin with Ronchaud, was preparing to return to Paris for the first time in more than a year. Taking stock, she found that none of her family or intimate friends had perished, and the building she lived in was not burned down. But she felt a grief that was inexpressible. She was unable to stay in Paris and experienced the first nervous attack we know of since the outbreak of the war. It lasted two months; she ended up with Claire at Versailles. By September she was visiting Tribert and sightseeing in the area. It was December before she really settled into her Paris apartment in the rue Malesherbes, after being an itinerant for eighteen months.

By that time new elections had fortified the republican group in the legislature and had consolidated its forces. Thiers had been declared president of the republic. Marie wrote to Ollivier that things had gone better than she had feared. Meanwhile, Juliette Adam, her former protégée, had become the premier hostess of republican Paris. Along with many of Marie's former regulars, Adam's salon eventually included all the republican statesmen of the new regime. As Marie reestablished her salon, old friends drifted back: Desiré Nisard, Mignet, Renan, Carnot, Victor Schoelcher, Dupont-White, Berthelot, Ernest Havet, Alfred Mézières, Henri Martin, Nefftzer, and Littré. Her friend Grévy presided over the legislative assembly. Viel-Castel continued to correspond; he was still at work on the eighteenth volume of his history of the Restoration, now four regimes behind. Prince Jérôme Bonaparte called on her when he was in Paris, but she did not want to see him because of the Bonapartist threat to the Third Republic. Once she met him in Parc Monceau, where she was walking with Dupont-White and Guy de Charnacé, and they debated political issues.

Her young followers, who were no longer so young, also returned to the salon—Söhnée, Boucher, Dolfuss, and Henneguy. Before the war the youngest member of the salon had been Edmond Schuré; he had visited the Wagners and came recommended by Cosima. The Alsatian had also visited Stern in Switzerland. Sorry to see her leave, he wrote, "Are you then destined to be the last of the illustrious women of our belle France? I hope not, but for me you will always be the most delightful."[29] Now he was in Paris.

Nefftzer, a supporter of the Orléans monarchy at heart, felt that this republic was the best possible. But he refused an article by Daniel Stern for *Le Temps* unless he could cut significantly the anti-Orleanist passages. Stern preferred not to publish it. Was this why Cosima, who heard from Marie about once a month, received instead a letter from Claire that her mother was ill again? She seems to have suffered an attack of spleen for at least two months in mid-1872. However, in October she was well again and writing to Ollivier: "After this disastrous war I expected plague, famine, bankruptcy and the rest. We are doing well, we are eating; we are paying the taxes; there is order in the streets, if not in our minds; we are back at work, and finally we are breathing. Perhaps God will take care of the rest!"[30]

The following month, after the Bourbon pretender to the throne had forbidden his followers to go along with any kind of republic and after Thiers's speech insisting that only a republic was possible, *Le Temps* published Stern's last article, a "Lettre à Littré." It was a response to an extract from Littré's newspaper *La Philosophie positive.* In it Stern placed herself in accord with him on the necessity of a conservative republic. Drawing on her experience of living in the provinces for much of the past few years, she asserted that people wanted peace and tranquillity. Despite the politicians and their cabals, despite the priests inspiring pilgrimages of repentance, the majority of the French had basic good sense. The achievements that she had named to Ollivier she named again and attributed them to the statesmanship of Thiers. For these reasons those who backed him would be returned in elections, even if the republic was not theoretically perfect. Thus in the early days of the Third Republic, Stern made the same choice she had made during the Second Republic, when she had supported Cavaignac—pragmatism over ideology.

In August of the same year she sent Cosima a copy of her Dutch history, *Histoire des commencements de la République des Pays-Bas,* which she had somehow found time to prepare for publication. Stern had been reading and preparing for this work ever since her first trip to Holland twenty years before. Having learned Dutch for the purpose, she also read widely in Spanish and French sources, even reading the American historian John Lothrop Motley in the original. She lived only to publish this first volume of the planned three-volume work.

As in her work on the revolution, Stern excelled in marvelous pen portraits of historical personalities. William of Orange, Olden Barneveldt, Maurice of Nassau on the one hand, and on the other, Phillip II and Alexander Farnese—each was given his due as the representative of a certain tendency in the history of the time. Phillip represented the past, absolutism, and Catholic dogma; William of Orange stood for the future, Protestantism, and republican liberty. Nor did Stern neglect the military details of sieges and battlefields. One also finds those descriptions of dramatic moments for which she was known—the last public execution ordered by the Inquisition in Gand or the skilfully developed recital of the martyrdom of Barneveldt.

The book received much positive comment for its severe and classical historical style. Stern decided to put it up for one of the Académie prizes, even though the history as projected was not complete. The candidature was taken in hand by the literary critic Desiré Nisard. Allart prodded her friend the historian Mignet. Stern's friends Littré and Viel-Castel were also members of the Académie française. As a result, Stern's work shared the Therouanne Prize, established "for the encouragement of historical works," with another book. Claire informed Cosima in May 1873. As Littré pointed out in his coverage of it in *Philosophie positive*, a history that deplored unnecessary bloodshed was a fitting one for recognition by the new moderate republic France was in the process of establishing.[31]

Although the prize had been awarded to Daniel Stern, everyone knew that it had been awarded to a woman in a field usually restricted to men. It was this that provoked Barbey d'Aurevilly to revile her as a bluestocking. But Stern was not upset. She had received high honors; the historian Mignet devoted a speech to the book's praise at the Academy in 1875. She wrote in her diary that year that she thought the principal attraction of her books was the feminine feeling for things combined with the masculine analysis of them—Germanic penetration combined with French clarity.

Cosima still kept a grudging admiration for her mother. She had in the past defended her when her siblings were harsh. But relations were difficult, partly because Cosima had become such a patriot of the new German Empire and Marie did not hide her feeling for the new French republic. It seems that Wagner tried to smooth things over. He continued to write to Marie, admired her history of Holland, and sent her every volume of his own works. When he finished the *Ring of the Nibelung* after twenty years of work, Cosima wrote to her mother that she considered it a vindication of her own life and efforts. Certainly, Marie recognized herself—or her old self—in her daughter! But Cosima felt deprived, because her mother was unable to give her daughter her dowry. Marie left it as a debt of honor in her will, for Claire to pay.

Cosima was also angry at Ollivier, who refused to hand over jewelry of Blandine's, which she claimed. Marie continued to write him. When he returned to Paris in 1874 he appeared at her salon. Ollivier had been elected to the Académie française before the war and now wanted to take his seat with the customary elegy to Lamartine, whom he had replaced. But he was not allowed to give his speech because he refused to remove a reference to Napoléon III. This did not prevent him from sitting. But feeling against him as an unabashed representative of the liberal empire was so extreme that some republicans boycotted Marie's salon, fearing to meet him there.

The monarchists had grown strong enough to overthrow Thiers in 1873, and Marshall MacMahon was elected president by the legislature, "keeping the seat warm for a king," as everyone said. The two pretenders to the throne, Bourbon and Orleanist, met in Germany and agreed that the Bourbon, who had no children, would reign as Henry V and would be succeeded by the Orleanist Count of Paris. Neither Ollivier nor Marie believed anything would come of it. Marie was most worried about a return of the clergy to power. She wrote, "It has been impossible for me to believe in the language used the past few days in Frohsdorf by the Count of Paris. . . . I ask myself . . . what Orléans gains from his renunciation, and whether he thinks that all of this will really be accomplished by invocation of the Sacred Heart of Jesus."[32]

In late 1874 the Bourbon pretender, Chambord, visited Versailles in the hope that this would bring about an uprising in his favor; it did not. Hortense Allart, who despised the republic, hoped for a return of the Orleanist monarchy. But Marie was convinced that the Orleanists would see their (literal) fortunes as safer in a conservative republic than in a monarchy. The following year, without a convention of any kind, the constitutional basis of the Third Republic was created by the Wallon amendment. Tribert became a member of the Senate. But Marie never lived to see her friend Grévy become president of the republic.

Stern now planned to publish her complete works, for which Renan undertook negotiations with Calmann-Lévy. She published her correspondence with Mazzini, leaving out, for the sake of her family, some of her more extreme anti-Catholic expressions. Also planned for publication were her correspondence with Sainte-Beuve and Ponsard, a second volume of her history of the Dutch republic, a new edition of *Esquisses morales,* and her memoirs. She renewed her contacts with Italy in the person of a young philologist, a professor of Sanskrit at Florence, Angelo de Gubernatis. He was editor of the *Rivista Europea* and wrote her for information, intending to include her in an article on French friends of Italy. The correspondence that ensued led to the idea of starting a new periodical that would bring the European countries together, "to form a European liberal opinion, independent in philosophy, politics, science and art,"[33] as Stern put it. In his devotion Gubernatis named a son after her. But when he arrived in Paris to meet her, she was not impressed; that was the end of their collaboration. Even in her old age and with a real admirer, Marie retained her standards.

To her great pleasure the poet Madame Ackermann, a widow, decided in 1873 to settle in Paris. An admiring friend, Ackermann called Stern "an Amazon of thought." The two women decided to attend the courses open to women at the Collège de France, given by the scientists Claude Berthelot and Claude Bernard and by the critic Ernest Havet. When Littré learned of this, he decided to attend with them. Marie also kept up her relations with Guy de Charnacé and helped him with his literary career, despite his separation from her daughter. Claire greatly resented what she considered her mother's disloyalty.

The new government brought Marie and her brother closer politically than they had ever been, as Marie was a more moderate republican and Maurice, basically an Orleanist, was willing to accept the republican form. His death of cholera, late in 1873, was a shock.[34] She wrote to Nefftzer that his loss made a terrible empty place in her life. "Despite great differences in character, tastes, opinions, we enjoyed each other's company." She was less affected when the Comte d'Agoult died in March 1875, at age eighty-five. But she wrote to Pictet: "I have just experienced one of those events which move one to the very bottom of one's thought and one's conscience. . . . He long foresaw his end and awaited it with the simplicity of a soldier and a calm Christian philosophy. . . . He left in the memory of all who knew him the image par excellence of a gallant man. In the most delicate of relations I have constantly found him loyal, disinterested, generous. I wear his mourning with respect and the profound regret that I could not equal him in his spirit of devotion and self-sacrifice."[35]

Her friend Hortense Allart, who had remarried in 1872, wrote Marie urging that she should do the same! Allart also still hoped to facilitate a renewal of relations between Marie and George Sand. Marie reread her letters from Sand and told Tribert, who agreed, that she saw in them two people who would never get along. She wrote Sand asking if Ronchaud could pick up her letters, since she was thinking of publication. Sand wrote back that she had burned all her papers at the approach of the Prussian army. Marie wrote in her diary, "Letter from G. Sand. The last, perhaps?" It was.[36]

The last reading of a work by Stern in her salon took place in 1875 in the presence of Edouard Thierry, administrator of the Comédie-Française. It was the now-lost play *Jacques Coeur*. The reading was also attended by Nisard, Renan, Berthellot, Havet, Ackermann, Mezières, Grévy, Viel-Castel, Schérer, Dr. Blanche, and others. Her salon remained full. Schuré later wrote that one could no longer see the superb Arabella of the past, whom one of her admirers had called a "centauress." She wore black silk, her white hair dressed with lace à la Mary Stuart; she sat in the corner of her boudoir holding a black fan. But you could see her past beauty, "and in her eyes the last gleam of the passions that still race under the cold cinders of the years." And when she stood up, "in her slim tall figure, in her majestic presence and her engaging smile, one seemed to see a dame of the eighteenth century."[37]

In this last year of her life Marie kept to a strict schedule. According to Ronchaud, she had always been the first, "before the birds, even before the children" to awake and watch the sun rise and the flowers open.[38] She took coffee with an egg for breakfast, and cold coffee with a little honey later in the morning. Lunch included an egg course, meat, and vegetables. At four she took some cold bouillon. Dinner at seven o'clock consisted of meat, vegetables, and either salad or dessert. For her time, it was a Spartan diet. During the morning Marie worked at her desk or wrote letters. She enjoyed walking along the river or in the park with friends during the afternoon but seldom went out at night anymore. In that year she visited Montmartre cemetery, stopping at the grave of her daughter Louise, and those of others she had known—Cavaignac, Delphine Gay, and Gautier.

"Speak to me of immortality," Marie had asked Pictet, whom she still considered a mentor in philosophy, when she had renewed her correspondence with him on returning to Paris. Years before, she had written to Herwegh, "There is an immortal breath whose organizing force will take on a more perfect form elsewhere, to accomplish what it has only dreamed or attempted in this world, That is my vague but unshakable hope."[39] Now, she wrote, to Pictet, like a true follower of Spinoza, "I have no terror whatsoever of death, but I love life passionately; the older I grow the more I feel its beauty, its poetry; the more my mind is filled with a desire to know, the more the love of God fills my mind."[40] Pictet himself was to die before she did. By this time Marie had lost many people close to her, beginning with three of her children, her mother, brother, and husband. Her half-sister Augusta, her nephew Leon Ehrmann, the tutor of her daughters Philippe Kaufmann, Ladislas Teleki, Charles Didier, and Prévost-Paradol had all killed themselves. Félix Lichnowski had been killed in the Polish revolution; her old confessor,

Abbé Deguerry, had been executed as a hostage by the Commune. She had also lost Vigny, Ponsard, and then Pictet.

Marie received word of his death on her seventieth birthday, December 30, 1875. She had written in her diary two days before, "I reflect with infinite joy on that great respect and sympathy with which everyone distinguishes me, on how many people recognize me without my knowing it. It is sweet after having been a *pariah* for so long."[41] Clearly, she had suffered from her anomalous position in society more than she had admitted. Now she felt that it was good to finish life admired by others. Her friends were amazed at her calm beauty. Ackermann told her, "You may be aged, but you will never be old" and, from Augusta Holmes, herself a beauty, "You will always be desirable." As Marie entered her salon in her seventy-first year, Madame de Pierreclos saluted the arrival of "the Queen of Denmark."[42]

Many years before, Marie had thought of and prepared for her death. In 1858 she had left directions with Ronchaud. After a few practical requests, such as keeping the neighbors quiet so that she could die in silence, she stated that she would die a republican and wanted to have a republican funeral, that is, without religious ceremony. She also asked that Ronchaud destroy anything negative that she had written about anyone. He should particularly arrange with Cosima to try to acquire and destroy any material that testified to bad relations between her parents. "I would like that great love to which she owes her life to be respected and honored after my death by those who have misunderstood or slandered it in my lifetime."[43] However, her final will, made in 1865, did not include the concern about memories of her life with Liszt; it also altered her funeral arrangements.

The main practical concern about her death was that her daughter and others should take the utmost precautions to see that she was in fact dead. All her worldly wealth was left to Claire, except for the forty thousand francs owed to Cosima. Her grandson Daniel Ollivier was to be the inheritor of all her literary property, in memory of his mother, Blandine. However, nothing was to be published without the aid and authorization of Ronchaud and Tribert. The personal papers were to go to Ronchaud, with the exception of the memoirs, which would go to young Daniel Ollivier as part of her literary property. Her personal property, with the exception of personal souvenirs, would go to Tribert and Ronchaud, to divide as they wished. (The two always worked in perfect harmony on her behalf.) As for the funeral, the will read: "Being born in the Protestant religion and having been raised Catholic without being consulted and contrary to the law of mixed marriages consented to by my parents, I ask that a pastor of the Protestant, that is, liberal church, Monsieur Fontanes . . . be asked to accompany my remains to the cemetery and say some edifying words."[44]

Marie de Flavigny, Comtesse d'Agoult, died quietly at noon on March 5, 1876. She was not buried at the Montmartre cemetery with the d'Agoult family, as she had asked in the earlier will, but in Père Lachaise cemetery. There the last members of the Commune had fought the troops from Versailles down to the last man and woman. One can find no explanation for her having been buried there; only Ronchaud, who arranged the funeral, could tell. With him, Claire, and Tribert, the coffin was followed by Girardin, Louis de Viel-Castel, Renan, Littré, Schuré, Schérer, Grévy, Henri Martin, and many other friends. Marie's last and youngest protégé, the student Victor Waille, could not restrain his tears. Fontanes, the Protestant pastor who had comforted her after the death of Blandine, presided. Ronchaud later arranged with the sculptor Henri Chapu to carve her gravestone with the figure of Thought Emerging. Claire's drawing of her mother is also incised into the stone.

C O S I M A learned of her mother's death by newspaper, because Claire, with whom she corresponded, did not have her new address. Unable to believe it at first, she telegraphed her stepsister. Before she received an answer, a telegram from Schuré advised her that Marie had been buried the day before. A more complete letter arrived from Tribert. Sadness moved her to make a visit to the grave of her brother Daniel, which she had not done for sixteen years. She even read the last book her mother had sent her—Hippolyte Taine's *Les Origines de la France contemporaine.* On the anniversary of her mother's death, she wrote to Tribert. By that time she had received her dowry and given it to Wagner to finance Bayreuth. Cosima was the only one of Marie's family who defended her in the years to come, when her father and occasionally her stepsister Claire vented their spleen.

Liszt wrote to Princess Sayn-Wittgenstein, "Barring hypocrisy, I could not weep for her more after her death than during her life. . . . Mme d'Agoult possessed to a high degree a taste, and even a passion, for the false—except at certain moments of ecstasy of which she could not afterwards bear to be reminded!" There was perhaps a little hypocrisy in his words to the more religious Emile Ollivier: "The memory I retain of Mme d'Agoult is a painful secret, which I confide to God while praying that he may grant peace and light to the soul of the mother of my three children."[45]

As was to be expected, *Le Temps* was the first to announce its associate's death. Schérer wrote the first obituary, Mézières the second. The latter wrote, among other things, "I still see her with her lovely face, its traits pure and severe, attentive to all being said around her."[46] Many of the obituaries followed those in the *Rivista europea* (De Gubernatis) and the *Revue politique et litteraire* (Schuré) by comparing her with Madame de Staël. Dolfuss waited more than a month before publishing his definitive article on her in *Le Temps*. Alluding to the events of her young life that determined her destiny, he concluded that Marie's dominant trait was sincerity. He called her a "daughter of Phidias and Plato," cosmopolitan and democratic. A thinking woman "who sculpted her thoughts into art," she always sought the great ideal behind the phenomena of life. Stern, he said, corresponded to the mission of the century, "in that she searched for the divine in the human, and spread the concepts of truth, justice and compassion. Her special role was to have brought together those likeminded persons, who without her would not have known of one another.[47]

Marie had typically tried to picture the phenomenon of her death in ideal form long before. The following is an extract of her poem "Oceano Nox," of September 1862:

> But she, calm and grave and with exalted brow
> Advances, intrepid,
> A pace, and yet another pace into the endless deep
> Of the ocean immense.
> She has yielded her life, and the God who awaits
> In the eternal mystery
> Takes her, immortal, and never returns her
> To the things of this earth.

∾ *Envoi* ∾

If you were a cultivated traveler in Western Europe in the nineteenth century, looking for a traveling companion who was schooled in all the social, political, and literary aspects of the countries on your itinerary—from the Netherlands to Italy, from the Germanies to France—you could not find a better one than the Comtesse d'Agoult. She would discuss with you the various aspects of these countries, from both the historical and contemporary points of view, in a way so clever that you would believe you knew more about these things than you had ever realized. And what you did know, she would draw from you by her educated questions. Those whom you met on the journey would be impressed by her beauty and aristocratic bearing; many would already know her, or would know people whom she also knew. As she traveled she seemed to move in a cosmopolitan world of those who constantly thought about, wrote about, or interpreted in art the time they were living in, in all its many aspects.

If you did not have the luck to travel with her, you might visit her on your way through Paris, where you would meet members of that very world. You would experience in her salon a continual seminar on important matters, an international exchange of ideas and information. You might become one of those who begged her for the more intimate hour before she was "at home" to the others, so as to receive for a while all her attention. If you were a man you might, in the middle decades of the century when her beauty was still amazing, fall in love with her. But if so, she would instruct you in that process by which she turned love that flared up into friendship that lasted. She only wanted the latter, having experienced the former and never really recovered.

Was it an artificial life, the one the countess led? Certainly, when compared to the active lives led by so many of her male friends, who were personally involved in the events of the time. It was not a totally satisfying life, and she never pretended to herself to be satisfied with it. If she had been a man. . . . But she was not and had therefore to limit herself to what a woman could hope to accomplish. For most women of her time, that meant either wearing herself out in fruitless efforts to participate in the male world, perhaps ending up in jail as did feminists of her time, or taking lovers and living in the male world vicariously, as did the typical outstanding women of the century.

What the countess really wanted, and she was mocked for it, was power, acclaim, esteem. Only the last was really open to her, and she built her life around it. She would rather have been famous as a great novelist, a great poet, a great political figure. But she knew she was not a creative genius, and the political world was not open to women. Power, yes, power would have been available to her had she been a man. She had the requisite knowledge and intelligence. She had even thought, for a short time during the 1848 revolution, that she might be able to exercise it through her relationship with Lamartine and Lamennais, or perhaps through her writings. But that was a short-lived dream. She was, after all, only a woman.

And so she did what a proud woman could do with the resources—the wit, the charm, the intelligence—that were hers. She became an intellectual and drew to herself other intellectuals from throughout Europe. It was one of the solutions available in the nineteenth century to women who wanted to transcend the normal female roles. But very few chose it or were even in a position to do so, given the requirements of education and financial independence. Those who did were undoubtedly liable to depression. Not only was it a second-best role, but it was difficult to know how successful one was at playing it. These conditions only exacerbated Marie's naturally depressive and even suicidal tendencies.

It is said that in the twentieth century many more women than men suffer from depression. Is it perhaps because women, in comparison to men, are still obliged to compromise, to settle for less, to forego power, and to a lesser extent, acclaim? It is significant that Marie, although she was esteemed in her lifetime, was soon forgotten after her death, unlike men at her intellectual level. Most women who read her story will find aspects of her life with which they can identify. For me, she has been an engrossing traveling companion for many years.

～ Notes ～

One ～ "Children born at midnight have a mysterious nature"

1. Richard Gutman, *Richard Wagner* (New York, 1968); also in Eleanor Perenyi, *Liszt, the Artist as Romantic Hero* (Boston, 1974), 16, hereafter cited as Perenyi.

2. "Notes pour *Mémoires*," Bibliothèque municipale de Versailles, Fonds de Charnacé, Ms. F. 770 (6), hereafter cited as BM Fonds de Charnacé.

3. When Napoleon's wife, Hortense de Beauharnais, was forming her royal household, the Bethmanns tried to acquire for their daughter a position of lady of honor, but de Flavigny refused to allow his wife to serve the Napoleonic regime in any way. When the family returned to France, they remained seated at mass during the *Domine, salvum fac impératorem*. Claude Aragonnès, *Marie d'Agoult, une déstinée romantique* (Paris, 1938), 16, 19.

4. Johann Nepomuk Hummel was at the time a star among musicians. He had lived with Mozart, worked with Beethoven, and was an intimate of Mendelssohn. Marie was highly praised for her masterly performance of his "Septuor" on the piano.

5. BM Fonds de Charnacé, Ms. F. 770 (6).

6. BM Fonds de Charnacé, Ms. F. 770 (6).

7. From *Règlements des Dames de Sacré-Coeur*: "The aim which should be adopted by the teachers is less to embellish and cultivate the minds of their students by human knowledge than to form their hearts to the love of religion and all the virtues which it inspires. . . . They should consider that the children and young persons who are raised within their houses are destined in the ordinary course of Providence to become wives and mothers of families. . . . Therefore, beside the principal study of religion, they will take up secular knowledge to the extent that it will be useful and necessary to a Christian person who ought to serve God in the world; the

accomplishments are permitted, following the rules of a sage discretion, and a particular attention should be given to form in the students the taste for domestic work and duties. . . . Beside the attention to reading and writing appropriate to all, they will be given some elementary lessons in grammar, history, geography and arithmetic; and one cannot neglect the development of their memory by making them learn by heart what is most important for them to know for the conduct of life and the pleasures of good society [bonne societé]." If the parents requested, and paid extra, and if the sisters considered it proper, foreign languages were possible. The point was "to banish entirely all that is liable to nourish only their pride." Jacques Vier, *La Comtesse d'Agoult et son temps*, 5 vols. (Paris, 1955–63), 1: 46–47, hereafter cited as Vier.

8. Daniel Stern, *Mes Souvenirs* (Paris, 1877), 176–78, hereafter cited as *Souvenirs*.

9. *Souvenirs,* 163.

10. *Souvenirs,* 308–09.

11. *Mémoires, Souvenirs et Journaux de la Comtesse d'Agoult,* 2 vols., ed. Charles F. Dupêchez (Paris, 1990), 1: 241, 399, hereafter cited as *Mémoires, Souvenirs et Journaux.*

12. *Mémoires, Souvenirs et Journaux,* 1: 184–89.

13. "Mémoires du Comte d'Agoult," in Jacques Vier, *Marie d'Agoult, son mari, ses amis, documents inédits* (Paris, 1950), 12, hereafter cited as *Marie d'Agoult.*

14. *Mémoires, Souvenirs et Journaux,* 1: 258.

15. Letter from Dieppe, July 1827, *Marie d'Agoult*, 18. He added that Vigny's mother-in-law (Lady Bunbury) was there also and was just about to give birth. "How could a mother-in-law forget herself to such a point!" (Comment une belle-mère peut-elle s'oublier à ce point!)

16. *Mémoires, Souvenirs et Journaux,* 1:15.

17. *Mémoires, Souvenirs et Journaux,* 1: 216–17.

18. *Marie d'Agoult,* 19–20.

19. *Cahier de notes* (red notebook), by Claire Charnacé, Bibliothèque municipale, Versailles, Fonds Feliciano d'Oliveira, Ms. F. 859, 184, hereafter cited as BM Fonds Feliciano d'Oliveira, Ms. F. 859, red notebook. In 1832 Marie tried to throw herself into the Seine and was saved by her nephew, Félix d'Amoureux, who adored her.

20. *Marie d'Agoult,* 15.

21. *Marie d'Agoult,* 14.

22. *Mémoires, Souvenirs et Journaux,* 1: 293.

23. She later wrote in her *Souvenirs:* "Saint-Preux, Werther, Oberman, Childe-Harold, Manfred . . . vous avez éclairé de vos splendides flambeaux ces pentes fatales qui mènent a l'abîme . . . nous nous sommes élancés sur vos traces, pensant vous atteindre et vous égaler; mais nous n'avons atteint que votre misère et nous n'avons égalé que votre ennui." The "we" was intended to indicate a whole generation of Romantics. Vier, 1: 87.

24. "Mémoires du Comte d'Agoult," in *Marie d'Agoult,* 119.

25. *Corinne* was the heroine of a novel by Madame de Staël.

26. Letter to Oriane de Montesquiou-Fézensac, October 27, 1831, in Vier, 1: 368, n. 8.

27. Jeanne Marie Bouvier de la Motte Guyon (1648–1717), French mystic. Put in a convent for her heretical ideas, released through the efforts of Madame de Maintenon, defended by Fénélon in a famous debate with Bossuet, she spent seven years in the Bastille and left collected works in forty volumes.

Two ∼ "To breathe the pure incense of sacrifice"

1. I owe this summary of Liszt's early life to Anthony Wilkinson, *Liszt* (London, 1975).

2. Vier, 1: 366, n. 350.

3. Robert Bory, *Une retraite romantique en Suisse* (Geneva, 1923), 19, hereafter cited as Bory, from Linda Ramann, *Franz Liszt*, 3 vols. (Leipzig, 1880–84), 1: 322. Liszt personally gave this description to Ramann.

4. Perenyi, 80, pointed out that this was not so much a description of Liszt as of Mrs. Radcliffe's Schedoni, Lord Byron's Giaour—the romantic hero in general. Since the memoirs in which they appear were written later in life, the description forms a double image—of Liszt, and of Marie as remembered herself, Romantic to a fault.

5. *Mémoires, Souvenirs et Journaux*, 1: 22–24.

6. *Correspondance de Liszt et Madame d'Agoult*, 2 vols., ed. Daniel Ollivier (Paris, 1933–34), 1: 21, 25, 27, 73, 83, 112, 77, hereafter cited as *Correspondance*.

7. Vier suggests (1: 156) that the Saint-Simonians may have been a source of Liszt's erotic brand of mysticism.

8. *Correspondance*, 1: 54.

9. Lamennais was a priest who turned republican and published a periodical, *L'Avenir*, calling Catholics to a new humanitarianism. His work was banned by the papacy, and many of his followers left him to avoid excommunication. Lamennais instead left the Church.

10. *Correspondance*, 1: 114.

11. Vier, 1: 144.

12. *Correspondance*, 1: 54–55.

13. *Correspondance*, 1: 38.

14. *Correspondance*, 1: 27, 29, 37, 46, 47, 50, 63, 52.

15. *Correspondance*, 1: 35.

16. *Correspondance*, 1: 66–67.

17. *Correspondance*, 1: 61, 45, 100.

18. He wrote her: "Your breath is still on my lips and my eyelids; the beating of your heart resounds constantly in mine and prolongs to infinity that intense double life that you have revealed to me, that we have revealed to one another." *Correspondance*, 1: 76.

19. Again, it was Sainte-Beuve.

20. *Correspondance,* 1: 96, 95.

21. *Correspondance,* 1: 72.

22. *Correspondance,* 1: 97–99, 77. With reference to "la grand scène," Liszt wrote: "Mon coeur se fond dans mes entrailles, lorsque je viens à espérer cette heure. Oh! de grâce dites-moi encore que vous ne voudriez pas vivre sans moi."

23. *Correspondance,* 1: 100–102.

24. Lamennais wrote *l'Indifférence* in 1833, which earned him the accusation of heresy. In 1834 he wrote *Paroles d'un croyant.*

25. *Correspondance,* 1: 122–26.

26. Perenyi, 95.

27. *Marie d'Agoult,* 38–42, letters of September 18, 1833, and January 24, 1834.

28. *Marie d'Agoult,* 172–75.

29. *Correspondance,* 1: 134–35.

30. This was copied out in a red notebook by her remaining daughter, Claire, after her death. She dates this material, because of certain spelling, in 1835 or soon afterward. BM Fonds Feliciano d'Oliveira, Ms. F. 859.

31. It was only established by Jacques Vier, in the 1950s, that it was indeed Marie d'Agoult, and not Liszt, who was primarily the author of these articles.

32. *Correspondance,* 1: 135–36.

33. The opponents of Marie, who picture her as cold and scheming, tend on the one hand to view her as having only recently given in to Liszt's desires, having held him off until she was afraid she would lose him and, on the other, to picture her as having been his lover for a long time but forcing the elopement by deliberately becoming pregnant. See Perenyi, 121.

34. *Mémoires, Souvenirs et Journaux,* 1:316, 2: 255–65.

35. *Correspondance,* 1: 136. "Von sechs bis 8 fuhrt mich Herr Knopp auf Land. Before or afterwards." Her daily agenda for 1835 notes on May 28, "Depart de . . . [last word slanting down page and illegible]." Bibliothèque nationale Manuscrits NAF 14320, hereafter cited as BN N.A.F.

36. *Mémoires, Souvenirs et Journaux,* 1: 202. There is one opinion that Liszt may not have left but may have awaited the results of his mentor's influence with Marie. This cannot be proved.

37. Letter from Lamennais, February 15, 1836, in Vier, 1, n. 112.

38. BM Fonds Feliciano d'Oliveira, Ms. F. 859, red notebook; see also Charles Dupêchez, *Marie d'Agoult, 1805–1876* (Paris, 1989), 315, n. 34, hereafter cited as Dupêchez.

39. Adrian Williams, *Portrait of Liszt by Himself and His Contemporaries* (Oxford, 1990), 578.

40. The letter is dated May 26, 1835. It was first published in Aragonnès, 73.

41. Williams, 578.

42. Probably the two had agreed to correspond through general delivery at the post office, which means he must have been waiting to hear from her. Otherwise, not

knowing his hotel, she would have been unable to contact him. We know that later, when they arrived in Geneva, Liszt immediately went to the post office to pick up mail.

43. *Correspondance,* 1: 136. The letter is dated June 2, 1835, from Basel.

44. *Correspondance,* 1: 136.

45. Perenyi, 123.

46. BM Fonds de Charnacé, Ms. F. 859.

47. Vier, 2: 1, n. 7.

48. Aragonnès, 79–80.

49. BM Fonds Feliciano d'Oliveira, Ms. F. 859, red notebook, 198, 195.

50. *Mémoires, Souvenirs et Journaux,* 1: 325.

51. *Mémoires, Souvenirs et Journaux,* 1: 327.

52. A letter from her brother indicated that he had heard about an embarrassing moment for the pair in the chateau at Wolfsberg, a pension they had visited on their journey, where a letter from him to his mother, who had planned to stay there, was given to Marie. Embarrassed, she left the desk, telling Liszt to pay the postage. He turned out all his pockets and had not even a bit of change. Finally, he cut a wildflower and presented it to the woman at the desk, much to the amusement of bystanders. The couple did not stay there long. *Memoires, Souvenirs et Journaux,* 2: 286, n. 61.

53. *Memoires, Souvenirs et Journaux,* 2: 336.

54. "Palma," in *Mémoires, Souvenirs et Journaux,* 1: 260. This passage and the alternate description of the decision to leave Paris together may have been parts of an earlier version of her novel *Nélida.*

55. Williams, 69–70.

56. *Mémoires, Souvenirs et Journaux,* 1: 339.

57. *Memoires, Souvenirs et Journaux,* 1: 70–71.

58. "Comme elle savait s'escrimer contre ces têtes grises, leur jeter de la poudre aux yeux avec ses paradoxes, ses tirades, et tout son appareil d'éloquence féminine" (Bory, 31). Compare the generous description of Marie as *salonnière* left by her husband in *Marie d'Agoult,* 18.

59. Two had been published, on May 3 and 17. Two more appeared on August 14 and 30.

60. "Réponse à Germanus le Pic," November 5, 1835.

61. Robert Bory, ed., *Correspondance de Franz Liszt et ses enfants Blandine, Cosima et Daniel* (Paris, 1936), 9, hereafter cited as *Liszt et ses enfants.*

Three ∾ *"This need to be loved totally"*

1. *Correspondance,* 1: 154.

2. *Correspondance,* 1: 156.

3. The caller was the Count Apponyi (Perenyi, 138).

4. *Correspondance,* 1: 174.

5. *Correspondance,* 1: 175; Marie d'Agoult, *Mémoires, 1833–1854,* ed. Daniel Ollivier (Paris, 1927), 74, hereafter cited as *Mémoires, 1833–1854.*

6. *Correspondance,* 1: 178; BN N.A.F. 1321.

7. *Mémoires, 1833–1854,* 66.

8. S. Rocheblave, "Une amitié romanesque: G. Sand et Mme d'Agoult," *Revue de Paris,* December 15, 1894, 7.

9. George Sand, *Correspondance,* ed. George Lubin (Paris, 1967), 3: 44.

10. Sand, *Correspondance,* 45.

11. Dupêchez, 85.

12. Sand, *Correspondance,* 3: 224.

13. Excerpts from this proposed treaty: "I. Il a été reconnu que George Sand est un enfant indiscipliné, taquin, mutin, hargneus, sournois, etc., auquel il sera donné force férules et *pensums* pour lui apprendre à parler et à écrire correctement. II. Que Marie trois-étoiles est un diamant, un cygne, un luth, une Péri, etc., et généralement tout ce qui constitue la créature que l'on ne saurait trop louer, chanter, vanter, encenser en prose et vers dans toutes les langues connues depuis le sanscrit jusqu'au bas breton. III. Ladite Marie concède à George que tous les aristocrates sont bons à pendre sous la condition que ledit George luis accordera que tous les républicains sont bons a noyer. . . . IV. Il a été convenu que la morale publique est un mot qui sonne creux. . . . V. Convenu que si George Sand venait à manquer de chemise, Marie trois-étoiles ferait une quête européenne au profit d'un *pauvre écrivain,* d'un *auteur indigent* de même que si ladite Marie se trouvait fatalement reduite à ne pouvoir payer sa cuisinière, ledit George écrirait au profit d'icelle un livre tendant à prouver que *tout va mal* dans *le plus mauvaise des mondes possibles* et qu'il n'est pas certain qu'il y ait un monde meilleur." Dupêchez, 87–88.

14. *Revue des deux mondes,* January 15, 1836.

15. Adophe Pictet, *Une course à Chamonix* (Geneva, 1838), later reedited by Robert Bory and published in *Une retraite romantique en Suisse;* see also George Sand's tenth "Lettre d'un voyageur," *Revue de deux mondes,* much of which is reproduced in *Correspondance Marie d'Agoult-George Sand,* ed. Charles F. Dupêchez (Paris, 1995), 85–111, hereafter cited as *Agoult-Sand.*

16. *Mémoires, 1833–1854,* 90.

17. Vier, 1: 400, n. 196.

18. Bory, 110–11.

19. Vier, 1: 232.

20. The "Bachelier" series was continued. A letter in praise of Berlioz appeared in *Le Monde* on November 11, 1836; Berlioz returned the favor in the *Gazette musicale* of December 25.

21. Vier, 1: 238.

22. An article on Lamennais by Pierre Leroux appeared on December 22. Lamennais's *Profession de foi* appeared on February 11, 1837. Vier, 1: 242.

23. Perenyi, 152–54.

24. Vier, 1: 237–38.

25. *Correspondance*, 1: 191.

26. Rocheblave, 28.

27. Rocheblave, 28.

28. Sand later suggested that Marie felt comfortable with her because she did not behave as a woman, making Marie feel like the only woman present. Vier, 1: 267.

29. Aragonnès, 102.

30. It was Musset's *La Confession d'un enfant du siècle.*

31. *Correspondance*, 1: 183.

32. The article was "Lettre d'un Bachelier à un poète voyageur," *Gazette musicale*, February 12, 1837; *Correspondance*, 1: 188–89.

33. Dupêchez, 94–95.

34. Dupêchez, 96, and footnote 52.

35. Sand, *Correspondance*, 2: 71.

36. *Agoult-Sand*, 146.

37. Perenyi, 152–54.

38. *Mémoires, Souvenirs et Journaux,* 2: 132.

39. George Sand, *Oeuvres autobiographique*, ed. Georges Lubin (Paris, 1971), 2: 990.

40. George Sand, *Journal intime*, ed. Aurore Sand (1926), entry for June 3, 1837.

41. Charles Didier, "Journal," *Revue des sciences humaines* (October-December 1959): 479.

42. *Mémoires, Souvenirs et Journaux,* 2: 138.

43. Rocheblave, 24; *Mémoires, Souvenirs et Journaux,* 2: 132.

44. The idea that music was a base for moral education, through the relation of harmony in music and in society, was quite common in France throughout the nineteenth century. See Phyllis Stock-Morton, *Moral Education for a Secular Society: The Development of "Morale Laïque" in Nineteenth-Century France* (Albany, N.Y., 1987), 77–78.

45. *Journal de commerce et des théâtres,* May 4, 1838. The reviewer also noted "a certain exterior charlatanism" that should be needed only by second-rate performers. This was not the only review of this period that thought Liszt overdid the virtuoso dramatics. Georges Herwegh, *Au printemps des dieux* (Paris, 1929), 31.

46. *Mémoires, Souvenirs et Journaux,* 2: 134.

47. *Mémoires, Souvenirs et Journaux,* 2: 136.

48. Vier, 1: 295.

49. Vier, 1: 140.

50. "Vme Lettre d'un bachelier à M. L. de R[onchaud]," dated September 20, 1837, in *Gazette musicale*, July 22, 1838.

51. *Gazette musicale*, July 22, 1838

52. *Mémoires, Souvenirs et Journaux,* 2: 150–51.

53. Dupêchez, 106.

54. *Correspondance,* 1: 205–211.

55. "Lettre d'un bachelier sur La Scala," *Gazette musicale,* May 17, 1838.

56. Bory, 126.

57. *Gazette musicale,* February 11, 1838.

58. Vier, 1: 259. Nevertheless, for a hundred years, Liszt biographers treated the series as written by him.

59. Vier, 1: 417, n. 160.

60. These comparisons are not confined to the Romantic period. John Julius Norwich wrote in 1992 that Titian was the Mozart of Venetian painting and Veronese its Liszt! H. C. Robbins Landon and John Julius Norwich, *Five Centuries of Music in Venice* (Schirmer, 1992). (Introduction in *New York Review of Books* by Robert Craft.)

61. Letter to Lehmann, June 22, 1839, in Solange Joubert, *Une correspondance romantique: Mme d'Agoult, Liszt, Henri Lehmann* (Paris, 1947), 15, hereafter cited as *Une correspondance romantique.*

62. Williams, 53. Unfortunately, in the portraits available from this period, her hair has darkened to brown.

Four ∼ "Such flights, such madness"

1. Dupêchez, 134.

2. Rocheblave, 32.

3. Sand, *Correspondance,* 4: 285–86.

4. Rocheblave, 35. Marie had met Mallefille in Switzerland and introduced him to Sand, who ridiculed him, much to Marie's annoyance, but he stayed on at Nohant as a tutor to Sand's children.

5. Rocheblave, 35; Sand, *Correspondance,* 1: 285–86.

6. Sand, *Correspondance,* 1: 291.

7. Vier, 1: 302.

8. Thérèse Marix-Spire, "Romantiques et la musique," *Revue des sciences humaines,* 564.

9. Dupêchez, 134.

10. Bory, 152.

11. Letter to Hortense Allart, quoted in Dominique Desanti, *Daniel, ou le visage secret d'une comtesse romantique, Marie d'Agoult* (Paris, 1980), 62, hereafter cited as Desanti.

12. Perenyi, 170; Marix-Spire, 560.

13. Vier 1: 424, n. 289; 2: 74.

14. Dupêchez, 136.

15. Sand, *Correspondance,* 4: 711.

16. Dupêchez, 137.

17. Letter from Marie d'Agoult to Liszt, January 21, 1840, in *Correspondance,* 1: 361.

18. Janka Wohl, *François Liszt, souvenirs d'un compatriote,* quoted in Desanti, 65–66. Also Liszt on Sand: "Elle engluait un papillon et l'apprivoisait dans sa boîte, en lui donnant des herbes et des fleurs—c'était la période d'amour. Puis, elle le piquait avec son épingle, alors qu'il se débattait—c'était le conge venant toujours de sa part. Après, elle en faisait la vivisection et l'empaillait pour la collection de héros de roman." Quoted in Dupêchez, 135.

19. *Mémoires, Souvenirs et Journaux,* 2: 165.

20. *Mémoires, Souvenirs et Journaux,* 2: 166–68.

21. *Mémoires, Souvenirs et Journaux,* 2: 170.

22. *Mémoires, Souvenirs et Journaux,* 2: 75.

23. *Correspondance,* 1: 218, 221–23.

24. *Mémoires, Souvenirs et Journaux,* 2: 307, n. 167.

25. *Correspondance,* 1: 217.

26. According to a letter she wrote to Ronchaud early in May, the problem involved an inflammation of the liver. Two doctors gave her different medicines, and she was finally cured with ice and leeches. *Mémoires, Souvenirs et Journaux,* 2: 308, n. 170.

27. *Correspondance,* 1: 226–32.

28. *Correspondance,* 1: 233.

29. *Mémoires, Souvenirs et Journaux,* 2: 250–51. This "Episode de Venise" comes from a fragment of the projected *Mémoires,* in which Marie changed the names and which remained unpublished until 1990.

30. *Mémoires, Souvenirs et Journaux,* 2: 198.

31. *Correspondance,* 1: 366.

32. *Mémoires, Souvenirs et Journaux,* 1: 332–33, n. 266.

33. *Correspondance,* 2: 291.

34. *Mémoires, Souvenirs et Journaux,* 2: 214–15.

35. That is, bound together like galley slaves (emphasis by the author). *Agoult-Sand,* 216.

36. *Mémoires, Souvenirs et Journaux,* 2: 180–81.

37. *Mémoires, Souvenirs et Journaux,* 2: 183–84.

38. Published in *L'Artiste,* September 2, 1838.

39. *Mémoires, Souvenirs et Journaux,* 2: 185.

40. *Mémoires, Souvenirs et Journaux,* 2: 218.

41. *Correspondance,* 1: 234.

42. Journal des Zyi, in *Mémoires, Souvenirs et Journaux,* 2: 213, 215.

43. *Correspondance,* 1: 238–41.

44. *Mémoires, Souvenirs et Journaux,* 2: 216.

45. *Mémoires, Souvenirs et Journaux,* 2: 188.

46. Perenyi, 190.

47. *Mémoires, Souvenirs et Journaux,* 2: 321, n. 207.

48. *Mémoires, Souvenirs et Journaux,* 2: 190–91. In June, Marie was to record meeting Allart happily nursing her baby, which was noteworthy because unusual for upper-class women of the time.

49. *Mémoires, Souvenirs et Journaux,* 2: 195–96.

50. *Mémoires, Souvenirs et Journaux,* 2: 194.

51. The following is taken from this "Journal d'un Enfant, Etude," in *Mémoires, Souvenirs et Journaux,* 2: 226–35.

52. *Mémoires, Souvenirs et Journaux,* 2: 225–26.

53. *Mémoires, Souvenirs et Journaux,* 2: 208.

54. *Mémoires, Souvenirs et Journaux,* 2: 201, 207.

55. Vier, 1: 314–15.

56. *Mémoires, Souvenirs et Journaux,* 2: 253.

57. *Mémoires, Souvenirs et Journaux,* 2: 333, n. 264.

58. *Mémoires, Souvenirs et Journaux,* 2: 252–53.

59. *Correspondance,* 1: 259.

60. *Correspondance,* 1: 264–83, 294–96.

61. *Correspondance,* 1: 262, 322–24.

Five 〜 *"I need rules, . . . the feeling of doing my duty"*

1. BM Fonds de Charnacé, *Mémoires inédites,* 184.

2. *Correspondance,* 1: 290.

3. A homeopath who had treated both Marie and her mother in the 1830s, Koreff ended up in trouble with the law in 1837. But he still retained the loyalty of many of his former patients. Marie was less enthusiastic about him as a person than were Liszt and Marliani. But she valued his medical advice.

4. *Correspondance,* 1: 300–303.

5. *Correspondance,* 1: 375.

6. *Correspondance,* 1: 393ff.

7. *Agoult-Sand,* 236.

8. Sand, *Correspondance,* 4: 804. It is not certain that this is the letter Marie received. Another long and bitter letter was written by Sand at this time, which, it is now agreed, was never sent.

9. In the long letter never sent, Sand developed this point. Marie had tried to care for Sand for Liszt's sake, although she actually hated her. Sand had chosen not to see Liszt anymore because she didn't want Marie to accuse her of stealing him from her, an idea that she had never entertained. Here Sand managed to imply that although she was totally faithful to Marie, Liszt might not be.

10. *Correspondance,* 1: 319–21.

11. He was the brother of Edward George Bulwer-Lytton, author of the well-known book *The Last Days of Pompeii.*

12. *Correspondance*, 1: 357, 365–66.

13. *Correspondance*, 1: 392–94.

14. Bulwer-Lytton had caused a scandal by leaving his wife, Lady Georgina, who had then written a novel about it.

15. It had a circulation of more than twenty thousand because of its low price, which was compensated by advertising.

16. As this was the name Sand had given her in indicating both her beauty and her faults, it was appropriate for a confessional. "Arabella" can be found in BM Fonds Feliciano d'Oliveira, Ms. F. 859.

17. *Emile Girardin inconnu*, 15.

18. *Emile Girardin inconnu*, 18–19.

19. BN N.A.F. 25187, fol. 11.

20. *Correspondance*, 2: 108.

21. Vincent Cronin, *Four Women in Pursuit of an Ideal* (London, 1965), 125–26.

22. Williams, 117–19.

23. *Correspondance*, 1: 360–62.

24. *Correspondance*, 1: 375–77.

25. *Correspondance*, 1: 396.

26. *Correspondance*, 1: 399.

27. *Correspondance*, 1: 402.

28. *Correspondance*, 1: 406–12.

29. This was unlikely in a physical sense because the princess was in poor health, being both syphilitic and epileptic.

30. *Correspondance*, 1: 423–26.

31. *Correspondance*, 1: 450.

32. *Une correspondance romantique*, 109–110.

33. *Correspondance*, 2: 21–21, 23–25.

34. *Correspondance*, 2: 33–36.

35. *Correspondance*, 2: 39–40.

36. *Emile Girardin inconnu*, 20, 22–23.

37. *Correspondance*, 2: 65–66.

38. This ceremony was an effort on the part of King Louis-Philippe, whose popularity was declining, to partake of the still widespread popularity of Napoleon.

39. *Emile Girardin inconnu*, 23–27.

40. *Correspondance*, 2: 59–61.

Six ∾ "Daniel, . . . the name of the prophet"

1. "Le Compagnon du Tour de France," *La Presse*, January 9, 1841; "Lettre d'un bachelier, le concert de Chopin," *Gazette musicale*, May 2; "Lettre d'un bachelier sur le concert à Hambourg," in the above, September 19.

2. BN N.A.F. 2588 445.

3. *Marie d'Agoult,* 74.

4. BN N.A.F. 2588 481, 484, 493.

5. *Marie d'Agoult,* 74.

6. *Marie d'Agoult,* 75.

7. Daniel Stern, *Essai sur la liberté considérée comme principe et fin de l'activité humaine* (Paris, 1847), 102, hereafter cited as *Essai sur la liberté.*

8. "La nouvelle salle de l'École des Beaux Arts peinte par M. Paul Delaroche," *La Presse,* December 12, 1841.

9. "La Cathédrale de Cologne," on December 22, 1841.

10. "Portrait de Cherubini par Ingres," on January 7, 1842; "Le Triomphe de la Religion par Overbeck," on February 25 of the same year.

11. Her articles appeared in *La Presse* on March 8, 20, and 27, 1842; April 6 and 22, 1842; March 15, 20, and 25, 1843; April 3 and 12.

12. Patricia Mainardi, *Art and Politics of the Second Empire: The Universal Expositions of 1855 and 1867* (New Haven, 1987), 75–76.

13. "D'un grand bien qui se fait dans un petit coin de France," *La Presse,* November 26, 27, and 28, 1844.

14. She managed to place an article, "Heine and Freiligrath," in *Revue des deux mondes,* December 1, 1844. Her three "Etudes sur l'Allemagne," one on the poet Platen and the other two on schismatic religion in Germany, were published in *Revue indépendante* in 1845.

15. "Meyerbeer: Chants religieux," *La Presse,* October 16, 1842.

16. "Ecrivains modernes de l'Allemagne: Mme d'Arnim," *Revue des deux mondes,* April 15, 1844.

17. *Au printemps de dieux,* 44.

18. *Une correspondance romantique,* 52.

19. Vier, 1: 317.

20. Williams, 168–70. These letters from Baroness Czettritz-Neuhaus to her daughter-in-law, reproduced in Emil Jacobs, "Franz Liszt und die Grafin d'Agoult," *Die Musik* (Berlin), October 1911. A partial translation exists in André de Hévesy, "Liszt et Mme d'Agoult," *La Revue musicale,* June 7, 1928.

21. *Correspondance,* 2: 118, 165.

22. *Correspondance,* 2: 175.

23. Williams, 174–76, 179–80.

24. *Une correspondance romantique,* 183–85.

25. "Hervé," *La Presse,* December 13, 1842. The work was also published with others in 1866 and 1883.

26. "Julien," *La Presse,* February 27 and 28, 1843, and again in the collections of 1866 and 1883.

Seven ∾ "Nonnenwerth, . . . the ashes of my hopes"

1. *Correspondance,* 2: 242–49, 293.
2. BN N.A.F. 14323. The date of this note is Christmas Day, 1843.
3. BN N.A.F. 14323.
4. *Au printemps de dieux,* 75.
5. *Correspondance,* 2: 327–29.
6. *Au printemps de dieux,* 64–65.
7. *Correspondance,* 2: 337.
8. *Correspondance,* 2: 338.
9. *Correspondance,* 2: 341.
10. *Liszt et ses enfants,* 21–22.
11. *Correspondance,* 2: 341.
12. *Une correspondance romantique,* 189.
13. *Au printemps de dieux,* 75, 77, 79.
14. Dupêchez, 167.
15. *Au printemps de dieux,* 84.
16. "D'un grand bien qui se fait dans un petit coin de France," in *La Presse,* November 26, 27, 28; "Profession de foi de deux poètes: Freiligrath et Henri Heine," *Revue de deux mondes,* December 1. The other article was on the German writer Karl Auguste von Platen, which appeared the following year in *Revue indépendante.*
17. BN N.A.F. 25182.
18. *Au printemps de dieux,* 67.
19. *Correspondance,* 2: 338–39.
20. Jacques Vier, *Franz Liszt, l'artiste, le clerc* (Paris, 1951), 154–55.
21. *Liszt et ses enfants,* 26, 29, 31.
22. Léon Seché, *Revue de Paris* (1907): 306–07.
23. *Revue indépendante,* January 25, February 10 and 25, March 10, 1846.
24. *Correspondance,* 2: 375. The date is April 14, 1846.
25. *Correspondance,* 2: 370–71.
26. Letter to Angelo de Gubernatis, quoted in Gugenheim, 110.
27. *Daniel Stern: Lettres républicaines du Second Empire,* ed. Jacques Vier (Paris, 1951), 17, hereafter cited as *Lettres républicaines.*
28. *Briefe aus Paris,* 2 vols. (Leipzig, 1842), 2: 38.
29. The three, under the rubric "Etudes sur l'Allemagne," included "Du nouveau schisme: Johann Ronge," "Le comte de Platen," and "Mouvement religieux: Les Amis de la Lumière."

Eight ∾ "The people is an eternal poet"

1. *Essai sur la liberté considérée comme principe et fin de l'activité humaine,* 2nd ed. (Paris, 1863), xx, hereafter cited as *Essai,* 2nd ed.

2. Proudhon's book was published in 1859.

3. Pierre-Joseph Proudhon, *Correspondance* (Paris, 1875), 1: 236.

4. *Essai*, 2nd ed., 101–102.

5. *Essai*, 2nd ed., 115, 104.

6. *Essai*, 2nd ed., 248–50.

7. He later noted in the margin of this letter, "Madame d'Agoult has since succeeded by talent; she has strength in her pen and elevation in her thought." *Le Cahier vert, 1843–1847* (Paris, 1973), 320.

8. Vier, 2: 204–05.

9. Gabriel Delessert, "Rapport de la préfécture de police sur les publications anarchiques de 1846," cited by Vier, 2: 296, n. 16. The above date may be incorrect, since the book did not appear until 1847, unless there was pre-censorship.

10. *Correspondance*, 2: 285–87.

11. *Correspondance*, 2: 390–416.

12. *Correspondance*, 2: 418.

13. These thoughts were recorded in her agenda for 1847, BN N.A.F. 14324. Italics by the author.

14. "Etats-Généraux de Berlin," April 25, 1847.

15. "Etats-Généraux de Prusse, Travaux de la Diète," *Revue indépendante,* June 27, 1847.

16. Daniel Stern, "Pensées sur le peuple," *Revue indépendante,* December 10, 1847.

17. Karl Gutzkow, *Briefe aus Paris,* 2: 38.

18. BN N.A.F. 14323.

19. Vier, 2: 40–42; *Correspondance,* 1: 380.

20. "Le Salon de Lamartine" appeared in German in *Allgemeine Zeiting Beilage* and in French in *Belgique musicale;* both articles anonymous.

21. Daniel Stern, "Pensées," *L'Artiste,* April 18, 1847.

22. Daniel Stern, *Esquisses morales* (Paris, 1849), 275–76, hereafter cited as *Esquisses morales.*

23. *Esquisses morales,* 84–91.

24. *Esquisses morales,* 179–80.

25. Daniel Stern, *Histoire de la révolution de 1848* (Paris, 1985), 18, 19, hereafter cited as *Histoire de la révolution.*

26. *Histoire de la révolution,* 32.

27. *Correspondance,* 2: 418.

28. *Histoire de la révolution,* 92–93.

29. *Histoire de la révolution,* 99.

30. *Histoire de la révolution,* 125.

31. *Histoire de la révolution,* 149.

32. *Histoire de la révolution,* 169, 173–75.

33. *Histoire de la révolution,* 261–63.

Nine ∾ *"Public affairs . . . a vain and irritating excitation"*

1. BN N.A.F. 14325.
2. BN N.A.F. 14325.
3. "Lettre républicaine au Prince de Joinville," *Courrier français,* May 27, 1848.
4. The reference is to the Protestant King Henry IV, who, kept from his capital by Catholic nobles for ten years in the late sixteenth century, finally conceded, "Paris is worth a mass," and became a Catholic.
5. "Lettre républicaine à Fanny Lewald," *Courrier français,* June 5.
6. "Lettre républicaine à Lamennais," *Courrier français,* June 11, 1848.
7. "Lettre républicaine à Adam Mickiewicz," *Courrier français,* June 23.
8. *Histoire de la révolution,* 618.
9. *Histoire de la révolution,* 608.
10. "Lettre républicaine à l'Assemblée nationale," *Courrier français,* June 30, 1848.
11. This "Letter to the Assembly on Socialism" was published in *Courrier français,* July 8, 1848.
12. "Lettre républicaine à M. Ronchaud," *Courrier français,* July 17.
13. "Lettre à républicaine à Emile Littré," *Courrier français,* July 28, 1848.
14. "Lettre républicaine à Fanny Lewald," *Courrier français,* August 1, 1848.
15. "Lettre républicaine au Général Cavaignac," *Courrier français,* August 17, 1848.
16. BN N.A.F. 14325.
17. *Courrier français,* December 7, 1848.
18. This child had been born after the assassination of his father, then heir to the Bourbon crown, and raised outside France during the Orleanist monarchy of Louis-Philippe.
19. "Lettre républicaine à Henri V," *Courrier français,* September 2, 1848.
20. "Lettre républicaine à Anselme Petetin sur l'éducation du peuple," *Courrier français,* September 12, 1848.
21. "Lettre républicaine aux ouvriers de Paris," *Courrier français,* September 23, 1848.
22. "Lettre républicaine à M. Lamartine," *Courrier français,* October 4, 1848.
23. *Correspondance,* 2: 399–400.
24. Dupêchez, 207–08.
25. *Esquisses morales,* 316–17.
26. "Lettre républicaine à Mazzini," *Courrier français,* October 22, 1848. Also, BN N.A.F. 25190.
27. "Lettre républicaine sur l'Allemagne, *Courrier français,* November 15, 1848.
28. "Lettre républicaine au peuple electeur," *Courrier français,* November 9, 1848. She is addressing the people here in positivist language. The domination of priests and the military is the first stage in the positivist interpretation of history.
29. BN N.A.F. 14326.
30. BN N.A.F. 14326.

Ten ∼ *"My research has been minute"*

1. BN N.A.F. 14326.

2. *Révolution*, iii.

3. "I have endeavored, in these my descriptions to satisfy everyone without besmirching the truth, but have probably satisfied no one. Nor would I be amazed should this be so, since I judge it impossible to satisfy many people in describing the events of their own times." *Histoire de la révolution*, 2–3.

4. Vier, *La Comtesse d'Agoult*, 3: 197–99.

5. *Journal des débats*, article by Cuvillier-Fleury, April 14, 1850.

6. *Revue des deux mondes*, review by Pontmartin, April 1, 1850.

7. *Revue sociale*, June 1850.

8. *Revue brittanique*, in the edition of May 1850.

9. *L'Opinion publique*, June 6, 1850.

10. *La République*, August 9, 1850.

11. *La Liberté de penser*, December 18, 1850.

12. Vier, 4: 79–80. "Color of the moment" may refer to Stern, in 1848, having appeared in her box for the performance of a play with a revolutionary theme wearing the red hat of revolution.

13. Vier, 4: 80.

14. *Correspondance*, 2: 341.

15. Vier, 3: 128.

16. Daniel Ollivier, ed., *Correspondance de Franz Liszt et sa fille Madame Emile Ollivier* (Paris, 1936), 87, hereafter cited as *Liszt et sa fille*.

17. *Liszt et sa fille*, 42–43.

18. *Liszt et sa fille*, 44–45.

19. *Liszt et sa fille*, 45–46.

20. *Lettres républicaines*, 68.

21. BN N.A.F. 14327.

22. *Liszt et sa fille*, 52–53.

23. *Liszt et sa fille*, 63–65.

24. "A propos de tout," BM Fonds de Charnacé, Ms. F. 771.

25. "A propos de tout," BM Fonds de Charnacé, Ms. F. 771.

26. *Au printemps de dieux*, 157–60.

27. *Histoire d'une amitié, Pierre Leroux et George Sand, d'après une correspondance inédite, 1836–1866*, ed. Jean-Pierre Lacassagne (Paris, 1973), 41.

28. Dupêchez, 230.

29. *Lettres républicaines*, 67.

30. Letter from Liszt to Agnes Street-Klindworth, in Franz Liszt, *Correspondance* (Paris, 1987), 291.

31. March 30, 1853. It had already been published in *La Libre Recherche*.

32. "Je voudrais introduire l'histoire vraie au théâtre et contribuer ainsi quelque peu à tourner l'esprit populaire vers nos annales où il aurait beaucoup à apprendre. Si j'avais un succès, la voie que je tente attirrerait de plus habile et nous finirions, peut-être, par avoir un théâtre national." BH Fonds Jules Michelet, tome XII, liasse A 4752 (12).

33. Desanti, 294.

34. Dupêchez, 241.

35. BN N.A.F. 25190.

36. Vier, 4: 31.

37. *Liszt et sa fille,* 112–13.

38. *Liszt et sa fille,* 112–13, 119, 121, 123–24, 125–26, 131–32.

39. *Mémoires, 1833–1854,* 222.

40. Dupêchez, 233.

41. Vier, 3: 130.

42. *Liszt et ses enfants,* 105–09.

43. *Liszt et ses enfants,* 142–43.

44. Jacqueline Bellas, "Liszt, prénom Daniel," *Actes du Colloquium international Franz Liszt,* Paris, *La Revue musicale* (1988), 223.

45. Dupêchez, 234.

Eleven 〜 "I love politics"

1. Vier, 1: 202. In 1840, when Pictet wrote his book *Une course à Chamonix,* about the trip with the Sand family and the Liszt couple in Switzerland, he resumed his correspondence with Marie, which continued until death.

2. Madame Ancelot, *Les Salons de Paris, foyers éteints* (Paris, 1857), 15–16.

3. Ferdinand Denis, *Journal,* ed. Pierre Moreau (Fribourg, 1932), 96, 112.

4. Dena Goodman, *The Republic of Letters* (Ithaca, N.Y., 1994), 102–104.

5. Dupêchez, 218.

6. This is a reference to a place in the novel of Madame de Staël and follows on Sainte-Beuve's reference to the same novel when he called Marie "the Corinne du quai Malaquai" in the early 1830s.

7. Dupêchez, 219.

8. Emile Ollivier, *Journal, 1846–69,* ed. Theodore Zeldin and Anne Troisier de Diaz (Paris, 1969), 1: 144–45.

9. *Liszt et ses enfants,* 131–34. Magnolet was the nickname given to the princess' daughter by the Liszt daughters.

10. Dupêchez, 232.

11. *Liszt et ses enfants,* 163–64.

12. *Liszt et ses enfants,* 140.

13. *Liszt et ses enfants,* 169–70.

14. *Liszt et ses enfants,* 181–82.

15. At her death, he noted in his journal: "Pas de talent. Petite âme." Dupêchez, 153–54.

16. Dupêchez, 242.

17. *Liszt et ses enfants,* 192.

18. Daniel Stern, *Dante et Goethe* (Paris, 1866), 398–99.

19. Henri-Frédéric Amiel, *Journal intime, l'année 1857* (Paris, 1965), 193.

20. *Liszt et ses enfants,* 152–54.

21. *Liszt et ses enfants,* 186–89.

22. *Liszt et ses enfants,* 189–95.

23. Ollivier, *Journal, 1846–69,* ed. Zeldin and Diaz, 1: 302–03.

24. *Au printemps de dieux,* 184.

25. BN N.A.F. 25179, fol. 274.

26. *Liszt et ses enfants,* 113.

27. Bory, 213–14.

28. Minutier central des notaires CX liasse 446; Duchâtel, 258–59.

29. Alfred Darimon, *Histoire d'un parti, les cinq* (Paris, 1885), 130.

30. *Au printemps de dieux,* 81–82.

31. BN N.A.F. 14336.

32. *Lettres républicaines,* 175.

33. BM Fonds de Charnacé, Ms. F. 770 (5), speaks of *raising* children to the fullest dignity of their natures. In her outline of the work on education (4) she speaks of the necessity of education for the success of a democracy.

34. *Oeuvres complètes d'Ernest Renan* (Paris, 1961), X, 185, 188.

35. *Au printemps de dieux,* 195.

36. *Le Siècle,* November 29, 1859.

37. *Le Siècle,* January 14, 1860.

38. *Le Siècle,* February 14, 1860.

39. *Le Siècle,* May 22, 1860.

40. Vier, 5: 135.

Twelve ~ *"Differently, but as completely as man"*

1. Dupêchez, 263.

2. Dupêchez, 263.

3. BN N.A.F. 14330, Journal 1861.

4. Franz Liszt, *Correspondance* (Paris, 1973), 436.

5. Ollivier, *Journal 1846–69,* ed. Zeldin and Diaz, 21–23.

6. Emile Ollivier and Carolyne de Sayn-Wittgenstein, *Correspondance, 1858–1887,* ed. Anne Trozier de Diaz (Paris, 1984), 369.

7. Juliette Adam, *Mes premières armes littéraires et politiques* (Paris, 1904), 370–71, hereafter cited as *Mes premières armes.*

8. BN N.A.F. 25188, fol. 7.

9. Having received the annulment of her marriage, the two had made plans to marry in Rome, soon after Liszt's return from Paris in 1861. But her daughter had married a Hohenlohe; a member of that family who was a bishop prevailed on the family to reverse the annulment. Three years later the princess's husband died, leaving the way clear. At that point, Liszt reverted to mysticism and took minor orders.

10. Dupêchez, 267. Was her memory of this occasion perhaps a dream?

11. Dupêchez, 284.

12. Juliette Adam, *Mes sentiments et nos idées avant 1870* (Paris, 1905), 26, hereafter cited as *Mes sentiments*.

13. *Mémoires, souvenirs et journaux,* 2: 21.

14. "L'ange nu du berceau qui appela Marie/Dit: Tu vivras d'Amère et Divine douleur;/Puis tu nous reviendras toute pure et guérie/Si la grace à genoux désarme le Malheur." Marcelline Desbordes-Valmore, *Bouquets et Prières* (Paris, 1843), 193.

15. BN N.A.F. 25181, February 17, 1874.

16. Suzanne Gugenheim, *Madame d'Agoult et la pensée européenne de son époque* (Florence, 1937), 92.

17. BN N.A.F. 16440, September 26, 1842.

18. BN N.A.F. 16440, April 26, 1846.

19. *Histoire de la révolution,* 174.

20. Vier, 3: 238.

21. It is interesting that socialist women later accepted the same argument—that economic justice in general should be the primary goal and that it would produce equality for women. As with the case of popular sovereignty, it was only partly successful.

22. BM Fonds de Charnacé, Ms. F. 768, September 15, 1851.

23. BM Fonds de Charnacé, Ms. F. 168, March 22, 1852.

24. BN N.A.F. 25181.

25. June 4, 1854, in Jacques Vier, "La Comtesse d'Agoult et Hortense Allart sous le Second Empire," *Archives des lettres modernes* 5, no. 33 (1960): 4.

26. *Archives des lettres modernes* 5, no. 33 (1960): 20.

27. Bibliothèque de l'Institut, fonds Spoelberch de Lovenjoul, E. 872, hereafter cited as Collection de Lovenjoul.

28. Undated, George Sand, *Correspondance,* ed. Georges Lubin (Paris, 1972), 9: 758.

29. Sand, *Correspondance,* ed. Lubin, 758.

30. Collection Lovenjoul E. 872.

31. Collection Lovenjoul E. 872.

32. BN N.A.F. 14330.

33. October 29, 1861, George Sand, *Correspondance, 1812–1876* (Paris, 1882), 16: 193.

34. Sand, *Correspondance, 1812–1876,* 4: 330.

35. Sand, *Correspondance, 1812–1876,* 4: 334.

36. *Idées antiproudhoniennes sur l'amour, la femme et le mariage* (Paris, 1858), 54.

37. BN N.A.F. 25181.

38. BN N.A.F. 25181.

39. BN N.A.F. 25181.

40. Adam, *Mes premières armes,* 87–88.

41. Adam, *Mes sentiments,* 136–37.

42. BN N.A.F. 25181, September 12, 1863.

43. Published as *Philosophie des Femmes* (Lausanne, 1859).

44. BM Fonds de Charnacé, Ms. F. 768.

45. Vier, 4: 52.

46. BM Fonds de Charnacé, Ms. F. 768.

47. BM Fonds de Charnacé, Ms. F. 769.

48. BM Fonds de Charnacé, Ms. F. 768.

49. *Esquisses morales,* 35–43.

50. *Essai sur la liberté,* 77–78, 124.

51. *Mémoires, 1833–1854,* 242–43.

52. *Esquisses morales,* 43, 67.

53. *Esquisses morales,* 53, 121–22.

54. *Au printemps de dieux,* 170–71.

55. Neither Mirabeau nor de Staël was a beauty.

56. *Dante et Goethe,* 193.

57. *Esquisses morales,* 63–65.

58. BN N.A.F. 25190.

Thirteen ⟋ "When a woman has created her life herself"

1. George Sand, *Histoire de ma vie,* 70.

2. Adam, *Mes premiers armes littéraires,* 462.

3. Dupêchez, 279. It might have been the Dutch poet Sirtéma de Grovestins, theologian and historian, who was writing a nineteenth-century elegy to folly. He wrote Marie praising first her Italian articles in 1861, then the second edition of her *Histoire de la révolution de 1848* in 1862. She leaned on him for aid in collecting material for her work on the Dutch revolution. Or it might have been the poet Hyacinthe du Pontavice de Heussey, with whom she visited Brittany in August 1862.

4. *Revue germanique,* May 1, 1863. The last of these poems envisioned her death.

5. *Dante et Goethe,* 3. The work had already been published in sections in *Revue moderne (germanique)* March 1, November 1, December 1, 1864, and May 1, June 1, October 1, 1865. Also in "La religion de Goethe," *Le Temps,* June 9, 11, 13, 1864.

6. *Dante et Goethe,* 90–91.

7. *Dante et Goethe,* 39, 307.

8. *Dante et Goethe,* 371.

9. BN N.A.F. 25188 (5055).

10. Gugenheim, 36.

11. BN N.A.F. 14324.

12. September 5 and 6, 1861. However, unlike Lamennais, Franchi was to return to the church, after Stern's death.

13. She certainly became aware of orthodox Protestantism; in 1864 *Le Temps* was involved in the defense of the pastor Athanase Coquerel, whom the Presbyterian consistory wished to defrock for heresy. However, all of the Protestants she knew were extremely liberal.

14. Edgar Quinet, *Revue des deux mondes,* May 1, 1854.

15. "Pouvoir et liberté," *Revue contemporaine,* April 15, 1855; "Quatre années de la vie d'un peuple libre," *Revue européenne* (1856); "La mort de Barneveldt, épisode de l'histoire de Hollande," *Revue germanique,* July 1 and August 1, 1859; "Vingt-cinq ans de l'histoire des Pays-Bas," *Revue germanique,* July 1, August 1, October 1, 1863; *La Hollande, son passé, sa liberté,* 1864.

16. BN N.A.F. 14330. The Papacy had lost the States of the Church to United Italy, except for the Vatican, and thus was no longer a political power. A movement in the Catholic Church was now pushing for a declaration of the infallibility of the Pope. This was not popular among all European bishops and came close to causing a schism. It was nevertheless successfully declared in 1870.

17. May 1, 1865.

18. Dupêchez, 283.

19. Vier, 256.

20. Marie d'Agoult, *Mes Souvenirs* (Paris, 1877).

21. *Mémoires,* 9.

22. *Dante et Goethe,* 216.

23. Dupêchez, 282.

24. *Mémoires,* 4.

25. *Mémoires, Souvenirs et Journaux,* 11–12.

26. Vier, 4: 267.

27. Vier, 3: 156–57.

28. The least expensive way to live in Europe, as one's meals are included in the price of the hotel.

29. Letter from George Sand to Henry Harisse, November 20, 1867, *Annales politiques et litteraries,* May 9, 1926.

30. In her agendas, BN N.A.F. 14322, 14323, 14325, 14327, 14328.

31. BN N.A.F. 14326, 14328.

32. Vier, 4: 13.

33. Vier, 4: 13.

34. *Au printemps de dieux,* 162, 165–66.

35. *Lettres républicaines,* 112.

36. Dupêchez, 261.

37. *Correspondance,* 2: 415–16.

38. BN N.A.F. 14329.

39. BM Fonds de Charnacé, Ms. F. 769 (232).

40. Jacques Vier, *La comtesse d'agoult et François Ponsard d'après une correspondance inédite, 1843–1867* (Paris, 1960), xxi, xx.

41. BN N.A.F. 25190 19.

42. Vier, 4: 75–76.

43. *Mémoires, Souvenirs et Journaux,* 1: 15.

44. Dupêchez, 282.

45. Vier, 4: 68–69.

46. Dr. Emile Blanche was what was known as an *alienist* in the nineteenth century. He treated many of the great names of France in his clinic—Gérard de Nerval, who came later and spent his time with occultism; Flaubert, Villiers de l'Isle Adam, Verlaine; and others who made short visits, like Hugo, Musset, Berlioz.

47. Vier, 4: 13.

48. Dupêchez, 287.

49. Dupêchez, 296.

50. Dupêchez, 292.

51. BM Fonds de Charnacé, Ms. F. 859.

52. BM Fonds de Charnacé, Ms. F. 859, July 3, 1869.

53. BM Fonds de Charnacé, Ms. F. 859, July 3, 1869. Claire did not do so. Going through her mother's papers after her death, she destroyed selectively, copying out only some of what she did not eliminate altogether.

54. BM Fonds de Charnacé, Ms. F. 859, July 3, 1869.

55. This is the opinion of her most recent biographer, Charles F. Dupêchez.

56. "Palma," in *Mémoires, Souvenirs et Journaux,* 2: 255 ff.

57. Vier, 2: 87–89.

58. Barbey d'Aurevilly, *Les Bas-bleues* (Paris, 1878).

Fourteen ～ "Apart, isolated, somewhat foreign as well"

1. In 1860, "Lettres écrites d'Italie" appeared in *Le Siècle* on January 14 and 23, February 14, May 28 and 29, June 11, July 3, and July 18. In 1861, on May 25, "M. Guizot jugée par M. de Cavour" was published; "Le Baron Ricasoli," on June 19; "Le libre-pensée en Italie, Ausonio Franchi," on September 5 and 6; "De l'esprit piémontais et son ascendant sur la révolution italienne," on December 10.

2. Daniel Stern, *Florence et Turin* (Paris, 1862), ix.

3. Also a Napoléon, Jérôme was known as "Plon-Plon." He espoused liberal causes and was a ladies' man.

4. Guggenheim, 340.

5. This may be an unfortunate term. Stern once forbade anyone to refer to her as Ollivier's mother-in-law. "Daniel Stern is no one's mother-in-law," she emphasized.

6. Vier, 5: 116.

7. "Un village dans la Jura," *Le Temps,* October 17, 18, 22, 26; November 2, 3.

8. Vier, 5: 83. The Salic Law supposedly originated with the medieval Salian Franks; it forbade the rule of women.

9. *Le Temps*, December 20, 1868.

10. *Lettres républicaines*, 321.

11. Vier, 6: 189.

12. During the Civil War in the United States, European forces entered Mexico in an attempt to force payment of bills owed to them. As the Civil War ended, other nations declined to face U.S. enforcement of the Monroe Doctrine, particularly since England was already in trouble for supporting the Confederacy. French troops remained there, and Napoléon III recruited a Habsburg prince to govern the state. However, the Mexicans themselves revolted and killed their prince.

13. Published on July 5, 19, and on August 7, 11, 1866.

14. The Germans had the breech-loading rifle. By 1870 the emperor had begun supplying some divisions with this weapon, but few in the army knew how to use it. The Germans also had universal military service, which the French did not.

15. Napoléon III was in such bad shape that he rouged his cheeks before reviewing the troops. He was to die, a few years later, in England after an operation on his gallbladder.

16. In one battle the German king, standing on a hillside watching waves of French soldiers with bayonets throwing themselves against the Germans, who mowed them down with artillery, cried out with his eyes full of tears, "Oh the brave fellows!"

17. Cosima Wagner, *Journal* (Paris, 1977), 1: 292, 293, 296, 300, 325. Cosima had also upset her father by turning Protestant when she married Wagner.

18. "Réponse à une lettre écrite de Heidelberg," *Le Temps*, September 13, 1870.

19. *Journal de Genève*, October 30, 1870.

20. Vier, 6: 17, letter to Eugène Poujade.

21. *Journal de Genève*, January 28, 1871.

22. Dated January 7, 1871, printed January 10.

23. "Lettre à Sir Henry Bulwer-Lytton, M.P.," *Progrès de Lyon*, January 10, 1871.

24. *Le Temps*, March 13, 1871.

25. Vier, 3: 294–95.

26. Dupêchez, 102.

27. Wagner, *Journal*, 1: 292, 293, 296, 300.

28. Wagner, *Journal*, 1: 325, 351–53.

29. Vier, 5: 67.

30. Vier, 6: 45.

31. *Philosophie positive* (July-September 1873).

32. Vier, 6: 49.

33. Vier, 5: 73.

34. This was one of the final waves of cholera that Europe experienced in the nineteenth century. Marie had left Paris to avoid this outbreak.

35. Vier, 6: 80.

36. Vier, 6: 79. Sand had not burned the letters.

37. See Edmond Schuré, *La Rêve d'une vie* (Paris, 1928), 95ff.

38. Louis de Ronchaud, "Etude sur Daniel Stern," preface to *Esquisses morales*, 3rd ed.

39. *Au printemps de dieux*, 189–90.

40. Charlotte Haldane, *The Galley-Slaves of Love: The Story of Marie d'Agoult and Franz Liszt* (London, 1957), 225.

41. BN N.A.F. 14332.

42. Vier, 6: 62–63.

43. Dupêchez, 220.

44. Signed "Marie de Flavigny, Comtesse d'Agoult. Enregistrée à 9ième bureau, folio 70. Ladite Dame, en son vivant, rentière, demeurrais à Paris, rue Malesherbes n. 38, où elle est décédée le cinq mars 1876," BN N.A.F. 16440 6. Also found in Minutier centrale des notaires CX, liasse 1064, no. 30.

45. Williams, 522–23.

46. *Le Temps,* March 9, 1876.

47. *Le Temps,* April 25, 1876.

~ *Sources* ~

Unless noted otherwise, Paris is the place of publication for the works listed below.

By Marie d'Agoult (Daniel Stern):

Nélida. 1846.
Essai sur la liberté considérée comme principe et fin de l'activité humaine. 1847. 2nd
    ed. 1863. 3rd. ed. 1880.
Lettres républicaines. 1848.
Esquisses morales. 1849.
Histoire de la révolution de 1848. 3 vols. 1851–53.
Marie Stuart. 1855.
Jeanne d'Arc. 1857.
Florence et Turin. 1862.
Dante et Goethe. 1866.
Histoire des commencements de la République des Pays-Bas, 1581–1625. 1872.
Mes souvenirs. 1877.
Nouvelles: Hervé, Julien, La boîte aux lettres, Ninon au couvent. 1883.
Mémoires, 1833–1854. 1927.
Mémoires, Souvenirs et Journaux de la Comtesse d'Agoult. 1990.
Plus 136 articles published in various French, German, Swiss and Italian periodi-
    cals, many of which are mentioned in the notes for this book.

Manuscript Sources

I list below only the archives and libraries that I personally have used.
    Bibliothèque nationale, Paris

Fonds Daniel Ollivier:
    N.A.F. 14320–14344, diaries and notebooks
    N.A.F. 25181–25184, letters by Marie d'Agoult
    N.A.F. 25185–25189, letters to Marie d'Agoult
    N.A.F. 25190, unfinished manuscripts
Bibliothèque historique de la Ville de Paris
    Fonds Jules Michelet, Tome XII, liasse A 4752 letters
Bibliothèque municipale, Versailles, Yvelines:
    Fonds de Charnacé:
        Ms. F. 768, letters
        Ms. F. 769, letters, notes on manuscripts, Preface to *Essai,* 2nd ed.
        Ms. F. 770, fragments of dramas, novels, *Esquisses morales, Pensées, Mémoires*
        Ms. F. 771, notes for articles
    Fonds Feliciano d'Oliveira:
        Ms F. 859, red notebook (*cahier rouge*), recopied and annotated by Claire
        Charnacé; letters; fragment of *Mémoires*, unedited, for May 31, 1835, and six
        weeks thereafter
Bibliothèque de l'Institut:
    Fonds Spoelberch de Lovenjoul, E. 872 letters to George Sand.

There is also correspondence of Marie d'Agoult in libraries and archives throughout France, Switzerland, East and West Germany, Poland, and Italy, as well as in personal collections.

Published Correspondence

Edited by Daniel Ollivier:
    Correspondance de Liszt et de Mme d'Agoult. 2 vols. 1933–34.
    Correspondance de Franz Liszt et de sa fille Madame Emile Ollivier. 1936.
    Autour de Madame d'Agoult et de Liszt. 1941.
Edited by Jacques Vier:
    Emile Girardin inconnu. 1949.
    Marie d'Agoult, son mari, ses amis. 1950.
    Daniel Stern: Lettres républicaines du Second Empire. Paris, 1951.
    Franz Liszt, l'artist, le clerc. 1960.

*Au printemps de dieux, correspondance inédite de la comtesse Marie d'Agoult et   du
    poète Georges Herwegh*, ed. Marcel Herwegh. 1929.
Correspondance Marie d'Agoult–George Sand, ed. Charles F. Dupêchez. 1995.
I Carteggio inedito di Madame d'Agoult con Angelo Gubernatis, ed. Petre Ciureanu.
    Geneva, 1969.
Lettres de Joseph Mazzini à Daniel Stern. 1872.

Sources

Correspondance de Franz Liszt et ses enfants Blandine, Cosima et Daniel, ed. Robert Bory, 1936.

Liszt, Franz. *Correspondance*. 1987.

Une correspondance romantique: Mme d'Agoult, Liszt, Henri Lehmann, ed. Solange Joubert. 1947.

Other letters appear in the articles cited in the notes to this book and in some of the biographies of Mme. d'Agoult.

Select Bibliography

Adam, Juliette. *Idées anti-proudhoniennes*. 1858.

———. *Mes premières armes littéraires et politiques*. 1904.

———. *Mes sentiments et nos idées avant 1870*. 1905.

Ackermann, Louise. *Pensées d'un solitaire*. 1903.

Aragonnès, Claude. *Marie d'Agoult, une déstinée romantique*. 1938.

Balzac, Honoré de. *Béatrix*. 1913.

Bory, Robert. *Une retraite romantique en Suisse: Liszt et la Comtesse d'Agoult*. 1930 (Geneva, 1926).

Boucher, Henri. *Souvenirs d'un Parisien*. 2 vols. 1908.

Brook, Ethel Saniel. *The Social and Political Ideas of Countess d'Agoult, Daniel Stern*. Ph.D. diss. Columbia University, 1969.

Charrier, Edmée. *L'Évolution intellectuelle feminine*. 1931.

Darimon, *Les cinq sous l'Empire*. 1885.

———. *Le Tiers-Parti sous l'Empire*. 1887.

Dupêchez, Charles. *Marie d'Agoult, 1805–1876*. Paris, 1989.

Gaultier, Abbé. *Exposé du cours complet des jeux instructifs*. n.d.

Goodman, Dena. *The Republic of Letters*. Ithaca, N.Y. 1994.

Grenier, Edouard. *Souvenirs littéraires*. 1894.

Gugenheim, Suzanne. *Madame d'Agoult et la pensée européenne de son époque*. Florence, 1937.

Gutman, Richard. *Richard Wagner*. New York, 1968.

Institutions de Sacré-Coeur. *Programmes des différents exercices qui seront soutenus par les élèves*. 1805.

Monod, Marie Octave. *Daniel Stern, Comtesse d'Agoult*. 1937.

Ollivier, Emile. *Journal*. Edited and annotated by Theodre Zeldin and Anne Trozier de Diaz. 1969.

Pariset, Georges. *La Revue Germanique de Dollfus-Nefftzer*. 1906.

Perenyi, Eleanor. *Liszt, the Artist as Romantic Hero*. Boston, 1974.

Pictet, Adolphe. *Une course à Chamonix*. 1840.

Proudhon, Pierre-J. *De la justice dans la révolution et dans l'église*. 4 vols. 1930–35.

Renan, Ernest. *La vie de Jésus*. 1863.

———. *Questions contemporaines.* 1868.

Rocheblave, Samuel. *Une amitié romanesque: George Sand et Madame d'Agoult.* 1894.

Ronchaud, Louis. *La politique de Lamartine.* 1878.

Royer, Clémence. *Introduction à la philosophie des femmes.* Lausanne. 1858.

———. *L'Origine des espèces de Charles Darwin.* 1862.

Sand, George. *Lélia.* 2 vols. 1833.

———. *Valentine.* 1833.

———. *Simon.* 1836.

———. *Lettres d'un voyageur.* 2 vols. 1837.

———. *Horace.* 1842.

———. *Bulletins de la République.* 1848.

———. *Souvenirs de 1848.* 1880.

———. *Histoire de ma vie.* 4 vols. 1856.

———. *Journal intime.* 1926.

———. *Correspondance,* ed. Georges Lubin. 1967.

———. *Oeuvres autobiographiques,* ed. Georges Lubin. 1971.

———. *Journal intime,* ed. Aurore Sand. 1926.

Vier, Jacques. *La Comtesse d'Agoult et son temps.* 6 vols. 1955–63.

Wagner, Cosima. *Journal.* Vol. 1. Paris, 1977.

Wilkinson, Anthony. *Liszt.* London, 1975.

Williams, Adrian. *Portrait of Liszt by Himself and His Contemporaries.* Oxford, 1990.

～ Index ～

Library of Congress Cataloging-in-Publication Data

Stock-Morton Phyllis, 1930–
The life of Marie d'Agoult, alias Daniel Stern / Phyllis Stock-Morton.
p.   cm.
Includes bibliographical references and index.
ISBN 0-8018-6313-9 (alk. paper)
1. Stern, Daniel, 1805–1876.   2. Authors, French—19th century—
Biography.   I. Title.
PQ2152.A38 Z92 2000
848'.709—dc21
[B]   99-047883